Microsoft Word for
Publishing Professionals

Microsoft Word for Publishing Professionals

Power-Packed Tips for Editors, Writers, Typesetters, Proofreaders, and Indexers

Jack M. Lyon

THE EDITORIUM

For my father, who was always a little surprised by my technical side

Please read this:

As the lawyers say, this book is provided for informational purposes only and without a warranty of any kind, either express or implied, including but not limited to implied warranties of merchantability, fitness for a particular purpose, and freedom from infringement. The reader (that's you) assumes the *entire risk* as to the accuracy and use of this book and the information therein. I don't anticipate any problems, but all computers and Microsoft Word installations are different, and I can't be held responsible for what might happen with yours. *Caveat lector!*

Note: Be sure to *back up your files* before trying *anything* in this book; then you'll have something to go back to if anything goes wrong. *You have been warned!*

ISBN 978-1-4341-0236-2

The Editorium, LLC
West Valley City, UT 84128-3917
www.editorium.com
editor@editorium.com

The names of any programs or companies mentioned in this book (including mine) are acknowledged as trademarks of their owners. The Editorium™ is a trademark of The Editorium, LLC.

The Editorium is not affiliated with Microsoft Corporation.

"Uncle Cosmo, why do they call this a word processor?"
"It's simple, Skyler. You've seen what food processors do to food, right?"

—Jeff MacNelly, Shoe

Contents

Navigation

Customizing Word

Editing

Revision Tracking and Comments

Styles

Footnotes and Endnotes

Proofreading

Indexing

Find and Replace

Macros

Miscellaneous Stuff

Preface

Most of the articles in this book came from *Editorium Update* (ISSN 1534-1283), my free email newsletter for publishing professionals who use Microsoft Word. Many of the articles include helpful comments (under "Readers Write") that readers have sent to me. I express my sincere appreciation to all who have contributed in any way. If you'd like to subscribe to the newsletter, please send a blank email message to editorium-subscribe@topica.com. I do not sell, rent, or give the subscriber list to anyone. Period.

Some readers may wonder about my choice to support Microsoft Word when other alternatives (such as the wonderful—and free—OpenOffice.org's Write program) are readily available. The fact is, I've had little choice; most editors and other publishing professionals were using Microsoft Word as their primary tool long before I started writing articles or creating add-in programs. That's understandable, as Word really is a marvelous piece of software. Unfortunately, it also has plenty of shortcomings, many of which I try to address in this book. (This book is not intended for use with Microsoft Word versions before Word 97.)

I'm grateful to all who have subscribed to the *Editorium Update* newsletter, purchased Microsoft Word add-ins from the Editorium, and sent feedback, questions, and suggestions for improvement. Even though I've never met most of you, I feel that I know you and that you are my friends. I've included a list (below) of those who have contributed to the Readers Write column of *Editorium Update;* I apologize if there's anyone I've overlooked. In particular, I appreciate the extraordinary help and support of Steve Hudson, Hilary Powers, Geoff Hart, Ron Strauss, Dan A. Wilson, and Eric Fletcher. That does not mean they endorse my work or this book.

Aaron Shepard	Bob Janes	Dave Gayman
Alan Seiden	Brad Hurley	David ("Bear") Chinell
Alice Falk	Brian Vicary	David King
Allene M. Goforth	Bruce White	David M Varner
Amanda Lucas	Callie Jordan	David Stacey
Andrea Balinson	Carolann Barrett	Debby English
Andrew Savikas	Caryl Wenzel	Derek Halvorson
Ann Redmon	Cher Paul	Donald Hawkins
Anna Marshall	Christopher Seal	Donna Payne
Anne K. Bailey	Chuck Tucker	Dorian Cougias
Anne-Marie Concepcion	Claes Gauffin	Dwight Purdy
April Karys	Clive Tolley	Ed Millis
Arnold Howard	Dan A. Wilson	Ed Nelson
Audrey Dorsch	Dan Goldstein	Ed Vesneske, Jr.
Bill Rubidge	Dave Erickson	Ellen Ellender

Eric Fletcher
Erika Buky
Erika Remmy
Francelia Sevin
Frazer Wright
Gary Frieder
Geoff Hart
Glade Lyon
Greg Ioannou
Gretchen
Hannah Hyam
Hélène Dion
Hilary Powers
India Amos
Iwan Thomas
James Spear
Jane Lyle
Janna DeVore
Jay A. Parry
Jeanne Pinault
Jeff Ross
Jeffrey White
Jenn Morris
Jim Cronin
Jim Pinkham
Joel Rosenberg
Johanna Murphy
John Eagleson
John Renish
Juanita Hilkin
Judy Stein
Julian Jenkins
Karen L. Bojda
Karen MacKenzie
Karen Slaney
Kathleen Much
Kathy Anderson
Katie Lewis
Keith Soltys
Kenneth Sutton

LeAnne Baird
Lew Golan
Linda Duguay
Linda Gray
Linda L. Kerby
Linda Northrup
Lindy M
Lou Burgoyne
Maarten Reilingh
Maggie Brown
Margaret Berson
Marie Shear
Mark Pool
Mark Taylor
Martha H. Bowes
Martin
Marty Spitzenberger
Mary C. Eberle
Mary L. Tod
Mary Russell
Meg Cox
Melissa Bogen
Michael C. Coleman
Mike Brown
Miriam Bloom
Nan Bush
Nancy Adess
Nancy Newlin
Nancyann Ropke
Ned Humphrey
Neil Hymans
Neman Syed
Niquette Kelcher
Pamela Angulo
Patrick LaCosse
Patsy Price
Paul Robinson
Peg Hausman
Peg Wier
Phil Rabichow

Preston Earle
Pru Harrison
Rebecca Evans
Renee DeCarlo
Rhana Pike
Rich Shattenberg
Richard H. Adin
Richard O'Regan
Rob Dilworth
Rob Little
Roger Shuttleworth
Rohn Solecki
Romke Soldaat
Ron Strauss
Rosalie Wells
Sage Rountree
Sam Mills
Sandee Lannen
Seth R. Beckerman
Sharon Key
Shirley S. Ricks
Stephen Riley
Steve Dobney
Steve Hudson
Susan Bullowa
Teresa N. Barensfeld
Terri Svilar
Terry Yokota
Thomas C Dixon
Todd A. Manza
Tony Dalton
Virginia Downs
Wallace Sagendorph
Walter Blum
William T. Buckley
Yateendra Joshi
Yehuda Yoel Zimmerman

Why This Book?

There are already two excellent books about editing on your computer:

Making Word Work for You: An Editor's Intro to the Tool of the Trade, by Hilary Powers:

 http://www.the-efa.org/res/booklets.html

Effective Onscreen Editing, by Geoff Hart:

 http://www.geoff-hart.com/home/onscreen-book.htm (electronic version)
 http://stores.lulu.com/store.php?fStoreID=1505747 (printed version)

If you don't own these books, you definitely should. Both provide information worth far more than their paltry price—information that will help you work faster and better, and with far fewer headaches. I heartily recommend that you buy them, study them, and use them. You'll be glad you did.

Now, I know what you're thinking: "If those books are so great, why did you publish this one?" Simple. Hilary and Geoff provide clear, structured guidance about how to use Microsoft Word to full advantage. Their approach is comparable to a well-organized automotive parts store: "Wiper blades? Sure! Second aisle on the left." I, on the other hand, run more of a salvage yard: "Hey, Bob, do we have a carburetor for a '65 Chevy Caprice? No? Do you think the one from this Impala might work?" Here you'll find an eclectic (and occasionally slightly repetitive) collection of disjointed techniques to make Microsoft Word do things its designers never intended and to fix things they didn't know were broken. Also, being of a somewhat philosophical turn of mind (like the old mechanic relaxing behind the counter), I'll occasionally throw in some thoughts about the publishing process and how some of these odd techniques can improve it. I hope you'll find it all very, very useful.

There's lots of good stuff in here—if you don't mind rummaging around to find what you need. You brought a wrench and a screwdriver, right?

Stuff You Should Know Before Using This Book

There are several things you should know about before using this book. If you don't, you might feel lost or overwhelmed, and we don't want that. So here you go:

Getting the Macros in Electronic Form

Nearly everything in this book is available in electronic form—macros, wildcards, sample text, and so on. Just go to http://blog.editorium.com and type the name of the article (such as "Repeating Macros") into the "Search" box, surrounding the name with quotation marks. In the Search results, you'll see the name of the article you're searching for. Click the name to open the article. Then you can select and copy the macro rather than laboriously typing it from this book.

Getting the *Book* in Electronic Form

Oh, I see. You want the book *itself* in electronic form. Well, all right. I'll personally send you the PDF (with hyperlinked contents, index, and internet addresses!) under the following conditions:

1. You buy the printed book.
2. You send an email message to editor@editorium.com with the following subject line:

   Jack, I bought the book!

3. You keep the PDF to yourself, for your own use, and not share it with anyone else. (I'm trying to make a living here, modest though it may be.)

I'd also welcome any comments you may have about the book.
Thanks for your cooperation and support, which I really do appreciate.

Editorium Programs

This book includes frequent mention of the add-in programs I've created for Microsoft Word: Editor's ToolKit, FileCleaner, NoteStripper, MegaReplacer, MultiMacro, RazzmaTag, and so on. Why? Because they're darned useful, that's why! And often they can be used in combination with the techniques outlined in this book to do some pretty amazing things. All of the programs are available for download on the Editorium website at www.editorium.com, and all have a free 45-day trial period. End of commercial.

Using Wildcard Find and Replace

Many of the articles in this book refer to finding and replacing with wildcards, which may be disconcerting if you have no idea what that is. But fear not! All is revealed in the section "Find and Replace." This section is fairly technical, but it's really, really important. Please take time to work through it; you'll be glad you did.

Using Macros

Many of the articles in this book include macros to automate repetitive tasks. Sometimes the macros are referred to as VBA programs or commands. "VBA" stands for "Visual Basic for Applications," which is the programming language built into Microsoft Word. (Don't worry; I'll try to keep things easy and clear.) The macros look something like this:

```
Sub CopyToSpike()
If WordBasic.GetSelStartPos() <> _
WordBasic.GetSelEndPos() Then 'Text is selected
WordBasic.Spike 'Add entry to spike
WordBasic.EditUndo 'Undo the cut
Else
WordBasic.MsgBox "Please select text before running this
 macro.", _
 "No Text Selected"
End If
End Sub
```

That particular macro copies text to the Spike. (See the article "I Like Spike.") However, you don't have to understand how the macro works in order to use it. Here's how to put it (or any other macro) into Word so it will be available when you need it:

1. Copy the text of the macro, starting with the first "Sub" and ending with the last "Sub." If the macro doesn't have those "Sub" lines at the beginning and end, skip step 8 in these instructions.
2. Click the "Tools" menu at the top of your Microsoft Word window.
3. Click "Macro."
4. Click "Macros."
5. Make sure "Macros Available In" shows "Normal.dot."
6. Type a name for the macro in the "Macro Name" box—probably the name used after the first "Sub." For this macro, that's "CopyToSpike."
7. Click "Create."
8. Delete the "Sub [macro name]" and "End Sub" lines that Word created in the macro window. The macro window should now be completely empty.
9. Paste the macro text at the current insertion point.
10. Click "File," then "Close and Return to Microsoft Word."

The macro is now stored in your Normal template, ready for use.
To actually run the macro, do this:

1. Click the "Tools" menu.
2. Click "Macro."
3. Click "Macros."
4. Click the name of your macro to select it.
5. Click the "Run" button. (If you wanted to delete the macro, you could press the "Delete" button instead.)

Warning: Before using any macro on a real document, test it on a backup *copy* of the document to *make sure* it does what you need it to do.

Assigning Macros to Menus, Toolbar Buttons, or Keyboard Shortcuts

Many of the articles in this book recommend using a menu, toolbar button, or keyboard shortcut to run a macro. How to do that will be covered in more depth later in the book, but for now, here are the procedures you'll need:

Menus

To assign a macro to a menu:

1. Click the "Tools" menu.
2. Click "Customize."
3. Click the "Commands" tab.
4. In the "Categories" list, on the left, find and click "Macros."
5. In the "Commands" list, on the right, find and click the macro you want to use and hold down the mouse button.
6. Drag the gray rectangle to the Word menu you want to use ("Edit," for example, or "Insert"). The menu will expand so you can see its entries.
7. Drag the gray rectangle to the position where you want your menu item to appear.
8. Release the mouse button. Your new menu item will appear on the menu, displaying the name of the macro.
9. Click the "Modify Selection" button or right-click the menu item you just added. A menu will appear.
10. Use the menu items to change the appearance of your new menu item until you're happy with it (see the explanations below).
11. When you're finished, click the "Close" button.

Your new menu item will appear on the menu you selected, displaying the name of the macro, and you can click the menu item to run your macro.

When you close Word, the program will ask if you want to save the changes you've made to the Normal (or other) template. In other words, do you want to keep the menu item you've added? If you do, click yes (this will also save any other changes you've made to the template).

Toolbar Buttons

To assign a macro to a toolbar:

1. Make sure the toolbar you want to use is showing. (You may need to click the "View" menu, click "Toolbars," and then put a checkmark next to the toolbar you want to display.)
2. Click the "Tools" menu.
3. Click "Customize."
4. Click the "Commands" tab.
5. In the "Categories" list, on the left, click "Macros."
6. In the "Commands" list, on the right, click the macro you want to use and hold down the mouse button.
7. Drag the gray rectangle (representing a toolbar button) to a suitable position on the toolbar you want to use. (A black "I-beam" will indicate the position of your new button.)
8. Release the mouse button. A new button will appear on the toolbar, displaying the name of the macro.
9. Click the "Close" button.

Now you can click the button to run your macro from the toolbar.

When you close Word, the program will ask if you want to save the changes you've made to the Normal (or other) template. In other words, do you want to keep the toolbar button you've added? If you do, click Yes (this will also save any other changes you've made to the template).

Keyboard Shortcuts

To assign a macro to a keyboard shortcut:

1. Click Tools > Customize > Commands > Keyboard.
2. In the Categories window, scroll down to and select "Macros."
3. In the "Macros" field, scroll down (if necessary) to the macro you want and select it. Any previously assigned keys now appear in the "Current keys" field.
4. Put your cursor in the box labeled "Press new shortcut key."
5. Press the key or key combination you want to use (INSERT, for example, or SHIFT + CTRL + H).
6. Click the "Assign" button.
7. Click the "Close" button.

Now whenever you press the keyboard shortcut you assigned, the macro will run.

When you close Word, the program will ask if you want to save the changes you've made to the Normal (or other) template. In other words, do you want to keep the keyboard shortcut you've added? If you do, click Yes (this will also save any other changes you've made to the template).

Word's Startup and Templates Folders

Some of the articles in this book refer to Microsoft Word's Startup and Templates folder. Unless you know how, finding those folders can be an exercise in frustration. So here's the scoop:

Startup Folder

To access the Startup folder:

1. On your computer desktop, double-click My Computer. (On a Macintosh, open your hard drive. Then continue with step 5, below.)
2. At the top of the window that opens, you'll see a "Tools" menu. Click that, and then click "Folder Options."
3. Click the "View" tab and make sure that "Show hidden files and folders" is selected. Then click the OK button.
4. Back in the window for "My Computer," double-click your local hard drive, probably "C."
5. Open the folders named, consecutively within each other, Documents and Settings > [your name] > Application Data > Microsoft > Word > Startup. (On a Macintosh, open Applications > Microsoft Office [2004] > Office > Startup > Word.)

Templates Folder

To access the Templates folder:

1. On your computer desktop, double-click My Computer. (On a Macintosh, open your hard drive. Then continue with step 5, below.)
2. At the top of the window that opens, you'll see a "Tools" menu. Click that, and then click "Folder Options."
3. Click the "View" tab and make sure that "Show hidden files and folders" is selected. Then click the OK button.
4. Back in the window for "My Computer," double-click your local hard drive, probably "C."
5. Open the folders named, consecutively within each other, Documents and Settings > [your name] > Application Data > Microsoft > Templates. (On a Macintosh, open Applications > Microsoft Office [2004] > Templates.)

By the way, some of the articles mention Word's Normal template (Normal.dot). That template is located in the templates folder.

Using This Book with Word 2007 and 2008

Many of the articles in this book explain how to customize Word for specific publishing tasks—something that was fairly simple before the release of Microsoft Word 2007 with its navigation "ribbon." In Word 2007, customization is difficult, so you may be wondering if the customization articles in this book are still relevant. Fortunately, most of them are, as long as you first install the ToolbarToggle add-in:

http://www.toolbartoggle.com/

The price is currently a measly $19.95, and if you're using Word 2007, I highly recommend that you download and purchase this program. If you use it for nothing more than the customization tips in this book, it will still pay for itself many times over. In addition, it automatically recreates the menus and toolbars of earlier Word versions (leaving the ribbon intact). That will be of great help as you use this book, which frequently refers to those menus and toolbars. If you don't care about customization (what?!?) but would still like to have the earlier menus and toolbars, the ToolbarToggle download includes a free "lite" version that provides just this.

If you're using Word 2008 (Macintosh), you're out of luck, as Microsoft has removed macro support completely from this version of Word. Enough people have complained about this, however, that it will probably come back in the future:

http://tinyurl.com/5v6wge

If you simply want to learn about Word 2007's ribbon equivalents to the earlier menus and toolbars, try the Word 2003 to Word 2007 interactive command reference guide:

http://office.microsoft.com/en-us/word/HA100744321033.aspx

For quick reference, here are some of the most frequently used menu items in this book and their equivalents in Word 2007:

- Tools > Customize. There is no real equivalent in Word 2007. You can, however, customize the Quick Access Toolbar by clicking Office Button > Word Options > Customize.
- Tools > Templates and Add-ins. The equivalent is Office Button > Word Options > Add-Ins. Then select Manage: Templates at the bottom of the dialog and click the Go button.
- Tools > Macros. On the ribbon, click View > Macros.
- Tools > Options. Click Office Button > Word Options > Advanced.

Personally, I'm going to avoid all the fuss. I'm sticking with Word 2003 on PC and Word 2004 on Macintosh—something I recommend unless you have truly compelling reasons to move to the newer versions. Actually, my favorite version is Word 2000, which can still be purchased online in various places (such as eBay).

Introduction

John Henry was hammering on the right side,
The big steam drill on the left,
Before that steam drill could beat him down,
He hammered his fool self to death.

American folk song "John Henry" pits man against machine in drilling a tunnel for the railroad. John Henry wins the contest, but the effort costs him his life.

You probably won't see that song on Billboard's Top 40 list, but its theme is still with us, as shown in the 2003 rematch between chess master Gary Kasparov and IBM's Deep Junior chess program. The Associated Press article for February 9 described the final moments:

"Kasparov played himself into a superior position but offered a draw on the 23rd move, surprising chess experts at the New York Athletic Club. Deep Junior turned down the offer but presented its own draw five moves later, and Kasparov readily accepted to boos from the crowd.

"Kasparov said he played better than Deep Junior in the deciding game and would have pressed for a win in a similar position against a human opponent. But, he said, he feared even a tiny mistake would have been severely punished by the computer."

Do you view technology as an opponent? For many editors, the answer is yes. Editors, indexers, and other publishing professionals seem extremely conservative about technology—perhaps with good reason. Their job is to ensure accuracy, clarity, and even beauty—and that requires a human mind. Editors are right to resist anything that gets in the way of those goals. And managers who believe that a spell check is as good as an edit or that a machine-generated concordance can take the place of an index need to be educated about the realities of the marketplace—realities that will surely come back to bite them if ignored.

It is also true, however, that editors who ignore the need to use technology do so at their peril. The field of publishing is changing rapidly, and editors need to keep up. If they don't, they'll be replaced—not by machines but by other editors who know how to use machines to their advantage and can thus work better, faster, and cheaper than their unplugged competitors.

I'm tempted here to give my lecture about how the lowly plow made civilization possible, with a recapitulation of Adam Smith's *Wealth of Nations* and the overwhelming role of technology in human progress. But I won't. Instead, I will ask: What have you learned this week about using your computer to help you do your job more efficiently? If your answer is "Nothing," may I encourage you to keep reading, ideally with your hands on the keyboard and this book at your side. I especially encourage you to read the articles on wildcard searching and replacing, which may be the most important tool you can acquire.

Finally, ask yourself: "What one thing could I do with my computer that would dramatically increase my effectiveness?" Then find out how to do it.

Michael Dertouzos, late director of MIT's Laboratory for Computer Science, had a slogan that I like: "Doing more by doing less." And Nolan Bushnell, founder of Atari, said, "[Those who are computer literate are] twenty times more valuable than [those who are not] because they're facilitated. It's like they have three robots working for them."

The truth is, you don't have to beat the machine; all you have to do is put it to work. I hope this book will help.

Readers Write

Dan A. Wilson:

In business talks and seminars aimed at corporate climbers and white-collar execs in the past several years, I've begun including this phrase at opportune times:

"Time was, and not too long ago, that the value of an individual to an organization increased geometrically when he or she became computer-literate. Today, literacy at the computer no longer pulls much weight: you have to be computer-sophisticated today, and that means simply that you must have come to regard the computer as far and away your most valuable tool, your ultimate enabler, your brain's second-in command. A brain with a pencil in its hand cannot compete—indeed cannot even credibly challenge—a brain with a computer and computer-sophistication at its disposal. Regarding the machine as an enemy, an obstacle, an unnecessary complication is lethal, and the individual who has that view of the computer is at least dying, if not already dead, in the world of business affairs, but probably doesn't yet know it."

David Varner:

I wanted to bring up your mention of wildcard searching as a skill. You said it "may be the most important tool you can acquire." Okay, I've read all your articles and tried the different tips. Heck, I've printed out all the articles. But it's not the same as having one dedicated wildcard text source. And so the question is, any chance you can point me to (or create/compile) a clear and straightforward, whole-enchilada wildcard search and replace manual? Or maybe I could just cut and paste all your wildcard articles together!

I responded: I've already done this, in a document named *Advanced Find and Replace in Microsoft Word*. It's available as a free download for anyone who wants it. This document is well worth your time, believe me. You can get the download here:

http://www.editorium.com/ftp/AdvancedFind.zip

I'd like to thank Bob Janes for formatting and editing the document and especially for compiling the reference section at the end.

Setting Up

Hardware for Editors

A few years ago I was shopping around for a new monitor—which got me thinking about what editors need in the way of computer equipment. If you work for a corporation, the powers-that-be probably think like this: "Editors just do word-processing, so they don't need much of a computer." Then they buy you something cheap and slow.

The truth is, editors need much more than a garage-sale castoff. If you're serious about editing on the computer (which you should be), you'll need the fastest machine you (or management) can afford. Why? Because you're doing much more than rearranging commas in a one-page letter. If you're like me, you're working on books with hundreds of pages, dozens of headings, complex formatting, and thousands of footnotes. And you're probably doing time-consuming stuff like this:

- Converting batches of files from one format to another (WordPerfect to Microsoft Word, for example).
- Running numerous search-and-replace routines to clean up text and make things consistent.
- Running macros (such as my add-in programs) to torture text and formatting into the form you need.

The most expensive resource you or your employer has is *your time.* If you have to sit idly by while your computer huffs and puffs its way through some automated procedure, you need to invest in a machine that will make you more productive.

Don't focus solely on speed, however. For someone who's editing for many hours at a stretch, other things are equally (or more) important:

Your monitor should be as large as you can get. Seventeen inches should be the *minimum* size. Back in the '80s, I wrote a 300-page book using a suitcase-sized "portable" computer with an *eight-inch* monochrome monitor. Never again. I'm currently working on a 22-inch widescreen LCD (thank you, Ron Strauss!). Sheer bliss. If you have to choose between a bigger, better monitor and a faster processor, you should probably go for the monitor, which you'll be looking at all day long. Not convinced? How valuable is your eyesight? By the way, ten minutes of *looking* at monitors at your local computer store will give you a much better idea of what you like than two hours of researching the Internet.

Your keyboard should be responsive, reliable, and comfortable to use. Keyboards are relatively cheap, so get yourself a good one. Doing so may spare you the pain and expense of having carpal-tunnel surgery, which more than one of my colleagues has had to endure.

Your mouse should feel good in your hand and not have to be babied along. If you have a bad mouse, you're probably not even aware of how much time you spend fighting it. You might also be interested in a trackball, mouse-pen, or other input device.

There are many other things to consider: desks, chairs, wrist pads, copy holders, and so on. You may not be able to afford everything you need all at once, but if you keep upgrading as you can, you'll be investing in your health, your comfort, and your productivity.

Readers Write

AUDREY DORSCH:

I put up with a temperamental mouse for years. (Don't ask me why except for ingrained thrift that resists replacing anything as long as it still functions.) When it finally gave up the ghost I treated myself to a Logitech cordless mouse with scrolling wheel and an extra, thumb-operated, button. All the buttons are programmable for whatever function I choose. What a joy. Worth every penny of the $85(CDN) it cost.

HILARY POWERS:

I get a lot of mileage out of an elderly voice command program called Kurzweil Voice Pro. It doesn't do continuous dictation—but I'm not really into dictation anyway, and it's fine for three or four words at a time.

It's brilliant for control of the machine, as it can fool virtually any Windows program into thinking its input is really coming from the mouse or the keyboard. "Page-down!" would do just what you want, with no special programming or training (beyond the basic read-in of the voice).

And you can record any sequence of keystrokes and call it anything you want. Fr'example, I have "Style-that!" pick up the selected text, move to the style sheet document, and drop the text there. Then (after I enter the part of speech or do whatever note-taking I need re the style item) "Head-on-back!" moves the insertion point in the style sheet to a new line, returns to the main file, and deselects the text.

There needn't be any externally obvious relationship between what you say and what you get—if your author makes a consistent mistake that's too complex to correct with a search&replace operation or a macro that runs through the whole file, but always takes the same keystrokes to fix once you find it, you can call it something satisfying like "Curl-up-and-die!" Then you put your insertion point where the sequence needs to begin, speak rudely to your computer, and watch it do the work. Very satisfying. . . .

I've actually bought L&H Voice Express, which is supposed to do all this and continuous dictation too, but haven't been able to make it work for me—mainly because I'm too comfortable with Kurzweil to go through the learning curve, but also because it seems to be much more sensitive to its microphone input. Headsets drive me buggy, and KV works happily enough with a good desk mike cantilevered out so it sits close to my mouth. L&H VE gets confused and grumpy with the same system, so it's not predictable enough to feel worth working with. L&H bought Kurzweil a couple of years ago, and was at least for a while selling the Kurzweil product as well as its own. Dunno if it's still available, but it might be worth a try.

The Need for Speed

In my last few years as a corporate employee, I felt compelled to edit faster and faster while still maintaining accuracy—probably something to do with the many rounds of layoffs. If you're feeling the same squeeze, I have some suggestions:

- Choose the fast way over the easy way. That sounds paradoxical, but it's often easier to spend *ten* minutes making corrections manually than it is to spend *five* minutes recording and running a macro to make the same corrections automatically. Human nature, I guess. But if you can keep breaking through your own resistance to change, all those new techniques will soon become second nature, and you'll be working at a higher and faster level.
- If you're still working on an old 233 MHz computer with 256 megs of RAM, get an upgrade, fer cryin' out loud! Buy a new computer—something fast, with, say, a 2GHz processor and 2G of RAM (I still recommend sticking with Windows XP and Word 2000 or 2003). If you can, get a computer with a dual-core processor, which is the equivalent of running two processors at the same time. That means you can do true multitasking, with one program performing a batch process on dozens of documents over *there* while you work manually on a single document over *here*. Another solution is to use two computers, one for batch processing and the other for manual work, transferring files back and forth between the two machines as needed. Over the past few years, desktop computers have become very powerful—and cheap:

  http://www.techbargains.com/

The latest Macs make me drool, but they're on the expensive side:

http://store.apple.com/1-800-MY-APPLE/WebObjects/AppleStore/

"But," you say, "I don't need a fast computer; all I'm doing is reading through one document at a time and making simple corrections." If that's true:

- Learn how to automate as many tasks as you can; that's what computers are for, and that's why you need one that's fast. If you're still editing as you would on paper, learn how to use macros and wildcard Find and Replace. Doing so will require an investment of time and effort, but you'll be amazed at the results.
- Spend a few minutes once a month researching new software that might make your life easier. There are wonderful programs out there, many of them free. As a friend of mine says, "If you keep doing things the same way, life will never get any better." For lots of interesting ideas, check out LifeHacker:

http://www.lifehacker.com

- Maintain your computer. How to do that is beyond the scope of this article, but there's plenty of information on the internet. I like Windows Secrets:

http://www.windowssecrets.com

- Set your mouse and keyboard to run as fast as you can stand. I always have mine at full blast. (See "Fast Moves" in this book.)
- Don't use directly applied formatting. Do use paragraph styles.
- See "Marking Spec Levels with Styles" and "Styles and Standardization."
- Make sure you've got the final version of the document you need to work on. I can't tell you how many times I've edited something only to have the author say, "Oh, that was a preliminary version." Editing once is fast; editing twice is slow.
- Educate your authors and clients. If old Professor Higgins always hits ENTER at the end of each line as if using a typewriter, pick up the phone, call the good professor, and explain why that's a bad idea. Don't just sullenly correct the same mistakes time after time. Why not give your authors a checklist of (1) things to do and (2) things not to do? It would make your life easier, and your work faster. I've included a few such items at the end of the instructions for my free Author Tools Template:

http://www.editorium.com/ftp/authortemplate.zip

- Educate yourself. Spend one hour each week (I like Friday afternoon) learning one new skill or technique that would make your work easier and faster—a great excuse to read this book!

Readers Write

BILL RUBIDGE:

One suggestion I would add, since it is so basic, is to use the keyboard rather than the mouse whenever possible. I'm not necessarily suggesting memorizing the keyboard commands—I'm just suggesting using the keyboard ALT keys to access the Word menus and move through them to the command you want. Once you display the keyboard commands, learning to use the keyboard instead of the mouse is pretty quick."

JUDY STEIN:

I seem to work most efficiently using a combination of keyboard and mouse. My main speed trick is the right-click edit menu: I've put my most frequently used menu items and macros on it (and gotten rid of the default items that I don't use often). [For instructions on how to do that, see "Customizing Shortcut Menus" in this book.]

Changing Word's Memory Allocation

Editors are often afraid to work on big documents in Microsoft Word. I routinely work on documents larger than 300 pages, so I'm not sure what all the fuss is about. I do believe in having plenty of RAM (random access memory) on a computer (I'm currently at 2 gigs), so that helps. Also, most of my documents don't include graphics, which can really bog things down in Word.

If you need to work on big documents with lots of graphics and find that Word often runs slowly or locks up, you may appreciate a tip from Word guru Woody Leonhard:

http://www.wopr.com

On page 270 of his book *Word 97 Annoyances,* Woody explains how to change Word's memory allocation. Here are the basic instructions:

1. Run Regedit (click Start button > Run > regedit).
2. When the registry editor opens, find the folder named HKEY_CURRENT-USER\Software\Microsoft\Office\11.0\Word\Options. [Note: That's for Word 2003; you may have 9.0, 10.0, 12.0, or something else, depending on your version of Word.]
3. Right-click on the Options folder and *back it up* by clicking Export, giving the export a name, and saving it to your desktop. Then, if something goes wrong, you can restore your original settings by importing the previously exported file.
4. Click Edit > New > String Value. Type in the name "CacheSize" and hit Enter twice. Type in 2048 and hit Enter.
5. Click Edit > New > String Value. Type in the name "BitMapMemory" and hit Enter twice. Type in 2048 and hit Enter.
6. Click File > Exit to leave the registry and save your changes.

What that does is tell Word to reserve 2048 KB of memory (instead of the meager default of 64) for documents (CacheSize) and graphics (BitMapMemory).

You don't have to use 2048, either; you can use lesser amounts, such as 1024. It's up to you. But the more you use, the less memory will be available for other programs that are running.

Don't mess with anything else in the registry. Doing so can cause all kinds of problems. And even for these settings, you change them at your own risk.

Macintosh users should simply be able to change the memory allocation for Microsoft Word.

Screen Settings for Editing

I finally went out and bought that new monitor—a 19-inch Sony that looked great in the store. But when I got it home and hooked it up, it didn't look so good. The characters in Microsoft Word looked jagged, and the toolbar icons were huge! Couldn't it do better than that? Then it struck me: on a monitor that was capable of 1600 by 1200 resolution, I was displaying 1024 by 768. No wonder! I quickly increased the resolution to the max, using the following procedure in Windows:

1. Right-click the Windows desktop.
2. Click "Properties."
3. Click the "Settings" tab.
4. In the "Screen area" box, move the slider all the way to the right.
5. Click the "OK" button.
6. Follow any additional on-screen prompts.

Wow, were those characters ever fine! And tiny! Maybe I'd gone a little overboard. I repeated the procedure, this time setting the resolution at 1400 by 1050. Much better! And still beautiful to look at. After doing some editing in Microsoft Word, however, I decided that the lettering on Word's menus was still a bit small for my middle-aged eyes. But I liked that high resolution. What could I do?

I increased the menu font size with this procedure:

1. Right-click the Windows desktop.
2. Click "Properties."
3. Click the "Settings" tab.
4. Click the "Advanced" button.
5. Click the "General" tab.
6. In the "Font Size" box, select "Large Fonts."
7. Click the "OK" button.
8. Click the next "OK" button.
9. Follow any additional on-screen prompts.

Better, but the menus could still be easier to read. How about putting them in bold? I tried this procedure:

1. Right-click the Windows desktop.
2. Click "Properties."
3. Click the "Appearance" tab.
4. Click the "Normal" menu in the sample display window.

5. On the bottom right, click the "B" (bold) button.

6. Click the "OK" button.

(Actually, while I was in there, I also selected "Icon" in the "Item" box and set its font to bold.)

For the first time in years, reading my computer's menus and icon labels was easy. I should have adjusted those settings a long time ago.

If you spend most of your day editing on the computer, trying to differentiate between opening and closing quotation marks, between em dashes and en dashes, you too may benefit by setting your computer display exactly the way you want it.

Readers Write

MAARTEN REILINGH:

To change screen resolution on a Macintosh, use the Monitor control in the Monitors and Sound control panel.

To change menu and other display fonts and font sizes, use the Appearance control panel (Fonts tab).

Control panels may be accessed in various ways depending on how your OS is configured, but usually they are available from the Apple pull-down menu. Once you open these control panels, everything else is pretty intuitive; just select the desired settings.

Typefaces for Editing

Just another pretty face? Nothing wrong with that. If you're editing in Microsoft Word, why not use a typeface that you're comfortable reading and that makes editing easy? (Unless, of course, you're editing documents that have already been carefully formatted for typesetting.) You can always apply the final typeface and formatting after your editing is finished (probably just by attaching a different template to the document).

Some typefaces lend themselves better to editing than others. Here are some things to look for in a typeface to use while you're editing:

1. Legibility. Are the characters clear and easy to read?
2. Universality. Is the typeface readily available at no cost or low cost, and on other computers as well as your own?
3. Are special characters easy to distinguish? These include the hyphen, the en dash, the em dash, and opening and closing quotation marks.

I first thought that Courier might be a good font to use in editing. It's nice and clear and can be found almost anywhere. Its hyphen and dashes, though, are practically indistinguishable, making it unsuitable for editorial work.

After considerable testing and exploration, I've found three typefaces that seem to work especially well for editing. You probably already have them:

1. Times [New] Roman (yep, that old chestnut).
2. Verdana.
3. Georgia.

Times Roman is actually a bit small and condensed (designed to fit lots of type into a newspaper column), but you probably won't find a face with more easily distinguishable quotation marks and dashes. The em dash is nice and long, the hyphen is tiny, and the en dash falls comfortably in between. You just have to make sure that you get the point size big enough so you can read it comfortably.

Verdana is a Microsoft sans-serif typeface that was designed for viewing on-screen, so it looks especially clean and legible on a computer monitor. Its quotation marks aren't as clearly distinguishable as those in Times Roman, but they're not bad, either.

Georgia is another Microsoft typeface that was designed for viewing on-screen, so, like Verdana, it looks great on a computer monitor. Unlike Verdana, it has serifs, making it a little easier to read.

Another excellent choice is the free Charis SIL:

http://scripts.sil.org/cms/scripts/page.php?site_id=nrsi\&item_id=CharisSILfont

Using one of these fonts, you may want to create a template that you attach to documents you're going to edit. If you don't want to create such a template yourself, please feel free to use the Typespec template that comes with my Editor's ToolKit program. Even if you don't use the program, you can still use the template, which was created using the Verdana typeface and has lots of styles for editorial markup. If you want to use a different typeface with the template, just open the template in Microsoft Word and change the Normal style to the font of your choice. Another approach is to use Times Roman, Verdana, or Georgia in the template you are currently using. You can always change back to the original font when you're ready for final formatting.

You may not have given much thought to selecting a typeface for use in editing, just using whatever your client has used by default. You'll probably find your work easier and more enjoyable if you use a typeface that you like and find easy to read. Why not give it a try?

Size and Zoom

A few years ago, I noticed that one of my colleagues, a fellow editor, was reading a document set in 10-point type, with the lines running all the way across his giant 21-inch monitor. He was having a terrible time "tracking" from the end of one line to the beginning of the next, and he was squinting, bending forward in his chair, and generally looking miserable.

"Why don't you shrink the window?" I asked.

"What?" he said.

"Size the window so it's not so wide. You'll be able to read more easily."

"How do I do that?" he asked.

"You know those three little boxes on the upper right? The left one minimizes the window, and the right one closes it."

"Yes."

"The middle one makes it so you can size the window." [My colleague was using a PC. On a Macintosh, grab the lower right corner of a window and drag to size it.]

"Show me," he said.

I took the mouse and clicked the middle "Restore" button (which looks like two cascading windows). Then I positioned the mouse pointer on the right-hand border of the window, pressed and held the left mouse button, and sized the window to about six inches across.

Next, I clicked View > Zoom and bumped up the Zoom size to 200 percent.

"How's that?" I asked.

"Lots better," he said.

If you usually edit a document with the Word window stretching all the way across your screen, you might want to change your strategy. If you were designing a book, you probably wouldn't allow a line length of more than about 24 picas (four inches). Otherwise, the text would be too wide to read comfortably. You won't torture your readers, so why torture yourself?

Another thing: If you work with a wide, wide window, you'll find yourself scrolling and scrolling and scrolling back and forth on a line. If your window is relatively narrow, you can often move to a certain word by scrolling one or two lines down (a keystroke or two) rather than 50 characters across. You may not realize how much time you spend scrolling through text, but it does add up.

Finally, remember that you don't have to look at text in its actual size. Zoom was invented for a reason. Go ahead, resize your text so you can read it from six feet away. Amaze your friends. Make your life easier. That's what all these tools are for.

Readers Write

DAN A. WILSON:

I think your position is the right one: it isn't a matter of *telling* people *how* to adjust, but of *reminding* them to *remember* to resize or zoom, or both. I, too, have seen countless cases of tennis-match-spectator neck syndrome caused by the use of a newly purchased monitor at full display max. Especially now that LCDs are so widely in use, it's important that users learn to adjust window sizes.

Almost all of my programs except Word and my browsers now run in windows that show my desktop wallpaper behind them on all four sides, because running them any larger than that on a 19-inch LCD is just plain silly unless you're viewing them from across the room. In Word, I either run single document pages at 80 to 90 percent zoom, or side-by-side pages at 75 percent, and the displays of the latter are *still* larger than those of pages at maximized display and 100 percent zoom on my 17-inch CRT on the other desk.

The advantage of the larger monitors today is that you can display *more;* using them to display the same old stuff *larger* is pointless for most programs, and an invitation to whiplash injuries.

Large LCD monitors have very high native resolution settings, and are optimized for those settings. Running a 17-inch LCD monitor at a resolution of 800 x 600 is not only bad for the monitor but bad for the eyes: even the best image available at that resolution on such a monitor will be fuzzy.

I use a 19-inch LCD with Word windows maximized but with my zoom set to 90% normally. Gives me a slightly larger-than-lifesize view of the page.

Most of the time, though, I use the taskbar right-click control to Tile Windows Vertically, so that I can have two different docs or two different views (or versions) of the same doc open side-by-side, each with its own toolbar. I set the zoom for each doc to 75 percent then, and the page on the screen is still about the size of an 8.5 x 11 sheet. This is great when I want to check text against the bibliography for presence and identity of entry info, for instance.

WILLIAM T. BUCKLEY:

Having received an e-mail containing a Word file, I opened it and was surprised to see that the "view" was not my usual 1-inch all around, but rather a depiction that put the first line at the absolute top of the viewable page, and the last line at the absolute bottom of the page. So I clicked on VIEW, expecting to see that the document had arrived in "normal" view. But no. It was checked off as my usual "print layout" view.

I couldn't figure that out, but proceeded to save the piece into a file on my hard drive and go on to the next piece of business. But when I next opened a file in Word, it came up in this no top/bottom margin view, which I was unable to alter. No matter what I did, I could not escape this depiction in "print layout" view.

So I first went into tools/options and clicked on something amounting to restore defaults. No good. Then I uninstalled/reinstalled Office XP, to no avail. Word still showed the same goofy top/bottom no margins.

Unable to figure an elegant solution, I produced a blank document with 1-inch margins on all sides and saved it. Then I created a shortcut and put that document on my desktop, next to my Word shortcut. Word was still behaving badly. But when I opened the 1-inch margin document and saved it to a second file, shut all applications down, and then opened the main Word software, the new piece came up with the appropriate 1-inch margins. Just to muddy the waters further, when I next opened the offending no-margin piece, then closed it, the view in a new document opened in the main Word application again came up with no top/bottom margin. It is as though some "toggle" function is at work. And it's driving me crazy.

Jack, can you please direct me on how to reset my main Word application to get rid of whatever influences came in on the offending e-mail piece that have so flummoxed my software? By the way, I run Norton Anti-Virus and it is updated by me almost daily—with default weekly updates.

I RESPONDED: I suspect what's going on there is that Word is set to hide white space. Basically, if you point your mouse at the top or bottom of a page, you'll see a little box with two arrows in it, one pointing up and one pointing down. If you let your mouse sit there a few seconds, you'll also see a ToolTip saying "Show White Space." If you then click your left mouse button, the display should return to normal. You can learn more by clicking Help and then searching for "Show or hide white space in print layout view."

BILL REPLIED: Your suspicions were accurate, and the corrective measure worked as advertised.

I must say that I don't see a lot of utility for this show/hide white space feature. But I guess the programmers have it for people who need the absolute maximum viewing area that they can squeeze onto their monitors. I found it perplexing (until you showed me how to escape it.)

Doing the Splits

One of the advantages of editing on paper is that you can lay out the various pages, one here, one there, for reference and comparison with each other. For example, you may need to refer to a certain paragraph on page 10 while editing a paragraph on page 300. On the computer, this is a problem. You can scroll back to page 10 for reference, but then you'll have to scroll forward again to page 300 to make your changes.

If you do this kind of thing a lot, you may want to try using Microsoft Word's Go To feature (CTRL + G) to jump to the specific pages you need. Many editors never even think about this; they just hold the Page Down key and scroll and scroll and scroll and scroll until they reach their destination. Go To may get you around more efficiently.

However, switching from one page to another over and over can get pretty tedious. Wouldn't it be nice if you could open the *same* document twice, with page 10 on the top of your screen and page 300 on the bottom? You can, with an often-overlooked feature called New Window. To use it, click the Window menu; then click "New Window." To see both windows at once, click the Window menu again; then click "Arrange All." You can tell the windows apart by looking at the title bar at the top of each one. Your original window's title will end with a 1. The new window's title will end with a 2.

You can move around each window freely, and you can have page 10 in the top window and page 300 in the bottom. Because each window contains the *same* document, any changes you make in one window will be reflected in the other. If you need to refer to more than two pages at the same time, you can open another new window. (If you're like many editors, you'd prefer to see the windows side by side, not one above the other. My Editor's ToolKit program includes an "Arrange Windows" feature that automatically arranges the windows for easy comparison.) You can switch from one window to the other by pressing SHIFT + CTRL + F6. To get rid of the second window, close it by clicking the X button on the window's upper right. (Be careful not to close Word itself, whose button is on the *upper* upper right.)

You can also compare different pages with Word's Split feature, which lets you split a single window and scroll the two halves independently. To use it, click the Window menu; then click "Split." Position the split by moving your mouse and clicking the left mouse button. You can switch from one pane to the other by pressing SHIFT + F6. To get rid of the split, click the Window menu; then click "Remove Split."

If you work on long documents (such as books) and need to compare pages often, you may need a larger monitor. I recommend 17 inches at a minimum. Once you've tried a 22-inch monitor, you'll never go back—at least not willingly. With a monitor that large, you can see a full page on your screen, and working on two documents side by side is a pleasure. You may never work on paper again.

Two Up

As a book editor, I often want to see the pages of a book I'm working on as "two up"—that is, two pages at a time, side by side on my screen. This is easily done in Print Preview, of course:

1. Click "File > Print Preview."
2. Click the "Multiple Pages" button—it's green and has four little pages on it.
3. On the little menu that pops up, point your mouse at the second of the first two pages, displaying the notation "1 X 2 Pages" at the bottom of the menu.
4. Click that second page.

Now two side-by side pages should be displayed on your screen.

You can actually work on these pages by clicking the Magnifier button (a toggle) on the Print Preview toolbar (second button from the left). Working in Print Preview always seems kind of clunky to me, however. So I've set up Word to display multiple pages in regular old Print Layout view (View > Print Layout):

1. Click "File > Print Preview."
2. Right-click the Print Preview toolbar and click "Customize."
3. Hold down the CTRL key (to copy rather than move) and drag the Multiple Pages button to a different toolbar—the Formatting toolbar should do nicely.
4. Click the Close button.

Now you have a copy of the Multiple Pages button on your Formatting toolbar. Click it, as explained above, to display pages two up. Pretty slick!

There's just one problem: Word displays those two pages with the odd page on the left and the even page on the right—exactly the opposite of what you'd see in a printed book. It's a little confusing, if you ask me. A workaround is to create a blank section page at the beginning of your document and number it as page 0. Here's how:

1. Place your cursor at the very top of your document (CTRL + HOME).
2. Click "Insert > Break."
3. Under "Section break types," click "Odd page."
4. Click the OK button.
5. Click "Insert > Page Numbers."
6. Click the Format button.
7. Under "Page numbering," click "Start at."
8. In the "Start at" box, enter a zero.
9. Click the OK button.
10. Click the Close button.

Now when you display pages two up, you'll see odd pages on the right, where they belong. I don't recommend showing pages two up while *editing* a document, but for page layout or overall document review, it's tough to beat. Just page down, review your pages, page down, review your pages, tweaking and refining as you go.

Readers Write

JULIAN JENKINS:

The same thing can be achieved by selecting "Two Pages" on the zoom menu (underneath the various choices of percentages to zoom to).

DONALD HAWKINS:

You might mention that even after you copy the Multiple Pages button to another toolbar, there's an extra step to getting two-up pages. You still have to pick the configuration you want (1x2 pages, 1x3, etc.)—it doesn't go directly to the 2-page display. And when you're done and want to go back to Normal view, you have to adjust the zoom back to 100%. (On my screen, print preview comes up at 49% zoom.)

AARON SHEPARD:

If you select "Different Odd and Even Headers and Footers" under File > Page Setup > Layout, Word will show odd pages on the right under Print Preview. In Word 98 for Mac, I'm going to Format > Document > Layout. Click "Different Odd and Even" and apply to the whole document. I think I first used it with Word 2001 for the Mac, but I'm not sure.

Word 98 doesn't have the option on the zoom menu. Simply choosing a small percentage for zoom does bring up multiple pages, but there's a difference: If I use the Multiple Pages button, the pages automatically expand to fit the window. That doesn't happen with the zoom setting.

CHUCK TUCKER:

I suggest a much simpler way to display pages Two Up. When I want to see two pages side by side in Word, I simply hold the CTRL key down and rotate the wheel on the mouse until I see two pages (or three or four or whatever) side by side. I can easily edit either page, move to other pages, etc. All I have done is change the zoom factor, and I don't need to go to Print Preview to do it.

I would also mention that Word 2003 has a new feature under the View menu called "Reading Layout" that automatically generates a Two Up display with side-by-side views of the pages. There is also an associated Toolbar. You can change the zoom factor in this view, and it remains two side-by-side pages. You can perform all usual edits on the pages. Scrolling down brings up the next two pages, etc. This feature is tied in with the Reviewing capabilities of Word—something I haven't pursued in any detail yet, but it looks like more reviewing features than were present in earlier versions.

Displaying Function Keys

Remember WordPerfect, with its cardboard template that showed which function keys did what? I liked it; you can tell because I created similar templates for my Editor's ToolKit and DEXter programs. But if you just want to see the function-key assignments in regular old Microsoft Word (2000 and above), there is a secret way:

1. Click Tools > Customize.
2. Click the Toolbars tab.
3. Put a check in the box labelled "Function Key Display."
4. Click the Close button.

At the bottom of your screen, you should now see a toolbar that displays Word's function-key assignments. You can move or float it just like any other toolbar. If you like, you can click the "keys" on the toolbar with your mouse while holding down the SHIFT key, the CTRL key, key combinations, and so on to reveal the various functions of the keys. But why not just use the keyboard?

As you type or edit, the toolbar will change. Different functions will become grayed out or even hidden, depending on what you are doing. It's a handy tool to see what functions are available on those keys.

If you want to *print* a list of the function-key assignments, do this:

1. Click File > Print.
2. In the "Print what" dropdown list, select "Key assignments."
3. Click the OK button.

You can also see a list on-screen:

1. Click Help > Microsoft Office Word Help.
2. Click the Answer Wizard tab.
3. Type "function keys" in the "Search for" box.
4. Press ENTER.
5. Click "Keyboard shortcuts for Word" in the Task Pane.
6. Click the items in which you are interested. A list of functions and their associated keys will be displayed. You can also click "Show All" at the top of the window to display *all* of the keys and their functions. Note that you can print this information by clicking the printer icon at the top of the window.

I highly recommend learning all of Word's keyboard shortcuts. No more reaching for the mouse!

Readers Write

Eric Fletcher:

Further to your article about displaying function keys, you can also generate a list of all mapped function keys via the Tools > Macros menu. In the "Macros in" box, choose "Word commands" then scroll down to choose "ListCommands" and click Run. The dialog that comes up lets you select either the current menu and keyboard settings (default) or all Word commands.

The resulting table presents each command alphabetically with the key and modifiers to get at it (as well as the menu where you can access it if applicable). Sort the table by key to see the keyboard mapping for the function keys.

On my system, choosing "all Word commands" generates a 30-page table—more than I care to print, but interesting to browse through to discover commands or keyboard shortcuts you may not have been aware of! (Did you know that CTRL + SHIFT + G brings up the Word Count dialog? I didn't.)

Unfortunately, the table doesn't include a description column, but if you want to find out what a command does, click on it in the Tools > Macros dialog and read the greyed-out description displayed at the bottom. If you click Run, it will invoke the command—the only way I could see the details for the oddly-named "Options Fuzzy" command!

The table will include any keyboard or menu assignments you may have made as well.

Visual Keyboard

Do you ever need to change your keyboard layout from one language to another? If so, you've undoubtedly noticed that your English-language keyboard doesn't always match the keyboard layout used by your computer. If this drives you crazy, you'll be happy to know about Microsoft's Visual Keyboard add-in. Visual Keyboard displays the keyboard for another language on your screen so you can see the character you're going to get *before* pressing the key. You can learn more about Visual Keyboard (and download the free software) here:

> http://tinyurl.com/rzle

And you can see a screen shot at Alan Wood's fabulous Unicode Resources site:

> http://www.alanwood.net/unicode/utilities_fonts.html\#visual

Once you've installed and activated the software, you can use Visual Keyboard by clicking its letters with your mouse. Or, you can simply use it as a visual reminder while typing on your regular keyboard. Pretty slick!

Show Me the Menu!

In the 1996 film Jerry McGuire, Tom Cruise shouts "Show me the money!" I know the feeling, but right now I want Microsoft Word to show me the *menu*—all of it! In Word's default state, many menu items are hidden until you click the little arrows at the bottom of a menu. For example, if I click the Format menu, only five items show up. If I click the little arrows down south, I get about four times that many. I'm really tired of having Microsoft decide what I can and can't see. If you are too, here's how to remedy the situation:

1. Click Tools > Customize. (If you can't see "Customize," try clicking the little arrows at the bottom of the menu. Heh.)
2. Click the Options tab.
3. See that check in the checkbox labeled "Menus show recently used commands first"? Get rid of it.
4. Click the OK button.

Now when you click on a menu at the top of your Word window, you'll see all of the menu items it contains.

(If you don't want to change this option, you can still just double-click a menu heading to view the full menu.)

Of course, Microsoft Word includes many more commands that aren't on *any* menu. You can learn more about that in the article "Hidden Features in Microsoft Word."

When Word Gets in the Way

If you've done much editing in Microsoft Word, you've probably noticed that some of Word's "helpful" features just get in your way. Luckily, Microsoft has made it possible to turn those features off, so that what you type is what you get. Here are some of the more common problems with some possible solutions.

PROBLEM: When you type a tab at the start of a paragraph, your tab turns into a first-line indent.

SOLUTION: Click "Tools," then "Options." Click the "Edit" tab. Uncheck "Use Tab and Backspace keys to set Left Indent." (The wording may be slightly different in your version of Word.) You might also consider modifying your paragraph styles to include a first-line indent. That way, you won't have to worry about tabs at all.

PROBLEM: Word adjusts spaces when you're cutting and pasting.

SOLUTION: Click "Tools," then "Options." Click the "Edit" tab. Uncheck "Use Smart Cut and Paste."

PROBLEM: Words that you type in lowercase sometimes become capitalized without your consent.

SOLUTION: Click "Tools," then "AutoCorrect." Uncheck "Capitalize First Letter of Sentences."

PROBLEM: You're trying to type a word (probably an abbreviation) that begins with two capital letters followed by lowercase letters. When you type a space or punctuation mark after the word, the second letter won't stay capped.

SOLUTION: Click "Tools," then "AutoCorrect." Uncheck "Correct TWo INitial CApitals." You might also want to uncheck "Correct accidental usage of cAPS LOCK Key."

PROBLEM: You're typing a list whose entries begin with (a), (b), and so on. When you type (c), you get the copyright character, a C in a circle. Or, Word mysteriously fixes your mistakes as you type, leaving you insecure about what else it might "fix."

SOLUTION: Click "Tools," then "AutoCorrect." Uncheck "Replace Text as You Type." If you really want to leave this feature turned on (not recommended for editing), you may want to edit the AutoCorrect entries to include only the items you really want Word to correct for you as you type.

PROBLEM: You're typing an enumerated list, and suddenly Word begins putting in the numbers for you. When you try to start an unnumbered paragraph, you still get a number!

SOLUTION: Click "Tools," then "Options." Click the "AutoFormat" tab. Click "Auto-Format As You Type." Uncheck "Automatic Numbered Lists." While you're at it, you might as well uncheck every other box in the window except for "Straight Quotes with 'Smart Quotes.'"

After you've made these changes, you, not Word, will be the editor-in-chief.

My Places

In the Open, Save, and Save As dialogs in recent versions of Word, there's a large vertical toolbar on the left-hand side of the dialog. The toolbar has buttons on it that make it easy to get to such places as My Documents and Desktop. Appropriately enough, the name of the toolbar is "My Places." Or maybe that's not so appropriate, since in any version of Word before 2002, there's no way to modify this toolbar—at least no way I've been able to find.

But in later versions there is a way to add places (folders) to the toolbar. Why should you care? Because doing so will give you quick and easy access to your latest editing projects without having to navigate all over the place. Here's how to add a folder you want to use:

1. Click the "File" menu and then click "Open," "Save," or "Save As."
2. In the dialog that opens, navigate to the folder you want to add to the My Places toolbar.
3. Click the folder so it's active.
4. Click the "Tools" menu at the top of the Save As dialog.
5. Click "Add to My Places."

That will add the folder to the My Places bar. You may need to click the down arrow at the bottom of the bar to see the folder you added. However, you can move the folder up in the list by right-clicking it and then clicking "Move Up." (You can also move it down by clicking "Move Down.") If you want to remove the folder from the bar, right-click it and then click "Remove." You'll notice that you can't remove the existing folders, such as My Documents; they're there to stay.

If you eventually accumulate too many folders to handle, you can better manage them by reducing the size of their icons (which, by default, are *huge*). To do so, right-click one of the folders and then click "Small Icons."

Readers Write

Claes Gauffin:

As you said, there are no ways to modify the My Places toolbar in earlier versions. But what you *can* do is modify the contents of, for example, the "My documents" folder to something useful. If you normally organize your different projects in separate folders, you simply create shortcuts of all these project folders and put the shortcuts into the "My documents folder." And presto! You suddenly have a swift way of reaching all your current work.

NAN BUSH:

An add-on I couldn't live without on Word 2000 is Woody Leonhard's WOPR Places Bar Customizer. With it, you can customize up to ten directory links on the Places bar. It's very easy to install and has worked flawlessly for me. As a technical writer juggling many documents, I can't imagine (well . . . yes, I can) trying to navigate without it. *Highly* recommended. I just looked it up to be sure of its availability and found the WOPR Places Bar Customizer and other WOPR products from:

http://www.wopr.com/html/order.shtml

Modifying Built-in Buttons in "My Places"

Dan A. Wilson

[Note: This article comes from Dan A. Wilson, a true gentleman and an editor's editor. Dan explains how to modify even the *built-in* buttons on Word's "My Places" toolbar. Don't want a "Desktop" button getting in your way? Dan explains how to remove it—and much more. I really appreciate Dan's generosity in supplying this information. If you're not already familiar with Dan's work, you'll definitely want to visit his Web site, the Editor's DeskTop, where he has still more useful information that every editor should read:

http://www.editorsdesktop.com/index.html

This information applies to Word 2002 (Word XP). The My Places bar was not fully customizable prior to the appearance of the 2002 (XP) version. It is easy to add new icons to the My Places bar in Word 2002, to re-order the icons, and to remove any icon(s) you have added, as Jack pointed out in the "My Places" article. But a small amount of registry tweaking will give you complete control over the My Places bar icons, and let you consign the standard, default icons to distant memory.

Entries on the My Places bar are contained in the following registry key:

HKEY_CURRENT_USER\Software\Microsoft\Office\10.0 [or whatever] \Common\Open Find\Places

The Places key contains the following two subkeys: StandardPlaces and UserDefinedPlaces. These subkeys contain the following keys:

StandardPlaces. This subkey contains five keys that correspond to the five default items that appear on the My Places bar.

Key Name	My Places Item
Desktop	Desktop
Favorites	Favorites
MyDocuments	My Documents
Publishing	My Network Places
Recent	History

UserDefinedPlaces. This subkey contains keys that correspond to items you have added to the My Places bar. Example:

Key Name	My Places Item
Place0	firstplaceadded
Place1	secondplaceadded
Place2	thirdplaceadded

The following values can be used for keys contained in the StandardPlaces key and the UserDefinedPlaces key:

Name	Type	Data Options
View	DWORD	{1=List, 2=Details, 3=Summary, 4=Preview}
ArrangeBy	DWORD	{1=Name, 2=Type, 3=Size, 4=Date}
SortAscending	DWORD	Boolean to sort ascending/descending
Index	DWORD	Relative position on the My Places bar
Show	DWORD	Zero to hide a Standard place

Okay, now, here's the trick: If you locate a DWORD "Show" in one of the StandardPlaces keys (or create a new DWORD "Show" in one of the StandardPlaces keys) and modify its value to "0", that folder will not appear in your Word MyPlaces bar in the Open and SaveAs dialogs. I'll explain this step-by-step below.

There must be at least one icon in the MyPlaces bar. If nothing else is there, Desktop will remain. But if there are other icons showing, you can get rid of the (essentially useless for most users) Desktop icon, the MyDocs icon, or any (or all) of the other default icons.

The standard, low-tech way to access the registry is:

1. Click the Windows Start button.
2. Click "Run..."
3. Type "regedit" (don't include the quotation marks).
4. Press Enter or click OK.

The Registry Editor opens.

To hide the Desktop item on the My Places bar, open this registry key (click the plus to the left of a key's name to expand it, then scroll down to the next subkey listed here and click the plus to its left ...):

HKEY_CURRENT_USER\Software\Microsoft\Office\10.0 [or whatever] \Common\Open Find\Places\StandardPlaces

Now, before you do anything else, save a copy of the registry key you are about to change. If anything goes wrong when you close the Registry Editor, all you have to do is locate your saved copy of the key (it has a name you assigned to it, and the extension .reg), double-click it, say Yes when you are asked whether you want to add this to the registry, and all will be the way it was.

Here's how you save a copy of a key: First, click the name of the key. In the example below, that would be the Desktop key. Click File in the Menu Bar at the top of the window, and click Export. Type a name of your choice in the blank, and navigate to a folder you choose to use as a storage folder for the saved-key file you are about to make. Now just click Save, and the key's entire image is saved as it is before you change anything. If you ever had to restore the key to its prior state, all you would have to do is double-click the name of the file you saved, answer Yes, and the changed key would be restored.

Now that the Desktop key is saved, let's change it. [Note: Be careful not to change anything else or go merrily messing around while you're in there. If you do, you could foul up your computer fairly seriously. Also, don't continue unless you've followed Dan's instructions for saving a copy of the registry key.]

1. Right-click Desktop.
2. On the Edit menu, point to New, and then click DWORD Value.
3. In the New Value#1 box, type Show, and then press ENTER.
4. Right-click Show, and then click Modify.
5. In the Edit DWORD Value dialog box, type 0 in the Value data box and click OK.
6. Close the Registry Editor.

That's it. Reboot.

If the StandardPlaces key you want to hide already has a Show item in the right-hand panel of the Registry Editor window, simply right-click the word Show, click Modify in the pop-up that appears, and type the number (not the letter) 0 in the value box, where the number 1 will already be selected, waiting to be changed. Once you have made a change, click OK and close the Registry Editor.

If the StandardPlaces key you want to hide does not already have a Show item, create one as above. You simply right-click the key you want to create a Show DWORD value in, and go from there. It's a snap.

I added a Show DWORD with a value of 0 (zero, not "O," remember) to each of the StandardPlaces keys when I had added several of my own folders to the My Places bar. I now have five (large) folder-icons showing in Word's My Places bar with no arrowhead at the bottom or top to indicate that there are more icons offscreen. I have icons for my folders called Admin, Editing, Current, Archives, and Computing. They're the ones I use most often in Word, and it's really handy and efficient to have them readily available in the My Places bar, so that I don't have to click through other folders to reach them.

After all, *handy* and *efficient* are descriptors it would be wonderful to be able to use for everything Word. This information can move you a step closer to that goal.

Document Preview

Maybe I'm just dense, but I've found another Word feature that I've been wanting but didn't know existed—document preview. If you've read the past couple of articles, you know I've been spending a lot of time poking around Word's Open dialog, and this is my latest discovery. To use the feature:

1. Click File > Open.
2. In the window on the left, find some Word documents and click one of them so it's selected.
3. The toolbar at the top of the Open dialog includes several buttons. At the far right is the "Tools" button. Next to it, on the left, is the Views button, which isn't labeled but looks like a tiny list of files. Just to the right of the Views icon is a tiny down-arrow. Click that arrow to see the different views that are available.
4. One of the views is called "Preview." Go ahead—click it.
5. Wow! In the window to the right, you'll see a preview of the document contents. You can even use the scroll bar on the right of the window to scroll through the document. On my computer, quite a few file types will work, including HTML.

Now you can see what's in a document *before* you open it, so no more opening a document just to find it's not the one you wanted. Very handy!

By the way, this feature works in Word 95 and up on the PC. The Open dialog in Word 2001 on a Macintosh has a "Show Preview" button, but on my Mac the feature never seems to show anything. Word 2004, on the other hand, automatically shows a thumbnail of a selected document.

Here's a bonus tip: In Word 2002 and later on PC, you can (and should!) change the size of the Open dialog by clicking and dragging the lower left corner with your mouse. Make that window as big as you like. Now you can really see those previews. Nice!

Readers Write

Phil Rabichow:

Just thought I'd mention something in follow-up to your article on Document Preview. You would think that if you open a document, go to File > Properties, and check the "Save preview picture," then you would have a picture as you describe in your article—one that you can see, read, and scroll through.

However, it's just the opposite! If you check that box, two things happen:

1. The file size grows.

2. You only see a snapshot in preview mode in the File > Open dialog box—and you can't scroll. The snapshot is so small (in Word 2000, anyhow), you can't read anything. Moral: never check that box.

JUANITA HILKIN:

One last tip on document preview. If you have a wheel mouse, hold down the CTRL key while you roll the wheel, and the view of your document will become larger or smaller depending on which way you roll the wheel. This makes it easy to quickly adjust the view on the screen but still lets you type in the document.

Document Properties

I've been thinking a lot lately about document management—that is, how to keep better track of all those Microsoft Word files I have floating around my computer. One tool I've neglected is Word's Properties feature. If you work in a law office, you probably know all about it. But if you work in a publishing house, you may not even know this tool exists.

To see the Properties feature in action, open a Word document (or create a new one). Then click File > Properties. The Properties dialog will open, and you'll see five tabs:

- General
- Summary
- Statistics
- Contents
- Custom

I'm not going to cover all of these tabs or their contents, but I would like to call your attention to the one that looks most useful for document management—the Summary tab.

Most of the items on the Summary tab are self-explanatory, but the important thing to note is that you can enter or modify any of them. In particular, I'm interested in the Subject, Category, and Keywords boxes. Why? Because if I type information into these boxes, I can do two very cool things. One of them is to search for files with a particular subject, category, or keyword.

Here's how:

1. Click File > Open.
2. Locate the "Tools" button on the upper right of the dialog. Did you know that was there?
3. Click "Find." Wow, is that a nifty dialog or what?
4. In the "Property" dropdown list, find the item you want to search, such as "Subject."
5. In the "Condition" list, find the conditions that fit the search you want to do, such as "Includes words" or "Begins with phrase."
6. In the "Value" box, type the words or phrase that you want to find in the property you selected from the "Property" list. Example: If I wanted to find all my files on the subject of elephants, I'd choose "Subject," "Includes words," and "elephant." Note that this won't find the *word* "elephants" in the text of a document. Rather, it will find all of the files whose Subject *property* includes the word "elephants."
7. Click the "Add to List" button. The search element you just defined will appear in the big box at the top of the dialog.
8. Click the "Find Now" button.

Word will search through your files and display those that match your search. Then you can open the files you want to work on. Note that you can narrow your searches by adding more than one item, that you can save your searches to use again later, and that there are various other features to help you refine your searches. You can learn more about each feature by clicking the Help button (labeled with a question mark) and then clicking the feature you want to know more about.

I mentioned that there were two cool things that can be done with document properties. One of them is searching. The other one is to sort by document properties in Windows Explorer. I'll reveal the details in the next article.

Readers Write

WILLIAM T. BUCKLEY:

When I went to test your instructions regarding document properties, I found they did not work, at least not on my setup.

I am using Word 2002 (10.4524.4219) SP-2, running on Win2K professional.

After I read your discussion of the usefulness of the document properties capability, I then moved on to your detailed instructions:

- I clicked File > Open.
- I located the "Tools" button on the upper right of the dialog.
- But, when I went to look for "Find" under "Tools," there was no such option available in the dialog.

So I am unable to go forward with your instructions. And I'm at a loss to explain why. Is it me, my Word software, my OS, all of the above, none of the above?

I RESPONDED: I really should have checked to see how the feature has changed in Word 2002, which now uses the term "Search" instead of "Find." Also, after clicking "Search," it's now necessary to click the "Advanced" tab, which will get you into the fancy features I described.

ERIC FLETCHER:

I see you've been delving into one of my favorite features of Word: the document properties dialog.

Several years ago we had a huge job coordinating publication of approximately 300 publications in three languages from numerous authors. Each publication would be in any of several different phases at any time so I knew document management was going to be critical. To deal with it, I set up a template with a "cover page" consisting of styled fields to show information from the document properties, then very fastidiously followed a rigorous naming convention with the "Show document properties when saving" option set on.

I've attached a sample document so you can see what I mean. [Note: To maintain privacy, I have not made this document available, but you should still be able to get an idea of what Eric is talking about from his comments.] Here are a few of the features:

1. The cover page has fielded info from the Summary part of the properties dialog. Title, subject, keywords, and comments are styled to display. The "comments" field has a running history of where the file has been. Our procedure copies the subject each time the file is saved with a new name (actually, it migrates through sets of folders; in our case, CHP-A through CHP-D as it moves through various set stages) and appends it to the end of the comments field so I keep the history with the file.

2. Some of the other fields are in the statistics tab: pages, words, creation date—and even some math to show things like average number of words per page (for our client's purposes originally but now very useful for quoting on similar work).

3. I set up a custom field "Default language" to identify the default spelling dictionary and display it on the cover page. We often do work in English, French, and Spanish, so it is helpful to be able to see at a glance what language is set as the default. The value and the setting is managed by a custom macro. (Custom fields can be very useful but the feature is poorly documented.)

4. Since we include the cover page for the client, we type any notes they need to see here so they can send the document off to their author without the notes if they choose. The page number references are fields referring to bookmarks, so we can be quite specific without having to worry about pagination differences. (Sometimes the files are sent electronically and printed at their site.)

5. Although this is a bit removed from the properties dialog, I've included sample portions of the proforma table of contents for the styled headings (we provide all levels at the interim stages so they can see the structure of their work—often handy for reducing confusion without having to be a heavy!) and the ToC for figures. The latter is seldom used in finals but we've found it helps a lot in author reviews since many of them are most keen to see that aspect of the text rather than re-reading the entire content.

I've cadged together various macros to generate summary documents using the properties fields: for example, I can list all files in the CHP-B stage in French and show the number of words. Such macros usually end up being job-specific, but they can be real lifesavers if there are large numbers of files. Of course, a well-thought-out naming convention is critical as well—but if you use the properties, you can greatly extend the number of variables to uniquely identify a particular file.

Oh, and a final tip: since I never use the Insert key, I map the File > Properties command to it. So, to see my properties dialog, I just hit Insert. (And if your finger slips going for Delete or Home, having a dialog pop up is pretty harmless—and reminds one of the usefulness of the feature!)

ANONYMOUS:

I accidentally found an article on Microsoft's MVP Site called "Using VBA, how can I get access to the Document Properties of a Word file without opening the document?" The link is:

http://www.mvps.org/word/FAQs/MacrosVBA/DSOFile.htm

This document has a link to a MS Knowledge Base article which has the DSOFile download. The article also has a link to a template to download and put in the Word Start Menu. When you do this it puts another option on the Tools menu to run the List File Properties. You then have to select which document properties you want to be listed. Bingo! The result is a table listing the document properties of each document in the folder. Actually, it only lists Word, Excel and PowerPoint documents. Fortunately for me, most of my documents are Word or Excel.

I have my document properties set up in the footnotes such as file name, subject, comments, author, etc. I wanted to keep an index of all documents so have manually entered the document properties for nearly 3,000 documents into an Excel spreadsheet. But now that I have the DSO file and template, I can run it to list the properties which I list in the spreadsheet and in the same order so that all I have to do is copy the table and paste it in the spreadsheet.

I keep all my new documents in the same folder until I have enough to put on disk. From now on, when I copy them to disk, I will run the properties list, paste it to the index, then either delete the documents or move them to another folder. That way, I will be sure that no document appears on the index more than once. The great thing about the Excel spreadsheet index is that I can sort by subject, or whatever.

This DSO file is going to save lots of time for me!

NED HUMPHREY:

Thought you might be interested in a bug report. Actually, it's not so much a bug as one of Word's irritating quirks. I call it:

HOW'D WE GET ONTO THAT SUBJECT?

I'm sure you're familiar with the way Word automatically inserts the first line of any new document in the Title box of the Summary (located in the Properties dialog box). Of course, the first line is often not suitable as a title at all. If that were the whole problem, I could live with it. But it creates further problems down the road.

There are two things wrong with it: First, the "title" persists even after the first line changes. That's not so bad. You can change the title at will, or simply ignore it . . . with one major exception. Which brings me to the second problem: Because I edit multiple documents and then immediately email them on to the graphics department every day using Outlook, I systematically rename files sent to me by my various authors so that the graphics people know what to do with them just by looking at the filenames (saves time in writing email explanations), and so I myself can easily find them in my archives. When I click on the "Send to Mail Recipient (as Attachment)" button, what I want to have happen is for the filename to be inserted as the Subject line in the new Outlook email. That works fine if there's no title entered in Summary. But if Summary contains a Word-generated "title," the email subject head defaults to that instead of using the filename. So I have the extra work, each time, of going to File/Properties/Summary/Title and deleting the (often nonsensical) title. Only then am I able to send the email with the proper subject head automatically inserted.

Of course, if you create all your documents yourself, you can avoid this by checking the "Prompt for document properties" box under Tools/Options/Save and then deleting the suggested title when the Properties dialog box pops up before saving a new document for the first time; but as most of my stuff comes from other people, I have to perform the above routine to get rid of previously created "titles."

What I would like Word to do is give you the option of turning off the "automatic titling" feature altogether.

STEVE HUDSON:

Looks like Ned is doomed. There's no way to turn that feature off. About the best bet would be to assign the following mini macro to a key or toolbar—

```
ActiveDocument.BuiltInDocumentProperties(wdPropertyTitle)=""
```

—as well as intercept the "send to" command and do likewise before actually doing the send.

Of course, a dangerous way around it is to include it in the autoopen event—but that means *all* documents will be untitled next save . . .

Sorting by Document Property

The previous article introduced the idea of using Microsoft Word to search for Word documents to which you've assigned certain properties, such as categories or keywords. Now we'll look at how to sort by those properties in a folder. I've learned, however, that this will not work in Windows 95 or 98. In XP, it works great, and it may work in some other versions.

Before you can sort by document properties, you'll have to assign those properties. Here's the basic procedure:

1. With a document open in Word, click File > Properties.
2. Click the Summary tab.
3. Enter the information by which you'll later want to sort. For example, you could enter a category, keywords, or a comment.
4. Save the document.
5. Repeat steps 1 through 4 for other documents. Note that you should really do these steps whenever you create a new document. Word can help you with this by automatically opening the Properties dialog the first time you save a document. To activate this feature, click Tools > Options > Save > Prompt for document properties.

You can also assign properties outside of Word by right-clicking a file in a folder and then clicking "Properties" and the Summary tab.

After assigning the properties you want to use, you can sort by those properties in Windows Explorer or any Windows folder. To do so:

1. Open the folder you want to use.
2. Click the View menu and then "Details." You should now see a line of buttons above your list of files. The buttons will have names like "Name," "Date Modified," and "Size." To sort your files by one of these properties, click the button for that property. For example, to sort your files by the date they were modified, click the "Date Modified" button.
3. Now, the good stuff. Take your mouse and right-click that button bar. Wow, look at all the properties you can include on the button bar!
4. For the really good stuff, click "More . . ." at the bottom of the menu.
5. Put a check in the box for the items you want to use, such as "Subject" and "Category." Then click the Okay button. Wow again! Now you can see those properties in your file list. (Note that you can apply these settings to all of your folders, if you like. To do so, click Tools > Folder Options > View > Apply to All Folders.)
6. Click the button for the property by which you want to sort. Pretty slick!

How can you use this feature? Well, how about keeping track of all documents from a particular author? Or maybe you'd want to group chapters that belong to a certain section of a book. How about using the feature as a document database that allows you to group all documents (from a variety of projects) by a particular subject? There are lots of possibilities.

On a Macintosh, life isn't quite so glorious. There's no way (that I know of) to sort by Word document properties in a folder (at least in OS 9.1, which I'm using). You can, however, sort by properties that you assign to files *outside* of Word. To do so:

1. Open the folder you want to use.
2. Click View > View Options.
3. Under "Show Columns," put a check in the box for the properties you want to display and sort. "Comments" and "Label" are really the only customizable properties available here. Note that you can also set these for all folders under Edit > Preferences > Views.
4. Select a file to which you want to assign properties.
5. Press COMMAND + I to bring up the General Information dialog.
6. In the Comments box, enter the text by which you want to sort. For example, you could type a category or keyword here.
7. If you like, click the Label button and assign a category such as "Essential," "In Progress," or "Project 1."
8. Close the dialog to save your changes.

Making Dashes Easy

While using Microsoft Word, I've often thought how great it would be if I could type two hyphens and get an em dash. Also, when I type a hyphen after a number, I want the hyphen to turn into an en dash to indicate inclusive numbers, like these: 3-10. Microsoft Word tries to address the em-dash issue with the AutoCorrect (as you type) feature, requiring three hyphens for an em dash and two hyphens for an en dash, but that's not very intuitive, and it's not how most people would type. (It comes from the LaTeX typsetting system.)

I decided to fix the problem myself with the following procedure:

1. Insert an em dash into my document (click "Insert," then "Symbol," then the em dash [eighth column, fifth row], then "Insert").
2. Select and copy the em dash.
3. Move my cursor so the dash is no longer selected.
4. Click "Tools."
5. Click "AutoCorrect" and the "AutoCorrect" tab.
6. Turn on "Replace Text as You Type."
7. In the "Replace" box, type two hyphens.
8. In the "With" box, paste that em dash I copied from my document.
9. Click OK.

Now when I type two hyphens together, I get an em dash. Pretty neat!

But how about that automatic en dash after a number? Well, it wouldn't be too hard to type in these AutoCorrect entries:

Replace 0- with 0– (that's zero followed by a hyphen, and then zero followed by an en dash)

Replace 1- with 1–

Replace 2- with 2–

And so on, up to 9.

The problem is, Microsoft Word sees each entry as a whole word, which means if I type a double- or triple-digit number followed by a hyphen, the hyphen doesn't change. Does that mean I have to insert all of those double- and triple-digit numbers by hand to make my dream come true? (There are 999 of them.) Well, since I'm a programmer, the answer is no. I'll just write a macro to do it. And I'll share it with you here.

The macro will create AutoCorrect entries for single-, double-, and triple-digit numbers. (In case you change your mind, I'll also include a macro to remove the entries. Please don't try to remove them by hand; it will take you forever and could cause problems if you try to run the "remove" macro later.)

Once you've run the macro, you'll get an en dash if you type a hyphen after a one-, two-, or three-digit number. You'll also get an en dash after a number like 3,435. Why?

Because Word interprets the comma as the end of a word, leaving the three digits together as another word. If you type an inclusive date, like "1951-52," however, the hyphen will remain a hyphen. That's probably all right because many editors prefer to include the full years anyway, like this: 1951-1952.

What about those times when you just want the hyphen after a number to be a hyphen? Type the number and hyphen (which will become an en dash). Then use CTRL + Z to undo the hyphen's metamorphosis. And, of course, you can always turn off "Replace Text as You Type" or run the macro that removes the digit-dash AutoCorrect entries.

Macros to Add Entries

For Microsoft Word on the PC

```
Dim a
Dim b
Dim c
On Error Resume Next
'SINGLE DIGITS
For a = 1 To 9
WordBasic.ToolsAutoCorrect ReplaceText:=1, _
Replace:=WordBasic.[LTrim$](Str(a)) + "-", _
With:=WordBasic.[LTrim$](Str(a)) + Chr(150), Add:=1
Next a
'DOUBLE DIGITS
For a = 1 To 9
For b = 0 To 9
WordBasic.ToolsAutoCorrect ReplaceText:=1, _
Replace:=WordBasic.[LTrim$](Str(a)) + _
WordBasic.[LTrim$](Str(b)) + "-", _
With:=WordBasic.[LTrim$](Str(a)) + _
WordBasic.[LTrim$](Str(b)) + Chr(150), Add:=1
Next b
Next a
'TRIPLE DIGITS
For a = 1 To 9
For b = 0 To 9
For c = 0 To 9
WordBasic.ToolsAutoCorrect ReplaceText:=1, _
Replace:=WordBasic.[LTrim$](Str(a)) + _
WordBasic.[LTrim$](Str(b)) + _
WordBasic.[LTrim$](Str(c)) + "-", _
With:=WordBasic.[LTrim$](Str(a)) + _
WordBasic.[LTrim$](Str(b)) + _
WordBasic.[LTrim$](Str(c)) + Chr(150), Add:=1
Next c
Next b
Next a
```

For Microsoft Word on the Macintosh

```
Dim a
Dim b
Dim c
On Error Resume Next
'SINGLE DIGITS
For a = 1 To 9
WordBasic.ToolsAutoCorrect ReplaceText:=1, _
Replace:=WordBasic.[LTrim$](Str(a)) + "-", _
With:=WordBasic.[LTrim$](Str(a)) + Chr(208), Add:=1
Next a
'DOUBLE DIGITS
For a = 1 To 9
For b = 0 To 9
WordBasic.ToolsAutoCorrect ReplaceText:=1, _
Replace:=WordBasic.[LTrim$](Str(a)) + _
WordBasic.[LTrim$](Str(b)) + "-", _
With:=WordBasic.[LTrim$](Str(a)) + _
WordBasic.[LTrim$](Str(b)) + Chr(208), Add:=1
Next b
Next a
'TRIPLE DIGITS
For a = 1 To 9
For b = 0 To 9
For c = 0 To 9
WordBasic.ToolsAutoCorrect ReplaceText:=1, _
Replace:=WordBasic.[LTrim$](Str(a)) + _
WordBasic.[LTrim$](Str(b)) + _
WordBasic.[LTrim$](Str(c)) + "-", _
With:=WordBasic.[LTrim$](Str(a)) + _
WordBasic.[LTrim$](Str(b)) + _
WordBasic.[LTrim$](Str(c)) + Chr(208), Add:=1
Next c
Next b
Next a
```

Macros to Remove Entries

For Microsoft Word on the PC

```
Dim a
Dim b
Dim c
On Error Resume Next
'SINGLE DIGITS
For a = 1 To 9
WordBasic.ToolsAutoCorrect ReplaceText:=1, _
Replace:=WordBasic.[LTrim$](Str(a)) + "-", _
With:=WordBasic.[LTrim$](Str(a)) + Chr(150), Delete:=1
Next a
'DOUBLE DIGITS
For a = 1 To 9
```

```
For b = 0 To 9
WordBasic.ToolsAutoCorrect ReplaceText:=1, _
Replace:=WordBasic.[LTrim$](Str(a)) + _
WordBasic.[LTrim$](Str(b)) + "-", _
With:=WordBasic.[LTrim$](Str(a)) + _
WordBasic.[LTrim$](Str(b)) + Chr(150), Delete:=1
Next b
Next a
'TRIPLE DIGITS
For a = 1 To 9
For b = 0 To 9
For c = 0 To 9
WordBasic.ToolsAutoCorrect ReplaceText:=1, _
Replace:=WordBasic.[LTrim$](Str(a)) + _
WordBasic.[LTrim$](Str(b)) + _
WordBasic.[LTrim$](Str(c)) + "-", _
With:=WordBasic.[LTrim$](Str(a)) + _
WordBasic.[LTrim$](Str(b)) + _
WordBasic.[LTrim$](Str(c)) + Chr(150), Delete:=1
Next c
Next b
Next a
```

For Microsoft Word on the Macintosh

```
Dim a
Dim b
Dim c
On Error Resume Next
'SINGLE DIGITS
For a = 1 To 9
WordBasic.ToolsAutoCorrect ReplaceText:=1, _
Replace:=WordBasic.[LTrim$](Str(a)) + "-", _
With:=WordBasic.[LTrim$](Str(a)) + Chr(208), Delete:=1
Next a
'DOUBLE DIGITS
For a = 1 To 9
For b = 0 To 9
WordBasic.ToolsAutoCorrect ReplaceText:=1, _
Replace:=WordBasic.[LTrim$](Str(a)) + _
WordBasic.[LTrim$](Str(b)) + "-", _
With:=WordBasic.[LTrim$](Str(a)) + _
WordBasic.[LTrim$](Str(b)) + Chr(208), Delete:=1
Next b
Next a
'TRIPLE DIGITS
For a = 1 To 9
For b = 0 To 9
For c = 0 To 9
WordBasic.ToolsAutoCorrect ReplaceText:=1, _
Replace:=WordBasic.[LTrim$](Str(a)) + _
WordBasic.[LTrim$](Str(b)) + _
```

```
        WordBasic.[LTrim$](Str(c)) + "-", _
        With:=WordBasic.[LTrim$](Str(a)) + _
        WordBasic.[LTrim$](Str(b)) + _
        WordBasic.[LTrim$](Str(c)) + Chr(208), Delete:=1
        Next c
        Next b
        Next a
```

Special Characters Made Easy (Sort of)

After reading the previous article, which offers an automatic way to insert dashes as you type, Sam Mills wrote: "Excuse me, but why can't you just type shift-option-hyphen to get an em dash as you type? and option-hyphen for the en dash?"

The answer, of course, is that you can (if you're using a Macintosh). PC users have it a little more difficult. To get an em dash, they have to hold down CTRL + ALT and then hit the hyphen key clear over on the numeric keypad. For an en dash, they have to hold down CTRL and then hit that distant hyphen key. Neither of these key combinations is very convenient, which is why I came up with an automatic way to create those dashes. Thanks, Sam, for pointing out the key combinations for those who want to use them on the Mac.

My Editor's ToolKit software provides two more ways to get dashes:

1. By holding down the ALT key and then pressing the M key to get an em dash or the N key to get an en dash-nice and easy.
2. By clicking the "Insert" menu and then the dash of your choice. (I've included the dashes right at the top of the menu.)

You can also get dashes by clicking the "Insert" menu, then "Symbol," then "Special Characters," and finally the dash you want to insert. While you're in there, take a look at the other "special characters" (as Microsoft calls them) that you can insert into your document. To the right of each character is a key combination that lets you insert the character from the keyboard.

For your convenience, these characters and key combinations are (in Word 2000):

Em Dash: ALT + CTRL + NUM-
En Dash: CTRL + NUM-
Nonbreaking Hyphen: CTRL + _
Optional Hyphen: CTRL + -
Em Space: [no key combination given]
En Space: [no key combination given]
1/4 Em Space: [no key combination given]
Nonbreaking Space: CTRL + SHIFT + SPACE
Copyright: ALT + CTRL + C
Registered: ALT + CTRL + R
Trademark: ALT + CTRL + T
Section: [no key combination given]
Paragraph: [no key combination given]
Ellipsis: ALT + CTRL + .

Single Opening Quote: CTRL + "
Single Closing Quote: CTRL + ' '
Double Opening Quote: CTRL + ' "
Double Closing Quote: CTRL + ' "
No-Width Optional Break: [no key combination given]
No-Width Non Break: [no key combination given]

If you try inserting these characters with their key combinations, you'll notice how clumsy some of them are, particularly the various quotation marks. Luckily, Microsoft Word makes it easy to assign new key combinations. To do so:

1. Go to the Special Characters menu by clicking the "Insert" menu, then "Symbol," then "Special Characters."
2. Click the character whose key combination you want to change.
3. Click the "Shortcut Key" button.
4. Press the key combination you want to use to get the special character. (For example, if you want to insert an em dash by pressing ALT + M, hold down the ALT key and press the M key.) The new key combination will appear in the box labeled "Press New Shortcut Key."
5. Click the "Assign" button.
6. Click the "Close" button.

Want to get crazy? Click the "Symbols" tab instead of the "Special Characters" tab. The "Shortcut Key" button is still there, which means you can assign anything in the symbols chart to the key combination of your choice. That's about as easy as it gets.

Canning Spam

For years I fought the battle against spam (junk email) but not at all effectively, even though I tried a couple of top-notch spam-filtering programs. My email address is plastered all over the place, and I was getting literally thousands of spam messages every day, requiring up to an hour to sift through and delete them. Then I tried SpamArrest, and I'm thrilled to say it's actually won the war.

When people send me an email message, they receive an email message in return that asks them to click a link to register themselves (a one-time operation) as someone who can send me messages. Spammers, of course, won't bother to do this, which means—that's right—no more spam. The completely online program (no downloads involved) provides complete control over how spam is handled, and it's very easy to use—including the ability to preregister family and friends.

If you'd like to know more, click here:

http://spamarrest.com/affl?1403707

And if you decide to sign up, please do so through the link above. Since I'm a SpamArrest affiliate, your support will help keep the Editorium alive and kicking. Thanks!

Navigation

Fast Moves

As I've trained editors working in Microsoft Word, I've noticed a strange phenomenon: Left to their own devices, some editors will scroll for pages using only the UP ARROW and DOWN ARROW keys (the cursor keys). That's like using a toothbrush to paint your house. This is going to sound pretty basic, but there's a whole hierarchy of keys you should use to move through a document. Here it is, from big movements to small:

- CTRL (COMMAND on a Macintosh) + HOME takes you to the top of your document.
- CTRL + END takes you to the bottom of your document.
- CTRL + G (Go To) takes you to a specific page.
- PAGE UP takes you up a screen.
- PAGE DOWN takes you down a screen.
- CTRL + UP ARROW takes you up a paragraph.
- CTRL + DOWN ARROW takes you down a paragraph.
- HOME takes you to the start of the line.
- END takes you to the end of the line.
- CTRL + LEFT ARROW takes you back a word.
- CTRL + RIGHT ARROW takes you forward a word.
- LEFT ARROW takes you back a character.
- RIGHT ARROW takes you forward a character.

Ordinarily, you shouldn't use keys that are lower on the hierarchy to make a move that is higher on the hierarchy. As an extreme example, you shouldn't use the RIGHT ARROW key to move (one character at a time) from the top to the bottom of your document. If you do, you're wasting time. For the same reason, you shouldn't use the RIGHT ARROW key to move forward even a single word. In the short run it won't matter much, but if you spend most of your day editing, those small movements will really add up. I'd guess that over the course of a year, you could measure them in miles. Want to increase your efficiency? Get into the habit of using the right key combinations for the movements you need to make. At first it may seem awkward, but after a while you'll notice a big difference in how quickly you can get around a document.

By the way, my Editor's ToolKit program adds one more item to the hierarchy:

- ALT + CTRL + LEFT ARROW takes you back a sentence.
- ALT + CTRL + RIGHT ARROW takes you forward a sentence.

Something else that will help you move around more efficiently is to increase your cursor speed. In a Windows environment, follow this procedure:

1. Click the Start button.

2. Click "Settings."

3. Click "Control Panel."

4. Double-click "Keyboard."

5. Set the repeat delay as short as it will go.

6. Set the repeat rate as fast as it will go.

7. While you're there, you may want to set cursor blink rate as fast as it will go (making it easier to spot your cursor).

8. Click "OK."

On a Macintosh, do this:

1. Click the Apple icon.

2. Select "Control Panels."

3. Select "Keyboard."

4. Set the key repeat rate as fast as it will go.

5. Set the delay until repeat rate as short as it will go.

6. Close the Keyboard dialog.

At first these new settings may seem impossibly fast. If you can stick with them, however, you should soon get used to them, and they'll definitely speed up moving around your document. That means you'll be working faster and more profitably, with more time to spend on the things that really matter. Good luck with your fast moves!

ED NELSON:

My newish keyboard has some added keys. One pair, between ALT and CTRL on each side, carries the MS logo. Maybe its only function is to add a new order of potential key combinations, but that might be a worthy addition if true.

I RESPONDED: Pressing this key is the equivalent of clicking the Start button on the Windows taskbar. I use it a lot, since I hate reaching for the mouse all the time.

ED CONTINUED: In addition, next to the right CTRL key is one with what looks rather like an icon(?). Looks like the representation of a sheet of copy with an arrow-cursor pointing toward the top.

I REPLIED: This key opens a "popup" or "context" menu. It's the equivalent of clicking the right mouse button.

NEIL HYMANS:

The two extra keys discussed recently can do much more than open the Start menu or simulate a right mouse click. When used in conjunction with a "key combination manager" (such as the amazing—and *free*—Winkey from http://tinyurl.com/ehlnw), they open up a world of possibilities for new hotkey combinations. [Note:

Some examples: I use WIN+W to start Word, WIN+X to start Excel, and many others that suit my needs, secure in the knowledge that they aren't conflicting with default key combinations of any other application.

MIKE BROWN:

You can use the Windows key for shortcut key combinations, but I find it most useful as OS shortcuts to useful functions.

My favorite functions are Windows + M to minimize all open windows to the Taskbar, Windows + R to display the Run dialog box (I like to run batch files from the Run dialog box), Windows + F to open the Find dialog, and Windows + E to open an Explorer window.

I use Macro Express (a program to create macros throughout the system or for any program), and I find the Windows key to be a great mnemonic aid for system-level macros.

If you have the Microsoft Natural keyboard or Intellitype software installed, there are tons of other combos:

http://support.microsoft.com/support/kb/articles/q126/4/49.asp

Using Word's "Go Back" Feature

If you're like me, you've often made an editorial correction in Microsoft Word and then, five pages later, changed your mind. But where was that correction? Word includes a feature that will take you back to your last change, then the change before that, and so on, cycling through the last four changes in your document.

The name of the feature is Go Back, although it's sometimes referred to as Previous Edit. Whatever Microsoft wants to call it, it's a handy feature to have. The problem is, it's a hard feature to find. You won't see it on a menu or a toolbar. Nevertheless, it's there, and you can use it by pressing SHIFT + F5.

When you press SHIFT + F5, you'll go back to your last change. What's less obvious is that if you made the change in a different document that's still open, Word will switch to that document and take you to the last change there. Neat! Not only that, but if you open a document you've worked on before, SHIFT + F5 will take you to the last change you made in *that* document. Amazing! Now you can find the place you left off editing in a document you've saved and closed. (If you're using my Editor's ToolKit program, you'll use the Go Back feature by pressing SHIFT + F10 rather than SHIFT + F5. You'll also find it on the Editor's ToolKit 1 toolbar and on the Edit menu, right under Go To.)

Go Back isn't a big, flashy feature. It's just one of those basic, practical tools that you'll use all the time—now that you know where it is.

Object Browser

Have you ever wished you had a way to move quickly from one footnote to the next in Word? How about from one edit to the next? One heading to the next? If so, you need to know about Word's Object Browser, which is poorly documented but richly useful.

The Object Browser lives at the bottom of the scroll bar on the right side of your Word window. It consists of three buttons— a double up-arrow on top, a small round button in the middle, and a double down-arrow on the bottom. The arrows take you to the next or previous something, and the button in the middle lets you pick what that something will be. Just click it to see and select the various options, which include:

- Go To
- Find
- Edit
- Heading
- Graphic
- Table
- Field
- Endnote
- Footnote
- Comment
- Section
- Page

That's a lot of stuff! Note that Go To will also take you to whatever you've selected in Word's Go To feature, which you can summon up by clicking the Go To button in the Object Browser (or by pressing CTRL + G). And that means you can add the following items to the list of things you can browse:

- Line
- Bookmark (selectable)
- Comment (selectable by reviewer)
- Field (selectable)
- Equation
- Object (selectable)

Similarly, the Find button will open the Find dialog, allowing you to search your document as usual. But after you've found the first instance of the thing you're searching for, you can use the Object Browser to jump to the next one. And the next one. And the previous one. Whatever.

This would really be slick if we just had some keyboard shortcuts to do our browsing instead of having to click those tiny buttons. Well, okay, the shortcuts are CTRL + PAGE DOWN and CTRL + PAGE UP. Enjoy!

Thanks to Meg Cox for suggesting this topic.

Go2Text Macro

When I'm editing in Word and see something I want to correct, I usually have to use the cursor keys (repeatedly) to get to it, or I have to reach for the mouse to select it. I finally got tired of both alternatives and created a macro called Go2Text, which instantly takes you to the character, word, or phrase you specify.

I'm giving away this macro! Please feel free to share it with friends and colleagues who might find it useful. After you've used it a few times, you'll wonder how you ever got along without it.

You can download Go2Text here:

http://www.editorium.com/ftp/Go2Text8.zip

The macro will work on both PC and Macintosh.

Once you've downloaded and unzipped (or unstuffed) the proper version of the program, you'll see the documentation, which is named GO2TEXT.doc. (Open it in Word to read it.) You'll also see the Go2Text template, which is named GO2TEXT.DOT. To use the template, follow this procedure:

1. Open it in Microsoft Word.
2. Double-click the large button that says "Double-Click here to Install."
3. Follow the prompts on your screen.

To use Go2Text to go to some text:

1. On your keyboard, press CTRL + SHIFT + G (which stands for "Go2Text").
2. In the box labeled "Enter Text," type the text you want to go to. It doesn't have to be far away. For example, if you see an error a few paragraphs down from your cursor, just type the first few characters of the error into the box.
3. Put a check in the boxes for any options you want to use.
4. Press Enter or click the OK button.

Go2Text will take you to the text you specified. It will also remember your entry and options for the next time you use the program.

To repeat the last action of Go2Text without having to retype the text, press CTRL + SHIFT + R (which stands for "Repeat"). The Go2Text dialog will not appear, but Go2Text will take you to the next occurrence of the text you specified earlier. You can repeat the action as many times as you like. See the program documentation for other options and niceties.

Go2Text vs. Find

A couple of readers asked (much more nicely than this), "Why the heck should I use Go2Text when Word's Find feature will do the same thing?" It's a fair question, and it's something I should have explained earlier.

The differences between Go2Text and Find are small (for the purpose of going to text), but to me they're significant, which is why I created the macro. Yes, Word's Find feature will take you to the text you wanted to find. But notice: after finding something, the Find dialog remains *open*. To work on the text you've found, you'll have to press the ESC key (or click the Cancel button) to get rid of the dialog. With Go2Text, that isn't the case. As soon as you press ENTER, the dialog goes away, saving you the annoyance of having to put it away manually.

Now notice this: After using the Find dialog, the text that was found is *selected*, which means you have to press the LEFT ARROW key to get in front of it—another unnecessary keystroke. Go2Text simply takes you to the beginning of the text without selecting it (unless you specify that it should be selected). This is also true when you press CTRL + R to repeat the macro, while pressing SHIFT + F4 to repeat a Find selects the text.

In summary, when text is found:

Go2Text	Find
Closes the dialog	Leaves the dialog open
Goes to the start of the text	Selects the text

To some people, these differences may not be important. But in my experience, those extra keystrokes add up fast in both time and frustration. If I can avoid them, I do. And if I have a dozen small macros for specific editing tasks, with each one saving me a couple of keystrokes, the effect on my work can be dramatic.

(Clarification: I don't mean to imply that Go2Text *replaces* Find or that it should always be used *instead* of Find. Find is a useful feature all on its own. Go2Text is for those times when you just want to jump quickly to some specific text without reaching for the mouse or cursor keys.)

I'm a big believer in exploiting the power of the computer to its fullest and in finding as many ways as possible to make work easier. Eventually, I hope to do all of my work with no effort. I'm kidding, of course, but that's sort of the idea. R. Buckminster Fuller, inventor of the geodesic dome, had a word for this: ephemeralization. He believed that with technological progress, we would continue to do more and more with less and less until we were basically doing everything with nothing. That sentence is a simplification of Bucky's philosophy, but I think it's true to his vision of the world.

Sentence to Sentence

Microsoft Word provides several keyboard shortcuts to help you move around a document, which is important when you're serious about editing efficiently. You may not know, however, that Word includes commands to move from sentence to sentence—highly useful for an editor! The commands aren't mentioned in Word's Help file, but, sneaky guy that I am, I found them for you:

SentRight (which will move to the next sentence)
SentLeft (which will move to the previous sentence)

To use these commands, you'll probably want to assign them to shortcut keys (or use my Editor's ToolKit program, which already has them assigned). Here's the procedure:

1. Click the "Tools" menu at the top of your Word window.
2. Click "Customize."
3. Click the "Keyboard" tab or button.
4. In the Categories list, find and click "All Commands."
5. In the Commands list, find and click the command, such as "SentRight."
6. With your cursor in the Press New Shortcut Key box, press the key combination you want to use. I'd recommend CTRL + ALT + RIGHT ARROW for SentRight and CTRL + ALT + LEFT ARROW for SentLeft, since these are probably not already in use on your computer.
7. Make sure the "Save Changes In" box shows Normal.dot.
8. Click the "Assign" button. (If you wanted to remove the key combination, you'd click the "Remove" button.)
9. Click the "Close" button.

That's it! Now you can merrily cruise from sentence to sentence as you edit your latest project. As you work, you'll probably notice that you can't hold down the SHIFT key and then select a sentence using the keys you've just defined. The commands, for some reason, don't allow it. However, you can overcome this problem with two other commands:

```
SentRightExtend
SentLeftExtend
```

You can assign these commands to some other key combinations. How about:

SHIFT + CTRL + ALT + RIGHT ARROW
SHIFT + CTRL + ALT + LEFT ARROW

That should make the commands work just the way you'd want them to.

Extending a Selection

Extend Selection, a terrific tool, is often overlooked because it's not included on a menu or a toolbar. It's also not covered well in Word's documentation (so what else is new?). Nevertheless, if you're editing in Microsoft Word, you'll find this feature invaluable.

Here's how it works: You're editing along and decide to delete the rest of the sentence. You could do it this way:

1. Hold down SHIFT.
2. Use your cursor key to move and move and move and move to the end of the sentence.
3. Press DELETE.

Or, you could do it this way:

1. Press F8 to turn on Extend Selection (or double-click the EXT box in the status bar at the bottom of your Word window).
2. Press the period key (.) to instantly select to the end of the sentence.
3. Press DELETE.

The second way is much faster, and when deadlines are looming, fast is good.

Extend Selection automatically selects to any character you type. If you hit the spacebar, it moves to the next space (probably selecting a word). Hit it again to extend to the space after that. Neat! Hit ENTER to extend to the end of the paragraph. Hit a character key to move to the next occurrence of a specific character. Use Word's Find feature to extend the selection to something far, far away. Once you've got that text selected, you can cut it, copy it, italicize it, style it, change its case, type over the top of it, or do almost anything else to it. You can even stick it on the Spike. (See "I Like Spike.")

In the meantime, you should know that hitting F8 several times in succession selects text all by itself. Here's the pattern:

1. Hit F8 once to turn on Extend Selection.
2. Hit it again to select the current word.
3. Hit it again to select the current sentence.
4. Hit it again to select the current paragraph.
5. Hit it again to select the whole document. Now that's a selection!

If you change your mind, you can cancel the selection by hitting ESCAPE and then pressing a cursor key.

The next time you need to select some text, don't reach for the SHIFT key. Instead, try Extend Selection.

Mousing Around in Microsoft Word

When I edit a document in Microsoft Word, I do everything I can from the keyboard. I avoid using the mouse because reaching over to get it interrupts the flow of work and slows me down. Sometimes, though, for a change of pace, I like to see how much editing I can do without even touching the keyboard, using the mouse as a sort of electronic pencil. If you're interested in trying this, here are some things to consider:

1. Using the mouse, you can (obviously) access any of the commands on Word's menus or toolbars, which include such things as changing case, changing format, cutting, copying, and pasting.

2. You can access the commands on Word's shortcut menu by clicking text with the right mouse button. For editing purposes, the most important commands are Cut, Copy, and Paste. (You can use the Cut command to delete text.) If you have Microsoft Bookshelf installed, you can use the Define command to look up words in the Bookshelf dictionary. In addition, Word 2000 includes a Synonyms command so you can replace a selected word with a suggested synonym or use Word's built-in thesaurus.

3. You can use the mouse to drag and drop selected words and phrases. You may need to turn this feature on under Tools/Options/Edit/Drag-and-drop text editing. Once it's on, you can select a word (double-click it), grab the word (hold down the left mouse button), drag the word to a new position (move the mouse), and place the word (let go of the mouse button). To copy the selection rather than move it, hold down the CTRL key with your left hand (if you're right-handed) before dragging the text.

4. You can use the mouse to copy and paste a word from nearby text rather than typing it in. You might also try resting your left hand on the keyboard (if you're right-handed) to type in the occasional space or other character. If you find yourself typing a lot, though, you may want to revert to using the keyboard instead of the mouse.

5. If you move through your document by dragging the vertical scroll bar, you'll see the page numbers in a small box at the right of your document window.

With some experimentation, I've learned which features I use most with the mouse, and I've placed them on the text shortcut menu (right mouse button) in my Editor's ToolKit program. Some of these are regular Word functions; others are unique to Editor's ToolKit. Here they are:

Cut
Copy

Paste
Delete (a single character or text you've already selected with the mouse)
Delete Word
Add to Spike
Insert Spike
Cap or Lowercase Word (toggle)
Make Word Italic or Roman (toggle)
Transpose Characters
Transpose Words
Apply Heading 1 Style
Apply Heading 2 Style
Apply Heading 3 Style
Apply Heading 4 Style
AutoStyle Block Quotation
AutoStyle List
AutoStyle Poem

Using all those features, you may be surprised at how much editing you can do without ever touching the keyboard. Give it a try! You'll soon be mousing around with the best of them.

Vertical Selection

You probably use your mouse to select text in Word all the time, but did you know you can select vertically as well as horizontally? For example, let's take the following text as an example:

> Circumstance does not make the man;
> it reveals him to himself."
> (James Allen, *As a Man Thinketh*)

You can easily select just the first few words of each line down through the whole quotation, something like this:

> Circumstance does
> it reveals him to
> (James Allen, *As*

To do so, just hold down the ALT key (PC) or OPTION key (Macintosh) as you select your text with the mouse. After you've made your selection, you can cut, copy, format, and so on.

Please note that if you're going to cut or copy and then *paste* the text somewhere else in your document, you must make enough room for the multiple lines to fit. They won't just go in at the insertion point the way regular text does. If you don't make enough room (by inserting carriage returns), the text will get mixed up with existing lines of text. This is difficult to explain, but if you try it you'll see what I mean.

Selecting text vertically is especially handy if you need to copy or format the first part of a list. I hope you find it useful.

Readers Write

KATIE LEWIS:

You know F8 is an alternative to holding down the SHIFT key for selecting text? It works well with the cursor keys, so is much more controlled than using the mouse. CTRL + SHIFT + F8 does the same thing for vertical selection. (Esc to turn off.)

I Like Spike

Remember when editors wore green celluloid visors and impaled pieces of paper on a shiny steel spike? Word, too, has a spike, but it's buried so deep that most Word users have never even heard of it. The Spike is a *cumulative* cut and paste. It lets you cut as many blocks of text as you want (like sticking them on a spike) and then paste them all at once in your chosen location. The text is pasted in the order in which it was cut-first in, first out. If you're rearranging massive chunks of text, you'll find the Spike exceedingly useful.

To use the Spike, do this:

1. Select the text you want to cut to the Spike.
2. Press CTRL+F3.
3. Repeat steps 1 and 2 for each item you want to add to the Spike.
4. Place your cursor at the spot where you want to insert the contents
5. of the Spike.
6. Press CTRL+SHIFT+F3.

The contents of the Spike will be inserted into your text, and the Spike will be empty once more. (Note: The Spike pastes each of its entries as a separate paragraph, so you probably won't want to unload it in the middle of a sentence somewhere.)

The Spike is actually an AutoText entry, which means you can see what's in it. To do so:

1. Click the Insert menu.
2. Click "AutoText."
3. In the list of AutoText names, click "spike."

You'll see the Spike's contents in the Preview box.

While you're there, you can insert the contents of the Spike into your document by clicking the Insert button. This will leave the contents of the Spike intact so you can use it again elsewhere if you need to. Or, you can accomplish the same thing like this:

1. Type the word "spike" into your document (remember, the Spike is an AutoText entry).
2. Press F3.

What if you want to *copy* rather than cut the text to add to the Spike? You can do it with a special Word macro that we'll discuss in the next article. In the meantime, I hope you like Spike!

Copying to the Spike

The previous article talked about Microsoft Word's Spike feature, which lets you cut as many blocks of text as you want (like sticking them on a spike) and then paste them all at once in your chosen location. But what if you want to *copy* rather than cut the text to add to the Spike? You can do it with a special Word macro called CopySpike—*if* you have the Macros8 template that comes with Word 8 (97 or 98) and you are using Word 8 or Word 9 (2000). I thought the macro was also in the Macros9 template for Word 2000, but it's not. And the Macros8 template isn't available at the Microsoft Web site. What's an editor to do?

Use my custom macro, which you'll probably want to assign to a keyboard shortcut:

```
Sub CopyToSpike()
If WordBasic.GetSelStartPos() <> _
WordBasic.GetSelEndPos() Then 'Text is selected
WordBasic.Spike 'Add entry to spike
WordBasic.EditUndo 'Undo the cut
Else
WordBasic.MsgBox "Please select text before running this
 macro.", _
"No Text Selected"
End If
End Sub
```

When you run the macro, the contents of the Spike will be inserted into your text, and the Spike will be empty once more. (Remember that the Spike pastes each of its entries as a separate paragraph, so you probably won't want to unload it in the middle of a sentence somewhere.)

If you do have Word 8 and the Macros8 template, just open the template in Word and follow the on-screen instructions to install and run Microsoft's version of the CopySpike macro. (You should find the template in C:\Program Files\Microsoft Office\Office\Macros.)

Line Numbers

I recently needed to use line numbers in a Word document to be reviewed by an author so we could discuss editing changes over the phone without saying things like "Page 289, second full paragraph, fourth line down." Using line numbers, we could say, "Page 289, line 23." Much easier.

If you'd like to do the same, here's how:

1. In Word, click File > Page Setup.
2. Click the Layout tab.
3. Click the Line Numbers button. Didn't know that was there, eh?
4. Put a check in the box labeled "Add line numbering."
5. Set "Start at" to 1, "From text" to "Auto," and "Count by" to 1.
6. Under "Numbering" select "Restart each page."
7. Click OK.
8. Click OK.
9. Make sure you're looking at Print Layout (View > Print Layout).

Line numbers!

Now you and your authors can be on the same page. Er, line. Enjoy!

Readers Write

DONNA PAYNE:

Line numbers in Word will not print next to each row of the table (only one of the rows), nor will it recognize text boxes and text boxes appropriately. I've suggested this as a fix to the Microsoft Word product development team.

Paragraph Numbers

Microsoft Word includes the ability to display line numbers in a document. Unfortunately, it *doesn't* include the ability to display paragraph numbers. And if you need to display paragraph numbers, that's a problem. So, here's a macro that will add a number, formatted as red and hidden, at the beginning of each paragraph:

```
Sub NumberParas()
Dim para, p
For Each para In ActiveDocument.Paragraphs
p = p + 1
para.Range.Select
Selection.MoveLeft Unit:=wdCharacter
Selection.Font.Hidden = True
Selection.Font.Color = wdColorRed
Selection.TypeText Text:=LTrim(Str(p))
Next para
End Sub
```

Formatting the numbers as red means they will stand out from the rest of the text on your screen. Formatting them as hidden means you can hide or display them as needed by clicking the Show/Hide button on the Standard toolbar (View > Toolbars Standard). (The Show/Hide button is the one with a paragraph mark—technically a pilcrow [¶]—on it.)

To get *rid* of the paragraph numbers, make sure they're showing. Then use Word's Find and Replace feature (Edit > Replace) to Find numbers (^#) that are red and hidden and Replace them with nothing.

Or, if the book you're working on actually needs paragraph numbers for reference in its final form, you could Find numbers that are red and hidden and Replace them with themselves (^&) formatted in some other way, such as superscript and not hidden. Better still, format them all with a character style so you can change them all at will and en masse.

Paragraph numbers may also come in handy if you want to use them as locators in a standalone indexing program such as CINDEX—

http://www.levtechinc.com/ProdServ/CINDEX.htm

—but want to use my DEXembed indexing program to automatically embed your entries into a Word document.

Customizing Word

Customizing Microsoft Word

When you first install Microsoft Word, it's set up for the "generic" user—someone who employs only the most basic features of this powerful program. For example, it displays the Standard and Formatting toolbars but not the AutoText or Reviewing toolbars. But if you're editing or typesetting in Word, you're not a generic user—far from it. You could probably *use* the AutoText and Reviewing toolbars. And maybe that Standard toolbar doesn't do much of anything for you. Don't be afraid to set up Word so that you can work as efficiently as possible. Here are some tips on how to do that:

1. During a typical workday, notice which features of Word you use the most. You might even make a list and put a check mark next to a feature each time you use it. Then count up the check marks for each feature at the end of the day.
2. If you're using menus or toolbars to access these features, learn and then use their keyboard shortcuts (see "Keyboard Shortcuts" in Word's Help file). Over the course of a year, this will save you an enormous amount of time because you won't be reaching for the mouse every thirty seconds. If the features don't have keyboard shortcuts, make your own, as explained in "Customizing Keyboard Shortcuts."
3. Explore Word's toolbars by clicking the "View" menu and then "Toolbars." Some of these (Control Toolbox, Visual Basic) may be completely meaningless to you. Others, however (Clipboard, Tables and Borders), you may find very useful.
4. Rearrange menu items and toolbar buttons in ways that make sense to you. Don't settle for Word's out-of-the-box arrangement. Word was *made* to be customized! Go ahead—pull off those buttons you never use. Move buttons from one toolbar to another. If you know that never in your life are you going to use the Letter Wizard, why keep it on your "Tools" menu? Get rid of it! Make your Word window as sleek and efficient as the cockpit of a jet. You can read the basic instructions for customizing toolbars and menus in "Macros on Buttons" and "Macros on Menus."
5. Go spelunking. Use Word's menus to explore features you may not have seen before. Check out Change Case, Word Count, Track Changes, and (if you're a keyboard junkie) Full Screen View. Some of these features will make you smile. When they do, remember where they are (make another list) or put them on menus and toolbars where you can find them again.
6. If you've recorded certain macros that you use a lot, make them easily accessible with keyboard shortcuts, toolbar buttons, and menu items.

If the idea of changing toolbars and menus scares you, just be sure to back up your Normal template (Normal.dot, which resides in your Templates folder). Then, if you need to, you can go back to your original configuration by replacing your new Normal template (where your customizations are stored) with your old, generic one. You can also keep your customizations (and macros) in your own add-in template, as explained in "Creating Add-in Templates."

Remember, too, that just because you remove a feature from a toolbar or menu doesn't mean it's really gone. You can always put it back if you need to. In the next few articles, I'll explain how to create your own toolbars and menus (not just modify existing ones) and add or remove features. After that, I'll show you the secret repository for *all* of Word's features—many of which are not on *any* menu, toolbar, or keyboard shortcut. If you're interested in customizing Word, you won't want to miss that.

Macros on Toolbar Buttons

If you've been recording your own macros, you may be interested in putting them on toolbar buttons for easy access. Here's how:

1. Make sure the toolbar you want to use is showing. (You may need to click the "View" menu, click "Toolbars," and then put a checkmark next to the toolbar you want to display.)
2. Click the "Tools" menu.
3. Click "Customize."
4. Click the "Commands" tab.
5. In the "Categories" list, on the left, click "Macros."
6. In the "Commands" list, on the right, click the macro you want to use and hold down the mouse button.
7. Drag the gray rectangle (representing a toolbar button) to a suitable position on the toolbar you want to use. (A black "I-beam" will indicate the position of your new button.)
8. Release the mouse button. A new button will appear on the toolbar, displaying the name of the macro.
9. Click the "Modify Selection" button or right-click the toolbar button you just added. A menu will appear.
10. Use the menu items to change the appearance of your button until you're happy with it (see the explanations below).
11. When you're finished, click the "Close" button.

Now you can click the button to run your macro from the toolbar.
Here's an explanation of the items on the "Modify Selection" menu:

- "Delete" deletes the selected button.
- "Name" lets you change the text displayed on the button (without affecting the name of the macro).
- "Copy Button Image" copies the icon from a selected button.
- "Paste Button Image" pastes a copied icon to a selected button.
- "Reset Button Image" resets a button to its default appearance, which is blank for a new button to which you've assigned an icon.
- "Edit Button Image" lets you create your own icons or modify existing ones. Be careful; it's easy to spend hours playing around in here.
- "Change Button Image" lets you select one of Word's built-in icons. I frequently use the smiley face to run a quick-and-dirty macro for a particular project.
- "Default Style" displays only the icon for a button that has both an icon and a text name.

- "Text Only (Always)" displays only the button's name, hiding the icon if you've assigned one.
- "Text Only (In Menus)" displays only the button's name if you drag the button to a menu rather than a toolbar (yes, you can do that).
- "Image and Text" displays both the icon and the button's name.
- "Begin a Group" separates the button from previous buttons with a thin, gray line.
- "Assign Hyperlink" lets you use the button to link to a Web page, a file, a picture, or other items, but that's a topic for another day.

When you close Word, the program will ask if you want to save the changes you've made to the Normal (or other) template. In other words, do you want to keep the button you've added? If you do, click Yes (this will also save any other changes you've made to the template).

Macros on Menus

The previous article explained how to put macros on toolbar buttons, but you may prefer putting them on menus instead. Here's how:

1. Click the "Tools" menu.
2. Click "Customize."
3. Click the "Commands" tab.
4. In the "Categories" list, on the left, find and click "Macros."
5. In the "Commands" list, on the right, find and click the macro you want to use and hold down the mouse button.
6. Drag the gray rectangle to the Word menu you want to use ("Edit," for example, or "Insert"). The menu will expand so you can see its entries.
7. Drag the gray rectangle to the position where you want your menu item to appear.
8. Release the mouse button. Your new menu item will appear on the menu, displaying the name of the macro.
9. Click the "Modify Selection" button or right-click the menu item you just added. A menu will appear.
10. Use the menu items to change the appearance of your new menu item until you're happy with it (see the explanations below).
11. When you're finished, click the "Close" button.

Your new menu item will appear on the menu you selected, displaying the name of the macro.

Now you can click the menu item to run your macro.

Here's an explanation of the items on the "Modify Selection" menu:

- "Delete" deletes the selected button.
- "Name" lets you change the text displayed on the menu (without affecting the name of the macro).
- "Copy Button Image" copies the icon from a selected button or menu item.
- "Paste Button Image" pastes a copied icon to the left of a selected menu item.
- "Reset Button Image" resets a menu item to its default appearance, which is blank for a new menu item to which you've assigned an icon.
- "Edit Button Image" lets you create your own icons or modify existing ones. Be careful; it's easy to spend hours playing around in here.
- "Change Button Image" lets you select one of Word's built-in icons. I frequently use the smiley face to run a quick-and-dirty macro for a particular project.
- "Default Style" displays the icon and menu name for a menu item that has both an icon and a text name.

- "Text Only (Always)" displays only the menu item's name, hiding the icon if you've assigned one. (The "Always" means this will be true even if you drag the item to a toolbar button.)
- "Text Only (In Menus)" displays only the menu item's name on the menu (but not if you drag it to a toolbar).
- "Image and Text" displays both the icon and the menu item's name.
- "Begin a Group" separates the menu item from previous menu items with a thin, gray line.
- "Assign Hyperlink" lets you use the menu item to link to a Web page, a file, a picture, or other items, but that's a topic for another day.

When you close Word, the program will ask if you want to save the changes you've made to the Normal (or other) template. In other words, do you want to keep the menu item you've added? If you do, click yes (this will also save any other changes you've made to the template).

Macros on Keyboard Shortcuts

David M Varner wrote, "I disagree with your implicit vote for using Word's menu to implement macros. Sorting through menu items is generally somewhat awkward, especially with time constraints always looming. A pretty good short-circuit for this snare is to use hot keys. Even if you prefer mousing in the menu, hot keys are a wonderful snap by comparison when considering time, and possibly crucial when a deadline is close."

Agreeing with David completely, I present herewith the procedure for assigning a macro to a keyboard combination:

1. Click Tools > Customize > Commands > Keyboard.
2. In the Categories window, scroll down to and select "Macros."
3. In the "Macros" field, scroll down (if necessary) to the macro you want and select it. Any previously assigned keys now appear in the "Current keys" field. (You might want to think twice before overriding existing assignments.)
4. Put your cursor in the box labeled "Press new shortcut key."
5. Press the key or key combination you want to use (Insert, for example).
6. Click the "Assign" button.
7. Click the "Close" button.

Readers Write

ED NELSON:

One of the possible virtues of Word is the capacity to program special keys. However, many are already assigned to some special function by Microsoft. Here are the "key maps" for all these assignments:

For PC:

http://support.microsoft.com/default.aspx?scid=kb;EN-US;Q211982

For Macintosh:

http://support.microsoft.com/default.aspx?scid=kb;EN-US;q177184

LINDA L. KERBY:

Despite the running joke about the Help file in Word, this is how I found the information that I think Ed was asking about. I went to Help > Contents & Index and typed in "keys" in the box in the popup screen. Then I went down in the menu to "shortcut keys" and found a whole array of options. I printed out the list and keep it handy in my Computer Log, along with the dates of when I updated my antivirus software and when I last defragged.

WALTER BLUM:

Yes, making your own macros or shortcut keys can be extremely useful. And yes, there are a lot of key combinations already in use, such as CTRL-C and CTRL-V and many more like them. But when making your own shortcuts, there's a simple way to find out if the key combination is already being used. You don't need a special list. Simply go to the Tools Menu, click on Customize, then click the box that says Keyboard. Under "Press new Shortcut key," do exactly that. If you want to see if CTRL-C is already taken, press those keys. Directly below, you'll see a message reading, "Currently assigned to:" and the key combination in use. If it's not in use, you'll see the word "Unassigned," which means you can use it.

MARY C. EBERLE:

Do you know if there is a way to convert the specialized keys on a typical Microsoft-friendly keyboard to do something useful? For example, I never launch programs from the start menu, at least not more than once. And if I needed to use the start menu, there is the trusty little mouse. Thus the start menu key is useless and even bothersome to me. But it would make a dandy key to run macros if I could redefine it. Do you know any tricks to make that key available to run macros in Word? [The answer? See "Readers Write" under "Fast Moves."]

I have written so many macros to use in my editing that many had to be assigned to hard-to-type key combinations. I recently purchased an X-keys auxiliary keyboard to which macros can be assigned. It has doubled my macro use and increased my productivity. Readers could check this product out at www.xkeys.com. I have even put the comma and colon on my X-keys keyboard because they often need to be inserted and are a pain because in using the regular keyboard for them, I have to take my hands off my mouse. Please note that the X-keys keyboard will work with both PC and Macintosh.

Creating Toolbars

A previous article talked about how to create toolbar buttons to activate your macros, but the fact is, you can create your own toolbars as well. Then you're not stuck with the toolbars that come with Microsoft Word. Here's how:

1. Click the "Tools" menu.
2. Click "Customize."
3. Click the "Toolbars" tab.
4. Click the "New" button.
5. In the box labeled "Toolbar name," type something like "My Macros."
6. In the box labeled "Make toolbar available to," select the template or document where you want your toolbar to live. This will probably be your Normal template (Normal.dot), which will make your toolbar available to any document. You could also select another template or document, however.
7. Click the "OK" button.
8. Click the "Close" button.

Now you can add macros to your toolbar as described in "Macros on Toobar Buttons."

Readers Write

Rob Dilworth:

After Adobe Acrobat Professional 7 was installed on a colleague's PC, he noticed that he could no longer customize his toolbars in Word. Specifically, if he removed a button from a toolbar or tried to add a template that added a button/pull-down menu to his menu bar, the customizations only lasted as long as his session in Word. Once he started Word again, the customizations were gone. Here are the workarounds:

- If the Acrobat add-ins (Adobe PDF and Acrobat Comments) are in Word, the user can save customizations to Word's toolbars by holding SHIFT on the keyboard; then, in the menu, by pressing File > Save All.
- The add-ins can be removed from Word by going into the Windows Registry. If the add-ins are removed, then Word works without any problems. Here's how to remove the add-ins:

Click Start > Run and type in "regedit"; then go to HKEY_LOCAL_MACHINE > SOFTWARE > Microsoft > Office > Word > Addins. Click LoadBehavior and set the value at 0. Once the value is set at 0, the add-ins won't load in Word.

Button Bonanza

Stars, pencils, light bulbs, puppy dogs, faces, diamonds, and hearts. What am I talking about? Toolbar buttons! Lots and lots of toolbar buttons!

If you like assigning macros to toolbar buttons, you're probably tired of the paltry handfull of images you can use on those buttons by default. But fear not! Word has hundreds of images available. You just have to know how to get to them. The only way I know is with a macro, and I'm perfectly happy to share it with you:

```
Sub MAKEBUTTONS()
HowManyToolBars = 10
HowManyButtons = 150
first = 1
last = HowManyButtons
On Error GoTo -1: On Error GoTo Warning
For toolbar = 10 To HowManyToolBars * 10 Step 10
TbarName$ = "Buttonbar " + _
WordBasic.[LTrim$](Str(toolbar / 10))
WordBasic.NewToolbar Name:=TbarName$, Context:=0
For button = first To last
WordBasic.AddButton TbarName$, 1, 1, "Bold", button, 0, ""
Next button
first = first + HowManyButtons
last = last + HowManyButtons
WordBasic.SizeToolbar TbarName$, 600
WordBasic.MoveToolbar TbarName$, 0, toolbar, (toolbar * 2) + 100
Next toolbar
GoTo Endmacro
Warning:
WordBasic.MsgBox "Buttonbar " + _
WordBasic.[LTrim$](Str(toolbar / 10)) + " already exists.",
"Delete Toolbar"
Endmacro:
End Sub
```

After you run the macro, you'll have 10 new toolbars, named Buttonbar 1, Buttonbar 2, and so on. Each toolbar will have 150 buttons. For the sake of programming simplicity, each button does the same thing: turn on bold formatting. But you can see a button's original function by resting your mouse pointer over it and waiting a few seconds for its tooltip to appear. You can also copy the images from any of the buttons to paste on any other buttons you want. For example, if you want to assign macros to custom toolbar buttons, you now have lots of button images to choose from. You can learn more about assigning macros to toolbar buttons in "Macros on Buttons."

If you decide you no longer need the toolbars and their many buttons, you can delete them by running this macro:

```
Sub DELETEBUTTONS()
HowManyToolBars = 10
On Error GoTo -1: On Error GoTo Warning
For toolbar = 10 To HowManyToolBars * 10 Step 10
WordBasic.ViewToolbars toolbar:="Buttonbar " + _
WordBasic.[LTrim$](Str(toolbar / 10)), Delete:=1
Next toolbar
GoTo Endmacro
Warning:
WordBasic.MsgBox "The toolbar does not exist.", "No Such
Toolbar"
Endmacro:
End Sub
```

If you really want to go crazy, you can step up the "10" in this line to create more than 10 toolbars:

```
HowManyToolbars = 10
```

And you can step up the "150" in this line to create more than 150 buttons on each toolbar:

```
HowManyButtons = 150
```

If you want to play around with this, please be judicious. The higher you set those numbers, the longer it will take to create the toolbars and buttons, and the more unwieldy they will become. I think 150 is pretty manageable for the number of buttons on a toolbar. You can set this to, say, 500, but that makes a *big* toolbar. And how many toolbars do you really need? The highest I've gone is 30, but I think 10 is plenty. It would be interesting to know how many images are actually available. After a while, quite a few of the images will be blank, and many of them will be duplicates.

WARNING: Be sure to adjust the macro that *deletes* buttons to correspond with the macro that *makes* buttons. To be more specific, the line "HowManyToolbars" should be set to *exactly the same number* in both macros. If you ignore this, you could end up deleting all those toolbars by hand (under View > Toolbars). Yow!

Thanks to Frazer Wright for suggesting this topic.

Creating Menus

Previously I explained how to create your own toolbars in Microsoft Word. You can create your own menus, too, as a place to activate macros or Word commands. Here's how:

1. Click the "Tools" menu.
2. Click "Customize."
3. Click the "Commands" tab.
4. In the "Categories" box (on the left), click "Menu" (you'll probably have to scroll down to find it).
5. In the "Commands" box (on the right), click "New Menu" and hold down your mouse button.
6. Drag your new menu (represented by a gray rectangle) up to Word's menu bar and drop it (by releasing the mouse button) where you want it to go. It will be displayed on the menu bar with the name "New Menu."
7. Back down in the "Customize" dialog, click the "Modify Selection" button. The customization menu will appear.
8. In the box labeled "Name," type the name for your menu, such as "Macros," and press your "Enter" key to make the change.
9. In the box labeled "Save in," select the template or document where you want your new menu to live. This will probably be your Normal template (Normal.dot), which will make the menu available to any document. You could also select another template or document, however.
10. Click the "Close" button.

Once you've created your menu, you can add macros to it as described in "Macros on Menus."

I've assumed that you're probably going to keep your new menus (and toolbars) in your Normal template, but that's not the best place to keep them, since the Normal template can become corrupted (you should back it up frequently, just in case). It's better to keep your menus and toolbars (and keyboard shortcuts and macros) in your own add-in template, as explained in "Creating Add-in Templates."

Customizing Shortcut Menus

Don't you love Word's shortcut menus? You know—the ones you get when you click the right mouse button. (If you're a Mac user, you can access the shortcut menus by holding down the CTRL key while pressing the mouse button.)

But did you know can customize the shortcut menus, putting the features you use most within easy reach? Here's how:

1. Click the "Tools" menu.
2. Click "Customize."
3. Click the "Toolbars" tab.
4. Scroll down the "Toolbars" list until you see the entry for "Shortcut Menus." Put a check in the checkbox next to it.

At this point, you'll see the "Shortcut Menus" menu bar in your Word window. It includes three menus: "Text," "Table," and "Draw." For now, click the "Text" menu. You can play with "Table" and "Draw" later.

You'll see a long list of the various text shortcut menus. Boy, there are lots of them! To see the one you usually get if you just click in the text of a document, click the one labeled "Text." Look familiar? If you're using my Editor's ToolKit program, you'll see a bunch of useful editing features. If not, you'll see the regular old Microsoft Word standards. You can add all kinds of commands, however, including Word features, macros, styles, fonts, and a bunch of other stuff. To do so:

1. Click the "Commands" tab in the "Customize" dialog, which should still be open on your screen.
2. Use the "Categories" and "Commands" lists to explore the various commands you can put on the shortcut menus. If you see something that catches your eye, use the mouse to drag it over to the text shortcut menu. If you change your mind, drag it off into your open document, where it will vanish into electron limbo. Want to use a different shortcut menu, such as "Comment"? Feel free.
3. Right-click an item on the menu to change its name, image, and so on. You can learn more about these options in "Macros on Menus."

Now, when you click that right mouse button, you'll see the features *you* put there.

Resizing Drop-Down Lists

I work a lot with styles in Microsoft Word, and I like being able to look up at the drop-down style list on the formatting toolbar to see the name of the current paragraph style. I also like giving my styles long, descriptive names, such as Normal Text 2, Normal Text 2 No Indent, Normal Text 2 Block Quotation, and so on. The problem is, Word's drop-down style list isn't wide enough to display the entire name of the style, so I usually end up looking at something like this:

Normal Text 2

—even when the name of the style should be displayed like this:

Normal Text 2 Block Quotation

I have the same problem with Word's drop-down font list, especially with font families that have long names and lots of members (Franklin Gothic Book, Franklin Gothic Demi, Franklin Gothic Demi Cond, and so on). Yes, I can click the arrow on the right of the list to see the full name, but I hate reaching for the mouse, especially when all I want to do is display something.

If you, too, have this problem, there's an easy way to fix it. You can resize the drop-down list to show the full name of a style or font:

1. Click the "Tools" menu.
2. Click "Customize." The Customize dialog box will appear.
3. Click inside of the drop-down list you want to resize. A black border will appear around the list window.
4. Move your mouse pointer to the right edge of the list window. Your cursor will change into a vertical bar with arrows sticking out of the sides (indicating that you can resize the window).
5. Click and hold your left mouse button.
6. Move the edge of the list window to the right until the window is the size you'd like it to be. Don't be shy—give yourself plenty of room.
7. Release the mouse button.
8. Click the "Close" button in the Customize dialog box.

Now, isn't that better? You may be surprised at how much frustration this saves from day to day. I know I was.

Readers Write

TONY DALTON:

I'd like to suggest a clarification in the instructions, which say:

1. Click the "Tools" menu.
2. Click "Customize." The Customize dialog box will appear.
3. Click inside of the drop-down list you want to resize. A black border will appear around the list window.

At this point you might be tempted to click one of the items in the dialog box itself, which won't work. Instead, click *outside* of the dialog box and inside of the drop-down list (such as the style list on the Formatting toolbar) that you want to resize.

STEVE HUDSON:

I have only one horizontal toolbar which has Style, Font (so I can tell which gallery I am using at the moment), and the file path. I have stretched the file path to its max, which is quite long. I also included undo/redo and highlight on this toolbar, as their drop-down nature means they have a nonstandard width.

Reassigning the Insert Key

It happens all the time: I'm editing merrily along in Microsoft Word only to discover that I've accidentally hit the Insert key, turning on Overstrike. Now I've typed over the top of a whole sentence and who knows what else. Aarrgh! I wish I could rip that key right off my keyboard.

After I calm down, I look for a less drastic solution. Sure enough, it's possible to reassign the Insert key so that instead of turning on Overstrike, it pastes something I've copied (just like pressing CTRL + V or clicking "Paste" on the Edit menu).

If you'd like to do the same thing, here's the procedure:

1. Click the Tools menu.
2. Click "Options."
3. Click the Edit tab.
4. Check the box labeled "Use the INS key for Paste."
5. Click the OK button.

(If, for some unfathomable reason, you still need to turn on Overstrike, just double-click the OVR box in the status bar at the bottom of your Word window. To turn it off, double-click the OVR box again.)

Finally, the Insert key is good for something!

It's still not perfect, though. Here's what happens: I'm editing merrily along in Microsoft Word only to discover that I've accidentally hit the Insert key, pasting a whole bunch of unwanted text here and who knows where else. Aarrgh! I wish I could rip that key right off my keyboard.

After I calm down, I look for a less drastic solution. Sure enough, it's possible to reassign the Insert key to almost anything! The question is, what should it be? I'll give you some possible answers in the next article.

Reassigning the Insert Key, Part 2

In the previous article, I complained about accidentally hitting the Insert key and thus turning on Overstrike by mistake. Microsoft Word lets you reassign the Insert key to paste the contents of the Clipboard, but that brings its own set of problems.

Reader Kathy Anderson suggested using the Insert key as an additional Delete key. Bruce from WinHelp IT Editing suggested using it to insert a commonly used symbol, such as the copyright mark. For instructions on how to do this, see "Special Characters Made Easy (Sort Of)."

These still don't solve my problem, however, which is my tendency to hit the key by mistake and then change the document without realizing it. If you, too, have that problem, here are some reassignments you might consider, with their "official" command names (which you?ll need later):

- OtherPane switches to and from another window pane, whether that be a notes pane, an annotations pane, or a split window-very handy if you do a lot of moving back and forth between one of those and your main document. Best of all, if no pane is open, it does nothing!
- ViewFootnotes opens and closes the notes pane at the bottom of your Word window. If you work with notes a lot, this would be a great feature to assign to the Insert key.
- ToolsWordCount displays the number of pages, words, characters, paragraphs, and lines in your document. See "Cut This by a Third" for a way to use this feature:
- ToolsThesaurus looks up a selected word in Word's built-in thesaurus, which I'd probably use a lot more if it were on a conveniently placed key rather than under the Tools menu.
- FormatChangeCase selects a word and lets you change its case.
- EndOfLineExtend extends the selection to the end of the line. After using this feature, you could press the delete key to delete to the end of the line.

There are many other candidates, too, which you can explore using a test document and the instructions below. I'll discuss one of my favorites, ExtendSelection, in a later article. In the meantime, here's how to assign a different feature to the Insert key if you're interested in doing so:

1. Click the Tools menu at the top of your Word window.
2. Click "Customize."
3. Click the Keyboard tab or button.
4. In the Categories list, find and click "All Commands."
5. In the Commands list, find and click the feature you want to assign to the Insert key (OtherPane, for example).

6. With your cursor in the Press New Shortcut Key box, press the Insert key on your keyboard.

7. Make sure the Save Changes In box shows Normal.dot.

8. Click the Assign button. (If you wanted to remove a reassignment, you'd click the Remove button.)

9. Click the Close button.

Readers Write

ANDREW SAVIKAS:

The primary motivation for most users when reassigning the Insert key is to avoid accidental invocation of the cursed Overtype feature; adding a new function to the Insert key is just a bonus. To accomplish the former semi-permanently, just intercept the command:

```
Sub Overtype()
' Do nothing (or do something else)
End Sub
```

Then users can re-assign or un-assign the Insert key at will, without any fear of Overtype returning.

DWIGHT PURDY:

While reviewing some of our long-ago discussions, I decided to go back to www.Phoebusnet.com to see if there was anything happening to their sMaRTcaPs program. As it turns out, there are some things which they have done with it, including branching out to your personal nemesis, the Insert key. The price for this gem is now $5.00. I couldn't resist that, so I downloaded it. If you hit the insert key, it tells you so! Ditto for Caps Lock and Num Lock, and all of them also respond audibly to holding them down for a moment. I haven't had time to explore what other little extras might be there, but this is a "must have."

ALAN SEIDEN:

Here's another caps lock fixer. The program is called AntiCapsLock. It is free to try, but costs $10 to have the program remember one's settings.

http://www.anticapslock.com/

We've set it up so that caps lock only toggles on or off when SHIFT is pressed along with the CAPS LOCK key. It works very well for a fussy computer user.

MARY C. EBERLE:

Here is a mechanical hint that may be helpful to some readers: I put an aluminum cap over the CAPS LOCK key to make it nonoperational. The aluminum cap is made from the open-and-close spout on a box of dishwasher soap. The triangular sides slip down on either side of the key. The pointed ends need to be cut off a little bit at a time until the right height is achieved so that when one accidentally keys the cap on top of the CAPS LOCK key, the key doesn't press down. I glued the aluminum cap on with heavy-duty double-sided sticky tape, but if one sometimes needs CAPS LOCK, the gluing is not necessary.

Style Aliases

As I edit in Microsoft Word, I mark the various typesetting spec levels with styles, which will later be converted by my QuarkConverter program so they can be used as style sheets in QuarkXPress. However, I hate reaching for my mouse to apply styles. So, to make applying styles easy, I sometimes rename the styles with an "alias," which I can quickly type using the keyboard. For example, if I had a style called "Block," I might give it the alias of "b." Here's how it works:

1. Click the Format menu.
2. Click "Style."
3. Click the name of the style you want to rename with an alias.
4. Click the Modify button.
5. In the "Name" box, add a comma to the end of the name, followed by the alias you want to use. (There should be no space after the comma.) For example, to give our Block style an alias of "b," your entry would look like this:

Block,b

6. Click the "OK" button.
7. Click the "Close" button.

Now, to apply the style, do this:

1. Make sure the Formatting toolbar is displayed (View/Toolbars/Formatting).
2. Press CTRL + SHIFT + S to activate the list of styles in the Formatting toolbar.
3. Type the style alias ("b").
4. Press the Enter key.

The currently selected paragraph will be formatted with the Block style.

Aliases aren't limited to one character, and you can use aliases with character styles as well as paragraph styles.

In addition to using aliases, you can use keyboard shortcuts to apply styles. We'll talk about that next.

Readers Write

STEVE HUDSON:

Style aliases are indispensable but can cause problems when exporting to a different format. This macro removes them (Word 2000+ for Windows):

```
Sub RemoveStyleAliases()
Dim sty As Style
For Each sty In ActiveDocument.Styles
sty.NameLocal = Split(sty.NameLocal, ",")(0)
Next sty
End Sub
```

Using Keyboard Shortcuts with Styles

Previously I explained how to use style "aliases," which make it easy to apply styles in Microsoft Word. Even easier is using keyboard shortcuts. I don't like the inconsistency of Word's standard ones, so mine are set up like this:

CTRL + SHIFT + 1 applies the Heading 1 style (Macintosh users would use OPTION rather than CTRL).
CTRL + SHIFT + 2 applies Heading 2.
CTRL + SHIFT + 3 applies Heading 3.

I've added the other heading styles as well—all the way through Heading 9 on CTRL + SHIFT 9.
Also on my computer:

CTRL + SHIFT + N applies the Normal style.
CTRL + SHIFT + B applies Block quotation.
CTRL + SHIFT + L applies List.
CTRL + SHIFT + P applies Poem.

In fact, for those last three, my Editor's ToolKit and WordSetter programs automatically style block quotations, lists, and poems as they should be for correct typographic control. For example, a four-paragraph block quotation actually needs *three* styles, not just one—like this:

First paragraph of the block quotation.
Middle paragraph of the block quotation.
Another middle paragraph of the block quotation.
Last paragraph of the block quotation.

On a typeset page, the positioning of each paragraph would be basically the same as it is here, with spacing above and below the block quotation.
To accomplish that, the first paragraph would need a style called something like BlockFirst, which would be set up to include, say, 6 extra points of spacing (leading) above it.
The second and third paragraphs, styled with BlockMiddle, would include *no* extra spacing above or below.
The third paragraph, styled with BlockLast, would include 6 extra points of spacing below it.
That may seem overly picky, but it provides enormous control over the formatting of a block quotation, and it's the right way to do it. The *easy* way to do it is to install my

Editor's ToolKit or WordSetter program, select the paragraphs of the block quotation you want to format, and press CTRL + SHIFT + B. Bingo! The whole block quotation will automatically be styled correctly. If you think that's neat, you should see how the programs style multiple-stanza poems (too complex to go into here).

If you want to assign your own key combinations to styles, you can do it like this:

1. Click the "Format" menu.
2. Click "Style."
3. In the "Styles" box, find and click the style you want to apply with a key combination.
4. Click the "Modify" button.
5. Click the "Shortcut key" button.
6. With your cursor in the box labeled "Press new shortcut key," press the key combination you want to use, such as CTRL + SHIFT + B.
7. Click the "Assign" button. The new combination will appear in the box labeled "Current keys."
8. Click the "Close" button.
9. Click the "OK" button.
10. Click the "Close" button.

To apply the style using the new key combination, do this:

1. Position your cursor on the paragraph you want to style
2. Press the key combination.

The paragraph will be formatted with the style you selected for that key combination.

Try not to get too carried away. Remember that you need certain key combinations for things other than styles. CTRL + F, for example, brings up Word's Find dialog, and ALT + E activates the Edit menu.

If you need to remove a key combination, that's easy too:

1. Click the "Format" menu.
2. Click "Style."
3. In the "Styles" box, find and click the style with the key combination you want to remove.
4. Click the "Modify" button.
5. Click the "Shortcut key" button.
6. In the "Current keys" box, click the key combination you want to get rid of.
7. Click the "Remove" button. The new combination will disappear.
8. Click the "Close" button.
9. Click the "OK" button.
10. Click the "Close" button.

And that's how to use keyboard shortcuts with style—oops, I mean styles.

Readers Write

NEMAN SYED:

A colleague of mine recently asked me if there was a keyboard shortcut to modify styles (I love keyboard shortcuts), and I showed him how to assign shortcut keys to Word commands and deal with the Task Pane. Office XP has very poor native keyboard alternatives for the Task Pane, to the point I hardly ever use them, with just a couple of exceptions:

- F6 toggles between the document and the Task Pane. You can then use up/down/tab/shift-tab/enter/alt-down (to open drop-down lists), etc.
- CTRL + TAB cycles through the Task Pane, toolbars, and menu, when you're in one of the Task Pane, toolbars, or menu. If you're in the document, it puts a tab.

Realizing that making these shortcuts may be useful for others, here's my solution: Assign the keyboard shortcut of ALT + M to the FormatStyleModify command.
Here's how:

1. Tools > Customize.
2. Commands > Keyboard.
3. From the Format category on the left, choose FormatStyleModify on the right.
4. Assign ALT + M or whatever keyboard shortcut you want in the "Press new shortcut key" box. If you choose something that already has an assignation, you'll see it noted in an unobtrusive manner below.
(4a. If desired, change the template from Normal.dot to whatever document/template you want this to apply to. Obviously this selection influences what machines this keyboard shortcut is available on; in Windows 2000 and above, this may only be for the current user. In my case I keep all my modifications, macros, etc. in a file called custom.dot which I automatically throw into Word's Startup folder whenever I'm on a new machine. It's portable and powerful. Note: Only open documents and their templates are eligible candidates here, so to use my personal approach you'll need to manually open whatever startup template/add-in you use to store all your customizations.)
5. OK your way back to your document.

Your ALT + M shortcut now modifies whatever style your cursor is sitting in. (Not surprisingly, character takes precedence over paragraph.) It certainly saves me time and trouble, and I hope it will for your readers, too!

Style Dialogs in Word 2002

The Styles and Formatting Task Pane in Word 2002 and 2003 is a useful feature, but, keyboard junkie that I am, I just hate reaching for the mouse every time I need to create or modify a style—and the Task Pane doesn't seem to work with the keyboard. Isn't there a way to get back Word's old Style dialog? Or better yet, how about a way to access Word's fancy Modify Style dialog (which has the most commonly used options right there) without having to drill down through the Task Pane and a couple of other dialogs?

The beauty of Word is that almost anything is possible, and although I'm unhappy with some of what Microsoft has done to increase the "marketability" of my favorite word processor, I'm glad they've had the good sense to leave in (and even add) some great features, even if they're sometimes buried pretty deep.

If you want to get back the keyboard-controllable Style dialog, do this:

1. Click Tools > Macro > Macros.
2. Click the "Macros In" dropdown list.
3. In the list, click "Word commands."
4. In the "Macro name" list, use the scroll bar to find "FormatStyle."
5. Click "FormatStyle."
6. Click "Run."

Wow! There's the friendly Style dialog, ready to be controlled through keyboard commands (or, if you insist, with your mouse). No Task Pane needed!

Of course, you're not going to want to drill down through Tools > Macro > Macros every time you want to use the dialog, so you might as well put the command on a toolbar button, a menu, or a keyboard shortcut.

While we're playing around with style commands, there are some others you might want to add to a toolbar, menu, or keyboard shortcut. If you work with styles a lot, you could even create a Styles menu or toolbar devoted entirely to these commands:

• FormatStyleModify (which lets you modify styles)
• FormatStyleNew (which lets you create new styles)
• FormatStyleGallery (which lets you see the styles in your various Word templates)
• FormatStyleVisibility (which lets you hide or display text depending on the style applied; where has *this* been all my life?)

Now are you happier with Word 2002? I know I am.

Note: If you're a Mac user, the procedure should be basically the same in Word X.

Readers Write

JIM CRONIN:

Prior to Word 2002, you could redefine a style by making direct formatting alterations in a paragraph then clicking on the style name in the toolbar's Style drop-down list and pressing Enter twice. This was a lot easier and quicker than using Word 2002's Task Pane. The solution is to click Tools > Options from the toolbar, select the Edit tab, and ensure that the "Prompt to update style" checkbox is selected.

ROMKE SOLDAAT:

Here are some other useful style commands to add to your custom Styles toolbar:

Apply Heading 1
Apply Heading 2
Apply Heading 3
Style by Example
Modify Style
Redefine Style
Rename Style
Delete Style
Style
Style Gallery

Also, here's a nifty little macro that you can add to your toolbar. The macro displays Word's Organizer feature, all set so you can organize styles:

```
Sub OrganizeStyles
With Dialogs(wdDialogOrganizer)
.DefaultTab = wdDialogOrganizerTabStyles
.Show
End With
End Sub
```

Hidden Features in Microsoft Word

Microsoft Word comes with lots of features, many of which do not appear on menus or toolbars unless you put them there. Some of these features aren't even documented. Nevertheless, some of them are very useful for editing, writing, typesetting, and other publishing tasks, and it's easy to explore them and put the ones you like on menus, toolbars, and keyboard combinations for easy access.

You can see (and run) *any* of Word's features like this:

1. Click the "Tools" menu.
2. Click "Macro."
3. Click "Macros."
4. In the "Macros in" box, find and click "Word commands."
5. In the "Macro name" list, you'll see all of Word's features.
6. Click a feature that looks interesting. You'll see a brief description of the feature in the "Description" box.
7. Click the "Run" button to run the feature.

If you want to add a feature to a menu, toolbar, or keyboard combination, feel free. The only difference in the procedures as explained in this book is that in the "Categories" list, you should click "All Commands" instead of "Macros."

One caution: Please don't try any of these features on a document with any importance. Just use a test document with some junk text until you understand exactly what a feature does and feel comfortable using it. Have fun spelunking!

Editing

Editing on the Computer

You may be wondering: *Why* should you edit on the computer? Because, to attain the same level of quality, it's cheaper than editing on paper—cheaper in money, time, and stress. I've heard editors complain that they don't like to edit on the computer because they "miss things." They may not realize it, but they miss things on paper, too. In my experience, editors who really understand the advantages of editing on the computer wouldn't go back to working on paper for anything. Here are some of those advantages, particularly in Microsoft Word, which I offer for those who don't understand them or who may need to convince others of their reality:

- Word's Find and Replace features help you attain complete consistency in matters of spelling, capitalization, and punctuation in a relatively small amount of time. To accomplish the same thing on paper, you'd have to comb through a manuscript several times, and even then you wouldn't be sure you'd caught everything.
- Word's Heading styles and Outline view let you see and revise the overall structure of a manuscript in ways that are practically impossible on paper. (Ah, the days of scissors and tape.)
- Word's spell checker makes it possible to catch even the most elusive of typos. It won't find correctly spelled words used incorrectly, but it sure will catch incorrectly spelled words. Editors should use this tool to full advantage.
- Word's macro features let you automate all kinds of nitpicky chores that would take hours to do by hand. I often plead with colleagues, "If you have some tedious, repetitive, mind-numbing editing task, please *tell* me so I can write a macro that will do it for you." Sometimes they do!
- Word's reference features (such as Thesaurus and Look Up Reference) let you instantly find synonyms, check definitions, and much more. In addition, all sorts of reference works are available on CD and online, so you can find information and check facts in a fraction of the time it used to take. One CD product, Microsoft Bookshelf, was made to work with Microsoft Word; it includes The American Heritage Dictionary, The Concise Columbia Encyclopedia, The World Almanac and Book of Facts, and other publications. If you also use Encarta or other CD-based reference works, I recommend that you install at least two CD-ROM drives on your computer for easy access. Better yet, put the electronic reference works directly onto that giant hard drive of yours.

Some useful reference Web sites include:

FreeByte's Guide to Free Online Reference: http://www.freebyte.com/reference/
The Reference Desk: http://rking.vinu.edu/ref.htm
Research-It!: http://www.itools.com/

OneLook Dictionaries: http://www.onelook.com/
Library of Congress: http://catalog.loc.gov/
Encyclopedia Britannica: http://www.britannica.com

And, of course, the Internet itself is a marvelous research tool.

- Editing electronically saves time (and thus lowers costs) throughout the production cycle, making you and your company more productive and more competitive. Here's why: If you edit on paper, somebody still has to get your corrections into electronic form for typesetting (and, nowadays, all sorts of electronic publishing). Some companies have typesetters key the whole edited manuscript. Others use the author's word-processor files, with typesetters keying in only the editor's corrections. Either way is a duplication of effort (and thus a waste of time and money), because the editorial changes are being made twice, once on paper and once electronically. Add to that the time and cost of proofreading (and correcting) the typesetter's work, and you begin to see the real extent of the problem. Why not just make the editorial changes electronically to begin with?

"Because," the papyrophiles exclaim, "we don't like making all those little changes on the computer." To which I say, "Why not? You make them on paper. And then check all of them on paper. And then send corrections back to the typesetter. And then check those corrections. Do you really like that better?" But okay, okay, I don't like making them either, on the computer *or* on paper. That's why I've created tools like FileCleaner, which avoids the whole ugly mess of manually eliminating double spaces between sentences, making sure punctuation following italicized words is also italic, making sure commas and periods are inside of quotation marks, and so on. By automating this kind of stuff, you make it easier to find substantive errors you might miss while messing with the miniscule. Editing on the computer doesn't turn editors into typesetters or technicians. It lets them focus on what good editors do best: grapple with meaning and clarity and communication.

If you're still working on paper, why not do yourself a favor? Learn to use the electronic tools that will make your work better, faster, and more fulfilling. You'll be glad you did.

Readers Write

SETH R. BECKERMAN:

There is a moderate list of web resources on the Council of Science Editors website:

http://www.councilscienceeditors.org/links.cfm

ALICE FALK:

The best place I've found for locating online works generally, not just references, is "The On-Line Books Page":

http://digital.library.upenn.edu/books/

There are online classical texts on the Perseus site:

http://www.lib.uchicago.edu/efts/PERSEUS/

The site has fantastic search capabilities—look for a phrase in all of Plato's works at once! switch back and forth between Greek and English!

When *Not* to Edit on the Computer

After I published the previous article, in which I hammered on "paper" editors fairly hard, LeAnne Baird wrote to remind me that there are times when editing on paper may be the best way to go. What are those times? Here are a few for your consideration:

1. When training is at least as important as efficiency. If you're trying to turn a proofreader into a copyeditor, or help a writer produce better copy, editing on paper lets the proofreader or writer see and absorb your changes. Yes, you can track revisions in Microsoft Word. But since a typeset document is eventually created from the edited Word document, there's no need for a proofreader to compare the two—or for a writer to make changes that have already been made.

2. Also, one of the main reasons for editing on the computer is to eliminate steps in the publishing process. So, if you're editing on the computer, you'll need to systematically teach the skills people learn naturally while proofreading or making corrections. Once source for training materials is EEI Communications (http: //www.eeicommunications.com/), which publishes a book called *The Copyeditor's Guide to Substance & Style*, by Mary Stoughton (http://www.eeicommunications. com/press/ss/).

3. When you're faced with a challenge that makes editing on the computer difficult or impossible. The problem could be anything from impaired vision to attention deficit disorder to carpal tunnel syndrome. Whatever it is, you'll need to find a way to work with it, and that might include editing on paper.

4. When you're doing a massive cut-and-paste job and simply need to see four or five or a dozen pages at once. Microsoft Word does a pretty good job of letting you see more than one document at a time, but unless you have a 35-inch monitor, paper may still be a more effective way to tackle the problem. See "Doing the Splits" for more information.

Interview with Hilary Powers

Hilary Powers and Jack Lyon

Here is an email exchange with on-screen editor and expert Word whacker Hilary Powers, to whom I owe many thanks, not just for this spectacular interview but also for her encouragement and suggestions in general. Pay attention; you're about to learn something.

JL: Why do you edit on the computer rather than on paper?

HP: The easy answer is, "That's what my clients want." But that's a cop-out, as I won't work with anybody who doesn't want on-screen editing. The computer can deal with the dogwork—it can handle the correction of mechanical things such as spacing after punctuation entirely unsupervised, and can do repetitive corrections of spelling idiosyncrasies and the like under my watchful eye a lot faster than I can take care of them by hand, and without missing anything. This leaves me free to concentrate on the flow of the language and on making sure that I understand the author and do only what will improve the text for the author's purposes. As a result, I can complete a job much more quickly onscreen than I could on paper, with (since I also work only on project rates) a corresponding boost to my income.

JL: What process do you use?

HP: It varies from job to job too much for a quick answer. I wrote out a basic guide for a class I taught a year or so ago, though; 2 pages single-spaced 12-pt Times Roman. Would you like a copy? [Hilary thoughtfully provided an updated version, and it's available here: http://www.editorium.com/process.htm]

JL: What features of Microsoft Word do you use the most? How do you use these features?

HP: (Aside from words-in-a-row, you mean?) VBA macros (my own as well as those provided by clients and purchased from the Editorium), customized menus ditto, hot keys, Track Changes, Find & Replace (including wildcards), and AutoText and AutoCorrect. All provide ways to get the computer to do things that would otherwise require me to use the keyboard and mouse. (Hot keys allow the keyboard to replace the mouse for menu selections and commands. The keyboard is faster than the mouse for such things.)

JL: What other programs do you use in the editing process?

HP: Kurzweil Voice Pro to run voice macros that move text to the style sheet and do other chores that have to be done one instance at a time. WinZip and Conversions Plus to deal with files, and CompareRite for clients who want WordPerfect edits. Frisk and McAfee for virus checking.

JL: Do you have any secret "power" techniques?

HP: Heh. If they wuz secret, I couldn't tellya, now could I? Here's one that I don't try to keep to myself: I set up a template for each client with menus that provide the same commands for the same functions, and load the client template as global whenever I work on a job for that client. Take queries, for example: everybody wants queries, but they want all sorts of different formats—some want inline boldface with various flag characters, others want Word Comments or separate styled paragraphs or even footnotes. I want to give them all exactly what they want, but I don't want to have to remember all the details. So every client template has a menu called "Queries" with ALT + Q for the hot key. The first item on that menu is always "1 Author," the second item is always "2 Editor," and the third is "3 Production"—with the numbers hot in each case—and any special stuff for that client further down the list. That means that when I run into something that requires a query to the author, all I have to do is press ALT + Q (the first item on a menu is selected automatically) and Enter, and I'm immediately positioned after the required salutation in a properly formatted query.

In the template I'm using at the moment, for instance, typing "ALT + Q ip inhyp hh " produces "[[AUTHOR: Is preceding sentence OK? In this hypersensitive age, it's useful to avoid 3rd-person-singular pronouns where feasible so as to keep the reader's mind on the matter at hand and off linguistic development and gender politics. . . . Even relatively neutral usages such as "his or her" can be distracting.]]" (with everything between the outer pair of brackets in boldface as the current client requires). Other special-purpose menus take care of typemarking code sequences and assorted repetitive chores. It's a sort of miniature version of "mass customization"—I work the same way all the time, but the effect is different depending on what the client wants.

JL: What is your "philosophy" of editing?

HP: The editor's job is to help the document serve the client's purposes in a way the client will find satisfactory. This involves a healthy dose of the Golden Rule (them as pays the gold makes the rules); I don't feel any compulsion to defend the English language against all comers or follow my own opinions as to perfect structure and style when the client has asked only for a light, mechanical edit. At the same time, the clients I keep are the ones whose rules make sense to me.

I'm usually working for a publisher rather than directly for the author of the work, and in that case my goal is still to keep the author happy—call the author's attention to anything I think has a chance of having shaded the meaning, explain what I'm doing in terms that convey my respect and appreciation for the work, and ask for authorization as needed—because a happy author makes for a happy publisher, but I'll also defend the publisher's house style to the author whether or not I agree with it unless applying it in a given instance will wreak such carnage that the publisher will look stupid as a result. It's a juggling act, but it's almost always possible to keep everybody happy with an edit. For more on queries and responses, check out http://www.editorsforum.org/forum_index_articles/editing_01_16_01.php at the Bay Area Editors' Forum Web site—the report on the January 2001 meeting includes a good writeup on a presentation I gave on the topic.

JL: What advice would you give to others who are editing on the computer?

HP: Stay alert—every time you spot yourself doing the same set of keystrokes or mouse moves more than twice on a job, look for a way to hand off all or part of the chore to the computer. It's well worth an hour's work to save yourself a minute on every job from now to the end of time. . . . As you go, you'll keep learning more about what the computer can do—and the better you know your tools, the more you can do with them. And every time you don't press a key or move your mouse, that's one less motion charged to your repetitive-stress account. (RSI is a Big Deal, and the time to deal with it is before it starts to be a problem. I'd like to be able to put in a 10-hour day from time to time the way I could when I first started, but 5 hours is a big day now and 8 hours is outright dangerous—despite a major ergonomic workstation and very careful techniques, all developed after I started to hurt.)

One more point: Never trust the computer to know more than you do about language, or about editing. It will "help" you into a hole in the ground, professionally speaking, if you get in the habit of running "Replace All" operations on files you don't subsequently reread, accepting its spelling recommendations without looking them up in the dictionary unless you recognize the correction as well as your own name, or adopting its grammar advice. (Well, I suppose that's "adopting its grammar advice for anything you don't know for absolute truth is an improvement in both the tone and the accuracy of the new text." But for most purposes the grammar checkers I've looked at are so flawed as to be outright dangerous to anyone who isn't far too confident to need them at all.) Microsoft Word is a fantastic tool for editing, but it's a tool; if it would do the job on its own, we'd all be hard up for work.

[Hilary Powers—who bills her editorial services business as "The edit you want, when you want it done!"—boasts of never having missed a job deadline, not even the one for the 325-page manuscript that arrived less than two weeks from its at-print date. The secret: maximum mileage out of the computer . . . plus a good sense of when to say no. She can be reached at www.powersedit.com but can't guarantee to have time to answer requests for advice.]

Editors and Preditors

In the publishing house where I used to work, we had several editors (who edited books, natch) and a few editorial assistants (who proofread, checked corrections, and so on). We edited in Microsoft Word, and most electronic manuscripts required a lot of cleanup. The editors did much of this themselves—turning multiple spaces into single spaces, changing double hyphens into em dashes, and so on. But I keep thinking that many such tasks could be relegated to someone less expensive than a full-fledged editor—sort of a "pre-editor," or, just for fun, "preditor."

The preditor's job would be to get electronic manuscripts ready for the editors, who could then focus more fully on editing. The preditor could do such things as:

1. Combine chapter files into one book file or split a book file into chapters, depending on how your editors like to work. Editor's ToolKit can automate this for you.
2. Rename files to fit your house standard, such as job number_chapter number (3298_0001.doc). If you don't have such a standard, you might want to create one. It will help streamline the publishing process and simplify archiving.
3. Apply to the files a document template formatted especially for editing:
4. Apply styles (or codes) to specify document structure and typesetting levels:
See "Marking Spec Levels with Styles," "Styles and Standardization, "Standard Style List," "Typefaces for Editing" and "Raw Codes."
5. Fix messed-up notes:
See "Fixing Bad Notes," "Restoring Missing Notes," "and "Restoring Superscript to Note Numbers."
6. Find and replace common editorial and typographical problems. My FileCleaner program can automate much of this.
7. Use wildcard and other searches to fix inconsistencies in editorial style, consulting with the project editor as needed. MegaReplacer makes this a snap and even includes scripts to fix common editorial problems. (See the "Find and Replace" section in this book.)
8. Run a spell check; it won't catch misused words, but it will catch the most elusive of typos. See "Spell Checkers."

At this point, those files should be squeaky clean—except for the actual editing, which editors can now do without worrying about such picayune problems as whether or not commas are inside or outside of quotation marks. Yes, I know that editors can't ignore such things, but a preditor can help free up editors' time so they can focus mainly on clarity, meaning, and communication.

The Problem of Proportion

One of the main problems editors have working on a computer is that they lose their sense of proportion about the manuscript. What do I mean by sense of proportion? While working on a paper manuscript, with the pages piled neatly on the desktop, editors know exactly how much work they've done: 112 pages, stacked on the left, are finished; 204 pages, stacked on the right, are left to edit. In my experience, they also know that chapter 3 is about, oh, half an inch from the bottom in the left-hand stack if they need to go back to it. And they know, semi-consciously, that the odd foreign word the author used was about twenty pages back and about a third of the way down the page. In other words, they have a "positional memory" that helps them find things. It's not as efficient as their word processor's "find" function, but it's not bad, either.

Editing on the computer throws all of this out of whack, because on the computer there are no discrete pages, just one long, solid mass of text that scrolls up and down. I know which "page" I'm on because Microsoft Word tells me the page number on its status bar. Still, when I fixed that misspelling, it was about half an inch from the top of the screen, but where is it now? And on what page?

Microsoft Word does include some tools that can help overcome this problem. If you've used Word's built-in Heading styles to mark your headings (which you should), you can use Word's Outline view to see your document's overall structure, navigate to the areas where you want to work, move paragraphs around, and "promote" or "demote" Heading levels. (To use Outline view, click the View menu item at the top of your Word window. Then click "Outline.")

I previously recommended the use of another tool, the Document Map. (To use it, click the View menu, then "Document Map.") The Document Map is like a table of contents that appears in a window on the left side of your screen. You can use the Document Map to see the structure of your document by expanding and contracting the heading levels that appear in it. Unlike Outline view, however, this will not change the display of the document itself. You can also click a heading level to jump to an area where you want to work. The Document Map is similar to Outline view but without the clutter. *But it does have problems.* If it can't find the formatting it needs to display document levels, it *creates* them—by automatically applying heading styles to the parts of your document it *thinks* are headings. For me, this is a deal-killer; I don't want Word doing *anything* automatically, so I no longer recommend this feature.

As I thought about other ways to solve the problem of proportion, I wondered what would happen if I could "lock" a document's pages, using manual page breaks to separate the text into discrete pages that fit nicely onto the screen. Seemed like a good idea. But the text would flow to a different page when I made changes. Solution: Set the page length to its maximum of 22 inches so there'd be plenty of room for text to shift without actually moving to a different page. You can do this manually, of course, but I've also created a Page Lock macro to do it for you. The macro is included in my Editor's ToolKit add-in, which also sets Word's Page Down and Page Up keys to go to the top of the page (like turning a manuscript page) rather than the next screen. (Nice!)

Using all of these tools together makes a real difference in the "feel" of editing on the computer. You can better understand the size and proportion of your document, and you'll have a better idea of where you last saw that funny misspelling your author is so fond of using. It may not be as direct and intuitive as working with a stack of paper, but it may be close enough.

Readers Write

PHIL RABICHOW:

I've been experimenting with the Document Map with Word 2000. Here's what I've found, assuming that you have lines that "look like" headings:

- If you open a document with headings already in it, Word doesn't add its own. I know that you've found this to be flaky, and I'm wondering if there are some other "rules" that Word follows.
- If you open a document with Doc Map turned off, nothing happens, of course. If you then turn on Doc Map, Word autoformats the file. You can press CTRL+Z once to undo the autoformat and make any edits you want without problems. [Note: This is a major discovery on Phil's part.]
- If you try to replace Level 1 paragraph formatting with Body Text formatting using Find/Replace, it won't work. You can click Replace All, and Word will tell you that it's making changes, but nothing happens. You must include the style definition (e.g., Normal) in the Replace box in order for it to work. And when you do that, it's not necessary to include a paragraph level in the Replace box for it to work. Once you do a Find/Replace, you can click the Doc Map on and off without Word making paragraph level changes.
- The only problem comes when Doc Map is turned on when you open a document. Since the Level 1 that Doc Map applies is direct formatting, you can select all (CTRL+A) and press CTRL+Q to remove all direct paragraph formatting (and leave all character formatting or styles). This will remove all Word's automatic changes, which isn't a problem provided you haven't applied direct *paragraph* formatting yourself to other parts of the document.

ROHN SOLECKI:

I think I've found something "new" in Word. Well, it is not documented in any of the Microsoft Word books I have, the online help, Microsoft Knowledge Base (but finding anything specific there is a minor miracle; I suppose it may be buried in there somewhere), or a Google search (first 26 entries) . . . so something "new"! What is this new thing? It is a way of providing fine control displaying levels in View / Outline. The previously documented methods I've found are:

1. default keyboard shortcuts, ALT + SHIFT + 1-9, +/- , A
2. outline toolbar, "+" and "-" buttons to open close a selected heading
3. outline toolbar, dropdown "Show Level #" list
4. outline toolbar, "Show Level" buttons (older versions of Word)
5. macros, assign macro to user defined toolbar buttons to recreate the old button method
6. click on the "+" sign beside the heading level in outline view

Now there is a 7th!

7. Document map.

I found that displaying the document map when in outline view provides finer control over the heading levels displayed. In the past I never used the document map with outline view. Why bother, they show the same thing, condensed headings. Occasionally I would use the document map because it provided a slightly more condensed (smaller text) view to jump around in the doc. The new thing I found is that I can use the document map to provide fine level control in the outline view. This is how:

1. Display outline view: View / Outline.
2. Concurrently, display the document map: View / Document map.

The two displays are "in sync" showing the same levels. The first 5 methods described above affect the whole document, and clicking on the "+" sign beside a level in outline view opens up everything below it, including the text, which is more detail than I want.

Right clicking in the document map displays a drop down with "+/-" signs and "Show Level" options. I've found the "+/-" options unpredictable in the document map, and the "Show Level" choices work exactly like the toolbar option (probably invoke same command) affecting the whole doc.

The "new" thing is that clicking on the "+" sign beside a heading in the Document Map only opens up the specific heading 1 additional level at at time, unlike when you do it in the Outline view, which opens up everything (including text!). And no matter how far down you click in the document map, it will only expand the associated outline view to display headings, never body text!

The result is that you can have the whole document in outline view displaying only level 1 except for 1 heading that you have drilled down as many heading levels as you want using the document map. I've gone down 6 or 7 levels to organize the headings.

It makes sense since both document map and outline view work with heading styles. And the one way fine control makes sense for the same reason. The document map can only display headings, never body text.

I have tested this in Word 2002/XP. I also tried it in Word 97. But Word 97 has (always had, in my experience) problems displaying in outline view. I found that it has a bad habit of arbitrarily displaying body text in the document map and outline view seemingly at random, making it hard to confirm this tip. Reapplying "Normal" style hides the unwanted displayed text, but it does not always "stick."

Editing in Full-Screen Mode

I've been editing a new project in Microsoft Word and decided to try something new—editing in Print Layout in Full-Screen mode. I didn't think I'd like it, but I do—a lot. If you want to try it, you can activate the feature by adjusting some items under the View menu, in this order:

1. Turn on Print Layout.
2. Set the Zoom level to "Whole page."
3. Click "Full Screen."

Whoa! Your Word menu bar has disappeared! That's okay; just move your mouse pointer to the top of your screen to bring the menu bar out of hiding. Move your mouse pointer back down, and the menu bar will vanish again, leaving a full page of your document floating over a gray background.

(To turn *off* Full-Screen mode, press the Escape key, or display the menu bar and again click View > Full Screen.)

What about your toolbars? They're probably still at the top of your screen, which keeps your document page from being displayed as large as possible. But who said toolbars have to stay at the top of the screen? You've now got lots of gray space at the sides of your page, and you can use that space to hold your toolbars. Just click and hold the vertical bar on the left of a toolbar, drag the toolbar to a new location, and release your mouse button. You can leave the toolbar "floating" in the gray space around your document (and resize it, if necessary), or you can "dock" it on either side of your screen.

With Full-Screen mode turned on, you'll immediately notice how tiny the type is in your document. "I can't work like this!" you'll say. And you'll be right. To overcome this problem, you'll need to attach a new template to the document—a template formatted especially for editing. I'd recommend making body type at least 18 points and headings even larger—whatever you need for nice, legible type, even if that means you no longer have as many words on a page. Don't worry; after you've finished editing, you can attach a template with the final formatting the document needs for publication. You can learn more about this in "Typefaces for Editing," "Attaching Templates to Documents," and "Creating Custom Templates."

Also, to really make this work, you'll need a big monitor. I do most of my work on a 22-inch screen, but a 19-incher will do. On 17 inches, it's iffy. If you're still using a 13- or 15-inch monitor, it's time to upgrade, and I'd recommend getting the biggest monitor you can afford (the ideal would be a big LCD). You can learn more about this in "Hardware for Editors" and "Screen Settings for Editors."

Some of the advantages of working in Full-Screen mode, are:

• You can see a full manuscript page on your screen.

- The information on your screen is "digital" rather than analog, resembling pages rather than scrolls. In other words, it's presented in discrete, self-contained batches, and hitting the Page Down key really does take you a full page down. (In my Editor's ToolKit program, it also places your cursor at the *top* of the next page; sweet!) You can more naturally perfect a page before moving on to the next one. You don't have that feeling of not knowing where you are or that you're in an unending, scrolling mass of words.
- The discreteness of the pages allows for positional memory and a better sense of proportion—editing seems more natural, like working on paper. You can learn more about this in "The Problem of Proportion."
- All the distraction of toolbars and menus is gone, leaving you free to concentrate on your editing.

As mentioned earlier, you can still access Word's menu bar by moving your mouse pointer to the top of the screen, but you can also access it by pressing the ALT key. Then you can activate menu items by pressing the key for the letters that are underlined on those items. For example, the File menu has an underline under the F, so you can press F to access the File menu. If you already know what those underlined items are (without looking), you can press both keys at once to access the menu: ALT + F.

Here are some additional tips for editing in Full-Screen mode:

1. Click Tools > Options > View and turn off the following items (to maximize the space on your screen):

- Status bar.
- Horizontal scroll bar.
- Vertical scroll bar.

2. Click View and turn off the ruler.
3. Get more text on a page by reducing the size of your margins under File > Page Setup.
4. If your pages aren't already numbered, insert page numbers. With the status bar gone, you'll need them to gauge your progress as you work through that manuscript.
5. Use Word's "Go To" feature (CTRL + G) to move around in your document.

All of this makes it possible to have a clean screen and see each page as a unit—a pretty nice way to edit! If you've never used Full-Screen mode, why not give it a try?

Readers Write

ERIC FLETCHER:

Your articles about working in full-screen mode articles prompt me to report on my very positive experiences with a second monitor. When an old system had to be retired, I added the surplus monitor to my main Windows XP system. There was an extra monitor port (not all video cards have them, but they are inexpensive if not), so I just plugged it in: WinXP detected it and I was in business! I've since added Ultramon (http://www.realtimesoft.com) to better manage the way I can switch windows between screens.

Now I can have two Word windows fully open for activities like editing and indexing. When I'm reviewing a new document, I typically put an outline view in one window while scrolling through it in the "Normal" view in the other. I routinely position toolbars and the taskbar on the second screen to keep them out of the way of my working screen, yet easily accessible.

A second monitor is also handy for non-Word tools: I usually have Excel running in the "scratch" monitor so I can access my useful conversions spreadsheet or do calculations; a browser assists in research; my thumbnail manager simplifies the task of accessing images . . . I now wonder how I managed with just a single monitor (and am seriously considering adding a third so I can have lower-order tasks like a video monitor window to be able to see vehicles coming into our driveway).

Of course, extra monitors need more desk space—but with LCD screens coming down in price, I expect to be able to have them hanging on the wall before too long!

My video card, the "dual-head" one from ATI in my system, has two monitor plugs, so installing the second monitor was a no-brainer. New ATI Radeon 7000 cards are going for about US$40 on eBay these days. You could add an even less-expensive second video card (my brother-in-law got one at a refurbished parts place for $5.00, and it works fine), but I'd opt for one of the dedicated single cards to avoid potential hardware conflicts.

The website for the multiple monitor software I use has a good resource area for technical details:

    http://www.realtimesoft.com/multimon/

BILL RUBIDGE:

You can invoke print preview with a macro, and set yourself to edit mode, with this bit of VBA:

```
ActiveDocument.PrintPreview
ActiveDocument.ActiveWindow.View.Magnifier = False
You might also use this bit of VBA to set a page-width zoom:
ActiveWindow.ActivePane.View.Zoom.PageFit = wdPageFitBestFit
I also believe you can enter full-screen view with this:
ActiveWindow.View.FullScreen = True
```

Full screen view is nice if you want to edit in a true WYSIWYG mode, without distraction from any tools, and if your computer is powerful enough or your document simple enough that editing in this mode works fast.

You also have access to all the standard Word commands in print preview mode, even if you can't see the icons and the menus. I avoid using the mouse and icons as much as possible, and just invoke the commands I want using the keyboard shortcuts for the menu bar.

One final suggestion—if you have a document set up to print on both sides of the page, so that you will have facing pages in the final bound document, you can set print preview to show two pages side by side. If you use full screen view, you can usually read the documents, if you have a big enough display and set the resolution to a good size like 1024 x 768. This view in edit mode is especially useful if you are trying to do nice layout in Word. You can adjust your page breaks to balance your layout across pages. (I recommend fixing page breaks with keep-with-next paragraph commands and start-new-page paragraph commands, rather than page breaks. That way, you won't have as much to undo if you make text edits and the content gets pushed around.)

CHRISTOPHER SEAL:

I find it annoying that when scrolling through a Word document in Print Preview mode that when the mode is closed the document reopens at the page where you were when you opened Print Preview. You could be at page 1, then go into Print Preview mode, scroll through checking page balancing or whatever, and then see some text you want to change on page 127.

So you exit Print Preview, find yourself at page 1, then find the text on page 127. It is so much quicker to edit the text in Print Preview mode when you see what you want to change. Here's how.

With the main document in Print Preview mode, open another Word document in Normal mode. Now refocus on the main document, which you left in Print Preview mode. The cursor is now an I-bar, allowing you to edit the text.

SEVERAL READERS:

There's an easier way to edit in Print Preview: click the Magnifier button (it looks like a magnifying glass over a piece of paper) on the Print Preview toolbar. You'll then be able to edit away. The Magnifier button is a toggle, so after you're through editing, you can click it again to return to Print Preview.

Editing from the Top Down

When I'm editing on the computer (which is most of the time), I'm most effective when I edit from the "top down." What that means is that I don't start changing commas and semicolons until I've done some other, more comprehensive tasks:

1. If each chapter of a book is a separate document, I pull all of the chapters together using the Add Documents feature of my Editor's ToolKit program. I like having all of the chapters in one document so I can see and work on the whole book at once. Later, if I need to split the document apart again, I use the program's Split Documents feature.

2. I apply my own document template (Typespec.dot, which comes free with Editor's ToolKit). This template uses a font that's easy on the eyes and includes all of the styles I'm likely to need. See "Typefaces for Editing" and "Attaching Templates to documents."

3. I replace directly applied formatting with paragraph styles. (Why more authors don't use styles to format their documents is beyond me, but that's the way it is.) If the author has been consistent, I can do this with Word's Replace feature, replacing 16-point Arial bold (for example) with Word's Heading 1 paragraph style (for example). If the author hasn't been consistent (which is usually the case), then I have to go through the document and apply at least some of the paragraph styles manually. The effort is worth it, however, because it means that the styles can be passed on to QuarkXPress when it's typesetting time or reformatted quickly and easily in Microsoft Word as needed. You can read more about this in "Marking Spec Levels with Styles."

4. After applying the heading styles (Heading 1 through Heading 9) in particular, I use Word's Outline View to look at the structure of the document. Does it make sense? Do chapter titles use consistent syntax? Are the different sections in some kind of logical order? If they're not, I can easily move them around in Outline View. You can read more about this in "The Problem of Proportion."

5. I run the document through my FileCleaner program to clean up double spaces, eliminate multiple carriage returns, remove any remaining directly applied formatting (but leave italic intact), and fix a host of other annoying (but common) errors.

6. Finally, I start editing the actual text of the document. As I do this, I watch for recurring errors. If an error shows up more than twice, I stop fixing it manually and take care of all of its occurrences in one fell swoop, using a macro or Word's Replace feature. I save my macros and find-and-replace strings for use on future projects, and I now have a large collection of these useful tools.

You may not want to follow my procedures exactly, but you might think about the steps you take in editing and see if there are some "top-down" procedures you could follow that would improve your speed, efficiency, and comfort.

Readers Write

ANN REDMON:

I've been using and enjoying many of your Editor's ToolKit features, but haven't tried the Add Documents feature for fear that the resulting document would just be huge and unwieldy. Is this not the case?

I REPLIED: It's true that the document is sometimes huge, but I think that having all of the book in one document is less unwieldy than messing around with, say, twenty different documents ("Let's see, where was that paragraph about . . . ?"). My computer has plenty of memory, so the hugeness doesn't bother me or crash my machine. I like being able to see the whole structure of a book in Outline View, and I like being able to do a quick Find and Replace that I know will standardize something throughout the book without having to go from chapter to chapter. All of this may just be a matter of personal preference, and you should probably do whatever works best for you.

Making Passes

No, no, not that kind of passes. I'm talking about making separate passes through a document to catch different kinds of errors. If you can catch them all in one pass, your mind is much more efficient than mine. I work much better and catch more errors by going through a manuscript several times, fixing different kinds of problems each time. This approach to editing works well on paper, but it works even better if you're editing on the computer. This is related to the article "Editing from the Top Down."

Here are some of the passes I make when I'm editing a document:

1. I do a spell check. Laugh if you will, but a spell check catches the most elusive of typographical errors—which means I don't have to. It saves time now and embarrassment later. You can read more on this topic in "Spell Checkers."
2. I scan for repeated errors, inconsistencies, and idiosyncrasies in punctuation (especially in citations), capitalization, and spelling. When I find something I don't like, I fix it globally with Microsoft Word's Find and Replace feature. This is much faster than doing all of this work by hand, and when I'm done, I'm not left wondering if I've missed an occurrence of one of the problems somewhere. You can learn more about searching in the "Find and Replace" section of this book.
3. I edit different kinds of items in separate passes. For example, I edit all of the chapter headings at one time, which ensures consistency and parallelism and all of that other good stuff. (If you use Word's built-in heading styles for chapter headings, you can see and edit them all at once in Outline View.) Then I edit the body text. Then I edit the sidebars. Then I edit the footnotes. Then I edit the bibliography entries. You get the idea. As I work, I make liberal use of Word's Find and Replace and macro features.

By the way, it's important to consider the order in which to make your passes. Can you really understand the sidebars if you haven't read the body text? If not, you'd better edit the body text first. Also, there's usually some going back and forth between items. For example, changes in the footnotes may require additional editing in the bibliography. So even if you're making passes, don't feel like you can't be a bit flexible. Editing on the computer, just as on paper, is as much an art as it is a science. And while the computer is a wonderful tool, don't forget that you're the one in charge.

Readers Write

DAN A. WILSON:

The principal difference between the amateur e-editors and the real professionals, in my opinion, is in the difference in their in-depth knowledge of the macro system and Find and

Replace system. The amateurs use the computer as an electric typewriter and continue to do all of the slogging work as though they were still editing on paper. The pros seize the power of the computer's systems and exploit it ever more fully with each passing project. [Dan A. Wilson is proprietor of The Editor's DeskTop (http://www.editorsdesktop.com/).]

PAMELA ANGULO:

Hint for making passes: I have a "Task" chart (a table, really) that I customize for each job. First, I fill in the details (number of pages, tables, figures, equations, and boxes) for each chapter, so I can track my progress. Below are check boxes for essential tasks: running the spellchecker, cleaning up spaces, checking and marking figure callouts, editing in-chapter headings, cross-checking references, editing references, editing figures and tables, editing boxes and appendices—all those niggling details that can't be remembered in one pass. I find this chart especially helpful if I have to put a job aside for any time longer than an hour (!); when I come back, I don't try to do things that I have already done.

And yes, I have a check-box grocery list on the fridge that I find very helpful in streamlining my shopping trips.

Divide and Conquer

Back in the days of working on paper, editors had to keep an eye out for all kinds of errors and problems—all at the same time. The human brain, which is wired to think about *one* thing at a time, often missed things, and editors were forced to comb through a manuscript over and over again. They also needed to keep style sheets (still a useful practice) to recall earlier decisions. Changing one's mind could have disastrous consequences; it often meant having to re-read the manuscript, unmaking previous decisions and implementing new ones.

If you're still working the same way on the computer, it's time to change. Researcher David Meyer from the University of Michigan explains why multitasking is so inefficient:

"People in a work setting who are banging away on word processors at the same time they have to answer phones and talk to their co-workers or bosses—they're doing switches all the time. . . . In effect, you've got writer's block briefly as you go from one task to another. You've got to (a) want to switch tasks, you've got to (b) make the switch, and then you've got to (c) get warmed back up on what you're doing."

You'll find more information about the university's study on multitasking here:

http://www.applesforhealth.com/HealthyBusiness/multihealth3.html
http://archives.cnn.com/2001/CAREER/trends/08/05/multitasking.study/

In the classic book *Wealth of Nations,* published in 1776, economist Adam Smith explained basically the same principle, but with the organization rather than the individual in mind. In fact, the first chapter in his book is titled "Of the Division of Labour." You can read the chapter here:

http://www.adamsmith.org/smith/won-b1-c1.htm

Smith illustrated his ideas with the example of manufacturing pins:

"A workman not educated to this business . . . could scarce, perhaps, with his utmost industry, make one pin in a day, and certainly could not make twenty. But in the way in which this business is now carried on, . . . it is divided into a number of branches. . . . One man draws out the wire, another straights it, a third cuts it, a fourth points it, a fifth grinds it at the top for receiving, the head; to make the head requires two or three distinct operations; to put it on is a peculiar business, to whiten the pins is another; it is even a trade by itself to put them into the paper; and the important business of making a pin is, in this manner, divided into about eighteen distinct operations. . . . I have seen a small manufactory of this kind where ten men only were employed, and where some of them consequently performed two or three distinct operations. . . . They could, when they exerted themselves, make among them about twelve pounds of pins in a day. There are in a pound upwards of four thousand pins of a middling size. Those ten persons, therefore, could make among them upwards of forty-eight thousand pins in a day. . . . But if they had all wrought separately and independently, . . . they certainly could not each of them have made twenty, perhaps not one pin in a day; that is, certainly, not the two hundred and fortieth, perhaps not the four thousand eight hundredth part of what they are at present capable of performing, in consequence of a proper division and combination of their different operations."

The principle can also be applied to editing, especially on the computer. Rather than trying to find and fix all problems at once, try going after one kind of problem at a time. For example, rather than putting all commas and periods inside quotation marks as you come to them, why not use Microsoft Word's Find and Replace feature to fix them all in one fell swoop? Once you've done that, you won't have to look for them or even think about them again, and you can be confident that you didn't overlook any. Then, go on to another kind of problem and fix that.

One approach to working in this way is to fix every instance of a certain problem the first time you encounter it. For example, if you're reading along and see "supersede" misspelled as "supercede," don't just fix the word and move on. Instead, use Word's Find and Replace feature to "Replace All." When you come to another problem, fix it in the same way. As you do this, you'll find that your manuscript is cleaner and cleaner the farther into it you read, because many of the errors you would have had to fix manually have already been fixed electronically. This, by the way, feels really good.

Another approach is to keep a list of errors and problems you commonly see and fix them all before you even touch anything else. My FileCleaner and MegaReplacer programs are ideal for this kind of work.

Whatever your approach, try looking for ways to focus on one thing at a time. Divide and conquer! Doing so will make your work easier, better, and more efficient.

Readers Write

HILARY POWERS:

If you're editing on a computer, separate passes are much faster than trying to do it all by hand. And Adam Smith had a point (you should pardon the expression) for his day—splitting up jobs as he describes did make for much higher production of basic manufactured goods. But a whole lot of 21st-century organizational development effort goes into undoing the damage the pin-factory mentality did to the human quality of working life and recreating occupations (like ours) that feed the mind and soul as well as the pocket.

Divide and Conquer, Part 2

I wrote earlier about increasing editorial efficiency by fixing one kind of problem at a time. This raises the question, "What kinds of problems lend themselves to this approach?" Some possibilities for your consideration:

- Fixing typographical errors with a spell check:

See "Spell Check."

- Editing all headings at the same time to make sure they match in tone and are parallel in construction:

1. Click View > Outline.
2. In the middle of the Outline toolbar, click the "Show Level" dropdown list (*not* the "Level" list, on the left) and select the depth of the heading levels you want to show.

- Editing all of your notes at once. See "Editing Notes in Microsoft Word" and "Editing Notes and Text Side by Side."
- Finding and replacing commonly made errors. See "Manual or Automatic?" "More Automatic Corrections," and "Even More Automatic Corrections."

Earlier I included a related article called "Editing from the Top Down." The idea was to start by editing the really big stuff (such as paragraph styling), then move down to medium stuff (spell check), and finally get down to the nitty-gritty of line editing. This is a good approach because (1) it gets rid of the messy stuff up front so you can concentrate on the details without distraction, and (2) it lets you concentrate on one thing at a time.

If that's "vertical" editing, then the approach suggested in today's article might be called "horizontal" editing. Both approaches are useful and will make you more efficient.

Just don't forget to actually *read* the manuscript after you've done all this wonderful electronic stuff.

Readers Write

Erika Remmy:

My second pass is usually to go through and fix en and em dashes—making sure the right kind of dash is used in each place and getting rid of stray spaces. (The copy I work with involves a lot of date spans, so there are always en dashes aplenty.)

I do it manually, with some search-and-replaces. (I can't figure out an automated way for a macro to specify what correction is needed in each instance. For example, " -" [space hyphen] could need to be an em dash or an en dash, or could be a situation where the hyphen is correct and the space in front of it just needs to be deleted. I could try to learn how to do dialog boxes, but I can't picture that method saving any time in this dash cleanup step, because there would be so many permutations to allow for.)

GRETCHEN:

I think people need to be reminded that "Replace All" can be dangerous if you have references. "Labour" might be the correct spelling in a reference. What I would do is start just above the references and do a backward replace.

[Another possible solution to this problem appears in "More Hidden Secrets."]

HILARY POWERS:

The Editorium wrote:

Editing all headings at the same time to make sure they match in tone and are parallel in construction:
1. Click View > Outline.
2. In the middle of the Outline toolbar, click the "Show Level" dropdown list (*not* the "Level" list, on the left) and select the depth of the heading levels you want to show.

Easier, and allows you to see the context at the same time:

1. Click View > Document Map.
2. Right-click on the pane that opens.
3. Select the heading depth you want to see.

Clicking on a heading in the pane moves the insertion point in the main document pane to that heading, so you can see what it modifies as you work on it while still seeing all its companion headings.

The idea was to start by editing the really big stuff (such as paragraph styling), then move down to medium stuff (spell check), and finally get down to the nitty-gritty of line editing.

Me, I run the spelling checker last, to make sure I didn't introduce any errors in the course of the job. I fix errors that jump out at me during the edit, but don't look for them - and my select-o-vision pretty much ignores things the spelling checker will catch, while zeroing in on unusual stuff and misused words likely to slide by it. It's gotta happen at the end, anyway, so why do twice what once will take care of?

Re Gretchen's "I think people need to be reminded that 'Replace All' can be dangerous if you have references. 'Labour' might be the correct spelling in a reference. What I would do is start just above the references and do a backward replace."

"Replace All" is dangerous, period. I use it a lot anyway, though. Safety tips: Except for the most mechanical sorts of changes, and for carefully vetted wildcard replaces, track changes should always be on when it's in use, and the relevant portion of the file should be selected if there are bits like reference sections where it's likely to do more harm than good. *And* never, ever use it on text that won't be read all the way through again.

Visible Punctuation

One of the problems of editing on-screen is that punctuation marks are harder to see than on paper. Is that speck on my screen a period or just spray from my diet soda? (Sorry. Didn't mean to gross you out.) There's an easy remedy for this—one I like a lot. Just create a character style that's big and bold and colorful. Then record a macro to find and replace punctuation marks with themselves, formatted with your character style. Here's how:

Creating the Paragraph Style

1. Click the "Format" menu.
2. Click "Style" (in Word 2002, "Styles and Formatting").
3. Click the "New" button (in Word 2002, "New Style").
4. In the "Name" box, type a name for your new style—"Punctuation," maybe, or "Jots and Tittles."
5. In the "Style type" box, select "Character."
6. Click the "Format" button.
7. Click "Font."
8. If it's not already selected, click the "Font" tab.
9. Under "Font," select a font you'd like to use, but make sure it has easily distinguishable punctuation marks. Times New Roman is my all-time favorite for this purpose.
10. Under "Font style," select "Bold."
11. Under "Size," select something nice and big. Try 18 points for starters (for text that is regularly 12 points). You can adjust this as you like.
12. Under "Font color," select red or blue—whatever you like.
13. Click the "OK" button.
14. Click the next "OK" button.
15. Click the "Close" button (except in Word 2002).

Recording the Macro

1. Click the "Tools" menu.
2. Click "Macro."
3. Click "Record New Macro."

4. In the "Macro name" box, give your macro a name, something like "BigPunctuation" (no spaces allowed in macro names).
5. If you like, assign the macro to a toolbar button or keyboard shortcut by clicking the appropriate buttons and following the prompts on your screen.
6. If necessary, click the "Close" button. You should now see the macro recording toolbar with its two buttons, which means Word is now recording what you do.
7. Click the "Edit" menu.
8. Click "Replace."
9. In the "Find what" box, enter some punctuation you want to include—let's say a comma.
10. In the "Replace with" box, enter the same punctuation you included in the "Find what" box.
11. Click the "Format" button (you may need to click the "More" button before this is available).
12. Click "Style."
13. Select your new style from the list.
14. Click the "OK" button.
15. Make sure the "Search" box says "All."
16. Click the "Replace All" button. That will replace all of your commas with themselves but formatted with your new style.
17. Repeat steps 7 through 16 for each punctuation mark you want to format with your new style. I recommend periods, commas, semicolons, colons, single quotation marks, double quotation marks, hyphens, en dashes, em dashes, and anything else you have trouble seeing. Don't overdo it, though. The point is to *see* the little stuff, not to get lost in a forest of overgrown punctuation.
18. Click the "Tools" menu.
19. Click "Macro."
20. Click "Stop Recording."

Now run the macro (Tools > Macro > Macros > [select the macro] > Run), and it will format your punctuation so it's easy to see. Of course, the macro will remain available for future use—you don't have to record it every time you do this.

A possible drawback to all of this is that the enlarged punctuation may expand your line spacing here and there, making your document look kind of funny. But if you can live with that, you'll probably come to like working with those "big commas." Another drawback is that any new punctuation you *type* in the document won't be big, bold, and colorful—unless you format it with the new style or run the macro periodically, but that seems like a lot of extra work to me. There is another solution, but that's a subject for another day.

"How do I get rid of the big formatting after I've finished editing?" you're now asking. The easiest way is just to delete the style from the document. But don't forget to do it! Otherwise, your client will think you're pretty weird. Here's the procedure:

1. Click the "Format" menu.
2. Click "Style" (in Word 2002, "Styles and Formatting").

3. Select the style you created earlier to format your punctuation.
4. Click the "Delete" button (in Word 2002, you must first click the dropdown arrow on the right of the style's name).
5. When Word asks if you really want to delete the style, click the "Yes" button.
6. Click the "Close" button (except in Word 2002).

Now all of your perfectly edited punctuation will be returned to its regular formatting. You'll thank me when you go to the optometrist.

Readers Write

HILARY POWERS:

I much prefer to edit in a font that has punctuation big enough to see . . . and everything else, too. If you have the typeface Lucida Console on your system, give it a try—it's both denser and easier to read than Courier New, and everything is clear. Even the dots for spaces with hidden characters turned on are the size of lentils. The similarity between en dashes and hyphens is the only problem for onscreen work, and that's easy to deal with. It looks awful on paper, though, so you do have to change it—basically, switch templates—before giving the file to anyone who plans to print it.

SUSAN BULLOWA:

I highlight all punctuation marks using Search and Replace. No font fuss. Next time, I plan to develop nested macros (if I can in Word).

In a book I just worked on, the author's I's, me's, and my's were all highlighted because my editor asked me to make the book a bit less egocentric! It worked like a charm.

KAREN MACKENZIE:

Great tip! I've already placed style and macro in my Normal.dot. But I did modify the replace so as to get it all in one fell swoop. The change as follows:
Wildcard search:

Search for: [,.;:'"] (What you listed, but I omit the hyphens and dashes—too much for me!).
Replace with ^& (this tells Word to put back what it found)

PHIL RABICHOW:

I enjoyed your technique for making punctuation stand out for those of us, er uh, those whose eyes may not be the sharpest (or to avoid eyestrain). I took your idea and expanded on it. I created a macro that would:

1. Create a character style called Standout that was Times New Roman, 18 points, bold, and red.
2. Handle the error in case the style already existed.
3. Replace all punctuation marks in one fell swoop with the new style.

Because of the error handling in 2. above, you can run the macro, add text with additional punctuation, and run the macro again. Also, instead of doing successive Find/Replace operations, it uses wildcards and Finds: [.,:;"""\?\!] i.e., all types of punctuation. The backslash in front of the question and exclamation marks finds those characters. The macro also finds all quotes (") and apostrophes. Although it doesn't show in an email, what appears to be 7 apostrophes are really 1 set of quotes, 1 apostrophe, 1 opening smart quote (ALT+0147) and 1 closing smart quote (ALT+0148). [On a Macintosh, the character numbers would be 210 and 211.] Replace contains: ^& (the operator for Find What Text) and is formatted for the Standout character style.

The macro is:

```
Sub BigPunctuation()
' BigPunctuation Macro
' Macro recorded 8/11/02 by Phil Rabichow
' Creates Standout style & replaces punctuation
' of selection with large red bold font
On Error Resume Next
ActiveDocument.Styles.Add Name:="Standout", _
Type:=wdStyleTypeCharacter
ActiveDocument.Styles("Standout").BaseStyle = _
"Default Paragraph Font"
With ActiveDocument.Styles("Standout").Font
.Name = "Times New Roman"
.Size = 18
.Bold = True
.Color = wdColorRed
End With
With ActiveDocument.Styles("Standout").Font
With .Shading
.Texture = wdTextureNone
.ForegroundPatternColor = wdColorAutomatic
.BackgroundPatternColor = wdColorAutomatic
End With
.Borders(1).LineStyle = wdLineStyleNone
.Borders.Shadow = False
End With
' Selection.HomeKey Unit:=wdStory
Selection.Find.ClearFormatting
Selection.Find.Replacement.ClearFormatting
With Selection.Find
.Text = ""
.Replacement.Text = ""
.Forward = True
.Wrap = wdFindContinue
.Format = False
.MatchCase = False
```

```
.MatchWholeWord = False
.MatchWildcards = False
.MatchSoundsLike = False
.MatchAllWordForms = False
End With
Selection.Find.ClearFormatting
Selection.Find.Replacement.ClearFormatting
Selection.Find.Replacement.Style = _
ActiveDocument.Styles("Standout")
With Selection.Find
.Text = _
"[.,:;""" & ChrW(8220) & ChrW(8221) & "'\?\!]"
.Replacement.Text = "^&"
.Forward = True
.Wrap = wdFindStop
.Format = True
.MatchCase = False
.MatchWholeWord = False
.MatchAllWordForms = False
.MatchSoundsLike = False
.MatchWildcards = True
End With
Selection.Find.Execute Replace:=wdReplaceAll
End Sub
```

Note that this macro will apply to a selection in case you only want to change some of the punctuation. If you remove the apostrophe before this line—

```
Selection.HomeKey Unit:=wdStory
```

—the macro will work on the entire document.

STEVE HUDSON:

[Steve provides this macro as an exercise in Visual Basic programming (and of course, it's useful, too!). It's a toggle, so you'll probably want to put the subroutine named SomeToolbarNameToggleBigPunctuation() on a toolbar button for easy access. You can learn how to do this in "Macros on Buttons." As you look through the macro, pay particular attention to Steve's comments, which explain what's going on. The macro is an excellent example of VBA, including find loops, wildcard matching, range objects, optional parameters, design analysis, and much more. Actually, the whole macro has many left-of-center concepts—for example, a Find that can return nothing yet still not have finished (it picks up the Chr$(7) that marks a table start, which can't be included in the wildcard entry). The macro also nicely changes the cursor and screen updating, and it backs out formatting changes. Steve is a master at this kind of stuff, so get ready to learn something. By the way, you'll note Steve's humor throughout.]

The past articles found and formatted punctuation by inclusion, which rules out Unicode and the like. So I figured a macro would be better with punctuation by exclusion in order to show up all sorts of strange dweebs.

The second problem was your suggestion to create a temporary style that mucks my document up with no subsequent hint of destruction.

The third was "How do I reverse this?" If I have a formula in character styling and another elsewhere in terminal screen, I can't find this style and kill it dead with a known something else. So I have to transpose my edits to have a safe working practice. Ack.

The fourth problem was not acknowledging No Proofing on styles.

So the first one is easy enough, we simply start the square brackets formula for the find with a ! and then what we are not interested in. Thus the string for a trivial solution is [!A-Za-z0-9^160]. Note the ^160 for the nonbreaking space; Word honours the ole caret at a higher priority than anything else. Basically, this finds anything *except* a letter, a number, or a nonbreaking space, but I've added additional characters in the macro itself.

The second is also easy. We all use *styles* like good little folk, so let's keep those in place and add—ooooh—*manual formatting*. We can hunt it down and undo it easy enough later by resetting that range to its underlying style again, so it's a temporary aberration for our temporary aberration. That's the third taken care of as well.

Now, the fourth and last—is there any way we can tell the Find to do only those styles with proofing set? Err, no. So we have to check this ourselves manually. Word's find falls down spectacularly with stuff like this. Easy enough, and should be faster as we are doing less styling work, which is expensive.

Now some little style notes—I prefer to use ranges and let the users have their selection object. It may be faster running selection.finds, dunno, duncare :-) It makes the resulting code smaller and easier to read and allows me sick puns—the last being the most important reason of course. What's the use of knowing all this junk if you can't have fun with it, I say. I know that some folks hate nonstandard variable naming, but I like code that is human readable.

Next, always reset stuff back to the way it was. If users do a Find, do they want your settings?

```
Public Sub SomeToolbarNameToggleBigPunctuation()
'Attach this to a button on a toolbar
'we use the toolbar name to start the sub so we know where
'this sub is called from
Static Toggle As Boolean
Toggle = Not Toggle
ProofReadBigPunctuation Toggle
End Sub
Public Sub ProofReadBigPunctuation(MakeBig As Boolean, Optional
Scope As Range)
'$Author: heretic [at symbol] tdfa.com
'$Short: If makebig is true, it makes punctuation marks BIG
'to aid proofreading as discussed by Editmeister Jack.
'If makebig is false, it removes this formatting
'$Known issues: Destroys original doc highlighting IF
'highlighting is used in the formatting process.
Dim HomeOnThe As Range 'Our findermatic
Dim Finished As Boolean
Dim Progress As Double 'enough space for calcs in big dox
'Be nice, don't assume system settings
```

```
Dim Cursor_pholder As WdCursorType
Dim ScreenUpdating_pholder As Boolean
'frilly bits: change the cursor whilst we work!
Cursor_pholder = System.Cursor
System.Cursor = wdCursorWait
'freeze the screen to speed things up
ScreenUpdating_pholder = Application.ScreenUpdating
Application.ScreenUpdating = False
'This basic technique can be used in as many ways as Bill
'has bux.
'--------------------------------
'Give our range a document range to hang off.
'The first .dupe is strictly speaking unnecc but a good habit
'to get into with range objects--the second one prevents us
'changing the passed scope without realising it!
'We avoid the other parts of the document by setting our
'ranges parent to be the range that is the content only.
'I regularly use Activedocument.Content too.
'Also note how we deal with no explicit scope being passed
'from that Optional parameter
If Scope Is Nothing Then Set Scope = _
ActiveDocument.StoryRanges(wdMainTextStory).Duplicate
Set HomeOnThe = Scope.Duplicate
'Collapse our range to a point at the start of the doc
'main body content, just like a cursor in a virgin document.
HomeOnThe.Collapse
'We don't have to clearformatting or anything as it's
'a whole new range. Just set up the find
'$Customize: the ! means NOT anything in the following list
With HomeOnThe.Find
'note we don't use If MakeBig = True then
If MakeBig Then 'errant chars
.Text = "[! 0-9A-Za-z^9^12^13^160]" '$Customize
.MatchWildcards = True
Else '$Customize: formatting
With .Font
.Color = wdColorRed
.Bold = True
End With
.Highlight = True
End If
End With
'Get started on a standard manual processing find loop.
While Not Finished
'let the poor user know where we are at
Progress = Int(HomeOnThe.End * 100 / Scope.End)
Application.StatusBar = "Restyling " & Format(Progress) & "%"
'ensure the statusbar change gets through
DoEvents
'the find!
With HomeOnThe.Find
.Execute Replace:=wdReplaceNone
Finished = Not .Found
```

```
End With
'Our range is now either null, meaning nothing found
'or it contains a range for us to examine
If Not Finished Then 'we caught one!
If MakeBig Then 'style if proofing on
If Not ActiveDocument.Styles(HomeOnThe.Style).NoProofing Then _
FormatFontGruesome HomeOnThe
Else 'unstyle
HomeOnThe.Font.Reset
HomeOnThe.HighlightColorIndex = wdNoHighlight
End If
End If
HomeOnThe.Collapse wdCollapseEnd 'so we keep moving along
Wend 'finished
'destroy our objects
Set HomeOnThe = Nothing
'reset our changes
Application.ScreenUpdating = ScreenUpdating_pholder
System.Cursor = Cursor_pholder
Application.StatusBar = "Finished"
End Sub
Private Sub FormatFontGruesome(Scope As Range)
'$Short: to make shtuff shtand out shorty, you
'gotta problem wid dat?
'$Customize: don't forget to keep this matched with the
'find requirements for the undo
'I don't like the thought of changing font name
'as that could change the displayed character
'Lets just make it BIG, BOLD and RED on a YELLOW background
With Scope.Font
.Color = wdColorRed
.Bold = True
.Grow
.Grow
.Grow
End With
Scope.HighlightColorIndex = wdYellow
End Sub
Sub TestProofReadBigPunctuationOn()
Dim i As Long
Application.ScreenUpdating = False
Documents.Add
DoEvents
For i = 27 To 1200
Selection.InsertAfter ChrW(i)
Next i
ProofReadBigPunctuation True
Application.ScreenUpdating = True
End Sub
Sub TestProofReadBigPunctuationOnSimple()
'run this on any trial doc to be sure
ProofReadBigPunctuation True
End Sub
```

```
Sub TestProofReadBigPunctuationOff()
ProofReadBigPunctuation False
End Sub
```

HILARY POWERS:

Remember I asked awhile back about automating the placement of serial commas? This doesn't do the whole job, but it takes a lot of the curse off of the problem of dealing with an AP author who's writing for a Chicago publisher. It goes to the next instance of the word *and,* backs up a space, and puts in a comma—ignoring *And* and *andiron* and the like. (I may do a partner for *or* one day, but that doesn't come up nearly as often.)

I have it assigned to the hot key ALT+/ and to a voice macro pronounced "seer-comm." So when I'm reading along and I see a spot that needs a serial comma coming up, I just say or key the command and the comma appears where it belongs, without the need to mouse to the exact spot. And if there was another "and" in the way that I missed seeing, well, that's what CTRL + Z is for.

```
'Serial Macro
'Macro written 02/27/03 by Hilary Powers; updated 3/12
Selection.Find.ClearFormatting
With Selection.Find
.text = "and"
.MatchCase = True
.MatchWholeWord = True
End With
Selection.Find.Execute
Selection.MoveLeft Unit:=wdCharacter, Count:=2
Selection.TypeText text:=","
```

MARTY SPITZENBERGER:

Here's a way to insert serial commas using a wildcard Find and Replace:

Type "([!,]) and>" (without the quotes) in the Find what field, and "\1, and" in the Replace with field. Put a check in the "Use wildcards" checkbox. Do Find Next. If the found text needs a comma, then do Replace. Since another Find Next is automatically performed after the Replace, exit the dialog box and do SHIFT + F5 to return to the point of text replacement so the manual review can continue. This sequence can be recorded and saved as a macro.

The Find What text above translates to the following: find a group of one character that is not a comma, followed by one space character, followed by "and", which is the end of the word. This approach avoids a match to something like "black andirons."

Obviously, this will still find "Jack and Jill", which doesn't need a comma, but then so does the previous macro. This approach does avoid the extra steps in the macro of moving the cursor to the end of the previous word to insert the comma. The Replace With text translates to: replace the selection with the found group/character that wasn't a comma, then a comma followed by a space character and "and".

An improved search string would find sentences with a serial comma error in the form "I like a, b and c." This wildcard Find What string is:

(, [!.,:\!\?^013]@) and>

This search string finds the following sequence of characters:
a comma,
a space,
one or more characters that do not include period, comma, colon, exclamation mark, question mark, or paragraph mark
a space,
"and", which is the end of the word
The appropriate Replace With string is unchanged:

\1, and

The search string limits the found text to appearing within one sentence of one paragraph, where the sentence contains a comma and then some other text without a comma immediately before " and". This way the search string avoids finding sentences in the form of "I like a and b." While it will incorrectly find sentences in the form of "Sadly, I like a and b.", it is still an improvement.

Another frequent task that can be simplified through wildcard search and replace is the deletion of extra paragraph marks inserted when a word-wrapped paragraph is converted to plain text. For example, my email as attached to your reply now has "> " at the beginning of each line and a paragraph mark at the end of each, with many short lines. Although transforming this text back into nice, word-wrapped paragraphs takes several steps, it is still quicker than doing each replacement manually:

1. Obviously, copy the desired text into a new word document.
2. Remove all of the "> " at the beginning of each line with this:

Find What: ^p>^032
(You can use a space character in place of the ^032 used here and elsewhere. I'm using ^032 to ensure that you enter a space.)
Replace With: ^p
Disable "Use wildcards"
Do Replace All
Note: The ^p at the beginning of the Find What is needed to avoid deleting a "> " string contained within paragraph text, which occurs here in the text representing key labels.

3. Review the text to ensure that there is a tab character starting each paragraph or a blank paragraph following each desired paragraph. Add any that are missing.

Note: Replacements in steps 4 and 5 are done to replace the paragraph mark with a space if a space isn't already before or after the para mark. The Find string also avoids replacing the paragraph mark if it is followed by a tab, under the assumption that this is an indented paragraph or a bullet.

4. Find What: ([!^013^032])^013([!^013^t^032])

Replace With: \1^032\2
Check "Use wildcards"
Do Replace All

5. Find What: ([!^013])^013([!^013^t])
6. Replace With: \1\2

Check "Use wildcards"
Do Replace All

Editorial Style Sheet

An editorial style sheet is a document an editor uses to keep track of style decisions. The Chicago Manual of Style explains:

"No style book will provide rules covering all matters of style encountered by the editor, and no editor worth the title will apply identical rules to every book manuscript. Therefore, to ensure consistency in the style used in a particular manuscript, and to aid the editorial memory, it is helpful if not imperative to keep for each manuscript a running account of special words to be capitalized, odd spellings, compound words with or without hyphens, and the like. For easy reference this style sheet should be in rough alphabetical order."

The manual then illustrates what such a style sheet might look like:

ABCD
city-state
drillmaster

EFGH
firepower
Hellenistic Age

IJKL
Kublai Khan

MNOP
manpower
Peace of Paris

QRST
riverboat
sea power

UVWXYZ
Zeitgeist

A useful tool, to be sure, but I prefer my style sheets to be in electronic form. This makes it easy to store them away, find them again, and search them electronically for specific style items.

My Editor's ToolKit program includes a template for such a style sheet, based on the one illustrated in the *Chicago Manual of Style,* but I'm going to share it with you at no charge. You can download it here:

http://www.editorium.com/ftp/stylesheet.zip

After you've unzipped or unstuffed the template, put it into Word's Templates folder. Then, the next time you need to create an editorial style sheet, click File > New and create a new document based on Stylesheet.dot.

Save your new document with a name like MyProjectStylesheet.doc. Then leave it open on your screen, using SHIFT + CTRL + F6 to switch between it and the document you're working on. Or, use the macro from Hilary Powers, below.

Readers Write

HILARY POWERS:

[Note: Hilary sent the following macro, which makes it possible to copy selected text (be sure to select it first) to an editorial style sheet with the touch of a key, and then move back to your main document with the touch of the same key.]

The macro relies on having two [and only two] files open at a time. The truly charming thing is that you can use one hot key for both chores: putting something on the style sheet and also priming the style sheet for its next use and returning to the main document.

```
Sub StyleThat()
' Macro adapted by Hilary Powers 1/30/04; updated 4/6/04
If Selection.Type = wdSelectionIP Then
GoTo HedBack
Else
Selection.Copy
WordBasic.NextWindow
Selection.PasteAndFormat (wdPasteDefault)
GoTo Final
End If
HedBack:
Selection.TypeParagraph
WordBasic.NextWindow
Selection.MoveRight Unit:=wdCharacter, Count:=1
Final:
End Sub
```

Editorial Style Sheet Macro

The previous article provided a style sheet that editors can use to keep track of style decisions while editing in Microsoft Word. Hilary Powers was kind enough to provide her StyleThat macro in the previous article, and here I've adapted that macro to work with the editorial style sheet. If you select some text in a document you're editing and then run this macro, it will switch to your editorial style sheet and paste the text under the alphabetical heading where it belongs: ABCD, EFGH, and so on. See "Editorial Style Sheet" for more information.

```
Sub StyleThat()
'Macro adapted by Hilary Powers 1/30/04; updated 4/6/04
'Adapted by Jack M. Lyon for use with editorial style sheet
If Selection.Type = wdSelectionIP Then 'No selection
GoTo HedBack
Else
FirstChar = Asc(Selection.Characters.First)
If FirstChar > 64 And FirstChar < 69 Then MySearch = "ABCD^p"
If FirstChar > 68 And FirstChar < 73 Then MySearch = "EFGH^p"
If FirstChar > 72 And FirstChar < 77 Then MySearch = "IJKL^p"
If FirstChar > 76 And FirstChar < 81 Then MySearch = "MNOP^p"
If FirstChar > 80 And FirstChar < 85 Then MySearch = "QRST^p"
If FirstChar > 84 And FirstChar < 91 Then MySearch = "UVWXYZ^p"
If FirstChar > 96 And FirstChar < 101 Then MySearch = "ABCD^p"
If FirstChar > 100 And FirstChar < 105 Then MySearch = "EFGH^p"
If FirstChar > 104 And FirstChar < 109 Then MySearch = "IJKL^p"
If FirstChar > 108 And FirstChar < 113 Then MySearch = "MNOP^p"
If FirstChar > 112 And FirstChar < 117 Then MySearch = "QRST^p"
If FirstChar > 116 And FirstChar < 123 Then MySearch =
"UVWXYZ^p"
If FirstChar > 90 And FirstChar < 97 Then MySearch =
"Comments:^p"
If FirstChar < 65 Or FirstChar > 122 Then MySearch =
"Comments:^p"
  Selection.Copy
  WordBasic.NextWindow
  WordBasic.StartOfDocument
  Selection.Find.ClearFormatting
  With Selection.Find
  .Text = MySearch
  .Forward = True
  .Wrap = wdFindStop
  .Format = False
  .MatchCase = True
  .MatchWholeWord = False
  .MatchAllWordForms = False
```

```
.MatchSoundsLike = False
.MatchWildcards = False
End With
Selection.Find.Execute
Selection.MoveRight
Selection.Paste
Selection.TypeParagraph
GoTo Final
End If
HedBack:
WordBasic.NextWindow
Selection.MoveRight Unit:=wdCharacter, Count:=1
Final:
End Sub
```

Note that you don't have to use the macro with *my* style sheet. It will work with any document in which you've included the following headings, each followed by a carriage return:

ABCD
EFGH
IJKL
MNOP
QRST
UVWXYZ
Comments:

Readers Write

ED VESNESKE, JR.:

I've tweaked Ms. Powers's original "StyleThat" macro (see below). Since I've never written a macro and have basically done this by poking around the VB help files and sussing out what was going on in the original, I thought I'd show you what I ended up with, for what it's worth.

Ms. Powers's StyleThat required only two docs open: no good for me. For one thing, I use NameSwapper.dot now, so I keep two style sheets, one just for names (thus, I actually need *two* macros, each pointing to a specific file). Besides, I often have files open for notes to author, endnotes or bibliography (if I've been asked to keep these in separate files by the client), etc.

Also, for some reason, neither Ms. Powers's macro nor your reworking of it were inserting a carriage return after pasting the selection; nor were they returning me to the original document afterward. Finally, I have no real need for the alphabetical headings incorporated in your rewrite (though, as a traditionalist, I like them): I just alphabetize everything via table sort. So I wanted a macro that would pick up a selection, go to a specific named file, move to the end of the file, paste, insert a carriage return, save the document for good measure, and go back to its starting point. By the way, I'm running Word 2002. Here's what I came up with:

```
    Sub SendToStyle()
    'SendToStyle Macro
    'Macro adapted by Hilary Powers 1/30/04; updated 4/6/04
    'Adapted by Ed Vesneske, Jr. 11/24/04
    If Selection.Type = wdSelectionIP Then
    GoTo Final
    Else
    Dim EditDoc As String
    EditDoc = ActiveDocument.Name
    Selection.Copy
    Documents("Style Sheet.doc").Activate 'Insert target document
  name
    Selection.EndKey Unit:=wdStory
    Selection.PasteAndFormat(wdPasteDefault)
    Selection.TypeParagraph
    ActiveDocument.Save
    Documents(EditDoc).Activate
    Selection.MoveRight Unit:=wdCharacter, Count:=1
    End If
    Final:
    End Sub
```

The macro allows me to use more than one (standard) style sheet, just by having different (standard) macros with different <Documents("mydoc.doc").Activate> lines. With the EditDoc declaration, I can also have more than one editing document open, and throw text into the style sheet(s) from any of them.

HILARY POWERS: I like Ed Vesneske's macro, and will keep it in mind if I need to deal with multiple sheets. Just thought it'd be useful to address this point:

> Also, for some reason, neither Ms. Powers's macro nor your reworking of it were inserting a carriage return after pasting the selection; nor were they returning me to the original document

That's because the "StyleThat" part of the published macro does only half the job. It goes to the style sheet and stops so I can take care of chores often needed there—untangle a whole list of words transferred at one go, add parts of speech, or comment on something about the given usage. The other part, originally a separate companion macro, "HedBack," puts in the carriage return, returns to the main document, and releases the selection.

I originally put StyleThat on the hot key CTRL + backslash and HedBack on ALT + CTRL + backslash, so it took very little by way of thought or effort to keep them straight. But less effort is better. The current version, with HedBack in an else clause, allows me to use CTRL + backslash for functions; if there's a selection, the macro moves it to the style sheet—and if there's not, it does the carriage return and file switch thang.

JIM PINKHAM:

You can also overcome the limitation on having only two Word docs open to make Hilary's macro run by simply specifying the windows you wish to switch between in the macro. For example, here's a snippet from one of mine:

```
Selection.SelectRow
Selection.Cut
Windows("Blue Rows.doc").Activate
Selection.Paste
Windows("Weekly Improvement Analysis March 22-28.doc").Activate
```

When I use this macro, I'll create a new "Weekly Improvement Analysis" doc each time—so I simply edit the file name accordingly.

PAMELA ANGULO:

As I read about the Editorial Style Sheet Macro, I wondered why anyone editing and creating a style sheet on a computer would be concerned about pasting copied style terms by letter or in alphabetical order. (Organizing terms by type—names, places, scientific terminology, etc.—now, that I understand.)

I copy terms to my style sheet as I go, in the order they present themselves—more or less from top to bottom of the manuscript. For some jobs (e.g., chapters by multiple authors for the same book, or individual articles for inclusion in a single magazine issue), I keep track of chapter, article, or author for each term as well. But however I handle the initial list, I sort the terms alphabetically later, *not* while I'm copying and pasting (too much time, and too much brain!).

I create different versions of the style sheet for different purposes: A single comprehensive alphabetical list for a multiple-part project allows me and the proofreader to cross-check terms across the entire project, which is always helpful; several individual alphabetical lists sorted by chapter, article, or author allow me to send only the relevant list to each author for review.

With Table > Sort in Word, arranging my style sheet in alpha order is a no-brainer, and I like that after a long day at the helm. :-) BTW, some people don't realize that this command will work on *any* list; the list doesn't have to be in a table.

A while back, a copyeditor posted to Freelance asking how to convert her style sheet into a table so she could sort it. It struck me *hard* then that one person's "no duh!" (it's soooo obvious) is very often another person's "no way!" (never would have thought of that).

MARY RUSSELL:

I'm working on a revision of an encyclopedia on world religions that already has a 108-page word list and a 1,000-page index of terms I need to check *everything* against. I'm using your style sheet macro to slap each term I want to check into the style sheet as I go and then doing a separate pass to check them all—and having them alphabetized saves me a lot of scrolling around in those files. By the way, I *love* your macro. I run the style sheet minimized and don't even have to switch back to my original document. You should really be selling this one. I'm usually more restrained, but this really is a great idea.

Meg Cox:

Joy Freeman on Freelance suggested a new approach that I think will alleviate the style sheet challenge considerably. I haven't tried it yet, but I'm going to on the next chapter I start. She gave her permission to repeat the approach here:

With each occurrence of a new name, search for the same and replace it with itself in a different color (say, blue). Then you know you've already encountered it and don't need to check it against the style sheet. That way you only have to take action with variations and first occurrences. If it's blue, move on through!

I suspect this approach will come in very handy the next time I have a manuscript with hundreds of unfamiliar personal, place, and organizational names, and it will help in simpler projects as well.

Another way it will help: Sometimes in a long chapter it's hard to remember whether the full name of a person or organization has appeared yet (my clients routinely ask for full version on first occurrence in each chapter, then shortened version thereafter). If the changing to blue is done chapter by chapter (and I think it could be handled quickly—I need to think macro on this), blue will mean the full version has already occurred and an abbreviation or last-name-only may be called for. Could be useful for long sets of notes too so I know when it's time to go with a short citation! (Lately I'm seeing plenty of chapters with 70 or more notes.) Oh, and good for parenthetical citations too, so I know what I've already checked against bibliography.

[Note: My RazzmaTag program would be very useful for this kind of thing.]

Meg Cox:

Some editors don't like to alphabetize an editorial style sheet as they go along. For me, it's essential if the style sheet is to be usable—especially in a book with a million personal and place names, and especially if it's about an unfamiliar geographical region.

Without keeping the style sheet in alphabetical order, I'm not going to spot the close-but-not-quite situations. Case in point: in my style-sheet-nightmare project, the author was rendering the names every which way. Was it Leon Mba or Leon M'ba? With an accent on the e or not? Denis Sassou-Nguesso with or without the accent, with or without the hyphen? Sassou-Nguesso as surname only, or just Nguesso? Or Sassou Nguesso? Some names appeared infrequently enough that I never would have been able to remember whether they had come up before and how they had been rendered. (This 700-page manuscript covered politics in 14 francophone African countries over a period of 120 years.)

Even in easier projects, it's the alphabetization that enables me to spot the inconsistencies as I go along so I can change them all to the same thing. In the 14-countries project, it would have been no easy matter to go back and search and replace later because the versions of the names varied too widely, so I had to decide on the first occasion of each inconsistency. If the author wanted to go with a version different from what I had settled on, once they were all consistent I would have been able to do a global search and replace. (Thank goodness in this case cleanup was in-house!)

If I wasn't working in history and political science, this wouldn't be as much of an issue.

As it turned out, I didn't come up with a good way to do what I wanted to do. Maybe I could have with more fiddling, but I finally needed to just give up and keep moving through all the names.

ERIC FLETCHER:

I was interested to see the tip from Meg Cox and Joy Freeman posting about highlighting all instances of an item. In a job some time ago, some very foreign names were being used throughout. I knew they would cause problems later in the spell check but unless I was careful, a slightly different spelling of the same name would easily slip past. For example, "Mkandawire" might also be "Mkandewire" . . . I wanted to avoid the tedium of clicking the Ignore button during spell check but still have a way to check the items.

So, in order to both flag a word as already seen and turn off proofing, I created the little macro below. To use it, I select the word (or words) and click the button associated with it. All identical instances (note the MatchCase) are set in green color with no proofing. The resultant green color shows that the word has already been encountered (as noted in your reader's tip).

However, what is particularly useful about this approach is that you can then later collect all of the flagged items in a single step—either for separate review or for use in a style guide. (This method only works for Word 10+.)

1. In the Find box, leave Find What empty but use Format to select the color (Green in my case).
2. Click the "Highlight all items found in:" box and choose Main Document. The Find button changes to Find All, and when you click it, all instances of the color green will be highlighted.
3. Now for the fun part: close the F&R dialog and choose Copy (CTRL + C); open a new document and paste (CTRL + V).

What you get is a list with each found item on a line of its own. You can then sort it and more easily review the list since all identical instances of the same item sort together. (...and I'm sure someone out there will even have a VBA script that could eliminate all duplicates in the sorted list!) [Note: You'll find such a script in "Working with Lists."]

Here's my macro:

```
Sub FlagThis()
'Flags current selection as green with no proofing throughout
the
  document. E Fletcher 2003-10-23
  Dim flagit As String
```

```
flagit = Selection
Selection.MoveLeft Unit:=wdCharacter, Count:=1
With ActiveDocument.Content.Find
.ClearFormatting
.Text = flagit
.MatchCase = True
With .Replacement
.Text = "^&"
.ClearFormatting
'-- colour and no proofing options for replace
.Font.Color = wdColorGreen
.NoProofing = True
End With
.Execute Format:=True, Replace:=wdReplaceAll
End With
Selection.MoveRight Unit:=wdWord, Count:=1
End Sub
```

Note that I have it set up so the cursor ends up at the end of the first word in the selection. If users want to just add color and not set the proofing off, the ".NoProofing = True" statement should be removed.

I also use a slightly modified version of this method to flag words set in a different language. My Quebec flag button sets the selection in my custom "French" character style [French (Canada) language and font color blue] so I modified the FlagThis macro to set all instances of the selection to the French style. The spell check switches languages on the fly so it checks properly in multiple languages. Then, before I print or release the final version of the file, I modify the style definition(s) to change the language color(s) to automatic.

If you were unable to run the style macros in the past few articles, you may find this message from Eric Fletcher helpful. I already knew about Eric's tip here, but I keep forgetting to implement it, in spite of Steve Hudson's efforts to educate me. Please accept my apologies. Eric wrote:

Your style listing macros came at a perfect time for me as I'd just received a large file full of oddball styles (actually, it was from a French version of Word so the style names were also all in French!).

However, I thought I'd pass along a tip about future macros. If users have the "Require variable declaration" option set (Tools | Options dialog in VBE), these macro won't run until they add the following line to declare the "sty" variable:

```
Dim sty As Variant
```

Defining variables is not entirely necessary but is recommended. If the option is set in VBE, it sets "Option Explicit" at the top of the macro editing window and forces all variables to be defined with Dim statements. I was tearing out what hair I have left trying to work out why some of my previously-working macros started displaying errors until I realized that it had happened after I'd followed someone's advice about setting the option.

Style by Microsoft

Recently a colleague said to me, "Look at this manuscript. All the ordinal numbers are superscripted." What he meant was that "1st," "2nd," "3rd," and so on had the "st," "nd," and "rd" in superscript. Then came an interesting question: "Do you think I should leave them that way?"

Now, I don't know about you, but I've never in my life been tempted to set ordinals with superscript, so my answer was basically "Are you kidding?" Later I started thinking about where the superscripts had come from: Microsoft Word's AutoFormat feature. And that led me to ponder a broader question: Are editors beginning to let Microsoft Word dictate editorial style?

It's tempting here to get off on a discussion of how the means of production influences the things produced, but instead may I just say that if we let Word dictate editorial style, we're in trouble. In my opinion, such "helpful" features as AutoFormat were created mainly as one more whizbang feature for Microsoft's marketing staff. The value to everyday users is negligible or worse. So I thought it might be helpful to identify "style by Microsoft" items to watch out for. Here's my list:

- The aforementioned superscript ordinals. You can learn how to turn off such items in "When Word Gets in the Way."
- Superscript note numbers in footnotes and endnotes. You can learn how to change these to regular numbers in "Changing Note Number Format."
- Automatic capitalization of articles, conjunctions, and prepositions when using Format > Change Case > Title Case. My Editor's ToolKit program solves this problem with its "Make selection title case" feature.
- Opening single quotation marks rather than apostrophes. For example, if I write "'Twas brillig, and the slithy toves," I want the character in front of the "T" to be an apostrophe, not an opening single quotation mark. My FileCleaner program (also included with Editor's ToolKit Plus) will correct most such problems.
- The tiny, ugly ellipses "character" (ASCII number 133 on PC, 201 on Macintosh). Brrr. If you need ellipses, properly spaced periods look vastly better. Again, File-Cleaner will fix the problem.
- Arial and Times New Roman. Everywhere I look, I see documents with headings in Arial and text in Times New Roman. Just because Microsoft uses these fonts as its default doesn't mean *you* have to. Go ahead, modify the styles in your Normal template. Be different! Be daring! Be tasteful!

Readers Write

[Quite a few readers sent additional Microsoft "style" nominations for the "hall of shame."]

KENNETH SUTTON:

Here's my nomination: "replace internet paths with hyperlinks." Bah!

INDIA AMOS:

How about this classic: e-mail addresses underlined (not to mention blue and hotlinked). Yecch! Have you ever *deliberately* clicked a linked e-mail address in a Word file? Me neither.

ANDREA BALINSON:

The "style by Microsoft" example that drives me crazy is "Internet and network paths with hyperlinks," which makes Web addresses appear underlined in blue. It's one thing if the document you're writing is designed to be read on a computer; in that case, having URLs as hyperlinks can actually be useful. Most of the time, though, I see printed letters, memos, and other paper materials in which the URLs are underlined—obviously because whoever created the documents didn't know or care enough to stop Word from formatting them as links.

LINDA GRAY:

I get rid of those hyperlinked URLs and e-mail addresses by pressing CTRL+SHIFT+F9 to unlink field codes. The publishing company I work for most often, Sage Publications, doesn't want any field codes in the Word files I send to them, so as part of my final check (and usually before that because they're a pain to work around), I press CTRL+A to select the whole file and then CTRL+SHIFT+F9 to unlink the field codes, which turns all those URLs and e-mail addresses into regular type without being linked to anything. It won't take care of any URL or e-mail address that's been underlined, but that's also easily changed by selecting the whole file and pressing CTRL+U—unless the file has text that needs to be underlined, which doesn't happen often in the work I do.

LEANNE BAIRD:

If you don't know that *'til* is a contraction of until, Microsoft spell checker only gives you *till* as an option, not *till* and *'til.*

CARYL WENZEL:

I have complained many a time of "style" imposed by Microsoft that is not accepted in an editorial style manual. Yet, someone at Microsoft thinks he or she is doing someone a favor by providing all these so-called helpful ideas. I routinely omit such formatting and follow traditional editorial guidelines. I just wish Microsoft would learn the same. In fact, even Microsoft publishes it own style manuals for the books its publishing arm produces, and many of these imposed styles are not allowed.

PEG HAUSMAN:

My pet peeve about Word's "help" is its default enforcement of the alleged rule against using "which" to introduce a restrictive (essential) clause in a sentence. I've appended a longish e-mail (below) that I sent to a local electronic discussion group a while back explaining why the rule doesn't hold water. But the short version is that it was originally simply a mild preference expressed by H. W. Fowler in his famous *Modern English Usage* (1926). The preference got picked up by AP and was soon presented as grammatical gospel, reproducing itself via journalism teachers all over the United States, in spite of the fact that it fails to reflect most normal educated usage.

Redmond has picked up this fiction and incorporated it into its Grammar function. Type a sentence like "The only document which really mattered was the one they neglected to send" into Word, and it will put the well-known wavy green underline under the fourth through the sixth words. A couple of investigative clicks will get you this message:

> If the marked group of words is essential to the meaning of your sentence, use "that" to introduce the group of words. Do not use a comma. If the words are not essential to the meaning of your sentence, use "which" and separate them with a comma.

I have two problems with this. One is that it is too dogmatic: If MS wants to help people abide by AP (and AP-influenced) rules, that's fine, but it should be noted as a matter of AP house style and not as law.

The other problem is that a lot of people won't get as far as the second click, so won't know what the wavy green line is about. They may, however, discover through experiment that adding a couple of commas will make the wavy green line go away. I've seen quite a number of restrictive clauses incorrectly garnished with commas for this reason, and the effect can be most confusing. If you add commas to the sentence above—"The only document, which really mattered, was the one they neglected to send"—it promptly sounds witless and absurd.

Fixing Typos Automatically

All this talk about editorial style sheets got me thinking again about lists of automatic corrections. Long ago, I provided a couple of such lists. For more information, see "Manual or Automatic?" "More Automatic Corrections," and "Even More Automatic Corrections." I now realize that those lists don't include nearly as many typographical errors as they could—errors like these:

abbout (about)
yeild (yield)
yera (year)
yoiu (you)
yoiur (your)

So here, for your editorial pleasure, is a giant list (more than 1,200 entries) compiled from various typo and AutoCorrect collections:

http://www.editorium.com/ftp/typolist.zip

The list is set up for my MegaReplacer program, with entries like this:

abbout|about+w
yeild|yield+w
yera|year+w
yoiu|you+w
yoiur|your+w

Words before the pipe symbol (|) contain the typos. Words after the pipe symbol are their replacements. And the +w at the end of each entry tells Word to search for "Whole words only." MegaReplacer will run such a list on the active document, all open documents, or all documents in a folder, fixing all of the typos in one fell swoop.

Of course, Word's spell checker will also catch these typos—if you want to click, click, click through them all manually. But why not put MegaReplacer to work while you do something more worthwhile? Of course, running that giant list on a bunch of documents could take a while, so you might want to (1) pare down the list to include only those entries you think you'll really need and (2) run it on fewer documents at a time. Or run it on a separate computer.

You might also want to use some of these entries (minus the pipe symbols and +w's) in your AutoCorrect list (some of them are probably already there). Feel free!

Listing Misspelled Words

I've been working on a really big set of really big books that use odd, archaic spellings. Wanting to modernize those spellings, I decided to create a macro that would list every word that Microsoft Word sees as misspelled. You'll find the macro a little farther down, but before using it, you'll need to tell the macro where the misspellings are to be recorded. There are three options:

OPTION 1: List the errors at the end of your document.

OPTION 2: List the errors in a new document.

OPTION 3: List the errors in the document in the next window, such as a new, blank document you've already created.

You'll specify the number of your option in the following line in the macro:

```
myOption = 1
```

If you use option 3, you can use my MultiMacro program to run the macro on a whole folder full of documents, which will give you a nice, long list of misspellings at the end of your MultiMacro list (assuming your documents have misspellings).

Once you've got that list, you can use it to *automatically* fix the misspellings. How? Stay tuned; I'll reveal the secret (and give you another macro) in the next article.

And now, here's the macro:

```
Sub ListSpellingErrors()
Dim myDoc As Document
Dim myErrorCount As Integer
Dim e As Integer
Dim myOption As Integer
'****************
'CHOOSE ONE OF THE FOLLOWING
'THREE OPTIONS:
'OPTION 1
'List the errors at the end of
'your document.
'OPTION 2
'List the errors in a new
'document.
'OPTION 3
'List the errors in the document
'in the next window, such as a new,
'blank document you've already created,
'or a MultiMacro list.
'Specify the number of your option
```

```
'in the following line:
myOption = 1
'*****************
'Macro specifies the current document:
Set myDoc = ActiveDocument
'Macro tells Word the document hasn't
'already been spell-checked
'(whether it has or not):
myDoc.SpellingChecked = False
'But if you want Word to remember
'spell-checking you've already done,
'put an apostrophe in front
'of the command above, which turns
'off the command.
'Macro counts the number of errors
'in the document:
myErrorCount = myDoc.SpellingErrors.Count
If myOption = 1 Then
Selection.EndKey Unit:=wdStory
ElseIf myOption = 2 Then
Documents.Add
ElseIf myOption = 3 Then
If Windows.Count >= 2 Then
WordBasic.NextWindow
Else
MsgBox "Only one document open."
GoTo EndMacro
End If
End If
'Now type the misspellings into
'the specified location:
For e = 1 To myErrorCount
Selection.TypeText Text:=myDoc.SpellingErrors(e)
Selection.TypeParagraph
Next e
If myOption = 3 Then
WordBasic.NextWindow
End If
EndMacro:
End Sub
```

Correcting Misspelled Words

So you've got your list of misspelled words; now how do you use it?

The way *I* recently used it on a multivolume typesetting project was to automatically fix a bunch of archaic (along with just plain wrong) spellings. Here's what I did:

1. Sorted the misspelled words alphabetically.
2. Removed duplicates.
3. Put each word beside itself, separated by a pipe symbol, so the lines looked like this:

fulfil|fulfil
fulness|fulness
kanyon|kanyon

3. Corrected the spelling of the words on the right side of the list:

fulfil|fulfill
fulness|fullness
kanyon|canyon

4. Used the list with my MegaReplacer program to automatically replace the misspelled words on the left with the correctly spelled words on the right—in all the chapters of all the volumes. Whew!

Of course, it would have been nice to have a macro that did steps 1 through 3 for me (sort misspelled words, remove duplicates, put each word beside itself). So I made one. And I'll share:

```
Sub MakeCorrectionList()
'Define variables
Dim Para1$
Dim Para2$
Dim aPara
'Sort words alphabetically
Selection.WholeStory
Selection.Sort
'Delete duplicate words
Selection.WholeStory
```

```
For Each aPara In ActiveDocument.Paragraphs
Para2$ = aPara
If Para1$ = Para2$ Then
aPara.Range.Delete
Else
Para1$ = Para2$
End If
Next
'Duplicate list side by side
'with pipe symbol separating
Selection.WholeStory
Selection.ConvertToTable _
Separator:=wdSeparateByParagraphs
Selection.Copy
Selection.InsertColumnsRight
Selection.Paste
Selection.Tables(1).Select
Selection.Rows.ConvertToText _
Separator:="", NestedTables:=True
'Add code indicating Match
'Case and Whole Word Only
Selection.HomeKey Unit:=wdStory
Selection.Find.ClearFormatting
Selection.Find.Replacement.ClearFormatting
With Selection.Find
.Text = "^p"
.Replacement.Text = "+&^p"
.Forward = True
.Wrap = wdFindContinue
.Format = False
.MatchCase = False
.MatchWholeWord = False
.MatchWildcards = False
.MatchSoundsLike = False
.MatchAllWordForms = False
End With
Selection.Find.Execute _
Replace:=wdReplaceAll
Selection.HomeKey Unit:=wdStory
End Sub
```

That last bit, "Add code indicating Match Case and Whole Word Only," is for use by MegaReplacer, and it will add +& at the end of each entry. In addition, at the bottom of the list, you'll get one final carriage return preceded by +&. You should delete that line before using the list with MegaReplacer.

You may find other uses for the macro as well—or at least pieces of it. For example, this part will delete duplicate paragraphs (i.e., single words on a line) in any list:

```
Sub DeleteDuplicates()
'Delete duplicate words (i.e., paragraphs)
Dim Para1$
Dim Para2$
```

```
Dim aPara
For Each aPara In ActiveDocument.Paragraphs
Para2$ = aPara
If Para1$ = Para2$ Then
aPara.Range.Delete
Else
Para1$ = Para2$
End If
Next
End Sub
```

And the following part will create a two-column table with the list of words in each column. You can then use the table as the basis for an index concordance. See "Making a Concordance," "Indexing with a Concordance," "Indexing with a Two-Column Concordance," and "Indexing with a Two-Column Concordance, Part 2."

```
Sub MakeConcordanceTable()
'Duplicate list side by side in a table
Selection.WholeStory
Selection.ConvertToTable Separator:=wdSeparateByParagraphs
Selection.Copy
Selection.InsertColumnsRight
Selection.Paste
End Sub
```

Making a Concordance

Have you ever needed to make a list of every word in a document? If so, here's a macro that will do it for you automatically. Basically, the macro marks an index entry for every word in your document, generates the index, and removes the page numbers, leaving you with an alphabetical list of words used (at the end of the document). It's sometimes interesting to see what Microsoft Word considers a "word"; periods, commas, and other unlikely items will be included.

To use the macro, open a document for which you need to make a concordance. (Be sure to keep a backup, just in case.) Then, run the following macro on the document (I've included comments to explain how it works):

```
Sub MakeCordance()
'Mark an index entry for each word in the document:
Dim myWord
For Each myWord In ActiveDocument.Words
ActiveDocument.Indexes.MarkEntry _
Range:=Selection.Range, Entry:=myWord
Next myWord
'Go to the end of the document:
Selection.EndKey Unit:=wdStory
'Mark place with a bookmark:
ActiveDocument.Bookmarks.Add _
Range:=Selection.Range, Name:="IndexStartsHere"
'Generate an index based on the entries marked earlier:
With ActiveDocument
.Indexes.Add Range:=Selection.Range, _
HeadingSeparator:=wdHeadingSeparatorNone, _
Type:=wdIndexIndent, RightAlignPageNumbers:= _
False, NumberOfColumns:=1, _
IndexLanguage:=wdEnglishUS
.Indexes(1).TabLeader = wdTabLeaderDots
End With
'Go back to the bookmark:
Selection.GoTo What:=wdGoToBookmark, _
Name:="IndexStartsHere"
'Select the index, from the bookmark
'to the end of the document:
Selection.EndKey Unit:=wdStory, Extend:=wdExtend
'Turn the index "field" into actual text:
Selection.Fields.Unlink
'Get rid of the page numbers after the index entries:
Selection.Find.ClearFormatting
Selection.Find.Replacement.ClearFormatting
With Selection.Find
.Text = ", [0-9]@[\^013]"
```

```
.Replacement.Text = "^p"
.Forward = True
.Wrap = wdFindContinue
.Format = False
.MatchCase = False
.MatchWholeWord = False
.MatchAllWordForms = False
.MatchSoundsLike = False
.MatchWildcards = True
End With
Selection.Find.Execute Replace:=wdReplaceAll
'Go back to the bookmark:
Selection.GoTo What:=wdGoToBookmark, _
Name:="IndexStartsHere"
End Sub
```

If you want to keep the page numbers, just leave out these lines:

```
'Get rid of the page numbers after the index entries:
Selection.Find.ClearFormatting
Selection.Find.Replacement.ClearFormatting
With Selection.Find
.Text = ", [0-9]@[\^013]"
.Replacement.Text = "^p"
.Forward = True
.Wrap = wdFindContinue
.Format = False
.MatchCase = False
.MatchWholeWord = False
.MatchAllWordForms = False
.MatchSoundsLike = False
.MatchWildcards = True
End With
Selection.Find.Execute Replace:=wdReplaceAll
```

For certain kinds of projects (catalogs, for example), you may be able to use a concordance to create an index of your document. You can learn more in "Indexing with a Concordance."

Need to create a concordance for a whole bunch of documents at once? Use my MultiMacro program to run the macro above on all documents in a folder. Or, you could use my WordCounter program, which includes a concordance feature with a frequency count of the words in a document or documents. In other words, WordCounter can now tell you *how many times* each word has been used. How might that be useful for editing? Stay tuned, and I'll reveal all.

Editing by Concordance

The previous article mentioned my WordCounter program, which can now tell you how many times each word has been used in a document—and I promised to show you how that might be useful for editing. The article also featured a macro that will create a concordance, or list of all words used, from a Word document. In the next article, I'll explain a very sneaky way to use that in editing.

Let's say you've run WordCounter's concordance feature on a document, including word frequency, so you've now got a report in a table that looks like this:

1,639 and
1,453 the
1,330 of

Notice that the table is sorted by word frequency, with the most frequently used words at the top. That doesn't seem very useful; who cares how many times "and" and "of" appear? On the other hand, it may give you an idea of your author's general verbosity and other faults. Lots of prepositions? As you edit, watch for strings of prepositional phrases. Lots of "is," "was," and "were"? The author's verbs may need strengthening, and you may need to root out the passive voice. Lots of capitalized "And" and "But"? Does it bother you to start a sentence with a conjunction? If not, has the author simply overdone it? How many times is "very" used? Fifty occurrences of "paradigm"? Good grief!

Now let's go to the bottom of the table:

3 manger
2 managment

Hmmm. In this business book, we've got "managment" appearing twice, and "manger" three times. The spell checker would have caught "managment" but not "manger." We now know that we should search for "manger" and replace it with "manager." And we might as well take care of "managment" while we're at it. You'll probably find some pretty strange fish in this end of the net, but without WordCounter, they might have gotten away. Find and replace as needed. If you have lots of them, I recommend fixing them en masse with MegaReplacer.

Now let's sort the table alphabetically by word. No, no, wait. First, select all those frequently used words at the top of the table and delete them. That will get them out of the way for what we want to do next. Here's how:

1. Select a whole bunch of words and numbers you want to get rid of.
2. Click Table > Select > Row.
3. Click Table > Delete > Rows.

Okay, *now* let's sort the table alphabetically by word:

1. Put your cursor in the table.
2. Click Table > Select > Table.
3. Click Table > Sort > Column 2, Text, Ascending.
4. Click OK.

Excellent. Now start looking through your list. What do you see? Multiple spellings for "realize/realise"? How about "President" and "president"? Sorting the table by word puts such variations near each other in the list so you can spot them easily. Then, in your main document, you can find and replace as needed.

Knowing how many times each word appears may also help in your decisions about editorial style. If both styles are acceptable, why not go with the one you have to fix the fewest number of times? Whatever your decision, using a word frequency list can alert you to editorial problems before you ever start editing, and it can help you achieve the editorial consistency you desire.

Readers Write

JUDY STEIN:

Eric Fletcher writes, "What is particularly useful about this approach is that you can then later collect all of the flagged items in a single step—either for separate review or for use in a style guide. (This method only works for Word 10+.)"

What's Word 10+? I assume it's something beyond Word 2000, because he goes on to talk about a "Highlight all items found in" box—but I don't have one of those.

I REPLIED: Word 10 is the same as Word 2002 is the same as Word XP. "Word 10+" means Word 10 and anything higher. Word 11, for example, includes Word 2003 (PC) and Word 2004 (Mac). Back in the good old days, Word was numbered with, well, numbers rather than years. So we had Word 2, Word 5, and Word 6. With Word 95, however, Microsoft decided to get fancy, but lots of folks still referred to it as Word 7. Word 97 (and 98) is thus Word 8, Word 2000 (and 2001) is Word 9, and so on. Word 2007 is Word 12.

MEG COX

I have solved my problem of viewing style sheet items in alphabetical order so I can spot near misses as I go along without having to scroll to the proper place each time to insert the new item. I also index books, so I have the SKY Index software. I knew this software would solve my problem, but I was stuck because every time I tried to shrink its window so I could tuck it in a corner of my screen, I would get an error message. Well, I decided to just shrink the window bit by bit, ignoring the recurring, and, as it turns out, benign, error message, until I had a nice compact little window to stick in the corner. Now the windows are sharing space nicely.

Now I can type or paste new entries in and immediately see them in context alphabetically next to other entries of the same category—personal name, foreign term, whatever. If I'm typing instead of pasting, autocomplete will let me know right away that the term has been encountered already (perhaps in a previous file if I'm using the color-coding method).

Now I'm wondering: I don't think a Word macro can open a window in another program and order a paste there. That would be very helpful.

Editing by Concordance, Part 2

The previous article explained some ways a concordance could be used in editing, with a promise that I'd show you a sneaky way to take that concept even further. So here goes.

There you are with a manuscript that needs editing, and lots of it. A cursory look reveals multiple inconsistencies and odd spellings, and you're going to have to fix them all. What to do? Try this:

1. Use my WordCounter program or the MakeConcordance macro in "Making a Concordance" to create a concordance, or word list, of all the words in the document. This time around, you don't need to worry about word frequency (although you can if you find that helpful). Instead, just make a list that looks like this:

and
managment
manger
of
the

And so on.

You could go through the list and manually delete all the commonly used words (such as "and," "of," and "the"), leaving you with the words you actually need to think about, but that would take a long, long time. A better way would be to use my MegaReplacer program to remove the commonly used words. And you could do that if you just had a list of commonly used words. You can download one here:

http://www.editorium.com/ftp/commonwords.zip

The list contains 2,256 entries (compiled from various sources) and is already set up for use in MegaReplacer. So use the list with MegaReplacer to delete all of the commonly used words from your word list, leaving you with just the real stuff.

Once you've got the real stuff (such as "manger" and "managment"), you'll find it much easier to go through the list and decide what needs to be changed. Please do so. As you find words like "managment" that need to be corrected, set *them* up for MegaReplacer as well:

managment|management
manger|manager

The bad goes on the left, the good on the right, with a pipe symbol in between. You may also want to add the good to your editorial style sheet, as explained in "Editorial Style Sheet" and "Editorial Style Sheet Macro."

Aside from misspellings, you'll also find inconsistencies in spelling, style, and capitalization that need to be fixed. Set them up the way you want them to be:

> realise|realize

When you come to words that are fine just as they are, add them to your editorial style sheet as needed and then delete them from the list,

When you're finished, you'll have a beautiful find-and-replace list that you can feed to MegaReplacer, which will go through your manuscript and automatically make all the changes you've specified. If this makes you nervous, you should know that you can have the program mark its revisions in case you later have any question about what was changed.

If you're looking for a way to speed up your work, you may find this technique useful. There's one way to find out. And you've got to admit that using a word list to modify a word list to modify a document is pretty sneaky.

Readers Write

Teresa N. Barensfeld:

Another good use for the concordance is for projects with vast reference lists. Sometimes the names are inconsistently spelled in the text or the ref list, but they're so close that it's easy to miss.

Meg Cox:

This is great stuff! My plan is emerging here:

1. Run Word Counter and go through the concordance and MegaReplacer process to make obvious changes. This would have been wonderful for fixing British spellings in this project (nearing completion) and the previous one. Take note of items that look troublesome but that I'll need to decide about when I encounter them in context.
2. Use my indexing software to construct my style sheet as I work through the book. (But begin by entering items from the concordance file that I know right off the bat need to be on the style sheet. I can create a tab-delimited file with the necessary items from the concordance and import it to save on typing or copying and pasting.) Using the indexing program is necessary because the concordance won't help me with items that are more than one word, and with the software I won't have to navigate to the right spot on the style sheet to compare new terms with earlier entries—the style sheet sorts itself in the top of the window as I enter terms at the bottom.
3. Note already-checked terms by finding and replacing to add different formatting or highlighting that I can remove later. Here there will be two levels: For references, I should do this while I still have all chapters combined. Then I can separate

the chapters and use the same process to indicate, for example, whether an organization with an acronym has appeared spelled out yet in the chapter, and whether a person has appeared yet with both first and last name in that chapter. In the case of end-of-chapter notes I would also somehow need to revisit the references and use the highlighting method to check for use of a full citation first time and short cite thereafter. I'll have to think about how to do that.

PAUL ROBINSON:

I edit in Word. After finishing a document, I calculate percentage mark-up by comparing a word count of the original document with a word count of the marked-up document. But this tells me only how many words I've added. I'd really like to be able to see how many words I've deleted as well. Then I could measure the heaviness of the editing by looking at the extent of both inserted and deleted words.

At present I count characters-with-spaces in the original text and then in the text with tracked changes. This gives me a very rough, comparative idea of the extent of the editing. To be able to count the number of inserted/deleted words (the revised words in total) would be a definite advance. To be able to count the inserted and deleted words separately would be even better! One could then report to a client as follows. "The editorial changes required were heavy (or light, as the case may be): insertions = m% of original word number, deletions = n% of original word number, which compares with my averages thus . . ." Moreover, one could suggest, if the number of deletions, say, was high, that the client was writing in a rather ponderous style; and so on—with all due tact, of course!

[Thinking that Paul has a great idea here, I created the following macro, which provides a count of both insertions and deletions.]

```
Sub CountRevisedWords()
Dim RevCount, WordCount, RevType, InsertedWords, DeletedWords, r
RevCount = ActiveDocument.Revisions.Count
For r = 1 To RevCount
WordCount = ActiveDocument.Revisions.Item(r).Range.Words.Count
RevType = ActiveDocument.Revisions.Item(r).Type
If RevType = 1 Then InsertedWords = InsertedWords + WordCount
If RevType = 2 Then DeletedWords = DeletedWords + WordCount
Next r
MsgBox "Inserted words:" & Str(InsertedWords) & " Deleted
words:" & Str(DeletedWords)
End Sub
```

WALLACE SAGENDORPH:

In the macro, what does that "r" stand for?

I RESPONDED: It doesn't really stand for anything (well, "revision number," maybe). It's an incremental counter. Here's how it works:

```
RevCount = ActiveDocument.Revisions.Count
```

That counts the number of revisions in the active document and stores the count in a variable named RevCount. (Remember X in algebra? That's all a variable is; it's a placeholder for some number.)

Then we have this:

```
For r = 1 To RevCount
(Something happens here)
Next r
```

That says to Word, "Starting with the number 1, do (something) however many times RevCount is."

"Next r" just increments r by 1.

So, let's say RevCount = 3, and the (something) was "Insert 'hello' into my document." The macro would insert this:

hello

Then it would make r become 2 instead of 1 (Next r).
Then it would insert this:

hello

Then it would make r become 3 instead of 2 (Next r).
Then it would insert this:

hello

When r got to 4, the macro would stop, because 4 is one more than Revcount (3), and you'd have something like this in your document:

hello
hello
hello

PAUL ROBINSON:

I've been meaning to get in touch to thank you properly for the revisions-counting macro. I'm very grateful for your help.

The macro takes a bit of getting used to. I find it takes an awfully long time to count the revisions in 5-10,000-word documents. In fact, so long, that at first I thought it wasn't working—one really should go and make a cup of tea and leave the computer to itself! This might be worth mentioning.

BILL RUBIDGE:

It's a funny coincidence about your macro to count revisions. I have been tinkering with this a little myself, and had put together the following macro. It hasn't been optimized at all, in part because I'm still thinking about how to use it to quantify the degree of revision.

For example, I would consider replacing one word with another, in the same position, to be a very minor revision. A letter change within a word (colour to color) even more minor. But if a revision is long enough (X characters) to indicate a new sentence, that would be an indicator to my client that I had done more work.

The one weakness of the word revisions tracking tool is that it does not allow us to track a different kind of revision—where text is simply moved from one place to another in a document. (DeltaView from WorkShare can do this for you, but the license is designed for large organizations, so the tool is typically used by law firms. And I don't know whether that "moved" information would be accessible as a count, or through VBA.)

Anyway, as a work in process, here's my draft macro.

```
Sub CountRevs()
Dim intWordCount As Integer
intWordCount = ActiveDocument.Words.Count
Dim intRevCount As Integer
intRevCount = ActiveDocument.Revisions.Count
If intRevCount = 0 Then
MsgBox ("This document has no revisions.")
Exit Sub
End If
Dim intCounter As Integer
intCounter = 1
Dim intInsertionCount As Integer
intInsertionCount = 0
Dim intInsertionLongestLen As Integer
intInsertionLongestLen = 0
Dim intDeletionCount As Integer
intDeletionCount = 0
Dim intDeletionLongestLen As Integer
intDeletionLongestLen = 0
Dim intOtherRevCount As Integer
intOtherRevCount = 0
Do While intCounter < intRevCount + 1
If ActiveDocument.Revisions(intCounter).Type = _
wdRevisionInsert Then
intInsertionCount = intInsertionCount + 1
If Len(ActiveDocument.Revisions(intCounter).Range) > _
intInsertionLongestLen Then
intInsertionLongestLen = _
Len(ActiveDocument.Revisions(intCounter).Range)
End If
Else
If ActiveDocument.Revisions(intCounter).Type = _
wdRevisionDelete Then
intDeletionCount = intDeletionCount + 1
If Len(ActiveDocument.Revisions(intCounter).Range) > _
```

```
intDeletionLongestLen Then
intDeletionLongestLen = _
Len(ActiveDocument.Revisions(intCounter).Range)
End If
Else
intOtherRevCount = intOtherRevCount + 1
End If
End If
intCounter = intCounter + 1
Loop
MsgBox ("Results of Revision Inventory: " & vbCrLf & _
"- " & intWordCount & _
" total words in the document (simple count)." & _
vbCrLf & "- " & intInsertionCount & _
" insertions, and longest insertion has " & _
intInsertionLongestLen & " characters." & _
vbCrLf & "- " & intDeletionCount & _
" deletions, and longest deletion has " & _
intDeletionLongestLen & " characters." & _
vbCrLf & "- " & intOtherRevCount & _
" other revisions (might be formatting, etc.).")
End Sub
```

DAVE GAYMAN:

Meg asked: "Now I'm wondering: I don't think a Word macro can open a window in another program and order a paste there. That would be very helpful."

Remembering that this was a stopper in a VBA project long ago—and I don't remember if it was because it could not be done, or simply that I could not master the commands to make it happen—I'd suggest MacroExpress (http://www.macros.com/index.htm), $50.

With MacroExpress, you simply record the key or mouse strokes (or both) to accomplish the task. In addition to recording the macro, users are also able to enter macros directly into an edit pane (much of which is done via select and paste) and they are able to edit the code that has been generated automatically. Before the recording begins, a sequence of dialogs lets you make choices, including whether you'll be capturing key strokes, mouse movement, or both; applicability—see next paragraph; hot keys; macro name, and so on.

Macros can be global (that is, work with all programs), program-specific, or window-specific. You can assign hot keys to the macro, as well as assign a password. In Meg's case, once Meg selects the target word, MacroExpress could copy the word, switch to (or launch, if it is not already open) the second window; if necessary position the cursor (for example, at the end); paste; then switch back to the Word window.

I've used MacroExpress to automate or semi-automate the process of eliminating duplicates in a long product order code list by cross-reffing against an Excel file; to set up glossary entries (including both making a new entry and applying of Word styles for formatting); and many small repetitive tasks.

Although I originally bought MacroExpress to create actions in Dragon NaturallySpeaking Preferred edition (a version level without macro capabilities), the order code duplicate finder gave me my $50 in value. It took a project that could easily have consumed three days and telescoped it into about an hour. Note that there is usually a variable amount of debugging to be done to make a macro more generic or to make it do everything you want it to do—the duplicate finder took about half an hour to set up and tweak, all told.

There's a support newsgroup where newbies are generally treated humanely (find it at http://www.pgmacros.com/newsgroup.htm). Users run the gamut from casual operators of the program (like me) to very serious macro wranglers with correspondingly complex automated tasks.

RICHARD H. ADIN:

I don't have a "within Word" answer for Meg, but I do have an answer that will work on a Windows PC: using MacroExpress (http://www.macroexpress.com).

I had three problems that needed solving and I couldn't figure out how to do it within Word:

1. How to copy a phrase from my text document to a style sheet and, if the phrase had an acronym, how to enter it twice on the style sheet—once as, e.g., World Health Organization (WHO) and then as WHO (World Health Organization);
2. I'm pretty sure that five chapters ago I had come across the acronym, e.g., WHO, and had spelled it out and added it to my style sheet. Now I've come across it again and it needs to be spelled out here, but I can't recall what it means. I wanted to quickly check the style sheet to see if it was spelled out, and if it was, then copy the spelled-out version and paste it in place in the text file; and
3. In books that follow the APA reference style (or any similar style) in which the text reference entry appears as, e.g., Smith, Jones, Adams, and Burley (1998), how to (a) verify that the entry is in the references; (b) check for and mark subsequent entries so I don't have to reverify that it exists or is correct each time I come across the entry in the text; (c) mark the entry in the references so I know (i) which references have been cited in the text and which haven't and (ii) I know that I have already checked that the reference is properly styled; (d) if the subsequent text entries are Smith, Jones, Adams, and Burley (1998) when they should be Smith et al. (1998), I can correct the erroneous entries; and, finally, (e) when done, I am returned to where I started.

Although the macros I have written in MacroExpress can yet be improved upon (and I am constantly improving them), they do work well as is. Below are the steps I take to run a macro for each problem.

PROBLEM 1: TO ADD MATERIAL TO THE STYLE SHEET: 1. Highlight the material to be added. If it is just a word or a phrase, highlight that; if it is a word/phrase with an acronym, highlight the spelled out word/phrase + the acronym, including the opening and closing parentheses.
2. Press F9 (this just happens to be the key to which I assigned the macro; MacroExpress lets you assign most any key combination).

3. In the dialog box that appears, enter only the place where you want to go. For example, in the WHO example, you want to go to the W section of the style sheet, so enter w and click OK.

4. You will be moved to the W section, and your cursor will blink where it is. BEFORE doing anything else, move the cursor to the beginning of the line where you want your selection to be entered. Do not add a return to make a line. If you already have entries, place the cursor at the beginning of the line that is to appear AFTER this entry is typed.

5. In the dialog box, make the appropriate choice. Choose Word for a word or phrase without an acronym; choose Word + Acronym for a word or phrase that has an acronym that needs to be entered; choose cancel to stop and return to the text file. Once you make your choice, the macro will paste your copied material at the insertion point on a new line. If you chose Word, you will then be returned to where you were in the text file. If you chose Word + Acronym, then

6. The macro will pause and tell you to move the cursor to the beginning of the line where you want the acronym to appear. Again, just move your cursor; do not add a line. When your cursor is in place, click Resume. The macro will paste the entry at the designated position, creating a new line, and will then move the acronym to the line beginning and put the spell out in the parentheses.

7. The macro will automatically return you to your place in the text file.

PROBLEM 2: CHECKING ON AN ACRONYM   1. Highlight the acronym—just the acronym, not any spaces before or after.

2. Press F10 (again, this was my choice).

3. The macro will take you to the style sheet and will highlight the first instance of the acronym. There is a slight delay so that you can see what is being highlighted in the style sheet, after which a dialog box appears. If the highlighted acronym is the correct one, click Yes; if it isn't, click No. Click Cancel to terminate the macro and return to the text file.

4. If you choose Yes, the cursor will move to the beginning of the spell out and pause.

5. Now highlight the complete spell out, including the acronym and the closing parenthesis, but not the paragraph marker.

6. Click Resume. The macro will return to the highlighted acronym in the text file and replace it with the spell out and acronym in parentheses.

7. If you chose No rather than yes, the macro will search for the next instance of the acronym; if it finds another instance, you will have the same three choices. If it doesn't find it, Word will tell you that it has not been found and ask you whether you want to search from the beginning of the document. Choose yes or no depending on where the search started. If you choose no, then also choose cancel in the Macro Express dialog box. It will cancel the macro, close the Find and Replace box, and return you to where you were in the text file.

PROBLEM 3: REFERENCE CHECKER 1. Highlight the first author's surname only (e.g., in Smith and Jones (1995) or Smith, Jones, Adams, and Burley (1998), highlight only Smith).

2. Press F7 (my choice).

3. The macro will take you to the beginning of the reference list and then search for the first instance of the name you highlighted, highlighting the name in the reference (e.g., Smith). A dialog box will appear asking if this is the correct reference. If it is, click Yes. (If you choose no, the macro will find the next instance of Smith.)

4. In the next dialog box, choose whether this is a reference that has either 1 or 2 authors or 3+ authors.

(a) If 1-2 is chosen, the highlighted name in the reference list will be colored green and the macro will then return to the text file and search for the next instance of Smith, which it will highlight. A dialog box will appear and ask whether this is the correct reference. If yes, a marker will be inserted following the name; if no, the macro will search for the next instance of Smith, at which time the dialog box will appear. The process repeats until the macro reaches the end of the document and finds no more instances of Smith, at which time you cancel the macro and are returned to where you began.

(b) If 3+ is chosen, the highlighted name in the reference list will be colored green and the macro will then return to the text file and search for the next instance of Smith, which it will highlight. A dialog box will appear and ask whether this is the correct reference and if it needs to be modified. Your choices are different from those in (a). If the listing is Smith, Jones, Adams, and Burley and it should be Smith et al., you choose Yes (make et al. and mark). If it is already Smith et al. but is the correct reference, you choose No (is et al. but needs mark). And if it is not the correct Smith, you choose Find next so that the macro will not mark this reference and will search for the next instance of Smith. The process repeats until the macro reaches the end of the document and finds no more instances of Smith, at which time you cancel the macro and are returned to where you began.

(c) Because you may have already found this entry and colored it green in another chapter, you can also choose to just search the main text file. In this case, you are returned to the main text file without marking the reference file, and the process proceeds as above.

When you are done editing the document, you simply search for the marker and replace it with nothing.

Because I work on a per-page or project fee basis, saving time is important. Do these macros save time? Absolutely. The steps look more cumbersome than they are—it's more difficult to explain the operation than to do it. Although the first two macros can be performed by using your mouse and keyboard to copy, switch between documents, paste, and switch documents again, my experience is that using the macros is much more efficient and faster. Even if I only save a few seconds each time, it adds up.

The third macro is a real timesaver because I accomplish several things simultaneously. (1) I verify that a reference is in the reference list and mark it (green highlight) so that when I get to the end of the project and now only have to check the reference list, I have already eliminated having to check most of the references—I only need to check those without the green highlight. (2) When I send the reference file to the author for review, I can tell the author that only those highlighted in green are cited in the text and ask what the author wants to do with the others. It becomes easy for the author to know which ones I mean. (3) By adding a marker to each occurrence of a reference in the main text, I speed things along because I know I have verified the reference already. It's a little slow in the beginning, but it speeds things as you move further along in the text. Imagine a 50-page chapter with scores of these references. How do you remember that Smith (1995) is OK but that Smith (1998) has not been verified?

MacroExpress has allowed me to make my keyboard more functional and to do things that were otherwise cumbersome. Just two quick examples of what I mean. (By the way, I primarily use Word, so all of the examples are of things that I do in Word. MacroExpress permits you to assign a macro to a specific application or to global, i.e., to every program.) Each of my clients has a different way to do things. Some want me to code with beginning and ending codes such as <BL> at the beginning of a bulleted list with </BL> at the very end of the list; some want me to apply a Word style to each paragraph; and some want specific codes used in specific series. MacroExpress lets me create different keyboards for different clients, and multiple keyboards for clients whose coding changes based on the series. Once I write a standard macro, for example, one that does the bullet list coding, I can import it into any number of keyboards and modify just the code, without modifying how it works, so that it inserts the codes the client wants.

In the case of the bulleted list, I press F6, and MacroExpress types <BL> and adds a bookmark. Then it pauses and tells me to move my cursor to the end of the bulleted list where I want the closing code placed. It doesn't matter whether the end is one line or 100 pages away; I move to it and click Resume, and MacroExpress types </BL> and then moves me back to the beginning of the list so I can edit.

I have one client who uses a standardized footnote system, e.g., every time a drug is named that is not FDA approved for the particular indication, the client wants a superscript 1 inserted in the text and then inserted as a new paragraph "1 This drug is not FDA approved for this indication." with the 1 superscripted and the Footnote style applied to the paragraph. With MacroExpress, I was able to write one macro that does it all. I place my cursor where I want the footnote reference inserted, press the assigned key combination, and in a split second it's done and I am returned to where I left off my editing. This ensures uniformity and that I don't forget to do something.

[Note: If you're interested in MacroExpress, you may also be interested in WinKeySim, which offers some of the same features. WinKeySim, however, is a freeware program for Windows 95 and later and Windows NT 4.0 and later. WinKeySim gives keyboard macro support for practically any Windows program that supports keyboard input. Generally speaking, if it can be done with the keyboard, it can be done with a WinKeySim macro: http://mwganson.freeyellow.com/winkeysim/]

Manual or Automatic?

When working electronically, editors often have to decide whether to make certain corrections manually or automatically, using such features as Find and Replace. Some corrections *have* to be made manually, but, in my opinion, editors often make more manual corrections than they should. For example, many editors change restrictive "which" to "that" by hand, making each change separately as it shows up in the manuscript. But how bad would it be, really, to change *every* "which" to "that" throughout the manuscript? You're going to read the manuscript all the way through anyway, right? So if you later come to a few "thats" that actually should be "whiches," you can fix them manually—which is much easier and faster than changing *hundreds* of "whiches" to "thats" by hand.

You have to use some judgment when doing this kind of thing. If a certain automatic correction will just make reading the manuscript too weird for you, don't use it. Or, you might try making the automatic correction with revision tracking turned on and showing—

Tools > Track Changes > Highlight Changes > Track changes while editing + Highlight changes on screen

—so that when you're reading through the document later, you'll know that the odd reading of that problem sentence is something you (rather than the author) introduced. Of course, if an automatic correction will result in *more* manual manipulation later on, you shouldn't use it.

Another possibility is to use wildcards in your Find and Replace corrections. In our "which" to "that" example, you could search for the word "which" whenever it *doesn't* follow a comma and replace it with "that," which would leave nearly all of the nonrestrictive occurrences ("blah blah, which blah blah") intact. Here's how:

1. Click the "Edit" menu.
2. Click "Replace."
3. In the "Find What" box, enter this:
4. ([!,]) which
5. In the "Replace With" box, enter this:
6. that
7. Put a checkmark in the "Use wildcards" checkbox (you may need to click the "More" button before you can do this).
8. Click the "Replace All" button.

Of course, if the idea of making such sweeping changes scares you, you can use the Find and Replace dialog to "Find Next" and "Replace" items individually, which still beats doing them all by hand.

Don't forget that there are certain corrections you'll almost *always* want to make, such as fixing commonly misspelled words. You'll probably want to make your own list, but here are some of my favorites:

Find What	Replace With
accomodate	accommodate
supercede	supersede
independant	independent
embarass	embarrass
annoint	anoint
occurrance	occurrence
accidently	accidentally
concensus	consensus
wierd	weird
mischevious	mischievous
definate	definite
transcendant	transcendent

To automate things even further, don't just do these replacements one at a time on job after job; instead, record them in a macro that you can use over and over again.

More Automatic Corrections

As I explained in earlier, editors who work in Microsoft Word can make many changes automatically (using Find and Replace) rather than making them manually. For more information on how to do that, see "Manual or Automatic?"

Here, I've provided a long list of corrections that you *might* be able to make automatically. Don't just use these blindly, however. Please look through the list to see which items would be most useful to you. Then you can record a macro that finds and replaces all of the items you've chosen. You can learn more about recording a find-and-replace macro in, well, "Recording a Find-and-Replace Macro."

Find What	Replace With
%	percent
&	and
a large number of	many
a small number of	some
absolutely	[nothing]
adjacent to	next to
admit of	admit
adventuresome	adventurous
albeit	though
all of the	all the
alongside of	along
already has been	has been
alright	all right
ameliorate	improve
amidst	amid
amongst	among
an historic	a historic
an historical	a historical
and also	and
anticipate that	expect that
append	add
arising from the fact that	because

assuredly	[nothing]
at present	now
at that point in time	then
at the time when	when
at this point in time	now
backwards	backward
be helpful	help
but rather	but
by itself	alone
cannot help but	can only
certainly	[nothing]
cognizant	aware
commence	start
component	part
consensus of opinion	consensus
currently	now
data is	data are
decidedly	[nothing]
depend upon	depend on
depending upon	depending on
despite the fact that	although
devoid of	without
different than	different from
disassociate	dissociate
divide up	divide
due to the fact that	because
due to	because of
e.g.,	for example,
eminently	[nothing]
end result	result
endeavor	try
ensue	follow
ergo	therefore
erstwhile	former
espouse	hold

et al.	and others
etc.	and so on
fifthly	fifth
filled up the	filled the
finalize	finish
first began	began
first of all	first
firstly	first
foreseeable future	future
forthwith	now
fourthly	fourth
fundamental	basic
general consensus	consensus
give an indication of	indicate
have a tendency to	tend to
have an effect on	affect
have an impact on	affect
have got to	must
henceforth	from now on
hereby	[nothing]
highly unlikely	unlikely
i.e.,	that is,
in addition to	besides
in excess of	more than
in order to	to
in spite of the fact that	although
in the event that	if
in the near future	soon
in view of the fact that	because
inasmuch	because
initiate	start
inquire	ask
irregardless	regardless
is a function of	depends on
is desirous of	wants

join together	join
lengthy	long
loth	loath
make a decision	decide
match up	match
may possibly	may
media is	media are
might possibly	might
miss out on	miss
more importantly	more important
must inevitably	must
must necessarily	must
neither of them are	neither of them is
never the less	nevertheless
none of them are	none of them is
none the less	nonetheless
numerous	many
on a daily basis	daily
on a monthly basis	monthly
on a regular basis	regularly
on a weekly basis	weekly
on a yearly basis	yearly
on an annual basis	yearly
owing to the fact that	because
presented in this	in this
preventative	preventive
previous to	before
prior experience	experience
prior to	before
quite	[nothing]
reason is because	reason is that
refer back	refer
rely upon	rely on
secondly	second
sixthly	sixth

take into consideration	consider
thankfully	[nothing]
the majority of	most
the reason is because	the reason is that
there are now	there are
thirdly	third
thusly	thus
together with	with
towards	toward
try and	try to
TV	television
underway	under way
until such time as	until
very	[nothing]
virtually all	most
which	that
while	although
whilst	while
will in the future	will
will take steps to	will
with the exception of	except

Readers Write

ELLEN ELLENDER:

If you are replacing "%" with "percent," you must specify that the replacement is "[space]percent" or you'll end up with text reading "75percent" instead of "75 percent."

ANNE K. BAILEY:

I would suggest that the replacement be "^spercent" (putting a nonbreaking space before the word "percent"). This would ensure that nowhere in the text would "75" (or whatever number) be dangling at the end of one line with the word "percent" at the beginning of the next. In my opinion, the nonbreaking space is extremely underutilized.

Even More Automatic Corrections

I'd like to thank Martha H. Bowes, Ned Humphrey, and Joel Rosenberg for sending more items for our "master list." (If I've missed anyone, I apologize.) I'm especially grateful to Microsoft Word genius Steve Hudson, who contributed most of the corrections in the list below.

I've set up the list with the pipe symbol (|) between entries so the list can be used with my MegaReplacer program.

And now, here's the latest installment, with the items to find on the left, and the items to replace them with on the right. Remember, don't use these blindly. Choose the items that will be most useful to you.

, and | and
a lot of | many
ain;t | are not
ain't | are not
aint | are not
app | application
apps | applications
aren;t | are not
aren't | are not
arn't | are not
at this moment in time | now
by using | with
can;t | cannot
cannot of been | cannot have been
can't | cannot
char | character
click | select
comm | communication
comms | communications
coudln't | could not
coudn't | could not
could of been | could have been
could of had | could have had
couldn;t | could not
couldnt | could not
couple of | several
coz | because
degrade | slow

dept | department
detailed | described
dev | development
devs | developers
didint | did not
didn;t | did not
didn't | did not
didnt | did not
diff | difference
diffs | differences
do not no | do not know
doc | document
docs | documents
doens't | does not
doesn;t | does not
doesn't | does not
doesnt | does not
don;t | do not
do'nt | do not
don't | do not
dont | do not
dosn't | does not
double click | double-click
dox | documents
eg | for example
epicenter | center
epicentre | centre
esp | especially

et cetera|and so on
etc|and so on
explained|described
func|functional
hadn;t|had not
hadn't|had not
hasn;t|has not
hasn't|has not
hasnt|has not
haven;t|have not
he;ll|he will
here;s|here is
I;d|I would
I;ll|I will
I'd|I would
I'd|I would
I'll|I will
I'm|I am
ie|that is
in order to|to
info|information
isn;t|is not
isn't|is not
it' snot|it is not
it snot|it is not
it;ll|it will
it'll|it will
it's|it is
let;s|let us
let;s|let us
made up|consists
may|can
mgr|manager
millenium/millennium
necc|necessary
needs to|must
op|operation
ops|operations
ot|to
para|paragraph
perm|permanent
peruse|study
perused|studied
perusing|studying
pref|preference

prefs|preferences
presently|at present
prod|production
QA|Quality Assurance
rep|representative
reps|representatives
res|resolution
right click|right-click
she;ll|she will
shoudln't|should not
shouldent|should not
shouldn;t|should not
shouldnt|should not
single click|single-click
spec|specification
specs|specifications
std|standard
succ|successful
sufficient number of|enough
teh|the
that has|with
thats|that is
they;l|they will
they;ll|they will
they;r|they are
they;re|they are
they;v|they have
they;ve|they have
they'l|they will
they'll|they will
they'r|they are
they're|they are
they'v|they have
they've|they have
theyll|they will
theyve|they have
trad|traditional
triple click|triple-click
twixt|between
uncheck|clear
untick|clear
utilise|use
utilize/use
via|by way of
visa versa|vice versa
wasnt|was not

we;d | we would
we;ll | we will
we;re | we are
we;ve | we have
we'd | we would
we'll | we will
we're | we are
we've | we have
wern;t | were not
wern't | were not
wernt | were not
what;s | what is
what's | what is
with regards to | about
won;t | will not

won't | will not
wo'nt | will not
woudln't | would not
wouldn;t | would not
wouldn't | would not
wouldnt | would not
you;d | you would
you;re | you are
you'd | you would
you're | you are
you've | you have
youare | you are
youve | you have
yr | year

Readers Write

STEVE HUDSON:

has the potential to -> can
cnr -> corner
gfx -> graphics
sfx -> sound effects
sth -> south
nth -> north

Semiautomatic Corrections

The past few articles have discussed corrections that editors can make automatically with Microsoft Word's Find and Replace feature. In addition, editors can save time by making "semiautomatic" corrections—in other words, by using Word's Find feature to locate "indicators" of possible problems and then fixing those problems as needed. For example, the word "are" is such an indicator. If you use Word's Find feature to locate occurrences of the word "are," you'll run into sentences like this one:

The editors are making corrections in the manuscript.

This can be edited to this:

The editors are correcting the manuscript.

Or maybe even to this:

The editors correct the manuscript.

In fact, any form of the verb "to be" ("be," "are," "was," "were") may indicate other problems (wordiness, passive voice, lack of a strong verb, unnecessary use of the present participle, and so on).

(Before I edited it, the previous sentence read, " In fact, any forms of the verb 'to be' are possible indicators of other problems . . . " See what I mean?)

Another indicator is the suffix "ly," which can be used to find sentences like this one: "He ran quickly down the street."

Weak, weak, weak. How about "He bolted down the street" or "He charged down the street" or "He blasted down the street"? If you're a writer, you'll find this trick particularly useful.

Other indicators are the phrases "there is" and "there are," particularly at the start of sentences. "There are three writers working on the project" can be edited to "Three writers work on the project."

Readers Write

Steve Hudson

[Here's a list of semiautomatic corrections provided by Microsoft Word expert Steve Hudson and edited slightly by me. Some of the items are for technical editing ("check," "tick," "up," "down"). Most, though, can be used in any situation.]

ATTEMPT TO KILL: aforementioned
empowerment
take
make
were
was
has been
will
would
should
could
be
that
used/use/using
follow
get/got
put
way
did
*ly

CAREFULLY AND MANUALLY CHECK: details (replace with "information")
check (replace with "set")
tick (replace with "set")
up (replace with "up arrow")
down (replace with "down arrow")
system (replace with something else if not being used generically)
say (replace with "show")
description (replace with "information")
explanation (replace with "information")
communicate (replace with "say," "tell," or "talk")
exponential (replace with "rapid")
feedback (does it mean anything?)
fortuitous (replace with "lucky")
input (does it mean anything?)
interface (replace with "connect)
paradigm (archetypal method? point of view? mindset?)
irony / ironic / ironically (implies the opposite of the literal sense)
linear (mathematical?)
synergy(increased energy through cooperative side-effects?)
and/or (rewrite to: ... and ... or ... or both)
that (restrictive & defining)
which (if nonrestrictive explanatory, set off in commas)
who (must be used with people)

NANCY ADESS:

"is in the process of..."
Attempt to kill this.
"grow your skills" "grow your organization" anything but grow your food!
Substitute: improve, expand.
"To better serve" "to better market" "to better any verb"
Substitute: To verb more effectively/more efficiently/more successfully
"Impact" used as a verb.
Change to "affect."

KAREN SLANEY:

period of timeperiod
made a decision|decided
OK|okay
O.K.|okay
email|e-mail
towards|toward
for awhile|for a while
literally|[nothing]
alot|a lot
each others'|each other's
one anothers'|one another's
he/she|he or she
him/her|him or her
my Mom|my mom
my Dad|my dad
someone that|someone who
[2],|,[2]
[2].|.[2]
reason why|reason
!!|!
!!!|!

MARY EBERLE:

I've been using AutoCorrect as a way to simplify my editing considerably. For example, if the author has used the verb "is" but the verb should be "are," I have an AutoCorrect entry that changes "isz_" (where the _ represents a space—the trigger for AutoCorrect to make the change) to "are"; I place the cursor right after the "is" and then access the

AutoCorrect feature with a function key that types "z space backspace" and the "is" toggles to "are." By using the same function key I can toggle "are" back to "is" ("arez" becomes "is"). I have set up numerous such pairs in my original AutoCorrect file. I used "z" because in English it doesn't form many words at the end of a word; if one just uses a space, AutoCorrect jumps in to "help" when it is not wanted.

You may wonder how I'm using a function key to accomplish the "z" thing. Well, I was actually using a key on my programmable X-keys keyboard.

One reason the z_space approach and the X-keys are helping me speed up my editing is that I don't have to take my right hand off the mouse, so I can quickly move to the next thing that needs to be fixed.

Further information: Just typing "z" and then "space" will invoke the "isz to are" or "arez to is" toggle. No backspace or macro is needed. I've been using the programmable X-keys for so long now that I'm not used to just using the regular keyboard. Anyway, I hope that this toggle idea is useful to you.

KATHLEEN MUCH:

You recommended: fortuitous (replace with "lucky")

You're right to check the usage, but what if the writer is actually using "fortuitous" correctly, to mean "by chance"? :)

I RESPONDED: Then the editor should leave it alone. :)

Kathleen makes a good point. Many such corrections should *not* be made automatically or without thought. Please be judicious and remember that the computer is a tool, a means to an end, and not an end in itself.

The Case Against Caps

As you've edited various manuscripts, you've probably noticed the propensity of some authors to type headings in all caps, as I've done with the title of this article. This holdover from the days of typewriting is, to put it bluntly, bad practice. Why? Because in typesetting or desktop publishing, putting a heading in all caps is a design decision, not an editorial one. Headings are generally set apart from body text with a different font or point size, not with capital letters.

If you leave headings in all caps, designers will change them anyway—probably by *retyping* them, and *without* telling you. If you're lucky, you'll catch any new typos and improper capitalizations *before* the publication goes to press. Personally, I don't like the risk. Fortunately, Microsoft Word makes it fairly easy to change all-caps to title case:

1. Select the heading you want to change.
2. Click the "Format" menu.
3. Click "Change Case."
4. Click "Title Case."
5. Click "OK."

If you did that with the title of this article, for example, you'd get this: "The Case Against Caps."

Unfortunately, as you've probably noticed, you'll still have to lowercase articles, prepositions, and conjunctions by hand to get proper title case. For example, you'd need to lowercase "Against" in the title of this article: "The Case against Caps."

Wouldn't it be nice to have a macro that took care of that automatically? My Editor's ToolKit program includes one. Just select the text you want formatted as title case and then run the macro (called "Make Selection Title Case"). Nouns, verbs, adjectives, and adverbs will be uppercased. Commonly used articles, prepositions, and conjunctions will be lowercased. Pretty neat!

What if a design calls for all caps? The caps should be applied through formatting, not typing all-cap characters. As I've said before, you should format headings with one of Microsoft Word's built-in heading styles, such as Heading 1. Then if you want headings to be set in all caps, you can do this:

1. Place your cursor in a heading formatted with the style you want to be all caps.
2. Click the "Format" menu.
3. Click "Style."
4. Click the "Modify" button.
5. Click the "Format" button.
6. Click "Font."

7. Put a check in the "All Caps" checkbox.
8. Click the "OK" button.
9. Click the next "OK" button.
10. Click the "Close" button.

All of the headings formatted with that style will now be in all caps.

Changed your mind? You can change the headings back to title case by reversing the procedure. And that may be the strongest argument in the case against caps.

Readers Write

Peg Wier:

I agree with you on all counts about the formatting of headings with all caps. I think you left out the most important case against all caps—THEY ARE HARD TO READ!

Steve Dobney:

As a keen keyboard shortcut user I make great use of SHIFT + F3 to toggle between capitalisation options.

Bruce White:

I have attached to a button the Change Case item from the Format menu. It changes the capitalization of selected text each time it is pressed to the next one in the sequence: UPPERCASE, lowercase, and Title Case.

For some reason Sentence case is not in the sequence. I suspect that you are meant to change it all to lower then select the first word and change it to title case.

Colin Wheildon's Type & Layout from Strathmoor Press (ISBN 0-9624891-5-8) has a bit to say against using uppercase. From his Table 5 on page 67:

Font	lowercase	Capitals
Roman old style	92%	69%
Roman modern	89%	71%
Sans serif	90%	57%
Optima	85%	56%
Square serif	64%	44%

These numbers are for legibility of printed material. The book includes the methodology used so that anyone wanting to see what results happen for online can follow the same approach.

Title Case Macro

During my other life as a copyeditor, I often find myself needing to change the case of words that an author has typed in all caps, LIKE THIS, in chapter titles and subheads. I often perform the task with the handy Cap Title Case feature in my Editor's ToolKit program, but I've also wished for a macro that would do most of the dirty work automatically throughout a document without having to select text. So, I decided to write one. Here it is:

```
Sub FixCaps()
Selection.Find.ClearFormatting
Selection.Find.Style = ActiveDocument.Styles("Heading 1")
With Selection.Find
.Text = ""
.Replacement.Text = ""
.Forward = True
.Wrap = wdFindContinue
.Format = True
.MatchCase = False
.MatchWholeWord = False
.MatchWildcards = False
.MatchSoundsLike = False
.MatchAllWordForms = False
End With
Selection.Find.Execute
While Selection.Find.Found = True
Selection.Range.Case = wdTitleWord
Selection.MoveRight Unit:=wdCharacter, Count:=1
Selection.Find.Execute
Wend
MsgBox "Finished!", , "Fix Caps"
End Sub
```

The macro goes through your document finding any words formatted with the Heading 1 paragraph style and changes them to title case. Of course, you'll still need to lowercase articles, prepositions, and conjunctions by hand, but at least the macro keeps you from having to change *everything* by hand.

If you're wondering why you'd want to change all caps to title case, please see "The Case against Caps."

Worried about all caps in other heading styles? You can modify the macro to find them by changing this line:

```
Selection.Find.Style = ActiveDocument.Styles("Heading 1")
```

For example, if I wanted to find text formatted with Heading 2 rather than Heading 1, I would change the line to this:

```
Selection.Find.Style = ActiveDocument.Styles("Heading 2")
```

You can also modify the case the macro will use to change the text it finds. Currently, it makes words title case, as specified in the following line:

```
Selection.Range.Case = wdTitleWord
```

Rather than using "wdTitleWord" (title case), however, you can use the following, if you prefer:

```
wdLowerCase 'which formats the words in lower case.
wdTitleSentence 'Which formats the words in sentence case.
```

Now the next time you need to change the case of a bunch of all-cap headings, you'll have an easy way to get the job done.

Title Case Macro, Version 2

The previous article featured a macro to change all-cap headings into title case. It had some drawbacks, though. It would do only one heading level at a time, and you had to specify which heading level you wanted it to work on. In addition, it didn't lowercase articles, prepositions, and conjunctions. What's really needed is a macro that will cycle through *all* of your heading levels (any paragraph styled with one of Word's Heading paragraph styles, such as Heading 1), make them title case, and lowercase articles, prepositions, and conjunctions unless they occur at the beginning or end of the heading. Oh, and one more thing: It should capitalize any word following a colon and a space. I'm giving away the store here, but here's the macro, which I hope you'll find useful:

```
Sub TitleCaseHeadings()
For h = 1 To 9
Selection.HomeKey Unit:=wdStory
Selection.Find.ClearFormatting
myHeading$ = "Heading" + Str(h)
Selection.Find.Style = ActiveDocument.Styles(myHeading$)
With Selection.Find
.Text = ""
.Replacement.Text = ""
.Forward = True
.Wrap = wdStop
.Format = True
.MatchCase = False
.MatchWholeWord = False
.MatchWildcards = False
.MatchSoundsLike = False
.MatchAllWordForms = False
End With
Selection.Find.Execute
While Selection.Find.Found = True
Selection.Range.Case = wdTitleWord
For Each wrd In Selection.Range.Words
Select Case Trim(wrd)
Case "A", "An", "As", "At", "And", "But", _
"By", "For", "From", "In", "Into", "Of", _
"On", "Or", "Over", "The", "Through", _
"To", "Under", "Unto", "With"
wrd.Case = wdLowerCase
End Select
Next wrd
wrdCount = Selection.Range.Words.Count
Selection.Range.Words(1).Case = wdTitleWord
Selection.Range.Words(wrdCount - 1).Case = wdTitleWord
```

```
strLength = Selection.Range.Characters.Count
For i = 1 To strLength
If Selection.Range.Characters(i) = ":" Then
Selection.Range.Characters(i + 2).Case = wdTitleWord
End If
Next i
Selection.Find.Execute
Wend
Next h
MsgBox "Finished!", , "Title Case Headings"
End Sub
```

If you're wondering why you'd want to use a macro like that one, please see "The Case against Caps."

Please note that you can modify the macro to specify the words you want to be lowercased. Here are the lines you'll need to change:

```
Case "A", "An", "As", "At", "And", "But", _
"By", "For", "From", "In", "Into", "Of", _
"On", "Or", "Over", "The", "Through", _
"To", "Under", "Unto", "With"
```

For example, if you wanted to add "Throughout," the modified lines might look like this:

```
Case "A", "An", "As", "At", "And", "But", _
"By", "For", "From", "In", "Into", "Of", _
"On", "Or", "Over", "The", "Through", _
"To", "Under", "Unto", "With", "Throughout"
```

You can also delete words. For example, if you wanted to delete "As," the modified lines would look like this:

```
Case "A", "An", "At", "And", "But", _
"By", "For", "From", "In", "Into", "Of", _
"On", "Or", "Over", "The", "Through", _
"To", "Under", "Unto", "With"
```

Don't worry about getting the lines too long. You won't. The lowlines _ at the end of each line just break up the macro for easy reading. You can delete them and the following paragraph returns to merge the four lines if you want to.

By the way, you don't have to reserve the macro for changing headings in all caps. You can use it on any headings that need to be changed to true title case. This does not, however, excuse you from editing your headings.

Thanks to Hilary Powers for suggesting the improvements.

Readers Write

HILARY POWERS:

Here's another wrinkle on the title-case macro:

```
Sub SentenceTitle()
' Macro written 3/20/2004 by Hilary Powers
Selection.Range.Case = wdLowerCase
Selection.MoveLeft Unit:=wdCharacter, Count:=1
Selection.Find.ClearFormatting
With Selection.Find
.text = ":"
End With
Selection.Find.Execute
Selection.MoveRight Unit:=wdCharacter, Count:=2
Selection.Range.Case = wdNextCase
End Sub
```

It's for converting two-part title-case titles to sentence case: Select everything but the first word and hit the hot key, and it all goes lowercase except the word following the colon. . . . A godsend for a 50-page reference list with mixed formatting that needs to go to APA. (A refined version would let you select the whole title and then uppercase both the first word and the word after the colon, but I got lazy.)

PRESTON EARLE:

Thanks for the improved Title Case macro. Is there a way to modify the macro such that it ignores a list of all-caps words like USA, NASA, MS (as in MS Word), and, perhaps, state abbreviations?

I RESPONDED: I've now modified the macro to do this. Here's the new version:

```
Sub TitleCaseHeadings()
For h = 1 To 9
Selection.HomeKey Unit:=wdStory
Selection.Find.ClearFormatting
myHeading$ = "Heading" + Str(h)
Selection.Find.Style = ActiveDocument.Styles(myHeading$)
With Selection.Find
.Text = ""
.Replacement.Text = ""
.Forward = True
.Wrap = wdStop
.Format = True
.MatchCase = False
.MatchWholeWord = False
.MatchWildcards = False
.MatchSoundsLike = False
.MatchAllWordForms = False
End With
```

```
Selection.Find.Execute
While Selection.Find.Found = True
Selection.Range.Case = wdTitleWord
For Each wrd In Selection.Range.Words
Select Case Trim(wrd)
Case "A", "An", "As", "At", "And", "But", _
"By", "For", "From", "In", "Into", "Of", _
"On", "Or", "Over", "The", "Through", _
"To", "Under", "Unto", "With"
wrd.Case = wdLowerCase
Case "Usa", "Nasa", "Usda", "Ibm", "Nato"
wrd.Case = wdUpperCase
End Select
Next wrd
wrdCount = Selection.Range.Words.Count
Selection.Range.Words(1).Case = wdTitleWord
Selection.Range.Words(wrdCount - 1).Case = wdTitleWord
strLength = Selection.Range.Characters.Count
For i = 1 To strLength
If Selection.Range.Characters(i) = ":" Then
Selection.Range.Characters(i + 2).Case = wdTitleWord
End If
Next i
Selection.Find.Execute
Wend
Next h
MsgBox "Finished!", , "Title Case Headings"
End Sub
```

The line that makes the difference is this one:

```
Case "Usa", "Nasa", "Usda", "Ibm", "Nato"
```

Feel free to modify that line to suit your needs. The items I've included are just examples. Notice, though, that for the macro to work, you must type your items not in all caps (USA) but in title case (Usa). That's because the macro has already put the whole *line* in title case, so you're now specifying words in title case that you want to be in all caps.

Fixing All Caps in Text

So now we have a macro that will set all headings in a Word document in true title case, with articles and prepositions lowercased. But what if you have a document in which an author has typed other stuff in all caps—author names in footnotes, or book titles in body text? It would be nice to have a macro that would look for anything in all caps and turn it to title case. I've modified the macro to do just that:

```
Sub FixAllCapsInText()
Selection.Find.ClearFormatting
With Selection.Find
.Text = "[A-Z]{2,}"
.Replacement.Text = ""
.Forward = True
.Wrap = wdFindStop
.Format = False
.MatchCase = False
.MatchWholeWord = False
.MatchAllWordForms = False
.MatchSoundsLike = False
.MatchWildcards = True
End With
Selection.Find.Execute
While Selection.Find.Found = True
Selection.Range.Case = wdTitleWord
Select Case Selection.Range
Case "A", "An", "As", "At", "And", "But", _
"By", "For", "From", "In", "Into", "Of", _
"On", "Or", "Over", "The", "Through", _
"To", "Under", "Unto", "With"
Selection.Range.Case = wdLowerCase
Case "Usa", "Nasa", "Usda", "Ibm", "Nato"
Selection.Range.Case = wdUpperCase
End Select
Selection.MoveRight Unit:=wdCharacter, Count:=1
Selection.Find.Execute
Wend
MsgBox "Finished!", , "Fix All Caps in Text"
End Sub
```

The key to the macro is this line:

```
.Text = "[A-Z]{2,}"
```

That tells Word to do a wildcard search for two or more capital letters in a row. If you like, you can make that number larger to avoid such common acronyms as USA and

NASA. A better way to take care of such items, however, is to list them in the following line of the macro:

```
Case "Usa", "Nasa", "Usda", "Ibm", "Nato"
```

If you'd like more information about wildcard searching, feel free to download my paper "Advanced Find and Replace in Microsoft Word":

http://www.editorium.com/ftp/advancedfind.zip

Thanks to Linda Northrup for suggesting this topic.

JOHANNA MURPHY:

The Title Case Headings Macro is awesome! Although I would need one where you only change one level at a time. Also, I have created other styles which are named OUT and OUTNUMBER (with only 5 levels) that we use a lot in our law firm. How can I change the macro to specify those style names?

I RESPONDED: To use different styles with the macro, do this:
1. Delete these two lines:

```
For h = 1 To 9
Next h
```

2. Modify this line—

```
myHeading$ = "Heading" + Str(h)
```

—to something like this:

```
myHeading$ = "MyStyle"
```

Italicizing a Whole Word

A couple of co-workers have recently started using Word 2003. Much to their annoyance, they found that they could no longer use one of their favorite features: put the cursor anywhere in a word and press CTRL + I to italicize the whole word. I, too, had vaguely wondered about this, but not enough to do anything about it. Thanks to Jay Parry for discovering the solution, which is:

1. Click Tools.
2. Click Options.
3. Click the Edit tab.
4. Put a check in the checkbox labeled "When selecting, automatically select entire word."

Now, when you press CTRL + I (or other wise turn on italic formatting), the entire word will be formatted without having to first select the word.

Readers Write

HILARY POWERS:

I started out to write, "That's a cure worse than the disease, as far as I'm concerned, at least for an editor. . . ." Then I double-checked the actual operation of the option, and discovered that it doesn't do what I thought it did at all. It doesn't force selection of whole words the way its name indicates; SHIFT + Arrow selects partial words just like it always did—so you can change, say, "raged" to "raging" by selecting the "ed" and typing over it.

Is that also a change? I have a vivid memory of watching the screen select whole words willy-nilly instead of parts in earlier versions of the program.

I RESPONDED: That's exactly what I was thinking, but it doesn't seem to be the case in Word 95, 97, 2000, 2002, or 2003. But now that you bring it up, it probably merits further investigation.

The Help file says:

When selecting, automatically select entire word:
Selects an entire word and the following space when you select part of a word.

But really, I see no difference whether the "feature" is turned off or on.

HILARY REPLIED: Have you really tried selecting a few letters out of a word in all the earlier versions? Or just looked to see if the italics thang worked as advertised? [Answer:

Yes, I tried selecting a few letters out of a word.] What we seem to have here is an undocumented change in function—the feature flat out does not do what the Help file says it does. And, as I said, I do think of it as operating as promised. Which is why I've always kept it turned off, as the alleged function is a disaster for an editor.

What it does now is select the entire word—but NOT the following space (or any internal punctuation, as with a URL)—when Word is left to make its own selection based on commands like CTRL+ I and CTRL + B, and that's dead useful—especially when you move an italicized word to the style sheet and then want to kill the italics there. When you make your own selection, it leaves you alone as a civilized piece of software should.

Magic Numbers

When I was in first grade, a magician came to our school, and I've been interested in magic ever since. One thing I've learned is that magic is largely psychological; it depends heavily on what magicians call "misdirection"—getting the audience to look at or think about something that furthers the magician's deception.

This principle can be used in software, too, as I recently discovered when putting together my free Author Tools template:

http://www.editorium.com/ftp/authortools.zip

Microsoft Word is notorious for getting automatically numbered lists out of whack, but the Author Tools template handles them quite nicely, mostly because of a little trick—Word's ability to reset the start of a list.

If you've used Word's automatically numbered lists, you've probably noticed that *any* lists in the document are actually part of the *same* list. So, if you make a list like this—

1. Bread.
2. Peanut butter.
3. Pickles.

—and then type some unnumbered text after it, as I'm doing with this paragraph—then the next list you make will look like this:

3. Chihuahuas.
4. Dachshunds.
5. Basset hounds.

The second list is numbered with the first, but obviously it shouldn't be. Fortunately, you can reset the numbering (and apply a numbered style) with this macro:

```
Sub ListNumberedStart()
With Selection.Paragraphs
.Style = "List Number"
With .First.Range.ListFormat
.ApplyListTemplate .ListTemplate, False
End With
End With
End Sub
```

For ease of use, you might want to attach the macro to a keyboard shortcut.

And now for the magical misdirection: Instead of using the macro to *restart* an existing list, use it every time you need to *start* a new list. If you need to continue an existing list, use Word's automatic numbering feature (which you'd usually use to start a list). Notice that this is exactly the opposite of what you might think should happen. But presto! It works!

By the way, when I talk about Word's automatic numbering feature, I am *not* talking about the buttons on the formatting toolbar, which will cause you no end of trouble. Instead, I'm talking about using paragraph styles that *include* the numbering—in this case, the one named List Number.

Quote, Unquote

I loathe Word's AutoFormat options, although I do use one of them—"Replace straight quotes with smart quotes." But sometimes, no matter how hard I try, I can't insert a quotation mark going the right direction. If I want a closing quotation mark, Word insists on giving me an opening one—or vice versa. If you've run into this problem, you know how maddening it can be. Wouldn't it be nice to type precisely the kind of "smart" quotation marks you need without having Word second-guess what you're doing? It turns out there's a built-in way to do that. Here are the key commands you need:

Opening Double Quotation Mark

To get an opening double quotation mark, press this key combination:

CTRL + '

(That little character on the end there is the single quotation mark on the key to the left of the "1" key on your keyboard.)

Next, press this:

SHIFT + '

(That little character on the end is an apostrophe. In other words, just type a quotation mark as you usually would.)

There's your opening double quotation mark.

Closing Double Quotation Mark

To get a closing double quotation mark, press this:

CTRL + '

Then press this:

SHIFT + '

Opening Single Quotation Mark

To get an opening single quotation mark, press this:

CTRL + '

Then press this:

'

Closing Single Quotation Mark

To get an closing single quotation mark, press this:

CTRL + '

Then press this:

'

Now that I've told you all of that, I've got to say that I don't much like those key combinations. They're hard to type, and they seem inconsistent. Luckily, Word allows us to create our own key combinations, so let's try setting up a more natural and consistent system:

1. Click Insert > Symbol > Symbols tab.
2. Make sure the "Font" list shows "(normal text)."
3. Make sure the "Subset" list shows "General Punctuation."

On the bottom row in the fifth column, you'll see an opening single quotation mark.
In the sixth column, you'll see a closing single quotation mark.
In the ninth column, you'll see an opening double quotation mark
And in the tenth column, you'll see a closing double quotation mark.
Now let's assign some keys:

1. Click the opening single quotation mark.
2. Click the "Shortcut Key" button.
3. Press the new key combination you want to use. I'm thinking this one:

CTRL + '

4. Click the "Assign" button.
5. Click the "Close" button.

While we're still in there, let's assign the rest of the quotation marks. To do so, repeat steps 1 through 5 for each quotation mark. Here are the other key combinations I'm going to use:
For the closing single quotation mark: ALT + '
For the opening double quotation mark: SHIFT + CTRL + '
For the closing double quotation mark: SHIFT + ALT + '
When you're finished, press that final "Close" button to put away the "Symbol" dialog.

That should do it. Note that you can continue to use Word's AutoFormat quotation marks if you want. But when you need to, you can easily specify exactly the kind of quotation marks you need to use.

Readers Write

LeAnne Baird:

I have a trick that wasn't my discovery, but I've passed it on to a lot of writers. To get a quotation mark to go the right way, type two of them in a row, then delete the first one. The second one stays as is, going the right direction. This is a slick workaround for people who remain unconvinced of the practicality of shortcut keys.

Derek Halvorson:

You've suggested in your latest update that Microsoft's use of CTRL + ' then ' (or SHIFT + ') for closing quotation marks is inconsistent, but it is actually completely consistent with their scheme for accented characters. You can add an accent aigu to any vowel by typing CTRL + ' before typing the vowel. So, you only have to remember that, any time you want a superscript accent that is slanted upwards from left to right, you need only key CTRL + ' first. If one follows your suggestion and makes CTRL + ' the shortcut key for a closing single quotation mark, then one loses the keyboard shortcuts for accented vowels. In this case it seems that there may be some sort of method to the Microsoft madness.

Automatic Dashes

Helpful as always, Microsoft Word will automatically insert em dashes for you—but with an interesting twist. I'll tell you what it is in just a minute. But first, here's how to turn on those automatic dashes if you want to use them:

1. Click the Tools menu.
2. Click "AutoCorrect."
3. Click the tab labeled "AutoFormat As You Type."
4. Under "Replace as you type," put a check in the box labeled "Symbol characters (--) with symbols (—)."
5. Click the OK button.

To see how the feature works:

1. Create a new document and type in a word.
2. After you've typed the word, don't hit the spacebar; instead, type two hyphens in a row.
3. Once again, don't hit the spacebar; instead, type another word.
4. *Now* hit the spacebar.

Wow, your two hyphens have turned into an em dash! What, you already knew you could do that? Okay, here's the interesting twist:

1. Create a new document and type in a word.
2. After you've typed the word, *do* hit the spacebar.
3. Type a single hyphen.
4. Hit the spacebar again.
5. Type another word.
6. Hit the spacebar again.

Wow, your single hyphen has turned into an en dash! What's going on here?

In the world of typography, there are several kinds of dashes, each with a different length. As the *Chicago Manual of Style* (5.105) notes, "There are en dashes, em dashes, and 2- and 3-em dashes. . . . Each kind of dash has its own uses." Chicago specifies that the em dash should be used to indicate "sudden breaks and abrupt changes" and "amplifying, explanatory, and digressive elements."

Some designers, however, beg to differ. Instead of using an em dash, they use an en dash surrounded by spaces. Robert Bringhurst argues for this in his book *The Elements of Typographic Style* (p. 80):

"The em dash is the nineteenth-century standard, still prescribed in many editorial style books, but the em dash is too long for use with the best text faces. Like the oversized space between sentences, it belongs to the padded and corseted aesthetic of Victorian typography. Used as a phrase marker – thus – the en dash is set with a normal word space either side."

In my opinion, Bringhurst is wrong. The whole point of the em dash is to indicate an abrupt change, and a long dash does that better than a short one. That's why Messrs. Garamond, Goudy, and Gill *designed* long dashes for their typefaces, fer cryin' out loud. The shorter en dash surrounded by spaces may look "prettier," but it is also less forceful, and form should follow function. That's my take on it, anyway.

The interesting thing is that Microsoft seems to be trying to accommodate *both* usages. If you type two hyphens in a row, you'll get an em dash. If you type space, hyphen, space, you'll get an en dash with spaces. Chicago or Bringhurst, take your pick. Thanks, Microsoft!

Thanks to Steve Hudson for suggesting this topic.

Readers Write

RICHARD O'REGAN:

I disagree with you on the use of the en dash. At least, over here, in "old Europe," the en dash, preceded and followed by a space, is used both in the UK and on the Continent. The em dash no longer sees the light of day.

LINDY M:

I share your preference for the em dash rather than the spaced en, but I do use the latter, for one reason: it's easier to control line breaks. With a nonbreaking space before the en dash I can ensure it always breaks at the end of a line rather than at the beginning. I can't find any way to attach an em dash to the end of a word other than spacing it, which would look excessive to my eye. I might add that some people firmly believe that dashes should appear at the beginning of a line, not the end. I don't. I should also confess that I use Word as little as possible. From what I've seen it handles em dash breaks elegantly, but some other word processors and page layout programs need help with this sort of thing, especially older versions.

Superscript Ordinals

In many of the manuscripts I edit, the author has used superscript for ordinal numbers, entering 1st, 2nd, 3rd, and 4th (and so on) as 1st, 2nd, 3rd, and 4th. Why? Because Microsoft Word by default inserts ordinal numbers using superscript—one of its many "helpful" features, which I explain how to turn off in "When Word Gets in the Way."

But if the superscript ordinals are already in the manuscript, you can't just turn them off. You have to figure out another way to get rid of that superscript. One way is to find and replace it (Edit > Replace) with "not superscript" (as Word phrases it). That will work fine unless the manuscript has superscript formatting you want to keep, in which case you have to find and replace each superscript item individually. Even that isn't so bad—unless the manuscript has footnotes or endnotes, in which case you might have to check hundreds of superscript reference numbers during your search. Ugh.

Faced with that very problem in an editing project, I figured out a simple way around it:

1. Make a backup copy of your document (always, always, always).
2. Click "Edit > Replace" to display the Replace dialog.
3. In the "Find What" box, enter the following wildcard string:

   [!^02]

4. Format the "Find What" box as Superscript. The easy way to do this is to press CTRL + SHIFT + = (on a Macintosh, click the "Format" button, then "Font," and put a check in the "Superscript" checkbox; you may first need to click the "More" button).
5. Format the "Replace With" box as Not Superscript/Subscript. The easy way to do this is to press CTRL + SHIFT + = two times in a row (on a Macintosh, click the "Format" button, then "Font," and clear the "Superscript" checkbox).
6. Put a check in the "Use wildcards" checkbox. (You may need to click the "More" button to make the checkbox available.)
7. Click "Replace All" (or "Find Next" and "Replace" if you want to try a few manually).

That will get rid of all superscript *except* on note reference numbers. The secret, of course, is that [!^02] code, which tells Word not to include note reference numbers in its search. You can learn more about searching with codes and wildcards in the "Find and Replace" section in this book.

"Cut This by a Third"

A longtime, highly skilled editor I know likes to keep track of how much she's tightened a manuscript, and she does it by counting words or pages as she works. This is especially useful if a publication (a magazine, for example) has only so much room for a particular article. But it may also be useful in editing long documents, such as books. After you've done it for a while, you'll get a feel for how much certain kinds of material need to be tightened, and you can use that as a guide in the amount of editing you do.

If you think this technique would be useful, Microsoft Word makes it easy to try. Before you start editing a particular document, do this:

1. Click "Tools."
2. Click "Word Count."

A dialog box will appear that shows the length of your manuscript in pages, words, characters, paragraphs, and lines. On a sheet of paper, jot down the number of pages (or words, if your document is short). Then, as you edit, check from time to time to see how you're progressing. Unless your space is limited, you don't consciously need to cut by a certain number of words or pages. Just edit as you ordinarily would. When you're finished, check the page count again. How did you do?

You might want to keep a record of your results for a variety of documents. Eventually, it will help you know ahead of time if you can get a chapter or article down to size through your regular editing, or if you'll need to get out the ax and start chopping. If you're negotiating with an author or client, that may be a useful thing to know. It may also be useful if you're making assignments to other editors: "Will you cut this by a third, please? I think that would be just about right."

Macro to Swap Table Cells

If you work with tables, you've probably wished for a way to automatically swap the contents of two adjacent cells. If so, here's a macro that will do the trick. Just put your cursor in the first of the two cells you want to transpose and then run the macro.

```
Sub SWAPCELLS()
WordBasic.SelType 1 'Get off any selected text
'In first cell
WordBasic.NextCell 'So you can select cell contents
WordBasic.PrevCell 'Select cell contents
If Asc(WordBasic.[Selection$]()) = 13 Then 'Cell is empty
WordBasic.MsgBox "This cell contains no text to invert.", "Cell
Empty"
GoTo Endmacro
Else
WordBasic.WW7_EditAutoText Name:="IMCell1IM", Context:=0,
InsertAs:=0, Add:=1
WordBasic.WW6_EditClear
End If
WordBasic.NextCell
'In second cell
If Asc(WordBasic.[Selection$]()) = 13 Then 'Cell is empty
WordBasic.MsgBox "The next cell contains no text to invert.",
"Next Cell Empty"
WordBasic.EditUndo 'Put the text back into the first cell
WordBasic.SelType 1 'Get off selected text
GoTo Endmacro
Else
WordBasic.WW7_EditAutoText Name:="IMCell2IM", Context:=0,
InsertAs:=0, Add:=1
WordBasic.WW6_EditClear
WordBasic.WW7_EditAutoText Name:="IMCell1IM", Context:=0,
InsertAs:=0, Insert:=1
WordBasic.WW7_EditAutoText Name:="IMCell1IM", Context:=0,
InsertAs:=0, Delete:=1
End If
WordBasic.PrevCell
'Back in first cell
WordBasic.WW7_EditAutoText Name:="IMCell2IM", Context:=0,
InsertAs:=0, Insert:=1
WordBasic.WW7_EditAutoText Name:="IMCell2IM", Context:=0,
InsertAs:=0, Delete:=1
Endmacro:
WordBasic.ScreenUpdating 1
WordBasic.ScreenRefresh
End Sub
```

Readers Write

VIRGINIA DOWNS:

Is there any such thing as a macro to convert all the tables in a document to text?

I REPLIED WITH THE FOLLOWING MACRO:

```
Sub Tables2Text()
Dim tableNew As Table
Dim rngTemp As Range
For Each tableNew In ActiveDocument.Tables
Set rngTemp = tableNew.ConvertToText(Separator:=wdSeparateByTabs)
Next tableNew
End Sub
```

STEVE HUDSON:

On AutoFormatting in Tables: You cannot add new table types to the Table AutoFormat list, nor can you edit existing ones.

However, you *can* get many more autoformat layouts by setting various properties of the autoformat to FALSE. For example, setting them all to false for table style normal gives you an invisible (borderless) table. By using grid with no first column, font changes, or first row, you get a nice boxed grid. You can also set the default line width for tables as well.

Anything more complex has to be handled by first inserting a table and then styling it up via macro. Ninety-nine out of a hundred times, this is accomplished by styling the table, then styling the first row, then styling the first column.

In Word XP we get table styles (they are making styles even more abominable by giving us different flavours), so I am guessing it *may* be possible to set autoformats of your own to a greater degree. Until they work properly however, I ain't investigating them.

An extract from my Word Spellbook:

Auto-formatting or custom default tables (Word 2000)

Highly specialized custom formats are difficult (when not impossible) to do. Very simple formats are somewhat easier and more likely to succeed. If you are prepared to bend your style guide to what is possible and what is not, you can get some satisfactory automatic results without having to resort to macros.

You can also just use Autotext entries to store a pre-formatted table in—you can drag these Autotext entries onto a menu if required.

As a quick aside, when dealing programmatically with tables, there are two subtle tricks. One is the .range.cells(n) object that serializes all the cells in the selected range. This tables(1).range.cells(k) is an easier way to address the collection. Secondly, you can do groovy table stuff via the selection object that you can't via a range . . .

Back to the plot. Inspect the Insert Table > AutoFormat dialog. To get all your tables inserted with invisible borders, select the simple 1 format and CLEAR all the little checkboxes. Voilà! Problem solved.

Whatever rows and columns I give it will be the default that is used from there on in when I tick "Use this as the default style."

To extend this concept, you are NOT limited to JUST the formats presented. You can also use just parts of them! We did this above and used NO PARTS to give us NO styling—or an auto-invisible table.

For example, many people could get away with Grid 5 with the font option cleared to make themselves a nice grid.

ROB LITTLE:

First, in 2002, any new table style becomes a table autoformat (it shows up in the table autoformat dialog).

Second, as for basing your table style on an empty style, use "Table Normal." Table normal is statically defined (like "Default Paragraph Font" for character styles) and cannot be changed by any user. (This is different than the "Normal" paragraph style which can be edited by users). "Table Grid" is the default table style because it includes a Grid border (among other things).

Here are a couple of things to know about table styles:

- Table styles cannot define "structural" elements of a table (merging of cells, etc). This means they cannot define the width of cells or the height of rows (changing the width of cells from row to row implicitly merges cells, for example).
- All table autoformats in Word 2002 are Table Styles and can be customized by the user. (New styles can be based on them, too.) Conversely, this means that anything you see done in the table autoformats can be built from scratch through the table styles user interface.
- Table styles define character, paragraph, and table/cell/row properties. These properties are evaluated *before* the paragraph style's properties (order of calculation is TableStyle + ParaStyle + CharStyle + DirectFormatting = Calculated Properties). For example: If your table style defines the "Whole Table" as being "Arial," then you'll see "Arial." If you apply a paragraph style that applies "Courier," then "Arial" + "Courier" = "Courier" (because the paragraph style wins).
- When you apply a table style, the character and paragraph properties of the table are *not* reset. This is different than paragraph styles, which reset the character properties of the paragraph before applying the paragraph (with some exceptions). So, if you have a table which has a lot of direct character/paragraph formatting (for example, fonts, sizes, justification, and so on), and you apply a Table Style (or Table Autoformat), that direct formatting will still be there (and will beat any table style properties). If you want to get rid of that direct formatting, select the table and choose Edit/Clear/Formats (or click Clear Formatting on the Styles and Formatting taskpane). This will reset the table contents to just the table style. (You can clear formatting before or after applying the table style; it makes no difference.)
- When you use the "Applies to" part of table styles (this is used in almost all autoformats), you are telling Word to run a set of rules against your table when it applies formatting. For example, if you tell it to format the "First Row" with bold text, then every time the table changes, Word makes sure to format the first row

with bold text—even if a new first row is inserted. In Word 2000 and before, the table autoformats were "static"—once the last row (for example) was formatted, if you inserted a new last row, you would end up with 2 rows looking like the last row. In 2002, the last row recalculates, and you get just one last row. This allows things like banding (every other row shaded, for example).

• There is a delicate interaction between table styles and the Normal style. Recall that the paragraph style is applied on top of the table style. This means that any formatting you have in your Normal style will almost always override your table style formatting (I say almost because not *all* styles are based on "Normal"). For example: If your Normal style has "Arial" in it, and you apply a table style that defines "Courier," you will see Arial. The paragraph style wins. There is a way around this, but it would take some space to explain, so I'll provide the solution if people ask for it (or I could leave it as an exercise for the reader). Are there really people still reading at this point?

• Because of the interaction between the Normal style and table styles, there is an even more delicate interaction with font sizes. First, you just plain can't force the table to use 10-point text. If you set the table style to 10 points, it won't apply it. I really don't want to try to explain why.

That's all I can think of off the top of my head. I think everything above is accurate, but it's late and its entirely possible that I flubbed something up. Feel free to send me comments or corrections.

Raw Codes

@Body:You probably think my word processor has gone wacko, inserting codes rather than applying formatting. But it hasn't. I'm just trying the technique described in this article—marking formatting with raw codes. Why would anyone want to do that? Consider this:

@ListFirst:1.<tab>Text formatting is misleading. It may <ital>look<rom> nice, but it comes with a price—the sacrifice of structure and control to appearance. Is your heading formatted with Heading 2 paragraph style, or is it formatted directly as Arial 14-point bold? The difference may not be immediately apparent. With codes, you know.

@ListMiddle:2.<tab>Using codes forces you to resist the "easy fix" of directly applied formatting. Come on, admit it: You sometimes center a heading with CTRL + e rather than modifying the paragraph style as you should. I know I do. But if I use raw codes, I don't even have to think about it. I just enter "@Heading 3:" and start typing away. My guilty feelings are gone (sob!).

3.<tab>Using codes is just plain <ital>easier<rom> than mucking about with styles and fonts and formats all the time. It's a simpler way to live. Try it! You might be surprised at how much you like it. If you're really going to make the attempt, you might want to record macros that insert your most common codes and then assign those macros to toolbar buttons or keyboard combinations.

4.<tab>Using codes for special characters means there's no more worrying about conversion problems from platform to platform.

5.<tab>Using codes ensures greater consistency from document to document—at least it does if you keep using the same codes. Ensuring consistency of styles is more difficult. Which ones are yours? Which ones did Word sneak in when you weren't looking? BodyTextUgly? Where did <ital>that<rom> come from?

6.<tab>Using codes makes it easy to tag your text by function and structure rather than by appearance. For example, instead of using a Heading 1 style, you can tag your text as @ChapterHead:, which actually says what your text is being used for.

7.<tab>Using codes means you can work in a simple text processor when you don't have access to Microsoft Word.

8.<tab>Using codes makes your formatting human readable! That's pretty remarkable, when you consider all of the hidden, proprietary formatting systems in the world.

@ListLast:9.<tab>Using codes makes it easy to translate your formatting into a variety of other formats: HTML. XML. Even Microsoft Word.

@Body:"And how," you ask, "can I turn codes into Microsoft Word formatting?" With my RazzmaTag program.

One of the most popular academic typesetting programs, TeX, is built around the concept of working directly with codes and then applying formatting based on those codes. Other programs, too, can import coded documents, including QuarkXPress, PageMaker, and

FrameMaker, and many publishers take advantage of that fact, asking their editors to work directly with codes. If you've never considered this possibility, now you can add it to your bag of tricks.

Readers Write

AMANDA LUCAS:

What is the difference between using raw codes in Microsoft Word as opposed to the Reveal Codes feature in WordPerfect?

I RESPONDED: Working with raw codes in Word is a completely different thing than working with Reveal Codes in WordPerfect. You might think of them as equivalents, as in this diagram:

Codes in Microsoft Word $\Longleftrightarrow$ WordPerfect Reveal Codes

But they're not. A better way to think about using codes in Microsoft Word is like this:

Coding systems (XML, XPressTags, TeX tags, Ventura tags, etc.)

$$\Downarrow$$

Rendering systems (Web browsers, QuarkXPress, TeX, Ventura, etc.)

Quite a few publishers, especially in academic and technical settings, work directly with codes (using basic text editors such as emacs) and then render their files into presentation documents (typeset docs, PDFs, etc.) using a separate program. I was trying to explain that Microsoft Word, too, could be used in that way. WordPerfect's Reveal Codes feature merely shows the coding underneath the program's WYSIWYG text. Working with raw codes, on the other hand, is a way to get specific about document levels and structure. It's not a substitute for Reveal Codes, which Word doesn't need if used correctly (in other words, if formatting is done with styles rather than applied directly to text).

AutoText Toolbar

AutoText provides an easy way to store and then reuse text, graphics, fields, tables, bookmarks, and other items. For example, my *Editorium Update* newsletter includes the same "Fine Print" section in every issue. All I have to do is save that as an AutoText entry, and I can easily insert it without retyping, copying, or pasting. Think of AutoText as your boilerplate library.

You can create, delete, and work with AutoText entries by clicking Insert > AutoText > AutoText. But the AutoText toolbar gives you quick access to AutoText entries that you use a lot. Since I work in a publishing house, I'm thinking particularly of manuscript markup tags or typesetting codes, as explained in "Raw Codes."

To display the AutoText toolbar, click View > Toolbars > AutoText. You can identify the toolbar among your many others by its wide button labeled "All Entries."

\HD1\Now, need to insert a Heading code? Click "All Entries" on the AutoText toolbar. Then click "Heading Tags." Then click "Heading 1" to insert the Heading 1 tag. What? You don't *have* an entry for "Heading Tags"? Let's fix that right now:

1. Create a paragraph style called "Heading Tags." Strange as it may seem, Word uses the style of the text you select as the group name for AutoText entries you create.
2. Type the text you want to store as an AutoText entry—\HD1\, for example.
3. Apply your new "Heading Tags" style to that text.
4. Select the text.
5. On the AutoText toolbar, click the "New" button.
6. Enter a name (at least five characters) for the entry—"Heading 1," in this case.
7. Click the "OK" button.

There, you've now got a "Heading Tags" group, and within that group you've got a listing for "Heading 1." Here's how to use them:

1. On the AutoText toolbar, click "All Entries."
2. Click "Heading Tags."
3. Click "Heading 1."

Presto! "\HD1\" appears in your document, formatted with the style you originally gave it. That's kind of neat, because it means you can make different text levels stand out by defining the style to use a specific font or color.

If you don't *want* your code to be formatted with a style, just format your text with the Normal style before creating your AutoText entry. Your entry will then appear under "Normal" when you click "All Entries" on the AutoText toolbar.

Insert Boilerplate

Boilerplate is text you can use over and over again as needed. For example, the Fine Print section of my *Editorium Update* newsletter is boilerplate. Here's a little-known but useful way to create boilerplate in Microsoft Word:

1. Create a new document to hold all of your boilerplate text.
2. Paste your boilerplate text into it (obviously enough).
3. Select each chunk of boilerplate text and apply a bookmark to it (Insert > Bookmark). Make the bookmark names short and easy to remember. You may even want to keep a list of the bookmarks for reference. (You'll see why in just a minute.)
4. Save your document with a name like "Boilerplate" in an easy-to-find folder.

Now, when you're working on some document and want to insert some boilerplate text, here's what to do:

1. Click Insert > File.
2. Navigate to your Boilerplate file and click it.
3. Click the "Range" button.
4. Enter the name of the bookmark for the chunk of boilerplate you want to use. Unfortunately, Word won't give you a dropdown list of the bookmarks, which is why you should use short, memorable bookmark names and keep a list of what they are.
5. Click the "Insert" button.

The boilerplate for the bookmark you entered will be inserted into your document.

Readers Write

Mary L. Tod:

How is the use of a boilerplate file with bookmarks different from or better than using Word's built-in AutoText feature?

I responded: Good question. It's different in that the entries aren't stored in a template but in a specific document. But is that an advantage over AutoText? Probably not. Is it better than AutoText? Probably not, since with AutoText you can pick and choose the entries you want to insert. However, it is one more item to include in your bag of tricks, and sometime it may come in handy, which is why I thought it might be worth mentioning.

DAVID KING:

The boilerplate article is a nice trick to get text inserted. What I use often is the auto insert feature which when attached to the normal template is always available. Or you can select a template to store it. I do not know how much text it can hold, but the nice feature is you have the option of storing formatting information by including the paragraph mark.

BRAD HURLEY:

I use AutoText to insert boilerplate, it's very fast and efficient.
First I type the boilerplate in a Word document and select the text.
Then, with the text selected, I go to Insert > AutoText > New
I give the entry an easy-to-remember and descriptive name, like "disclaimer."
From then on, whenever I start to type the word "disclaimer" in a document, Auto-Text pops up and suggests the boilerplate text; to insert the whole shebang all I have to do is hit the Enter key.
If I have a lot of different boilerplates for different purposes and can't remember all their names, I can quickly find and select the right one by going to Insert > AutoText and reviewing the entries in the menu. It stores any entries you've created according to the style of the original text. So if you were using Normal style when you created the boilerplate text, you'll find your AutoText entry in the Insert > AutoText menu under "Normal."

Sample Text

Working in Microsoft Word, I often need some "junk" text to play around with, for various reasons:

- I'm designing a document and don't want to get bogged down in what the text actually says.
- I'm creating a template with various paragraph styles and need to see what they will look like.
- I'm creating a macro and need some text for testing purposes.
- I'm trying to learn more about some feature of Microsoft Word and don't want to practice on a real document.

Microsoft Word includes an undocumented feature that generates lots of sample text To use it, type the following line into a Word document:

```
=Rand(1,1)
```

Then press the ENTER key.
Word will insert the following text into your document:

The quick brown fox jumps over the lazy dog.

(As you probably know, this sentence includes every letter in the alphabet and is sometimes used for typing practice.)
Need more than one sentence? You can specify how many sentences you need by changing the last number in the Rand statement. For example, if you needed five sentences, you could type this—

```
=Rand(1,5)
```

—which would produce this:

The quick brown fox jumps over the lazy dog. The quick brown fox jumps over the lazy dog. The quick brown fox jumps over the lazy dog. The quick brown fox jumps over the lazy dog. The quick brown fox jumps over the lazy dog.

Need more than one paragraph? You can specify how many paragraphs you need by changing the first number in the Rand statement. For example, if you needed two paragraphs (with five sentences in each one), you could type this—

```
=Rand(2,5)
```

—which would produce this:

> The quick brown fox jumps over the lazy dog. The quick brown fox jumps over the lazy dog. The quick brown fox jumps over the lazy dog. The quick brown fox jumps over the lazy dog. The quick brown fox jumps over the lazy dog.
>
> The quick brown fox jumps over the lazy dog. The quick brown fox jumps over the lazy dog. The quick brown fox jumps over the lazy dog. The quick brown fox jumps over the lazy dog. The quick brown fox jumps over the lazy dog.

In other words, the first number specifies the number of paragraphs you want to insert; the second number specifies the number of sentences you want to include in those paragraphs.

If you're tired of that quick brown fox, you can use the traditional Latin "Lorem ipsum dolor . . . ," which has been used as placeholder text for centuries:

> Lorem ipsum dolor sit amet, consectetuer adipiscing elit, sed diam nonummy nibh euismod tincidunt ut laoreet dolore magna aliquam erat volutpat. Ut wisi enim ad minim veniam, quis nostrud exercitation ulliam corper suscipit lobortis nisl ut aliquip ex ea commodo consequat. Duis autem veleum iriure dolor in hendrerit in vulputate velit esse molestie consequat, vel willum lunombro dolore eu feugiat nulla facilisis at vero eros et accumsan et iusto odio dignissim qui blandit praesent luptatum zzril delenit augue duis dolore te feugait nulla facilisi.

If you're curious about this, it's a garbled quotation from Cicero's *De Finibus Bonorum et Malorum* (*On the Ends of Good and Bad*), book 1, paragraph 32, which reads, "Neque porro quisquam est, qui dolorem ipsum, quia dolor sit, amet, consectetur, adipisci velit," meaning, "There is no one who loves pain itself, who seeks after it and wants to have it, simply because it is pain." The book was popular during the Renaissance, when the passage was used in a book of type samples for that wonderful new technology, printing.

Sample Text in Autotext

In the previous article I explained how to use Word's Rand feature to create sample text ("The quick brown fox jumps over the lazy dog") that you can use for various purposes. I neglected to mention that for the Rand feature to work, "Replace text as you type" must be turned on under Tools > AutoCorrect. If you tried using Rand but nothing happened, you don't have it turned on. Of course, you may not *want* it turned on because then Word automatically makes certain "corrections" that you may not want. If you're editing in Word, that can be a disaster. For more information on how to prevent such problems, see "When Word Gets in the Way."

If you turn off "Replace text as you type," you can still use the traditional "Lorem ipsum dolor sit amet" sample text. Subscriber Karen L. Bojda of Bojda Editorial & Writing Services sent this helpful suggestion for doing so:

"Depending on your layout, repeating the 'quick brown fox' creates columns of words and rivers instead of a nice sample layout. So I just made an AutoText entry for the 'Lorem' text, which works whether AutoCorrect is on or not."

Thinking that this was a great idea, I immediately followed suit. Now, whenever I need some sample text to work with, I just type the word "lorem" into my document and press the F3 key. Presto! If you'd like to do this, here's how to set it up:

1. Copy and paste the "Lorem" text into a Word document (I've included a nice, long version at the end of this article).
2. Select the "Lorem" text.
3. Click the "Insert" menu at the top of your Word screen. In Word 95 or earlier, click the "Edit" menu.
4. Click "AutoText."
5. Click "New."
6. In the box labeled "Please name your AutoText entry," type "lorem."
8. Click the "OK" button.

Now, when you need some sample text, do this:

1. Type "lorem" into your document.
2. Press the F3 key.

The "Lorem" text will be inserted into your document.

Karen also sent this caution: "If you're going to address AutoText entries in an upcoming newsletter, I found the way Word files them by style to be at first baffling and then annoying, and I think a heads-up about that would be worthwhile. I avoid adding AutoText entries casually. Instead, I first create a style that has a meaningful name, such as 'sample text' or 'math symbols.' Then I format the text I want to add using that style, so that the AutoText entry gets filed under a heading that is more meaningful than 'Normal' or 'Body Text.' The style itself can then be deleted."

Here's a three-paragraph version of the "Lorem" text that you can use to create an AutoText entry (after deleting the extraneous email carriage returns at the ends of the lines):

Lorem ipsum dolor sit amet, consectetuer adipiscing elit, sed diam nonummy nibh euismod tincidunt ut laoreet dolore magna aliquam erat volutpat. Ut wisi enim ad minim veniam, quis nostrud exerci tation ullamcorper suscipit lobortis nisl ut aliquip ex ea commodo consequat. Duis autem vel eum iriure dolor in hendrerit in vulputate velit esse molestie consequat, vel illum dolore eu feugiat nulla facilisis at vero eros et accumsan et iusto odio dignissim qui blandit praesent luptatum zzril delenit augue duis dolore te feugait nulla facilisi.

Ut wisi enim ad minim veniam, quis nostrud exerci tation ullamcorper suscipit lobortis nisl ut aliquip ex ea commodo consequat. Duis autem vel eum iriure dolor in hendrerit in vulputate velit esse molestie consequat, vel illum dolore eu feugiat nulla facilisis at vero eros et accumsan et iusto odio dignissim qui blandit praesent luptatum zzril delenit augue duis dolore te feugait nulla facilisi. Lorem ipsum dolor sit amet, consectetuer adipiscing elit, sed diam nonummy nibh euismod tincidunt ut laoreet dolore magna aliquam erat volutpat.

Duis autem vel eum iriure dolor in hendrerit in vulputate velit esse molestie consequat, vel illum dolore eu feugiat nulla facilisis at vero eros et accumsan et iusto odio dignissim qui blandit praesent luptatum zzril delenit augue duis dolore te feugait nulla facilisi. Lorem ipsum dolor sit amet, consectetuer adipiscing elit, sed diam nonummy nibh euismod tincidunt ut laoreet dolore magna aliquam erat volutpat. Ut wisi enim ad minim veniam, quis nostrud exerci tation ullamcorper suscipit lobortis nisl ut aliquip ex ea commodo consequat.

Fancy Sorting

Back in my WordPerfect days, I used to enjoy the program's ability to do all kinds of fancy sorting. Microsoft Word has never been able to duplicate that, but it can still do more than you might think.

Let's say you've got a list of names, like this:

Kit Carson
Annie Oakley
William Cody

You probably know that you can sort them by first name under Table > Sort. But what if you want to sort them by last name? Yes, it *is* possible. Here's how:

1. Select the list.
2. Click Table > Sort.
3. Click the Options button.
4. Under "Separate fields at," select "Other."
5. In the box next to "Other," type a space (indicating the space between first and last names).
6. Click the OK button to go back to the "Sort Text" dialog.
7. Under "Sort by," click the drop-down arrow and select "Word 2."
8. Under "Then by, click the drop-down arrow and select "Word 1."
9. Click the OK button.

Your list should now be sorted like this:

Kit Carson
William Cody
Annie Oakley

Pretty slick!
What if some of your names have more than three parts?

Samuel Langhorne Clemens

Simple. Sort by Word 3, then Word 2, and then Word 1. Word lets you sort by up to three words, in any order, as long as they're separated by the same character (such as a tab, comma, or space). It may not be Perfect, but it's probably better than you thought.

Working with Lists

In my previous life working at a publishing house, I often compiled and edited lists of book titles, authors, type specs—all kinds of things (such as a list of nearly 1,400 book titles for a giant electronic publishing project). A typical list looked like this:

To Kill a Mockingbird
Jane Eyre
Old Man and the Sea
Great Gatsby
Moby Dick

(I removed the initial "The" from The Old Man and the Sea and The Great Gatsby so they'd sort properly. You may also want to do this with "A" and "An.") To sort such lists:

1. In Microsoft Word, select the paragraphs making up the list to be sorted.
2. Click the Table menu.
3. Click "Sort" or "Sort Text."
4. Under "Sort by," select "Paragraphs."
5. Under "Type," select "Text."
6. Select "Ascending."
7. Click "OK."

Wow, that works great! But wait a minute. I've got Great Gatsby in here three times! And Moby Dick twice! I wonder how many other duplicates I've got. Isn't there a way to delete them automatically? In fact, there is. Just use this trusty macro:

```
Dim Para1$
Dim Para2$
WordBasic.StartOfDocument
WordBasic.ParaDown 1, 1
Para1$ = WordBasic.[Selection$]()
WordBasic.CharRight 1
While WordBasic.AtEndOfDocument() = 0
WordBasic.ParaDown 1, 1
Para2$ = WordBasic.[Selection$]()
If Para1$ = Para2$ Then
WordBasic.WW6_EditClear
Else
Para1$ = Para2$
WordBasic.CharRight 1
End If
Wend
```

Hidden Articles

In the previous article, I presented the following list of book titles, noting that I'd removed the initial "The" from The Old Man and the Sea and The Great Gatsby so they'd sort properly:

To Kill a Mockingbird
Jane Eyre
Old Man and the Sea
Great Gatsby
Moby Dick

A reader wrote to ask if there isn't a way to preserve the initial articles (like "The") but still sort correctly, mentioning that he'd had to delete opening quotation marks from items in a list so the items wouldn't be sorted to the top.

It would certainly be possible to write a macro that would take care of such items. Another approach, however, would be to format initial articles as Hidden. Let's say you're working with a list like this (notice the articles on the third and fourth items):

To Kill a Mockingbird
Jane Eyre
The Old Man and the Sea
The Great Gatsby
Moby Dick

You could use Microsoft Word's Find and Replace feature to find "The" (using Match Case) and replace it with "The" in Hidden format:

1. Click the "Edit" menu.
2. Click "Replace."
3. If it's available, click the "No Formatting" button.
4. Type "The " in the "Find what" box (include a space after the word).
5. Type "The " in the "Replace with" box (include a space after the word).
6. If it's available, click the "More" button.
7. Check the "Match case" box. (Uncheck any of the other boxes.)
8. Click the "Format" button.
9. Click "Font."
10. Check the "Hidden" box.
11. Click the "OK" button.
12. Click the "Replace All" button.

13. Click the "OK" button when Word tells you how many items it found and replaced.
14. Click the "Close" button.

You could repeat this for anything else you want to be ignored when you sort the list, such as "A," "An," quotation marks, and so on. (You could even record all of these together as a macro.)

Now sort your list (Table/Sort Text). When you're finished, it should look like this:

Great Gatsby
Jane Eyre
Moby Dick
Old Man and the Sea
To Kill a Mockingbird

But wait! We're not done yet. Now we'll get our articles (etc.) back by reversing the Find and Replace routine we used to hide them:

1. Click the "Tools" menu.
2. Click "Options."
3. Click the "View" tab.
4. Check the "Hidden text" box (under the "Formatting marks" heading).
5. Click the "OK" button (revealing the hidden text so it can be found).
6. Click the "Edit" menu.
7. Click "Replace."
8. If it's available, click the "No Formatting" button.
9. Type "The " in the "Find what" box (include a space after the word).
10. If it's available, click the "More" button.
11. Check the "Match case" box. (Uncheck any of the other boxes.)
12. Type "The " in the "Replace with" box (include a space after the word).
13. Click the "Format" button.
14. Click "Font."
15. Clear the "Hidden" box.
16. Click the "OK" button.
17. Click the "Replace all" button.
18. Click the "OK" button when Word tells you how many items it found and replaced.
19. Click the "Close" button.

Now your list will look like this, which is what you were after in the first place:

The Great Gatsby
Jane Eyre
Moby Dick
The Old Man and the Sea
To Kill a Mockingbird

Hidden text is useful for other things, too—but we'll talk about that another day.

More Hidden Secrets

In the previous article, we talked about using Hidden formatting to make sure a list sorts properly. But Hidden formatting is useful for other things as well.

Let's say you're editing a scholarly book with dozens of block quotations from old journals. The author has consistently misspelled several geographical and personal names, so you fire up my MegaReplacer program to find and replace them all in one fell swoop (or you get ready to do them one at a time, by hand).

But wait! Although you want to replace the *author's* misspellings, you *don't* want to replace the original misspellings in the block quotations. They need to be reproduced verbatim. And you certainly don't want to okay every replacement by hand in this, long, long book.

Hidden formatting to the rescue!

Being the astute editor that you are, you've already formatted the block quotations with a style—named Block, let's say. (If you're not using styles for formatting, I beg you to learn how *today*. It will save you enormous amounts of time.) All you need to do now is set formatting in the Block style to Hidden. Here's how:

1. Click the Format menu.
2. Click "Style."
3. In the Styles box, click "Block."
4. Click the Modify button.
5. Click the Format button.
6. Click "Font."
7. Check the box labeled "Hidden."
8. Click the OK button.
9. Click the next OK button.
10. Click the Close button.

Whoa! All of your block quotations will have disappeared—if you're not displaying hidden text. If you *are* displaying hidden text, hide it, like this:

1. Click the Tools menu.
2. Click "Options."
3. Uncheck the box labeled "Hidden text."
4. Click the OK button.

Now, with your block quotations hidden, you can find and replace the misspellings in the rest of your text. Pretty slick!

Once you're finished, don't forget to reset your block quotations so they're no longer hidden. To do so, follow the first procedure used above, but this time *uncheck* the box labeled "Hidden." All of your block quotations will reappear, with their misspellings gloriously intact.

Now there's a "hidden" secret worth knowing!

Readers Write

NEIL HYMANS:

Like all writers, my working copy is littered with half-finished sentences and gems-to-be that I want to retain until I'm absolutely sure I won't need them . . . but they are a real distraction when I'm trying to read back clean text. My solution is to make them disappear and reappear at will.

I have a global *character style* called "Hidden" (it is a character style so it won't overwrite the existing paragraph style). It only has two attributes: the text is hidden, and plum coloured for higher visibility. I apply it using a simple hotkey combo (ALT+D works for me), but it is easy enough to create a toolbar button or menu command to apply the style to a selection, to suit personal preferences.

By default, Word doesn't display hidden text. I recorded two simple macros: one to display hidden text, another to hide it. Once again, these can also be configured to work from hotkeys, menu commands or toolbar buttons according to preference.

When I despatch one of my creative gems to the literary boneyard, I apply the "Hidden" style with ALT + D. In Word's default mode, it vanishes instantly from the screen. When I get desperate for inspiration, I click the button to display the boneyard again, and there it is. Should I decide to reclaim the text, I simply select it and reapply the appropriate paragraph style.

Best of all: it takes about two minutes to create this facility on any version of Word.

Finally, there is an important caveat on this tip: don't rely on hidden text if trashed text is potentially sensitive. Turn the hidden text display on, then copy the public text to a new file for review (or better still use the amazing "Editioning" template—thanks for that tip, by the way!). [You can learn more about the "Editioning" template in "Editioning Software."]

Converting Text Boxes to Text

I've recently needed to help several people convert Microsoft Word text boxes to text. Is there something in the wind? Whatever is going on, if you're having to copy and paste, copy and paste, to get that text out where you can use it, you'll appreciate the following macro, which pulls text-box text out as regular text and styles it with a character style named "OnceABox," colored red for easy identification. To (eventually) get rid of the red, just delete the character style. (Thanks to Geoff Hart, David Chinell, and Janna DeVore for inspiration.)

If you have lots of documents that need to be converted, you might consider running the macro with my MultiMacro program.

And now, the macro. Enjoy!

```
Sub ExtractTextBoxes()
Dim NoStyle As Boolean
Dim aStyle As Style
Dim aShape As Shape
Dim i As Integer
'Check for "OnceABox" character style
NoStyle = True
For Each aStyle In ActiveDocument.Styles
If aStyle.NameLocal = "OnceABox" Then
NoStyle = False
Exit For
End If
Next aStyle
'If necessary, create "OnceABox"
'character style
If NoStyle Then
ActiveDocument.Styles.Add Name:="OnceABox", _
Type:=wdStyleTypeCharacter
With ActiveDocument.Styles("OnceABox").Font
.Color = wdColorRed
End With
End If
'Style textboxes and convert to frames
For Each aShape In ActiveDocument.Shapes
If aShape.Type = msoTextBox Then
i = i + 1
aShape.Select
aShape.ConvertToFrame
Selection.Style = _
ActiveDocument.Styles("OnceABox")
End If
Next
```

```
'Clean and delete frames
For i = ActiveDocument.Frames.Count _
To 1 Step -1
With ActiveDocument.Frames(i)
.Borders.Enable = False
With .Shading
.Texture = wdTextureNone
.ForegroundPatternColor = _
wdColorAutomatic
.BackgroundPatternColor = _
wdColorAutomatic
End With
.Delete
End With
Next
End Sub
```

Readers Write

BRAD HURLEY:

I usually use bibliographic software for references (EndNote, which integrates nicely with Word), but occasionally I have to edit documents that use Word's endnotes and footnotes. Is there any way to insert footnotes or endnotes into text boxes? We frequently prepare documents with sidebars, which we create with text boxes, but there doesn't seem to be any way to add footnotes to them if we need to cite a reference. Maybe there's a better solution for creating sidebars than using text boxes?

I REPLIED: As you've already learned, text boxes don't support footnotes or endnotes. However, frames do.

So if you can use frames rather than text boxes, that should solve your problem. To get a frame in Word 2000, you have to click Tools > Macro > Macros and then select "Word commands" in the "Macros in:" dropdown list. Then click "InsertFrame" in the "Macro name:" box. Then click the "Run" button. Finally, use your mouse to draw the frame in your document.

Please note that this kind of frame is not to be confused with the Format > Frames command, which creates HTML frames for use in Web pages.

RENEE DeCARLO:

Changing text into text box—select the text and click the Text Box icon at the bottom of the screen.

Page Layout Template

Typesetters usually like to see a sheet of paper showing the page layout for a book they are about to typeset. This saves them from having to guess the location and pagination the editor has in mind for an epigraph, dedication, preface, introduction, and so on. For years our editors created page layouts by hand, drawing little boxes and writing in their instructions about what text goes on which page. But wouldn't it be nice to create a page layout in Microsoft Word? Now you can. Just download this custom template:

http://www.editorium.com/ftp/pagelayout.zip

To use the template:

1. Put it in Word's Templates folder. If you don't know where that is, you can find out by clicking Tools > Options > File Locations > User Templates.
2. Click File > New.
3. In the Task Pane, click "[Templates] On my computer."
4. Under the General tab, find and double-click Page Layout.dot to create a new document.
5. Save your new page layout with a name of your choice—something like "MyProject Page Layout.doc."
6. Modify the page layout as needed for the book you're working on. Each box is a bordered table, and you can freely copy and paste the boxes as needed—for back matter, for example. You can also change the contents of the boxes and the page numbers underneath. If necessary, you can modify the template itself to meet your needs.

Using a page layout should help your typesetter, but it should also help you as you plan the layout of your book. Enjoy!

Wordperfect Weirdness

I work with lots of authors who use WordPerfect. Sometimes they pass their documents on to colleagues who use Microsoft Word. That wouldn't be a problem if the authors would first save their documents in Word format. But they don't, and their colleagues work on the documents in Word, pass them around to others, and then give them back to the authors, who send them to me.

When I open these documents they look okay—except that some of the characters look kind of funny. The quotation marks and apostrophes are a little crooked, and the em dashes are thick and bold. What's going on here?

What's going on is that these aren't regular ANSI characters. You can prove this by selecting one and then pressing CTRL + SPACEBAR to remove any directly applied formatting. When you do, the character will turn into some other character. With this particular kind of weirdness, an opening quotation mark (for example) will become a capital A. You could Find and Replace these with real quotation marks, but your document may have hundreds—even thousands—of *real* capital A's that you want to preserve.

Here's a list of the pseudo-characters (the ones I've identified; there could be more) and their corresponding true identities:

Character Disguised As	True Identity (sort of)
Em dash	C
En dash	B
Opening quotation mark	A
Closing quotation mark	@
Opening single quotation mark	>
Closing single quotation mark (apostrophe)	=

Another way to prove something weird is happening is to put your cursor in front of one of these characters and then run the macro you'll find in "What's That Character?"

The macro will tell you that the ANSI number is 40—which is really the number for an opening parenthesis. That will be true whether you're checking a pseudo-quotation mark, em dash, en dash, whatever. So you can't Find and Replace them by using character number 40, either, since your document may contain legitimate parentheses.

What's needed is a way to Find and Replace a character that is an A (or whatever) *and* has the ANSI number 40. At the end of this article is a macro that will do just that, for all the weird characters in question.

Now, if you run into this WordPerfect weirdness, you'll have a way to fix it.

If you remove directly applied formatting and the character (such as an em dash) *doesn't* change to something else (such as a C) but instead to a less-bold version of the same thing (which can happen), then the macro won't fix it.

```
Sub FixWPWeirdness()
Dim a
Dim i
Dim FalseChar$
Dim TrueChar$
Dim ThisChar
Selection.HomeKey Unit:=wdStory
Selection.Find.ClearFormatting
Selection.Find.Replacement.ClearFormatting
'Check for platform
a = InStr(WordBasic.[AppInfo$](1), "Macintosh")
For i = 1 To 6
'Set find and replace variables
Select Case i
Case 1
FalseChar$ = "C"
If a Then
TrueChar$ = Chr(209)
Else
TrueChar$ = Chr(151)
End If
Case 2
FalseChar$ = "B"
If a Then
TrueChar$ = Chr(208)
Else
TrueChar$ = Chr(150)
End If
Case 3
FalseChar$ = "A"
If a Then
TrueChar$ = Chr(210)
Else
TrueChar$ = Chr(147)
End If
Case 4
FalseChar$ = "@"
If a Then
TrueChar$ = Chr(211)
Else
TrueChar$ = Chr(148)
End If
Case 5
FalseChar$ = ">"
If a Then
TrueChar$ = Chr(212)
Else
TrueChar$ = Chr(145)
End If
```

```
Case 6
FalseChar$ = "="
If a Then
TrueChar$ = Chr(213)
Else
TrueChar$ = Chr(146)
End If
Case Else
End Select
'Find and replace characters
With Selection.Find
.Text = FalseChar$
.Forward = True
.Wrap = wdFindContinue
.Format = False
.MatchCase = True
.MatchWholeWord = False
.MatchWildcards = False
.MatchSoundsLike = False
.MatchAllWordForms = False
End With
Selection.Find.Execute
While WordBasic.EditFindFound()
ThisChar = Asc(WordBasic.[Selection$]())
If ThisChar = 40 Then
WordBasic.EditClear
WordBasic.Insert TrueChar$
End If
Selection.Find.Execute
Wend
Next i
End Sub
```

Readers Write

After reading the article on finding and replacing weird WordPerfect characters, Jane Lyle, managing editor at Indiana University Press, sent the following macro, which does its work by searching for characters formatted in the WP TypographicSymbols font.

```
' WPTyp Macro
' Macro recorded 10/25/2001 by Jane Lyle
Selection.Find.ClearFormatting
With Selection.Find
.Replacement.Font.Name = "Times New Roman"
.Font.Name = "WP TypographicSymbols"
.Text = ""
.Replacement.Text = ""
.Forward = True
.Wrap = wdFindContinue
.Format = False
.MatchCase = False
```

```
.MatchWholeWord = False
.MatchWildcards = False
.MatchSoundsLike = False
.MatchAllWordForms = False
End With
Selection.Find.ClearFormatting
Selection.Find.Replacement.ClearFormatting
With Selection.Find
.Replacement.Font.Name = "Times New Roman"
.Font.Name = "WP TypographicSymbols"
.Text = "A"
.Replacement.Text = """"
.Forward = True
.Wrap = wdFindContinue
.Format = True
.MatchCase = False
.MatchWholeWord = False
.MatchWildcards = False
.MatchSoundsLike = False
.MatchAllWordForms = False
End With
Selection.Find.Execute Replace:=wdReplaceAll
Selection.Find.ClearFormatting
Selection.Find.Replacement.ClearFormatting
With Selection.Find
.Replacement.Font.Name = "Times New Roman"
.Font.Name = "WP TypographicSymbols"
.Text = "@"
.Replacement.Text = """"
.Forward = True
.Wrap = wdFindContinue
.Format = True
.MatchCase = False
.MatchWholeWord = False
.MatchWildcards = False
.MatchSoundsLike = False
.MatchAllWordForms = False
End With
Selection.Find.Execute Replace:=wdReplaceAll
Selection.Find.ClearFormatting
Selection.Find.Replacement.ClearFormatting
With Selection.Find
.Replacement.Font.Name = "Times New Roman"
.Font.Name = "WP TypographicSymbols"
.Text = ">"
.Replacement.Text = "'"
.Forward = True
.Wrap = wdFindContinue
.Format = True
.MatchCase = False
.MatchWholeWord = False
.MatchWildcards = False
.MatchSoundsLike = False
```

```
.MatchAllWordForms = False
End With
Selection.Find.Execute Replace:=wdReplaceAll
Selection.Find.ClearFormatting
Selection.Find.Replacement.ClearFormatting
With Selection.Find
.Replacement.Font.Name = "Times New Roman"
.Font.Name = "WP TypographicSymbols"
.Text = "="
.Replacement.Text = "'"
.Forward = True
.Wrap = wdFindContinue
.Format = True
.MatchCase = False
.MatchWholeWord = False
.MatchWildcards = False
.MatchSoundsLike = False
.MatchAllWordForms = False
End With
Selection.Find.Execute Replace:=wdReplaceAll
Selection.Find.ClearFormatting
Selection.Find.Replacement.ClearFormatting
With Selection.Find
.Replacement.Font.Name = "Times New Roman"
.Font.Name = "WP TypographicSymbols"
.Text = "B"
.Replacement.Text = "^="
.Forward = True
.Wrap = wdFindContinue
.Format = True
.MatchCase = False
.MatchWholeWord = False
.MatchWildcards = False
.MatchSoundsLike = False
.MatchAllWordForms = False
End With
Selection.Find.Execute Replace:=wdReplaceAll
Selection.Find.ClearFormatting
Selection.Find.Replacement.ClearFormatting
With Selection.Find
.Replacement.Font.Name = "Times New Roman"
.Font.Name = "WP TypographicSymbols"
.Text = "C"
.Replacement.Text = "^+"
.Forward = True
.Wrap = wdFindContinue
.Format = True
.MatchCase = False
.MatchWholeWord = False
.MatchWildcards = False
.MatchSoundsLike = False
.MatchAllWordForms = False
End With
```

```
Selection.Find.Execute Replace:=wdReplaceAll
Selection.Find.ClearFormatting
Selection.Find.Replacement.ClearFormatting
With Selection.Find
.Replacement.Font.Name = "Times New Roman"
.Font.Name = "WP TypographicSymbols"
.Text = "?"
.Replacement.Text = """"
.Forward = True
.Wrap = wdFindContinue
.Format = True
.MatchCase = False
.MatchWholeWord = False
.MatchWildcards = False
.MatchSoundsLike = False
.MatchAllWordForms = False
End With
Selection.Find.Execute Replace:=wdReplaceAll
Selection.Find.ClearFormatting
Selection.Find.Replacement.ClearFormatting
With Selection.Find
.Replacement.Font.Name = "Times New Roman"
.Font.Name = "WP TypographicSymbols"
.Text = "Y"
.Replacement.Text = ". . ."
.Forward = True
.Wrap = wdFindContinue
.Format = True
.MatchCase = False
.MatchWholeWord = False
.MatchWildcards = False
.MatchSoundsLike = False
.MatchAllWordForms = False
End With
Selection.Find.Execute Replace:=wdReplaceAll
```

Revision Tracking and Comments

Tracking Trick

If you've done much editing in Microsoft Word, you've probably used Track Changes (Revisions), which marks deleted and added text so you can review (or let someone else review) your editing. If you haven't used it, here's how to turn it on:

1. Click the "Tools" menu.
2. Click "Track Changes."
3. Click "Highlight Changes."
4. Put a check in the box labeled "Track changes while editing." (While you're there, you can also decide whether or not to show ["highlight"] changes on your screen or in the printed document.)
5. Click the "OK" button.

Or, what the heck, just double-click the "TRK" box in the status bar at the bottom of your screen. You can also right-click the box to set various options.

One of the options is what color to use to designate deletions and additions—blue, turquoise, and so on (scroll down to see the more unusual colors). The most interesting color is the one labeled "By author." What's it do? Well, my own "author" color, by default, is red. If, however, I open a document from you, your tracked changes will show up in a different color, probably blue. So "By author" tells word to assign a different color to changes from a different user. How does Word know the document is from a different user? Because of the name that was specified under Tools > Options > User Information > Name when the document was created.

And that suggests an interesting trick. If you're going to track changes, why not track different *kinds* of changes in a way that will be helpful to you? The most obvious application of this idea would be to track big changes (such as moving paragraphs around) and small changes (such as moving commas around) separately. All you have to do is change the name under User Information to something like "Big Changes" before getting out the cleaver, and to something like "Little Changes" before getting out the tweezers. The obvious advantage of this is that little changes then show up in a different color *inside* of big changes, which doesn't happen if you make all of your changes using the same user name (and thus the same color).

You can even record each name change in its own macro and assign those macros to menus, toolbar buttons, or keyboard shortcuts for easy access.

After you've finished marking big and little changes (or whatever), don't forget to set your user name back to your actual name.

Now, there are plenty of changes you probably don't want to track at all. For example, before I ever start reading a document, I first clean up multiple spaces, multiple paragraph breaks, and lots of other stuff that gets in the way of real editing. I do this with Track

Changes turned off (using my FileCleaner and MegaReplacer programs) because I don't consider these to be significant changes. I don't want to review them, and I don't think my authors care about reviewing them. I do, however, want to have any significant changes available for review, and the tracking trick of changing the user name makes this eminently doable.

Macros for Intuitively Reviewing Tracked Revisions

Here's the problem with reviewing tracked revisions: Whether the text is marked for insertion or deletion, it's *still there* on my screen. And to make it go away (or to retain it) requires a *different* action for an insertion than it does for a deletion. I understand Microsoft's reasoning on this, but they could have handled it in a more intuitive manner.

Consider: If I want to accept deleted text, that means the text will be deleted. If I want to reject deleted text, that means the text will be retained. Conversely, if I want to accept inserted text, that means the text will be inserted. If I want to reject inserted text, that means the text will be deleted. No wonder I get confused. Here's a grid that shows what happens to the text on my screen:

Revision Type	Accept	Reject
Insertion	Retained	Deleted
Deletion	Deleted	Retained

When I'm reviewing revisions, my brain actually has to make three decisions for every revision it encounters:

1. How is the text marked—as a deletion or an insertion?
2. Do I want to keep the displayed text or get rid of it (whether marked for deletion or insertion)?
3. So do I accept the revision or reject it?

Really, all I should have to think about is number 2: Do I want to keep the displayed text or get rid of it? Then Word should be smart enough to deal with my decision in the appropriate way. Unfortunately, this is not the case. So let's fix it with the following two macros:

```
Sub KeepRevision()
Dim revType
On Error GoTo EndMacro 'In case text isn't a revision.
revType = Selection.Range.Revisions(1).Type
If revType = 1 Then
Selection.Range.Revisions(1).Accept
ElseIf revType = 2 Then
Selection.Range.Revisions(1).Reject
Else
GoTo EndMacro
End If
EndMacro:
End Sub
```

```
Sub KillRevision()
Dim revType
On Error GoTo EndMacro 'In case text isn't a revision.
revType = Selection.Range.Revisions(1).Type
If revType = 1 Then
Selection.Range.Revisions(1).Reject
ElseIf revType = 2 Then
Selection.Range.Revisions(1).Accept
Else
GoTo EndMacro
End If
EndMacro:
End Sub
```

I highly recommend attaching these macros to a couple of keyboard shortcuts for ease of use. On my computer, KeepRevision is attached to CTRL + ALT + UPARROW (the UP cursor key). KillRevision is attached to CTRL + ALT + DOWNARROW (the DOWN cursor key).

In addition, I've attached the Microsoft Word command ToolsRevisionMarksNext to CTRL + ALT + RIGHTARROW and ToolsRevisionMarksPrev to CTRL + ALT + LEFTARROW.

These four keyboard shortcuts make a very nice combination. You can use them to:

1. Find the next (or previous) revision (either deletion or addition).
2. Permanently keep or remove the revised text (as opposed to accepting or rejecting the revision).

Easy and intuitive. Maybe you'll like it!

Readers Write

HILARY POWERS:

Regarding your tracking-review macros: I think they'd drive me crazy. Maybe I've been doing this too long, but my thought process runs purely to "keep this change" and "don't keep this change" without reference to whether the underlying text will thereby be restored or removed.

This probably works for me because I never, ever review each and every revision and decide upon its fate individually.

When I go through an edited manuscript after the author has indicated what should happen to it, I first move from one of the author's comments or adjustments to the next, eyeballing for the author's tracking color. In each case, I fix that part of the manuscript so it does what the author wants (which may or may not be precisely what the author asked for). In the process, I try to delete all the queries I've put into the text.

Then I simply approve all the changes remaining in the manuscript, holus bolus—after which I have a whole array of very quick scans to make sure that no queries escaped and nothing else bad happened as a result.

For me, that's intuitive.

Ed Nelson:

We must accept the changes, but reject the inserts to get equivalent results, the omission of the text under consideration.

Sometimes the problems we see come from outside circumstances conflicting with the way our mind sees the issue in the first place. Here's what I'm trying to get at:

We may see the issue as being "What is this command going to do to the text before me?" And what the commands do *does* seem opposite to each other. But if we see it as "What will this command do to the established procedure?" the result isn't so weird. To overcome the Insert process, the new text gets omitted. To overcome the prior editorial correction, the new text (a different item in this case) also gets omitted.

Contradictory procedures are both being overcome. Consistent, No?

Pasting Tracked Revisions

One of the oddest things in Microsoft Word is its seeming inability to copy and paste text that includes tracked revisions. If you want to see what I'm talking about, try this:

1. Create a new document.
2. Type a few lines of text.
3. Turn on revision tracking. (Double-click the TRK box in the status bar so the TRK turns black. Yep, TRK stands for "tracking." At this point, the Reviewing toolbar should appear at the top of your Word window.)
4. Delete a few words here; add a few words there. You'll see your revisions in color, since they're tracked.
5. Copy some text that includes tracked revisions.
6. Create a new document.
7. Paste your text into the new document.

Hey, where are the tracked revisions? Well, they didn't get copied (and thus didn't get pasted). But what if you really need to copy them? As usual, there's a trick. Just turn *off* revision tracking *before* copying the revised text. (Double-click the TRK box in the status bar so the TRK turns gray.) Then, when you paste the text (into a document with tracking turned off), all of your revisions will be there.

Why do you suppose Microsoft made Word that way? A bug? Could be. But maybe, just maybe, it's a feature, giving you a choice about whether or not to copy and paste revisions. But if that's true, why not copy revisions when tracking is on, and *not* copy revisions when tracking is off? That would be more logical. Shoot, maybe it is a bug. If so, now you know how to squash it.

Readers Write

Hilary Powers:

It's a feature. Lots of times I'm working along, and I want to pull something from the main document, which has tracking active, to the style sheet—and I want the final version of whatever-it-is, not any changes I may have made in it. That wouldn't be feasible with the apparently logical system. Keeping only the final version is the more likely choice, so it makes sense to have to do something to keep the tracking.

But it's a feature only in Word 2000+; in Word 97, there's a genuine bug: you can't copy tracking AT ALL. If you want to reproduce a passage with tracking intact, you have to bookmark it, then use Insert, File, Range (bookmark name) to put the bookmarked passage into a file that has tracking turned off. (If you want the whole file, you can simply Insert it without the Range bit.)

HANNAH HYAM:

You can also copy and paste tracked changes using the Spike:

1. With Track Changes ON, select the text you want to paste and cut it to Spike (CTRL + F3). If you only want to copy, not cut it, press CTRL + Z immediately after to restore the text.
2. Turn Track Changes off and insert the text where required (CTRL + SHIFT + F3). The changes are retained.
3. Don't forget to turn Tracked Changes back on to continue editing.

FRANCELIA SEVIN:

On my Mac in Word 2001, toggling the track changes on/off doesn't work. I still cannot copy and paste text and include the tracked changes. I have upgraded with the latest patches for 2001 and that hasn't made any difference.

HILARY POWERS: That sounds like the PC Word 97 tracking-copy bug, alive and well in Mac Word 2001. If so, the PC workaround—bookmarking the material and inserting it in its new spot (with tracked changes turned off in the receiving document)—should work just fine. To move something in the same document, save the bookmarked file under a different name, then reopen the active file and turn off tracking, insert the bookmarked passage from the copy, and delete it from its original location. Then turn the tracking on again, and you're back in business.

KAREN BOJDA: This is a known "issue" (bug) in Word 97/98. It's been fixed in Word 2000 and higher. A workaround is to insert the text (Insert > File) into the new document rather than paste it. If you don't want to insert the whole doc, bookmark just the part you need and then enter the bookmark name into the 'Range' box of the Insert dialog.

I can confirm that this works in Word 98 on the Mac. You have to save a copy of the file under a different name, since Word won't let you insert a file (or even a bookmarked part of a file) into itself. It might be a cumbersome workaround, but I've used it and been grateful to know about it.

ERIKA BUKY:

On a Macintosh pasted revisions are made permanent? Actually, I was pleased to discover the other day that it ain't necessarily so. Using Word 2001, I was able to paste 35 pp. of marked-up bibliography into the main document using the Spike.

As you're aware, putting something on the Spike deletes it from the original document, though you can undo that change once the text has been spiked.

[See "Copy to Spike" and "I Like Spike."]

Pasting Tracked Revisions, Part 2

Pasting tracked revisions works in various ways depending on whether tracking is turned on or off (Tools > Track Changes). On a Macintosh, you have only one option: If you copy text with revisions and paste it somewhere, the revisions are made permanent in the pasted text. On a PC, several things can happen, based on whether tracking is turned on or off as you copy and paste. Here's what happens (strikethrough indicates a deletion; underlining indicates an addition.):

• Original text with tracked revisions:

This ~~is a~~ test.
This is a <u>good</u> test.

• Copy with tracking OFF, paste with tracking OFF: Existing tracking is retained.

This ~~is a~~ test.
This is a <u>good</u> test.

• Copy with tracking ON, paste with tracking OFF: Tracked revisions are made permanent; text is pasted as regular text.

This test.
This is a good test.

• Copy with tracking OFF, paste with tracking ON: Tracked deletions revert to *original* text (danger!); tracked additions are kept; text is pasted as a tracked addition.

This is a test.
This is a good test.

• Copy with tracking ON, paste with tracking ON: Tracked revisions are made permanent; text is pasted as a tracked addition.

This test.
This is a good test.

The moral of our story? When you're copying and pasting text with tracked revisions, be sure to turn tracking on or off for both copy and paste, based on the result you want to achieve.

Marking Revisions for Review in WordPerfect

A few years ago, one of the editors I work with needed to show tracked revisions to an author she's working with. The problem was, the author used WordPerfect, not Microsoft Word. We tried opening the marked-up Word document with WordPerfect, but no go. Additions were there, marked in red, but deletions had reverted to regular text. Saving the document in various formats and then opening in WordPerfect brought us no joy. What to do? Well, how about a macro that checks and formats each revision? If it's an insertion, color it blue and accept it; if it's a deletion, mark it with strikeout, color it red, and accept it. Then save the document in Rich Text Format (RTF). When it's opened in WordPerfect (or any other word processor that accepts RTF), all of the changes will be visible. Here's the macro, which I hope you'll find useful:

```
Sub FormatRevisions()
Dim ThisRevision As Revision
For Each ThisRevision In Selection.Range.Revisions
Application.Run MacroName:="ToolsRevisionMarksNext"
If ThisRevision.Type = wdRevisionInsert Then
With Selection.Font
.Color = wdColorBlue
End With
ThisRevision.Accept
GoTo Continue
End If
If ThisRevision.Type = wdRevisionDelete Then
With Selection.Font
.StrikeThrough = True
.Color = wdColorRed
End With
ThisRevision.Reject
GoTo Continue
End If
Continue:
Next ThisRevision
End Sub
```

Comments to Text

I've been asked by several readers if there's a way to convert Word comments (Insert > Comment) to document text. It depends on what "convert" means. If you just need to get the text of a bunch of comments, you can open the Comments pane (View > Comments), select all, copy, and then paste to a new document. Easily done.

If you want to turn comments *into* text in the document where the comments live, here's a macro that will do the job:

```
Sub Comments2Text()
Dim objComment As Comment
For Each objComment In ActiveDocument.Comments
objComment.Reference.InsertAfter " <" & objComment.Initial _
& ": " & objComment.Range.Text & "> "
objComment.Delete
Next
End Sub
```

Before running the macro, be sure to back up your document, just in case.

As written, the macro puts the initials and text of each comment, in angle brackets, into the document text and then deletes the comment.

If you don't want to use angle brackets, you can change them to some other character or string of characters by modifying the following two lines (note that there's a space before and after the brackets, which you can omit if you like):

```
objComment.Reference.InsertAfter " <" & objComment.Initial _
& ": " & objComment.Range.Text & "> "
```

If you don't want to delete the comments, just remove this line:

```
objComment.Delete
```

If you wanted to, you could use parentheses—

```
objComment.Reference.InsertAfter " (" & objComment.Initial _
& ": " & objComment.Range.Text & ") "
```

—and then use my NoteStripper program to turn the parenthetical comments into footnotes.

You could also use my Puller program to pull items in brackets or parentheses into another file.

Finally, you could format items in angle brackets (or other delimiters) to make them stand out from text. Red would be nice. Here's how:

1. Back up your file, just in case.
2. Click Edit > Replace.
3. In the Find What box, enter this:

\<*\>

4. In the Replace With box, enter this:

^&

5. Click the More button if it's there.
6. With your cursor in the Replace With box, click Format > Font > Font color > red.
7. Click the OK button.
8. Put a check in the "Use wildcards" checkbox.
9. Click the Replace All button.

All of your bracketed comments should now be red.
Thanks to Jenn Morris for suggesting this topic.

Readers Write

ANNA MARSHALL:

Do you or any of your readers have a macro that will take comments out of the comments area and paste them into the running text of a document?

I RESPONDED: I received not just one macro but *three,* one from Steve Hudson and two from Clive Tolley. Many thanks to them! Before using these "in the real world," try them on some test documents to make sure they do what you want. You can also edit the macros if necessary to better suit your needs.

```
Sub CommentsToInline()
'Copies comment initials and text inline between square
brackets,
'leaving original comments in place.
Dim C As Comment
Dim S As String
For Each C In ActiveDocument.Comments
S = C.Range.Text
S = " [" & C.Initial & ": " & S & "]"
C.Reference.InsertAfter S
Next
Set C = Nothing
End Sub
```

```
Sub CECopyComments()
'Copies the open file's comments to another file
'and saves this under the same name + '_COM'
'VBA routine written by Clive Tolley, 18.05.03
Dim Doc1 As String
Dim DocName As String
Dim DocPath As String
Dim i As Integer
Doc1 = ActiveDocument
i = Len(ActiveDocument.Name)
DocPath = ActiveDocument.Path + "\"
DocName = Left(ActiveDocument.Name, i - 4)
If ActiveDocument.Comments.Count >= 1 Then
ActiveDocument.StoryRanges(wdCommentsStory).Copy
End If
Documents.Add
Selection.Paste
ActiveDocument.SaveAs FileName:=DocPath + DocName + "_COM.doc"
End Sub


Sub CEIncorporateComments()
'Removes comments and incorporates their text
'into the main text of the document,
'adding a space before.
'VBA routine written by Clive Tolley, 22.05.03
Dim i As Integer
If ActiveDocument.Comments.Count < 1 Then
MsgBox "There are no comments in this file!"
Else
For i = 1 To ActiveDocument.Comments.Count
ActiveDocument.Comments(1).Range.Copy
Selection.GoTo What:=wdGoToComment, Which:=wdGoToAbsolute,
Count:=1
Selection.Collapse Direction:=wdCollapseStart
Selection.TypeText " "
Selection.PasteSpecial DataType:=wdPasteText
ActiveDocument.Comments(1).Delete
Next i
End If
End Sub
```

Deleting Multiple Comments

While editing in Word, you may use Word's Comments feature (Insert > Comment) to insert questions for your client—or possibly your client has used comments to insert questions for you. In either case, there will probably come a time when you need to remove the comments so the file can be used for typesetting. But deleting comments one at a time can be a real pain.

The solution? A trusty macro, of course. Here's a simple macro that will delete all the comments in a document:

```
Dim aComment
For Each aComment In ActiveDocument.Comments
aComment.Delete
Next
```

But what if there are comments you don't *want* to delete? For example, what if the only comments you want to remove are the ones you created? The following macro will do the trick:

```
Dim aComment
For Each aComment In ActiveDocument.Comments
If ActiveDocument.Comments(1).Initial = "JML" Then
aComment.Delete
End If
Next
```

Just put your own initials in the macro in place of "JML" and off you go—comments deleted; problem solved.

Readers Write

GREG IOANNOU:

In Word 2003 and 2007, no macros are needed to delete multiple comments. From Word's help files:

- To quickly delete all comments in a document, click a comment in the document. On the Review tab, in the Comments group, click the arrow below Delete, and then click Delete All Comments in Document.

It is a bit more complex for just one reviewer:

- On the Review tab, in the Tracking group, click the arrow next to Show Markup.

- To clear the check boxes for all reviewers, point to Reviewers, and then click All Reviewers.

Click the arrow next to Show Markup again, point to Reviewers, and then click the name of the reviewer whose comments you want to delete.

- In the Comments group, click the arrow below Delete, and then click Delete All Comments Shown.

Printing Comments but Not Markup

In earlier versions of Microsoft Word, it was possible to print comments separately from tracked revisions. You can still do that with Word 2002 and later versions, but how to do so is no longer obvious. Here's the trick:

1. Click View > Toolbars > Reviewing.
2. On the Reviewing toolbar, click the Show button.
3. Remove the checkmark from "Insertions and Deletions." This will turn off the display of tracked revisions (but leave them intact if you want to redisplay them later).
4. Click File > Print > Print what > List of markup.

Word will print a list of your comments without including your revisions. Fairly easy, once you know how.

Here's another way of approaching the problem:

1. (Temporarily) accept all revisions. This is now trickier than you might think:

a. Click View > Toolbars > Reviewing.
b. On the Reviewing toolbar, click the down arrow to the right of the Accept Change button.
c. Click "Accept all changes in document."

2. Click File > Print > Print what > List of markup.
3. Click OK, which will print comments alone, because the document no longer includes any revisions.
4. Close the document *without saving,* thus preserving your revisions.

Simple but effective.

Thanks to Dan Goldstein for suggesting this topic.

Deleting Multiple Bookmarks

Bookmarks in a Word document are useful for many things, such as, well, marking your place, marking ranges for index entries, and marking text for cross-references. But they can also get in the way—for example, if you've finished editing a document for a client and have several dozen bookmarks you've created but now need to delete, or if you're getting ready to import a Word document into QuarkXPress or InDesign, which don't like bookmarks.

The usual procedure for deleting bookmarks is to click Insert > Bookmarks, select a bookmark, and click the Delete button—over and over and over again, since Word won't let you select more than one bookmark at a time.

The solution? A trusty macro, of course. Here's a simple one that will delete all the bookmarks in a document:

```
Dim aBookmark
For Each aBookmark In ActiveDocument.Bookmarks
aBookmark.Delete
Next
```

But what if your client included bookmarks that you don't *want* to delete? What if the only bookmarks you want to remove are the ones *you* created? Well, if you've started those bookmarks with a unique identifier, such as your initials, the solution is easy. For example, my initials are JML, so I name my bookmarks something like this:

```
JMLchapter12
JMLsection14
```

Then, when I'm finished editing, I run the following macro to delete them:

```
Dim aBookmark
For Each aBookmark In ActiveDocument.Bookmarks
If Left(aBookmark.Name, 3) = "JML" Then
aBookmark.Delete
End If
Next
```

Just put your own initials in the macro in place of "JML" or use some other unique code such as "zzz" (yes, the macro is case-sensitive).

Bookmarks deleted; problem solved.

Revision-Tracking Format in Word 2002

Before Word 2002, it was possible to set revision-tracking colors and formatting separately for inserted and deleted text. The procedure was simple:

1. Click Tools / Track Changes / Highlight Changes / Options.
2. Select "Mark" (bold, italic, underline, or double underline) for "Inserted text."
3. Select "Color" (various) for "Inserted text."
4. Select "Mark" (bold, italic, underline, or double underline) for "Deleted text."
5. Select "Color" (various) for "Deleted text."
6. Click the "OK" button.

In Word 2002, however, this feature works only for "Inserted Text." "Deleted text" automatically follows suit, and there seems to be no way to set the two independently. To make matters worse, Strikethrough is no longer among the listed marking options. How annoying! Fortunately, there's a hidden way to overcome these limitations. I've exploited it in the following macro, which you can easily modify to meet your own needs:

```
Sub SetTrackingFormat()
With Options
.InsertedTextMark = wdInsertedTextMarkUnderline
.InsertedTextColor = wdBlue
.DeletedTextMark = wdDeletedTextMarkStrikeThrough
.DeletedTextColor = wdRed
End With
End Sub
```

The macro is currently set to mark insertions as blue text with underline, and to mark deletions as red text with strikethrough. To change this, replace the "Underline" on the end of "wdInsertedTextMarkUnderline" or the "StrikeThrough" on the end of "wdDeletedTextMarkStrikeThrough" with any of the following:

Bold
ColorOnly
DoubleUnderline
Italic
None
StrikeThrough
Underline

Then replace "wdBlue" or "wdRed" with any of the following:

wdBlack
wdBlue
wdBrightGreen
wdByAuthor
wdDarkBlue
wdDarkRed
wdDarkYellow
wdGray25
wdGray50
wdGreen
wdNoHighlight
wdPink
wdRed
wdTeal
wdTurquoise
wdViolet
wdWhite
wdYellow

Then run the macro (Tools / Macro / Macros). Hah, hah! Once again Microsoft Word must bend to your will!

Readers Write

DAVID STACEY:

The general public react to the use of different colors when marking their documents. Do you have any recommendations about the choice of colors? (Too much red seems to cause them stress.) I'm now using red for strikethrough and blue for insertions.

I REPLIED: I think this is a good question, and I like the idea of using blue for insertions. How about using 25% gray for strikethrough? (You have to scroll down in the list of colors to see this one.) That would help communicate the idea that the text has been deleted because it would be lighter than the surrounding text.

HERE'S AN EXCHANGE BETWEEN MIRIAM BLOOM AND ME:

MIRIAM: When comparing (merging) documents in MS Word for Windows XP, is there a way to format different font colors for the "delete" vs. the "add" function? I used to be able to do it in older versions of both Word and WordPerfect, but now I can't figure out how to do it in either.

JACK: As far as I can tell, Microsoft has removed this feature from Word 2002, which makes me very grumpy indeed. In fact, I'm unhappy with nearly all of their "enhancements" having to do with merged documents and tracked changes.

MIRIAM: Moreover, I can't figure out how to do it after the fact because find-and-replace doesn't seem to work on merged documents.

JACK: That's because "red underlined" (for example) for revision tracking is a different kind of formatting. If you simply format some text as red underlined using the Font dialog, you should be able to find and replace it, even in a merged document.

MIRIAM: Is there an alternative way of searching it—or any way at all of getting around the color problem short of going through documents and redlining them manually?

JACK: You can use Word's Reviewing toolbar to go to each new change, but this won't alter appearance. You could go back to Word 2000, which allows you to use separate colors for insertions and deletions.

KEITH SOLTYS:

I was interested to note your macro for setting Word 2002 to mark deleted text as strikethrough. In versions of Word prior to 2002, I've usually set deleted text to be hidden. I was surprised to see that Word 2002 didn't allow you to change the option for this; I guess they really want you to use the balloons, a "feature" that I detest. (They also broke comments; there's a market for an addon to make Word 2002 comments work the same way that Word 2000 did).

However, I did run into a really interesting bug that you might not be aware of. If you are using Word 2000 and have your revision tracking options set so that revision tracking is on and deleted text is shown as hidden, this setting gets carried forward into your Word 2002 document. You can't change it through the interface, only through VBA.

In this case, and if you are not using balloons, you may run into pagination issues. What happens is that in print layout view, Word may insert spurious blank pages when it finds deleted text. Pagination will be OK in normal view, but in print layout you will get any number of blank pages added into your file. It gets even more interesting—if you go to print preview, your file may balloon in size to several thousand pages.

The conditions for this to happen are quite specific. You must have revision tracking set so that deleted text is marked as hidden and revision tracking must be set to Final Showing Markup, and you must be in Print Layout view and not using balloons.

The fix is to use VBA to change how Word shows deleted text from hidden to strikethrough. You can also accept the changes in the file. Or set revision tracking to Final, or use balloons.

I encountered this bug not long after "upgrading" to Word 2002. I posted a message about the problem to the word-pc list and was contacted by someone from Microsoft, who eventually confirmed that it was indeed a bug.

Comments and Tracking in Word 2002

If you've started using Microsoft Word 2002, you've probably seen the little "balloons" that display your comments and tracked changes. In my opinion, these are pretty much useless in a professional environment. For example, if you get many deletions on a page, Word will abbreviate the balloon messages, so printing these for an author to review is of little help. Yes, you can print the changes separately (File > Print > Print what: > List of markup), but trying to compare this list with the document is cumbersome.

Online review isn't much better. An author can use the Reviewing toolbar to go from change to change or comment to comment in the Reviewing Pane, but that's not how real people read. I want to see the corrections and comments clearly marked inline—just as they were in previous versions of Word.

Good news: After mucking around in the bowels of the program, I've discovered a fix for revision tracking:

1. Click the "Tools" menu.
2. Click the "Track Changes" tab.
3. Under "Balloons," uncheck the box labeled "Use balloons in Print and Web Layout."

Wow, what an improvement! No more balloons, and revision tracking is handled inline the way it used to be. To print your document showing tracked changes, do this:

1. Click the "File" menu.
2. Click "Print."
3. Under "Print what:" select "Document showing markup."

Now for the bad news: There is no fix for comments—at least not that I can find. In previous versions of Word, each comment had an inline reference (like "[JML3]") and a corresponding reference at the beginning of the comment. That was a good system, easy to use and understand.

With Word 2002, these references have gone away, so it's now difficult to figure out what part of the text a comment refers to. You can move from comment to comment using the browser arrows at the bottom right of your screen, but that's a poor substitute. Even worse, there seems to be no way to print comments at all without enabling those stupid balloons. Microsoft, are you listening?

If you know of a way around this problem, please let me know. If not, you can always resort to typing coded inline comments [[like this one]] that can later be deleted with a wildcard Find and Replace:

Find what:

\[\[*\]\]

Replace with:

[nothing]

Maybe if we all wrote to Microsoft about this, they'd stop gumming up a perfectly useful word processor. Maybe we should send balloons.

Readers Write

ERIKA BUKY:

It's not much of a workaround for people with only one computer and the current version of Word, but I you can import files with comments into a previous version of Word (97 or 2000), and the comments will print in the old, rational way.

NANCYANN ROPKE:

Woody's Office Watch has had several articles about comments and tracking in Word 2002.

http://www.woodyswatch.com/wowmm/archtemplate.asp?v3-n06
http://www.woodyswatch.com/wowmm/archtemplate.asp?v3-n02

MEG COX:

Don't take my balloons!

I love the balloons. I used to have a terrible time working with tracked changes showing. It was too hard to follow the final version in the middle of all that mess. But if I didn't show changes, I would forget to toggle track changes back on when I needed to, and I'd wind up with untracked paragraphs. Everything's much easier with the balloons, and I think much clearer for the reader—even the comments as long as they stay on the same page as the text.

I agree that the balloons become less useful when the changes become denser. Word should indeed provide an easy-to-find alternative.

Styles

Marking Spec Levels with Styles

An important part of editing is marking type specification levels in a manuscript. The Chicago Manual of Style describes the process like this:

"Each item in the opening of an article or of a preface, chapter . . . , appendix, or other section of a book (title, chapter number, etc.) is marked for its particular type size, style, and placement. . . . Specifications for text, subheads, block quotations, and similar elements must also be given, at least at the first occurrence of each. Thereafter, handwritten 'codes' added during editing identify similar elements for the typesetter. . . . Increasingly, however, a much more abbreviated form of markup is being used that relies on the typesetter to follow directly the design layouts and detailed list of specifications provided by the publisher's design department. All the editor need do is provide, during editing, the traditional codes for elements that would not be obvious to the operator. The various levels of subheads, for instance, must be indicated for the typesetter, usually by circled alphabetical or numerical codes (A, B, C or 1, 2, 3, etc.)." (14th edition, 2.135.)

A footnote adds this:

"Such codes written by hand on the manuscript correspond to the codes used on electronic manuscripts, which are part of the electronic files; both serve the same identifying function. If a manuscript (or printout) coded by hand is to be produced electronically, the handwritten codes are translated into electronic codes."

Now, if you're editing directly in Microsoft Word, you don't *have* any handwritten codes. So how are you going to mark spec levels?

@BODY:Some editors mark them by entering typesetting codes directly into the manuscript, as I've done at the beginning of this paragraph. If you're a QuarkXPress user, you'll probably recognize that code as an XPress Tag.

XPress translates XPress Tags into style sheets, which work a lot like styles in Microsoft Word. Entering all those codes seems like a lot of work, though, even if you have each code in a macro and assign the macros to function keys. Those codes also mess up the pristine appearance of your beautiful Word document, and they may confuse authors and reviewers. There ought to be a better way.

Well, you could just mark spec levels with styles. For example, you could mark part titles with Word's Heading 1 style, chapter titles with Heading 2, and subheads with Heading 3. If you're typesetting in Microsoft Word (some people do), applying styles should take care of all of your paragraph-level formatting.

If you're typesetting in QuarkXPress, however, you may want to try my QuarkConverter program (which is also included with Editor's ToolKit Plus). QuarkConverter adds XPress Tags for all the styles in a document, for character formatting (such as italic and bold), and for various typographic niceties, and it converts special characters (which include dashes and quotation marks) from PC to Macintosh or vice versa. It also converts Word index entries into QuarkXPress index entries, which means you can index in Word but have page numbers in your index reflect the pagination in your QuarkXPress document.

Readers Write

Jenn Morris:

I have 150 Word Documents that were extracted from Quark for Mac. I need to open them in Word for PC and make some changes. One change involves the fonts. In Quark, postscript fonts were used, and the individual fonts for bold, italics and bold italic were used instead of using Quark's attribute styles. This causes Word for PC to not recognize that the font is styled. However if I highlight some text, the original font name will appear. (For example, "Baskerville Bd BT" appears in the font window.) Manually I do a Search & Replace based on Format and Font name by pasting the above font name into the Find Font line, and then in the Replace field I have the format Font name blank but I apply the Bold style. Eventually all of the text will be converted to Times New Roman, so if I don't do this I will lose all the bold and italics.

I tried recording a macro to convert all of the fonts used in the original Quark doc, but it doesn't work.

I also have other macros, along with the font ones, that I am trying to run using MultiMacro on the whole 150 documents to try and automate things. Any help would be greatly appreciated.

I responded: Word is notorious for not accurately recording macros that find and replace formatting. I run into this all the time, and it drives me nuts. Here's a macro that should work:

```
Sub ReplaceAFont()
Selection.Find.ClearFormatting
Selection.Find.Replacement.ClearFormatting
Selection.Find.Font.Name = "Baskerville Bd BT"
Selection.Find.Replacement.Font.Bold = _
True With Selection.Find
.Text = ""
.Replacement.Text = ""
.Forward = True
.Wrap = wdFindContinue
.Format = True
.MatchCase = False
.MatchWholeWord = False
.MatchByte = False
.MatchWildcards = False
.MatchSoundsLike = False
.MatchAllWordForms = False
End With
Selection.Find.Execute Replace:=wdReplaceAll
End Sub
```

Actually, you can paste the body of the macro (that is, all but the first and last lines) over and over between the first and last lines, each time modifying these lines as needed:

```
Selection.Find.Font.Name = "Baskerville Bd BT"
Selection.Find.Replacement.Font.Bold = True
```

Another example:

```
Selection.Find.Font.Name = "Courier New"
Selection.Find.Replacement.Font.Italic = True
```

In addition to Bold and Italic, you can use:

Underline
Shadow
Strikethrough
Superscript
Subscript

And so on.

You can also combine replacement items, using two in the same macro:

```
Selection.Find.Font.Name = "Courier New"
Selection.Find.Replacement.Font.Bold = True
Selection.Find.Replacement.Font.Italic = True
```

Of course, you *could* create a separate macro for each kind of formatting—

```
Sub ReplaceThisFont()
Sub ReplaceSomeOtherFont()
```

—and then run them all at once with MultiMacro.

Or you could put all the different formats in one macro and use MultiMacro to run that macro on multiple files.

Styles and Standardization

In the early days of printing, the "source" for the words on a printed page was the metal type used in the press. Once the pages had been printed, the type was removed from the printing forms and resorted into bins, completely destroying the source text. Producing a new edition of the book meant setting, proofreading, and correcting the type all over again—an enormous investment of time and money.

Too often people still do essentially the same thing today, even though we now have the technology (and the necessity!) to preserve source text (which is now electronic) and create new editions from it in a variety of forms:

- Printed books.
- Web pages.
- Electronic reference libraries.
- PDF (Adobe Acrobat) documents.
- Palm and PocketPC documents.
- Dedicated e-book reader documents.

And so on.

Form Follows Function

Because people often need to produce a document (or parts of a document) in a variety of forms, a document's structure is far more important than its appearance—and in fact, its appearance should be derived from its structure. This is true because a document's appearance will change depending on the form in which it is presented. For example, a document presented on the printed page may look very different from the same document presented on a Web site.

In traditional typesetting, a chapter heading might be designed and typeset as 24-point Palatino. However beautiful that may be, it gives us no clue that the type is a chapter heading—information that would be crucial on a Web page or in an electronic reference library, where chapter headings might be used for linking, navigation, and so on. In other words, the heading's *function* is much more important than its *form*. Even in a particular printed book, if one chapter heading is set in 24-point Palatino, *all* of the book's chapter headings should be set in 24-point Palatino, because that signals the reader that any type so displayed *is*, in fact, a chapter heading. In type design, as in all other kinds of design, form should *follow* function.

Now consider what would happen if you had to put 300 different books together for an electronic reference library or Web site and needed to display all of the chapter headings for navigational purposes in a single table of contents. If chapter headings were electronically marked *as* chapter headings, it would be a piece of cake. If not, it would be a nightmare.

That's why it's no longer adequate to simply set type as 24-point Palatino. Instead, the type's *function* needs to be designated in a consistent, standardized way. Fortunately, that is not hard to do. In Microsoft Word, it's done with styles.

Using Styles

Paragraph styles are a way to specify the function of a block of type and then assign a form (the type's appearance) to that function. As an example, consider the subheading above, "Using Styles." In a book, it might be formatted with a paragraph style named Heading 3, designating the line as a subheading. Heading 3 might format the line as 16-point Verdana type. However, it would be easy to redefine Heading 3 as 28-point Garamond, which would completely change its look. Nevertheless, it would *still* be styled as Heading 3—a subhead—and that can be useful in many ways.

For one thing, it would allow you to *change your mind* about a document's appearance. Let's say you've directly formatted (without styles) all of your main headings—102 of them, to be exact—as 24-point Arial, but the managing editor now thinks they should be bigger—28 points instead of 24. Let's also say you've used 24-point Arial elsewhere in your document, so you can't just find and replace the formatting you need to change. What does that mean? It means you now have the painful task of selecting and reformatting every single one of those 102 headings—unless, of course, you've used styles, in which case you can adjust the heading style with a few clicks of the mouse, *automatically* changing all 102 headings at once.

Using styles has other advantages, too:

- You can easily find one style and replace it with another. This is much simpler than having to search for directly applied formatting, such as 24-point Arial bold no indent.
- You can see and change the structure of your document in Outline view and Document Map.
- You can use the styles to automatically generate (or—after the author has added a new chapter—regenerate) a table of contents.
- You can use the styles to create automatic headers, footers, and cross-references.

If you're not using styles, you're spending a lot more time on formatting than you need to, and you're missing much of the power of Microsoft Word. In addition, you're making it difficult to reuse electronic text for other purposes—something we will all increasingly need to do.

Standard Style List

Because of this problem, you should consider marking type levels using a standard list of styles that will work well in your publishing environment. That doesn't mean every publication needs to *look* the same, since designers can *define* the styles any way they want. It does mean:

- Every publication should use styles from a standard list.
- No other styles should be used. In other words, don't just make up new ones as you go along. If you *need* a new one for a certain function not covered by the standard list, consult with others in your organization (such as typesetters and designers) so that everyone can be consistent.
- Styles should be used consistently from document to document. For example, you might always have Heading 1 be a part title, no matter what publication you are working on. Heading 2 could always be a chapter title. Heading 3 could always be a first-level subhead. And so on. If you then used the Heading 1 style for a chapter title or the Heading 2 style for a subhead, you would be at variance with the standard list, and that could cause problems in the future. Try not to think of a book as a single publication. Each book may eventually be part of a larger electronic *library* of books; if so, those books will need to be consistently produced.
- Text should not have directly applied formatting. For example, don't just select a heading and format it as 20-point Helvetica. Instead, apply the correct style for that heading and then *define* the style as 20-point Helvetica. In the short run, this may be a pain. In the long run, it will save enormous amounts of time, money, and frustration.

Stand by, and I'll share my standard list of styles.

Readers Write

SUSAN BULLOWA:

If you have the Styles and Formatting Task Pane open In Word 2002 and you hover the arrow cursor over the paragraph mark to the right of the style name, the tool tip with all of the style's attributes appears. I find the tool tip information useful because it usually displays more detail than the listing of attributes in the Modify Styles dialog box. When the tool tip appears and I want to record the information, I press the Print Scr button and paste the picture into Paint. In that way, I can print the information for myself while I build my spreadsheet of style attributes.

ERIC FLETCHER:

I discovered a feature of Word 2002 that I'd hitherto overlooked—and it was so useful I thought I should share it with you.

With Word's task pane set to "Styles and formatting" and the bottom pull-down set to "Formatting in use", you are presented with what at first appears to be an often long and useless list of all of the variations of different formatting within the document. But when you select one of the items in this list (labelled "Pick formatting to apply"), instead of clicking on the format summary to apply it, right-click it and examine the pull-down menu that appears. From it, you can choose Modify and some other options, but the top line both shows how many instances of the selected format occur in the document AND gives you the opportunity to select all of them at once. Once selected of course, you can apply a style or do some other action on the whole set.

As an example, when I noticed that the panel listed both "Heading 3" and "Heading 3 + underline", choosing to select all 11 instances of the latter let me change all eleven of the instances of underlining contained within the Heading 3 style to no underline and italic instead—in one single action.

Of course, I could have done the same thing with find and replace but this is much faster and lets me see formatting issues that I might otherwise have overlooked. For example, I frequently end up selectively tweaking character spacing (condensing the font) or slightly reducing inter-paragraph spacing in several places throughout a document to manually adjust to fit text for a final print layout. Getting rid of such things for subsequent use of the content is complicated because they are not evident. This task pane feature makes it simple: all of the variations are listed and I can do all of it from the panel without potentially losing other formatting I do want to retain. (As would be the case with superscripts and the like if they were within a selection and I just used CTRL + Space to reset the font for example.) My panel showed all such variations as "Condensed by 0.1 pt" as well as "Condensed by 0.25 pt" and "Block indent + Before: 5 pt" so it was easy to reset them to the normal conditions. As you do so, the list gets shorter until (ideally) you are left with only the standard style list with allowable variants like italics within them.

In addition to Formatting in use, the other options at the bottom of the task pane in this view let you see Available styles (just the styles), Available formatting (the styles plus variants), All styles (your own plus default ones), and Custom (lets you select what to display). All-in-all, a very powerful tool for anyone who is serious about managing style usage in a Word document.

ERIC FLETCHER (REDUX):

Late last year as part of a message I sent you regarding styles, I mentioned my use of Word 2002's Task Pane. I've been using it a lot and have found it to be an extremely useful tool in more ways than I'd thought. But don't rely on the built-in Help: it is particularly sparse and almost makes it look like the feature was added at the last moment. Here are some of my observations in no particular order.

1. I've made a tool button to be able to pop the Task Pane up whenever I need it. I have two monitors, so I float the task pane (and other toolbars) in the second one most of the time. However, on my wife's single monitor, a button makes it easier to be able to hide and restore the Task Pane (instead of the View | Task Pane menu). You can use a preset button or make your own.
2. The Clipboard panel holds up to 24 elements as you cut or copy. A 25th pushes the first off the stack. You can paste any item by clicking on it, but be aware that a right click lets you delete a clipboard item. This is handy when you need to cut something in a series of copies, or if you inadvertently copy something you don't really need. The feature has the utility of the old "spike" function but lets you

manage the contents in a way Spike never did. Excel users should note that the Word and Excel task panes share the same content, so copying between the two is easy. (Very handy for ad hoc copying of addresses from Excel to Word when a mail merge is too much bother!)

3. The Styles and Formatting panel (S&F) has some very useful features for cleaning up document formats. If you've ever examined a Word file in a text editor, you may have noticed how all formatting is collected at the end and each different instance has pointers back into the text where it is to be applied. S&F appears to use this to great advantage: each different instance of any type of formatting can be listed in the S&F panel depending on what you choose to show via dropdown at the bottom of the panel.

The feature is not particularly intuitive, so open a document and try it. Consider a document with a few levels of headings and some manually applied formatting. Bring up the Task Pane and set it to the S&F panel. When you click on a subhead—say Heading 3—in the text, the S&F panel will display the style name at the top. If the selection is a variant of the defined style, the difference(s) will be noted: for example, "Heading 3 + Garamond" when I set a Heading 3 to the Garamond font. But click to the right side of the box and pull down the list to see the options:

Select all XX Instance(s) lets you select all instances within the document but also gives you a *count* of how many there are. (This is very useful if you need to do a count of instances of a particular style: how many bibliographic references are there in this document? Is this the only time I used a Heading 5?)

- Clear Formatting removes formatting from the selection.
- New Style brings up the dialog to make a new style based on the selection.
- Modify Style lets you change the style definition.
- Reveal Formatting switches to a different panel to give you all the specific formatting details.

But with the selection still in the modified Heading 3, scroll down and look at the options available for the "Heading 3" style: "Update to match selection" lets you modify the defined style to match the selection in one step. Very useful!

The other different option is Delete. This removes the style definition but doesn't delete the formatted content. In fact, it appears to have the same effect as the "Clear formatting" style selection. Particularly if I am in the process of preparing a template, I like to go through and remove any unnecessary style definitions before finalizing it.

4. When there has been a lot of "fiddling" done to make pages fit, a document can often have numerous variations on style (for example, "Body Text + Condensed by 0.1pt" or "Body Text + Before: 4pt"). If you need to re-use such copy, these variations can create headaches later. Use the S&F panel to browse through and eliminate all such variants. (I use it to remove all extraneous variations to prepare copy for conversion to HTML since I then don't have to deal with manually removing all the code Word prepares for me.)

5. Use the "Show" dropdown in the S&F panel to manage what formatting is displayed. The "Formatting in use" shows only the formatting used within the document (styles and variants of them); "Available formatting" adds the styles defined for the currently-applied template; "Available styles" lists only the styles and without the variants; and "All styles" displays the styles from the current template plus the names of Word's "built-in" styles. This latter option is lengthy, but you can pare it down by choosing "Custom . . ." and selecting which styles you want to have displayed.

6. Use the Custom pulldown to define what variants should be displayed (font, paragraph, bullet & numbering) and to add the "Clear formatting" option to the style list (which also puts it at the top of the style toolbar pulldown, incidentally). The selection of styles to make visible or not changes by the category selected. Finally, you can save the options in the template so it is set for other or later use.

7. The Reveal Formatting panel (RF) shows all the details about the format of the current selection. If you select "Distinguish source style" at the bottom of the panel, the display shows the underlying style and any differences—showing the detail much as the variants are shown in the S&F panel. The pulldown options for the selection let you clear formatting, choose all other similar formatting in the document, but also change the format to match the surrounding text. I'm not entirely sure what rules are used for this: a word set with French language was set to English but only if I selected the whole word; but a word set in green was changed to black when the selection was within the word.

8. Select something and then turn on the "Compare with another selection" checkbox. A second box appears, and when you make a second selection, the panel itemizes the differences.

My documents are cleaner and smaller since I've incorporated the Task Pane into my set of Word tools.

Standard Style List

Every editor (and publishing house) needs a standard style list. Here's mine. As you look at the list, keep in mind that it was developed for styling books. If you work mostly on journals or magazines, your list will probably look quite different. I'm sharing my list primarily to give you an idea of what a fairly complete standardized list might look like. If you can use it or adapt it for what you do, great.

You'll notice that my style names are long. I've made them that way because I don't like trying to decipher names like HD1NI and BQ2. In some situations, however, that kind of brevity might be important, so do whatever works best for you. Sometimes, I've modified the names of built-in Word styles by adding a comma and then some descriptive text.

I've also modified the drop-down style list on Word's Formatting toolbar so it's nice and wide to accommodate those long style names. See "Resizing Drop-Down Lists."

I keep my styles in a template that I attach to any document I need to edit, and I've formatted the styles so they're easy on my middle-aged eyes. You can learn more about that in "Typefaces for Editing."

I'm also fond of using color in heading styles so I know at a glance whether I'm dealing with a first-, second-, or third-level subhead. You can learn more about that in "Glorious Color."

As you review the list, you might wonder why I have so many variations of styles for block quotations, poetry, and a few other items. These are necessary for decent typography, as explained here:

http://www.editorium.com/editkit/TH_49.htm

The style named Normal,Text 1 is the basic body text for any book. It's named Normal,Text 1 rather than Normal for ease in importing documents into QuarkXPress, which uses a style named Normal that isn't always compatible with Word's Normal style. Many editors prefer to use a style named something like "Body Text" for the same reason.

Some of the styles end in "NI," which stands for "no indent." I use these to mark text that should have no paragraph indent. For example, Block Quote Start NI marks the first paragraph of a block quotation that begins somewhere in the middle of the paragraph being quoted. Normal Text 1 NI is used after a block quotation to mark text that does not begin a new paragraph but continues the thought of the text before the block quotation. Using these styles is the equivalent of writing "No paragraph" or "No indent" on a paper manuscript.

The name of each style is followed by a description of its function. The styles marked with an asterisk are the ones I use most often. If you'd like to see an actual Word template that includes such styles, you'll find one (named Typespec.dot) included with my Editor's ToolKit Plus program. Feel free to use the template and modify it to suit your needs.

And now, here's the list:

Bib Subhead: Subheading separating different kinds of bibliographic entries. For example, a bibliography might include different entries under the subheadings of "Books," "Periodicals," and "Archival Materials."

Bib Text: The text of a bibliographic entry, such as "Pyle, Howard. *Salt and Pepper.* Harper and Brothers, New York, 1885."

*Block: A block quotation of one paragraph (indented).

*Block NI: A block quotation of one paragraph (not indented).

Block Heading: A heading at the beginning of a block quotation.

Block Subhead: A subheading between paragraphs of a block quotation.

*Block First: First paragraph of a block quotation (indented).

*Block First NI: First paragraph of a block quotation (not indented).

*Block Middle: Middle paragraph of a block quotation. The quotation may include more than one of these.

*Block Last: Last paragraph of a block quotation.

Block Source: Citation following a block quotation (usually someone's name).

Block Poem: A single line of poetry inside a block quotation.

Block Poem Heading: Heading before a poem inside a block quotation (usually the poem's title).

Block Poem Subhead: Subheading between stanzas of a poem inside a block quotation.

Block Poem First: First line of a poem inside a block quotation (possibly indented).

Block Poem First NI: First line of a poem inside a block quotation (possibly not indented).

Block Poem Start: Starting line of any poetry stanza but the first inside a block quotation (possibly indented).

Block Poem Start NI: Starting line of any poetry stanza but the first inside a block quotation (possibly not indented).

Block Poem Middle: Middle line of any poetry stanza inside a block quotation (possibly indented). The stanza may include more than one of these.

Block Poem Middle NI: Middle line of any poetry stanza inside a block quotation (possibly not indented). The stanza may include more than one of these.

Block Poem End: Ending line of any poetry stanza but the last inside a block quotation (possibly indented).

Block Poem End NI: Ending line of any poetry stanza but the last inside a block quotation (possibly not indented).

Block Poem Last: Last line of a poem inside a block quotation (possibly indented).

Block Poem Last NI: Last line of a poem inside a block quotation (possibly not indented).

Block Poem Source: Citation following a poem inside a block quotation (usually someone's name).

*Book Byline 1: A book's author. Used on the book's title page.

*Book Byline 2: A book's second author. Used on the book's title page.

Book Byline3: A book's third author. Used on the book's title page.

Book Byline4: A book's fourth author. Used on the book's title page.

*Book Publisher: A book's publisher (such as Random House or HarperCollins). Used on the book's title page.

Book Puff: A testimonial for the book. Used on the half-title page or jacket.

Book Puff Source: The name of a person giving the testimonial. Used under a book puff.

Book Puff Source Affiliation: The position or affiliation of a person giving the testimonial. Used under a book puff source.

**Book Series:* The title of a series to which a book belongs, such as *The Lord of the Rings* (by J.R.R. Tolkien).

**Book Subtitle:* A book's subtitle, such as *There and Back Again* (whose title is *The Hobbit*). Used on the book's title page.

Book Subsubtitle: A book's subsubtitle (yes, these do show up from time to time). Used on the book's title page.

Book Teaser: A line of marketing or explanatory copy. Used on the book's title page.

**Book Title:* A book's title, such as *Fellowship of the Ring* (by J.R.R. Tolkien). Used on the book's title page.

**Caption:* The caption under a photograph or other graphic.

**Chapter Number:* The number of a chapter. See "Heading 1,Chapter Title."

Chapter Quote: A quotation at the beginning of a chapter.

Chapter Quote Source: A citation for a chapter quote. This is usually someone's name.

Chapter Subtitle: A subtitle after a chapter title (Heading 2,Chapter Title).

Chapter Subsubtitle: A subtitle after a chapter subtitle.

Colophon: A statement, usually on the last page of a book, describing elements of the book's production.

**Copyright:* A book's copyright notice.

**Dedication:* A book's dedication.

**Endnote Reference:* A superscript reference number that refers to an endnote.

**Endnote Heading:* A heading that introduces some endnotes, either at the end of a chapter or in a notes section at the back of the book. An example is "Notes to Chapter 12."

Endnote Subheading: A subheading between sections of endnotes.

**Endnote Text:* The text of an endnote.

Epigraph: A saying or quotation that introduces a book ("Caveat lector").

Epigraph Source: The source of an epigraph, usually someone's name.

**Folio:* A book's page number.

**Footnote Reference:* A superscript reference number that refers to a footnote.

**Footnote Text:* The text of a footnote.

Glossary Subhead: A subheading in a glossary.

Glossary Text: The text of a glossary entry.

**Heading 1,Part Title:* Heading for a major section of a book. Using this level for part titles makes it possible to browse a book's sections in Microsoft Word's Outline View or Document Map.

**Heading 2,Chapter Title:* Heading for a chapter title. Using this level for chapter titles makes it possible to browse a book's chapters in Microsoft Word's Outline View or Document Map.

**Heading 3,Subhead A:* Subheading level A.

Heading 4,Subhead B: Subheading level B.

Heading 5,Subhead C: Subheading level C.

Heading 6,Subhead D: Subheading level D.

Heading 7,Subhead E: Subheading level E.

Heading 8,Subhead F: Subheading level F.

Heading 9,Subhead G: Subheading level G.

*Index 1 (Subject): Text of an entry in a subject index.

Index 2 (Scripture): Text of an entry in a scripture index.

Index 3 (Custom): Text of an entry in some other kind of index.

Index Subhead: Subheading indicating a grouping of index entries. For example, an index to a biography of Mark Twain might include such subheadings as "Mark Twain, early life of" and "Mark Twain, writings of."

Jacket Blurb Book: Text of marketing copy (blurb) on a book jacket.

Jacket Blurb Author: Text of "about the author" copy on a book jacket.

Jacket Continued: Line of text explaining that the jacket blurb is continued on the back flap.

Letter Date: Date of a letter quoted in the text of a book ("June 10, 1900").

Letter Place: Place of a letter ("Boston").

Letter Salutation: Salutation of a letter ("Dear Ella").

Letter First: First paragraph of a letter.

Letter Middle: Middle paragraph of a letter. There may be more than one of these.

Letter Last: Last paragraph of a letter.

Letter Signature: Signature of the person writing a letter ("Your affectionate husband, William").

List: An item in a "list" consisting of a single item.

*List First: The first item in a list of items.

*List Middle: A middle item in a list of items. There may be more than one of these.

*List Last: The last item in a list of items.

*List Bullet: An item in a bulleted "list" consisting of a single item.

*List Bullet First: The first item in a list of bulleted items.

*List Bullet Middle: A middle item in a list of bulleted items. There may be more than one of these.

*List Bullet Last: The last item in a list of bulleted items.

List Number: An item in a numbered "list" consisting of a single item.

*List Number First: The first item in a list of numbered items.

*List Number Middle: A middle item in a list of numbered items. There may be more than one of these.

*List Number Last: The last item in a list of numbered items.

*Normal,Text 1: The normal text level of the body of a book.

*Normal Text 1 First: The first paragraph in a chapter or following a subheading. Used when the paragraph requires special formatting, such as extra leading.

*Normal Text 1 NI: Normal text, not indented. Usually used after a block quotation when the subject of the paragraph has not changed.

Normal Text 2: The second text level of the body of a book. Usually used to designate long passages from a second author.

Normal Text 2 First: The first paragraph in a chapter or following a subheading in a second text level. Used when the paragraph requires special formatting, such as extra leading.

Normal Text 2 NI: Second text level, not indented. Usually used after a block quotation when the subject of the paragraph has not changed.

Normal Text 3: The third text level of the body of a book. Usually used to designate long passages from a third author.

Normal Text 3 First: The first paragraph in a chapter or following a subheading in a third text level. Used when the paragraph requires special formatting, such as extra leading.

Normal Text 3 NI: Third text level, not indented. Usually used after a block quotation when the subject of the paragraph has not changed.

Note Text: The text of an "author's note" at the end of a book or chapter; not to be confused with endnote or footnote text.

Note Subhead: A subheading in a note.

Note Subsubhead: A subsubheading in a note.

*Part Number: The number of a major section of a book. See "Heading 1,Part Title."

Part Quote: A quotation at the beginning of a section.

Part Quote Source: A citation for a part quotation. This is usually someone's name.

Part Subsubtitle: A subtitle after a part title (Heading 1, Part Title).

Part Subtitle: A subtitle after a part subtitle.

Poem: A single line of poetry ("April is the cruelest month").

Poem Heading: Heading before a poem; usually the poem's title ("The Waste Land").

Poem Subhead: Subheading between stanzas of a poem ("What the Thunder Said").

*Poem First: First line of a poem (possibly indented).

*Poem First NI: First line of a poem (possibly not indented).

*Poem Start: Starting line of any poetry stanza but the first (possibly indented).

*Poem Start NI: Starting line of any poetry stanza but the first (possibly not indented).

*Poem Middle: Middle line of any poetry stanza (possibly indented). The stanza may include more than one of these.

*Poem Middle NI: Middle line of any poetry stanza (possibly not indented). The stanza may include more than one of these.

*Poem End: Ending line of any poetry stanza but the last (possibly indented).

*Poem End NI: Ending line of any poetry stanza but the last (possibly not indented).

*Poem Last: Last line of a poem (possibly indented).

*Poem Last NI: Last line of a poem (possibly not indented).

Poem Source: Citation following a poem (usually someone's name).

Pull Quote: A quotation set apart from the body text for emphasis.

Running Head First: First running head in a chapter, where such a running head needs different formatting from the other running heads (it may be centered, for example, while the others are left- and right-justified).

*Running Head Even: Running head on a left-hand (verso), even-numbered page.

*Running Head Odd: Running head on a right-hand (recto), odd-numbered page.

Sidebar Text: Text in a separate text box used as a direction, additional information, or tip.

Sidebar Head: Heading for sidebar text.

Table Heading: Heading that introduces a table.

Table Subhead: Subheading in a table.

Table Subsubhead: Subsubheading in a table.

Table Text: Text of a table.

Readers Write

Eric Fletcher:

Wow, your style list would be a great reference for parts of books, let alone for managing the format!

I have a couple that we use that you might also consider.

Photo box   Used to identify an image by its file name or reference number. I usually have this set up in red text with a red box around it because if you zoom out (CTRL + Scrollwheel), they are very visible even when the rest of the copy turns to black lines. When we are trying to "populate" a book with images, it can be a handy way to see if there are any gaping holes. If we are doing the layout with the images in Word, this is handy because I can put in the file name, then convert it to the includepicture field after we've dealt with the text of the file. If we are providing the images, we can provide information that helps in the layout (file name on CD, pixel dimensions & colour depth; identity and format of original art...)

Editorial note   Used for a note to the editor (or reviewer) about something we came across during the layout or editing. We have it set the copy in a light green filled box in Arial Narrow type so it is very visible on screen and quite visible if printed. It is also easy to spot in a very reduced view (as above) but I also have an associated button that finds the next "Editorial note" style to be able to quickly review them. The editorial note has been much more useful to us than Word's comments or review functions as many of our documents get sent out as paper copies. As well, many are being reviewed by people whose first language is not English (or French) so we often find ourselves having to be "diplomatic" in querying the intended meaning. (Some of the content is very technical so we cannot presume to be subject matter experts even if we see something that is clearly not correct—I'm sure you've had this experience now and then . . .) This style enables us to copy a sentence and rework it as a "suggestion." If they agree, they don't have to write it themselves—and we don't have to try to decipher their writing!

Bill Rubidge:

Eric Fletcher explains that he uses an "Editorial Note" style. We use something similar, but the style is called "Open Issue". (Actually, the name has a prefix, so that all the styles we use are sorted together in the list and distinguishable from styles that may come from other templates or users). The style highlights items with color, as Eric's does, but we do one thing more.

At the end of our documents, we insert a page break and then type a title "Open Issues". Below that, we generate a TOC based only the Open Issue style (not any headings—TOC field {TOC \t "wbrOpenIssue,1"}). This gives us a complete list of these open issues for the entire document, to ensure that none are overlooked.

By the way, we also insert these Open Issue paragraphs (which are sometimes just queries) ABOVE the item in question, and the Open Issue style has the paragraph set to "keep with next". This helps make the page number refs in the Open Issue TOC more accurate.

If you really want to get complicated, on multi-file projects (we deal with about 40 files per book), it may be easier to just extract the open issues from the file and put them into another document. For now, I just do this using the open issue TOC at the end of each file, but have a macro that copies it (fields unlinked) to the clipboard and then opens up our Open Issue file (in Excel, for easier sorting). Based on posts in the Word PC listserve, I think involving Maggie Seneca, I think you could also harvest all the Open Issue items in the file and automatically write them to another file (rather than the manual paste we're using).

You might refer to the macro that Bryan and Pieter helped Eve Golden with, back in the Daily Word Tips list. I think the last posts about it were from November 20. That macro searches for text highlighted in a certain way, and copies all that text and appends it to a separate file.

REBECCA EVANS:

I have been designing and typesetting books for a living since 1976. Being able to use style tags in today's programs is certainly a blessing compared to keeping a spec sheet beside you so you can hand key specs as you re-type a book from a typemarked manuscript.

My comment on the style naming issue is that I have found I do not need list tags that add space after the list (NL End), just the tag to begin the list and for the interior paragraphs. All I need after lists, boxes, and the like, are two Body Text tags with added space above them, one with a paragraph indent and one without, because any paragraph style other than Body Text—heads, extracts, boxes, summaries, other lists—already includes space above.

Of course this assumes that spacing is consistent within a design so that you don't have +12' below a BL and +6' below an NL. And, I realize this may not be applicable to documents other than books. However, in my experience with textbooks, I have found those two extra Body Text styles to be all the "exit" styles I need.

On another note, I use two character style names because that lets me reduce the width of the style tag window (I use Ventura Publisher and keep the style list docked and open on screen), leaving more screen width to display page spreads. This is not an issue if you use a style drop down menu but I thought I'd throw in my two cents on that one too.

ROHN SOLECKI:

I also have a favorite style you might want to pass on. Although it may not be useful to the publishing industry, it is handy for internal documentation in companies that still use "green screen" computer terminals. Green screen terminals are the old style fixed pitch font, by default 24 line by 80 character displays (but optionally up to 27 lines by 132 characters).

Rather than doing a graphic screen capture I do a Edit / Select All, Edit / Copy to capture the text, paste to Word, then apply my "Screen Print" paragraph style to reasonably simulate the appearance of text on the computer terminal. This style has 3 main advantages over pasting a graphic screen capture:

- It uses orders of magnitude less space, which is important if you have lots of screens to capture.
- It is editable, so if something on screen changes you don't have redo the capture.
- Since it is editable, it is easy to apply character formatting like highlighter or font colors to highlight specific sections (without having to use a separate graphics program).

DETAILS OF SCREEN PRINT PARAGRAPH STYLE: Paragraph Formatting - Flush Left, Keep with Next, Keep lines together, Border: box (single line), Shading: 5%, Indent: Hanging 0.25 Right 0", Widow and Orphan Control. Font Formatting - Courier, 10 pt, Condensed 0.5 pt.

Reasons for choices:

- The Box Border and 5% Shading simulate the look of the screen.
- Keep Lines together and Keep with next ensure that the whole screen capture stays on same page.
- Hanging indent is optional if a line wraps for some reason, for example, capturing from a 132-character display.
- Courier is fixed pitch so characters line up as they did on screen.
- 10 pt Condensed 0.5pt so that an 80-character line will fit on a page with reasonable margins (less than the default 1.5" both sides) without wrapping.

STEPHEN RILEY:

I used to do something similar to Rohn Solecki's tip "back in the day." Another great advantage is being able to cheat and edit the data you have captured. It's sometimes a heck of a lot easier to do this than to setup meaningful data in whatever application you are documenting. As an extra snippet, this was when I was documenting green-screen Unix apps. Screen capture was via a terminal emulator (Reflection?) running on a PC. For report files, print to .txt file and FTP from server to PC. I used a similar style definition tweaked for 132 chars and using a landscape page.

LEANNE BAIRD:

The paragraph naming scheme below is a pain to implement because legacy documents may need to have their styles replaced, but we bit the bullet and did it in one team I was on just because it is *such* an elegant solution—so elegant that I've used it at every new company since we did the first one, and so have many of the other team members in *their* subsequent assignments. (Note: I've never used a complete template that didn't have more than 100 and less than 120 styles. Seems always to come out about the same regardless of the subject matter or document type!)

1. Rename each paragraph (and character) style with a two-letter prefix followed by a space. Begin master and reference page styles with z or x +[letter or number] to send them to the bottom of the list.
2. Tag paragraphs from the keyboard by pressing F9, entering the prefix, and pressing Enter (or you may need to press one or two down arrows, see below). The desired style is applied.

This strategy makes the shortcuts easy to memorize through frequent use because we try hard to be logical, with the exception of "aa body," so named because it can always float to the top of the list. If you're forced to scroll for something, at least you can get close with F9+one key.

aa	body
b1	bullet 1st level
b2	bullet 2nd level
bp	bullet para
bp	bullet para 2 (F9+bp+Down Arrow)
h1	heading 1
h2	heading 2
tb	table body
th	table heading
t1	table bullet 1
tp	table bullet 1 para
s1	step 1
s2	subsequent steps
zc	Chapter name
zn	Chapter number

I am about finished with a Word template with customized style and table-insert toolbars so that our non-writer internal customers can easily use the same styles to produce consistently styled documents. These documents then (ZIP!) import right into FrameMaker and lay themselves out with only minor nudges for print and PDF, and (ZIP!) right out through WebWorks Publisher to reformat as online Help systems.

By the way, for organizations looking toward the XML future, these are the considerations in style naming according to the quick-and-dirty search I did. Some of the major databases (SQL, Oracle, Sybase) do not support underscores in XML tag names, and for SQL processing XML tag names must start with two alpha characters. Of course, use no special characters, and this includes hyphens. Mixed case would seem to be OK, but the suggestion is that all the style names be mixed case if some are. (I can't imagine why this would make a difference, but who knows what lurks inside those database engines.) Also, in the XML naming specs, titles should not be longer than 30 characters for Sybase and Oracle, 18 for Informix.

Roger Shuttleworth:

Some folks suggest that you should keep paragraph (and character) format names to one word. One reason for this is that XML tags cannot contain spaces, and you may want to (ZIP!) them across to XML in some way in the future, perhaps as attributes. So I use an underscore rather than a space, and run the words together, such as RI_ReferenceInfo.

Steve Hudson:

Here are my standard style lists for a variety of publication types, including formatting for the styles:

Publish Type: Draft   Body Text: Generic + Font: Arial, Hyphenate, Outline numbered, Tabs: 0 cm

Body Text C: Generic + Font: Arial, Centered, Hyphenate

Body Text R: Generic + Font: Arial, Flush Right, Hyphenate

Code: Default Paragraph Font + Font: Courier New, 10 pt, Underline color: Auto, No Proofing, Raised 1 pt, Font color: Auto, English (Australia), No effect, Pattern: Clear

Copyright: Generic + Font: Arial, 7 pt, Space before 0 pt after 0 pt, Hyphenate

Default Paragraph Font: The font of the underlying paragraph style + English (Australia)

Emphasis: Default Paragraph Font + Font: Bold, Not Italic, Underline color: Auto, Font color: Auto, No effect, Pattern: Clear

FollowedHyperlink: Default Paragraph Font + Font: Not Italic, Underline, Underline color: Auto, No Proofing, Font color: Gray-50%, No effect, Pattern: Clear

Footer: Header +

Generic: Font: Times New Roman, 10 pt, English (Australia), Kern at 10 pt, Flush left, Line spacing single, Space before 3 pt after 3 pt, Widow/orphan control, Keep lines together, Suppress line numbers, Don't hyphenate

Glossary: Default Paragraph Font + Underline color: Auto, Font color: Auto, No effect, Pattern: Clear

Header: Generic + Font: Arial, Tabs: 7.3 cm centered, 14.64 cm right flush

Heading 1: Heading 4 + Font: 26 pt, Indent: Hanging 0.74 cm, Space before 18 pt after 21 pt, Level 1, Outline numbered, Tabs: 0.74 cm

Heading 1 No TOC: Generic + Font: Verdana, 26 pt, Bold, Space before 18 pt after 21 pt, Keep with next, Not Keep lines together

Heading 2: Heading 4 + Font: 22 pt, Indent: Hanging 0.74 cm, Space before 18 pt after 15 pt, Level 2, Outline numbered, Tabs: 0.74 cm

Heading 2 No TOC: Generic + Font: Verdana, 22 pt, Bold, Space before 18 pt after 15 pt, Keep with next, Not Keep lines together

Heading 3: Heading 4 + Font: 16 pt, Indent: Hanging 0.74 cm, Space before 18 pt after 15 pt, Level 3, Outline numbered, Tabs: 0.74 cm

Heading 4: Generic + Font: Verdana, 12 pt, Bold, Space before 6 pt after 6 pt, Keep with next, Not Keep lines together, Level 4

Heading 5: Heading 4 + Space before 3 pt, Level 5

Heading 6: Heading 4 + Space before 3 pt, Level 6

Heading 7: Heading 4 + Space before 3 pt, Level 7

Heading 8: Heading 4 + Space before 3 pt, Level 8

Heading 9: Heading 4 + Space before 3 pt, Level 9

Heading-table-centred: Heading-table-left + Centered

Heading-table-left: Generic + Font: Arial Narrow, 13 pt, Bold, Hyphenate

Heading-table-right: Heading-table-left + Flush Right

Hyperlink: Default Paragraph Font + Font: Not Italic, Underline, Underline color: Auto, No Proofing, Font color: Blue, No effect, Pattern: Clear

Index 1: Generic + Font: Arial, Hyphenate

Index 2: Generic + Font: Arial, Indent: Left 0.74 cm First 0.74 cm, Hyphenate

Index 3: Generic + Font: Arial, Indent: Left 1.48 cm First 1.48 cm, Hyphenate

Input: Default Paragraph Font + Font: Tahoma, 9 pt, Bold, Underline color: Auto, No Proofing, Font color: Auto, No effect, Pattern: Clear

KeyPress: Default Paragraph Font + Font: Tahoma, 9 pt, Bold, Underline color: Auto, Not Small caps, All caps, No Proofing, Font color: Auto, No effect, Pattern: Clear

List Bullet: Font: Arial, 10 pt, English (Australia), Kern at 10 pt, Indent: Hanging 0.74 cm Flush left, Line spacing single, Space before 3 pt after 3 pt, Widow/orphan control, Keep lines together, Suppress line numbers, Outline numbered, Tabs: 0.74 cm

List Number: Font: Arial, 10 pt, English (Australia), Kern at 10 pt, Indent: Hanging 0.74 cm Flush left, Line spacing single, Space before 3 pt after 3 pt, Widow/orphan control, Keep lines together, Suppress line numbers, Outline numbered, Tabs: 0.74 cm

List Number Outline: Font: Arial, 10 pt, English (Australia), Kern at 10 pt, Indent: Hanging 0.74 cm Flush left, Line spacing single, Space before 3 pt after 3 pt, Widow/orphan control, Keep lines together, Suppress line numbers, Outline numbered, Tabs: 0.74 cm

Microline: Normal + Font: 1 pt, Font color: White

Normal: Font: Arial, 10 pt, English (Australia), Kern at 10 pt, Flush left, Line spacing single, Widow/orphan control, Keep lines together, Suppress line numbers

Output: Default Paragraph Font + Font: Verdana, 9 pt, Underline color: Auto, No Proofing, Font color: Auto, No effect, Pattern: Clear

Page Number: Default Paragraph Font + Font: Arial, Bold, Underline color: Auto, No Proofing, Font color: Auto, No effect, Pattern: Clear

Subtitle: Title + Font: 18 pt, Space before 12 pt, Keep lines together

Terminal Screen: Generic + Font: Courier, 8 pt, No Proofing, Indent: Left 0.55 cm Right 0.55 cm, Space before 1 pt after 0 pt, Border: Top(Single solid line, Auto, 1 pt Line width), Bottom(Single solid line, Auto, 1 pt Line width), Left(Single solid line, Auto, 1 ...

TextBox: Generic + Font: Arial Narrow, Bold, Space before 0 pt after 0 pt, Hyphenate

TextBox C: TextBox + Centered

TextBox R: TextBox + Flush Right

Title: Generic + Font: Tahoma, 36 pt, Bold, Centered, Space before 72 pt after 12 pt, Not Keep lines together

TOC 1: Generic + Font: Verdana, 12 pt, Bold, No Proofing, Space before 18 pt, Keep with next, Not Keep lines together, Tabs: 0 cm, 14.64 cm right flush ...

TOC 2: TOC 1 + Font: Not Bold, Space before 3 pt after 0 pt, Keep lines together

TOC 3: TOC 2 + Font: 10 pt, Indent: Left 0.74 cm

TOC 4: TOC 3 + Indent: Left 1.48 cm, Space after 3 pt

TOC 5: TOC 2 + Font: 10 pt, Space after 3 pt

TOC 6: TOC 5 +

TOC 7: TOC 5 +

TOC 8: TOC 5 +

Version: Subtitle + Font: 14 pt, Not Bold, Space before 6 pt after 3 pt

PUBLISH TYPE: HELP   Body Text: Generic + Font: Arial, 12 pt, Hyphenate, Outline numbered, Tabs: 0 cm

Body Text C: Generic + Font: Arial, 12 pt, Centered, Hyphenate

Body Text R: Generic + Font: Arial, 12 pt, Flush Right, Hyphenate

Code: Default Paragraph Font + Font: Courier New, 12 pt, Underline color: Auto, No Proofing, Raised 1 pt, Font color: Auto, No effect, Pattern: Clear

Copyright: Generic + Font: Arial, 7 pt, Space before 0 pt after 0 pt, Hyphenate

Default Paragraph Font: The font of the underlying paragraph style + English (Australia)

Emphasis: Default Paragraph Font + Font: Bold, Not Italic, Underline color: Auto, Font color: Auto, No effect, Pattern: Clear

FollowedHyperlink: Default Paragraph Font + Font: Not Italic, Underline, Underline color: Auto, No Proofing, Font color: Gray-50%, No effect, Pattern: Clear

Footer: Header +

Generic: Font: Times New Roman, 10 pt, English (Australia), Kern at 10 pt, Flush left, Line spacing single, Space before 3 pt after 3 pt, Widow/orphan control, Suppress line numbers, Don't hyphenate

Glossary: Default Paragraph Font + Underline color: Auto, Font color: Auto, No effect, Pattern: Clear

Header: Generic + Font: Arial, Tabs: 7.3 cm centered, 14.64 cm right flush

Heading 1: Heading 4 + Font: 28 pt, Space before 18 pt after 21 pt, Level 1

Heading 1 No TOC: Generic + Font: Verdana, 28 pt, Bold, Space before 18 pt after 21 pt, Keep with next, Keep lines together

Heading 2: Heading 4 + Font: 24 pt, Space before 18 pt after 15 pt, Level 2

Heading 2 No TOC: Generic + Font: Verdana, 24 pt, Bold, Space before 18 pt after 15 pt, Keep with next, Keep lines together

Heading 3: Heading 4 + Font: 18 pt, Space before 18 pt after 15 pt, Level 3

Heading 4: Generic + Font: Verdana, 14 pt, Bold, Space before 6 pt after 6 pt, Keep with next, Keep lines together, Level 4

Heading 5: Heading 4 + Space before 3 pt, Level 5

Heading 6: Heading 4 + Space before 3 pt, Level 6

Heading 7: Heading 4 + Space before 3 pt, Level 7

Heading 8: Heading 4 + Space before 3 pt, Level 8

Heading 9: Heading 4 + Space before 3 pt, Level 9

Heading-table-centred: Heading-table-left + Centered

Heading-table-left: Generic + Font: Arial Narrow, 13 pt, Bold, Keep lines together, Hyphenate

Heading-table-right: Heading-table-left + Flush Right

Hyperlink: Default Paragraph Font + Font: Not Italic, Underline, Underline color: Auto, No Proofing, Font color: Blue, No effect, Pattern: Clear

Index 1: Generic + Font: Arial, 12 pt, Hyphenate

Index 2: Generic + Font: Arial, 12 pt, Indent: Left 0.74 cm First 0.74 cm, Hyphenate

Index 3: Generic + Font: Arial, 12 pt, Indent: Left 1.48 cm First 1.48 cm, Hyphenate

Input: Default Paragraph Font + Font: Tahoma, 11 pt, Bold, Underline color: Auto, No Proofing, Font color: Auto, No effect, Pattern: Clear

KeyPress: Default Paragraph Font + Font: Tahoma, 11 pt, Bold, Underline color: Auto, Not Small caps, All caps, No Proofing, Font color: Auto, No effect, Pattern: Clear

List Bullet: Font: Arial, 12 pt, English (Australia), Kern at 10 pt, Indent: Hanging 0.74 cm Flush left, Line spacing single, Space before 3 pt after 3 pt, Widow/orphan control, Suppress line numbers, Outline numbered, Tabs: 0.74 cm

List Number: Font: Arial, 12 pt, English (Australia), Kern at 10 pt, Indent: Hanging 0.74 cm Flush left, Line spacing single, Space before 3 pt after 3 pt, Widow/orphan control, Suppress line numbers, Outline numbered, Tabs: 0.74 cm

List Number Outline: Font: Arial, 12 pt, English (Australia), Kern at 10 pt, Indent: Hanging 0.74 cm Flush left, Line spacing single, Space before 3 pt after 3 pt, Widow/orphan control, Suppress line numbers, Outline numbered, Tabs: 0.74 cm

Microline: Normal + Font: 1 pt, Font color: White

Normal: Font: Arial, 12 pt, English (Australia), Kern at 10 pt, Flush left, Line spacing single, Widow/orphan control, Suppress line numbers

Output: Default Paragraph Font + Font: Verdana, 11 pt, Underline color: Auto, No Proofing, Font color: Auto, No effect, Pattern: Clear

Page Number: Default Paragraph Font + Font: Arial, Bold, Underline color: Auto, No Proofing, Font color: Auto, No effect, Pattern: Clear

Subtitle: Title + Font: 18 pt, Space before 12 pt

Terminal Screen: Generic + Font: Courier, 8 pt, No Proofing, Indent: Left 0.55 cm Right 0.55 cm, Space before 1 pt after 0 pt, Border: Top(Single solid line, Auto, 1 pt Line width), Bottom(Single solid line, Auto, 1 pt Line width), Left(Single solid line, Auto, 1 ...

TextBox: Generic + Font: Arial Narrow, Bold, Space before 0 pt after 0 pt, Hyphenate

TextBox C: TextBox + Centered

TextBox R: TextBox + Flush Right

Title: Generic + Font: Tahoma, 36 pt, Bold, Centered, Space before 72 pt after 12 pt

TOC 1: Generic + Font: Verdana, 12 pt, Bold, No Proofing, Space before 18 pt, Keep with next, Tabs: 0 cm, 14.64 cm right flush ...

TOC 2: TOC 1 + Font: 10 pt, Not Bold, Proof Text, Space before 3 pt after 0 pt, Not Keep with next, Tabs:Not at 0 cm, 14.64 cm

TOC 3: TOC 2 + Indent: Left 0.74 cm

TOC 4: TOC 3 + Indent: Left 1.48 cm, Space after 3 pt

TOC 5: TOC 2 + Space after 3 pt

TOC 6: TOC 5 +

TOC 7: TOC 5 +

TOC 8: TOC 5 +

Version: Subtitle + Font: 14 pt, Not Bold, Space before 6 pt after 3 pt

PUBLISH TYPE: PRODUCT   Body Text: Generic + Font: Arial, Hyphenate, Outline numbered, Tabs: 0 cm

Body Text C: Generic + Font: Arial, Centered, Hyphenate

Body Text R: Generic + Font: Arial, Flush Right, Hyphenate

Code: Default Paragraph Font + Font: Courier New, 10 pt, Underline color: Auto, No Proofing, Raised 1 pt, Font color: Auto, No effect, Pattern: Clear

Copyright: Generic + Font: Arial, 7 pt, Space before 0 pt after 0 pt, Hyphenate

Default Paragraph Font: The font of the underlying paragraph style + English (Australia)

Emphasis: Default Paragraph Font + Font: Bold, Not Italic, Underline color: Auto, Font color: Auto, No effect, Pattern: Clear

FollowedHyperlink: Default Paragraph Font + Font: Not Italic, Underline, Underline color: Auto, No Proofing, Font color: Gray-50%, No effect, Pattern: Clear

Footer: Header +

Generic: Font: Times New Roman, 10 pt, English (Australia), Kern at 10 pt, Flush left, Line spacing single, Space before 3 pt after 3 pt, Widow/orphan control, Keep lines together, Suppress line numbers, Don't hyphenate

Glossary: Default Paragraph Font + Underline color: Auto, Font color: Auto, No effect, Pattern: Clear

Header: Generic + Font: Arial, Tabs: 7.3 cm centered, 14.64 cm right flush

Heading 1: Heading 4 + Font: 26 pt, Space before 18 pt after 21 pt, Level 1, Numbered, Tabs: 0 cm

Heading 1 No TOC: Generic + Font: Verdana, 26 pt, Bold, Space before 18 pt after 21 pt, Keep with next, Not Keep lines together

Heading 2: Heading 4 + Font: 22 pt, Space before 18 pt after 15 pt, Level 2

Heading 2 No TOC: Generic + Font: Verdana, 22 pt, Bold, Space before 18 pt after 15 pt, Keep with next, Not Keep lines together

Heading 3: Heading 4 + Font: 16 pt, Space before 18 pt after 15 pt, Level 3

Heading 4: Generic + Font: Verdana, 12 pt, Bold, Space before 6 pt after 6 pt, Keep with next, Not Keep lines together, Level 4

Heading 5: Heading 4 + Space before 3 pt, Level 5

Heading 6: Heading 4 + Space before 3 pt, Level 6

Heading 7: Heading 4 + Space before 3 pt, Level 7

Heading 8: Heading 4 + Space before 3 pt, Level 8

Heading 9: Heading 4 + Space before 3 pt, Level 9

Heading-table-centred: Heading-table-left + Centered

Heading-table-left: Generic + Font: Arial Narrow, 13 pt, Bold, Hyphenate

Heading-table-right: Heading-table-left + Flush Right

Hyperlink: Default Paragraph Font + Font: Not Italic, Underline, Underline color: Auto, No Proofing, Font color: Blue, No effect, Pattern: Clear

Index 1: Generic + Font: Arial, Hyphenate

Index 2: Generic + Font: Arial, Indent: Left 0.74 cm First 0.74 cm, Hyphenate

Index 3: Generic + Font: Arial, Indent: Left 1.48 cm First 1.48 cm, Hyphenate

Input: Default Paragraph Font + Font: Tahoma, 9 pt, Bold, Underline color: Auto, No Proofing, Font color: Auto, No effect, Pattern: Clear

KeyPress: Default Paragraph Font + Font: Tahoma, 9 pt, Bold, Underline color: Auto, Not Small caps, All caps, No Proofing, Font color: Auto, No effect, Pattern: Clear

List Bullet: Font: Arial, 10 pt, English (Australia), Kern at 10 pt, Indent: Hanging 0.74 cm Flush left, Line spacing single, Space before 3 pt after 3 pt, Widow/orphan control, Keep lines together, Suppress line numbers, Outline numbered, Tabs: 0.74 cm

List Number: Font: Arial, 10 pt, English (Australia), Kern at 10 pt, Indent: Hanging 0.74 cm Flush left, Line spacing single, Space before 3 pt after 3 pt, Widow/orphan control, Keep lines together, Suppress line numbers, Outline numbered, Tabs: 0.74 cm

List Number Outline: Font: Arial, 10 pt, English (Australia), Kern at 10 pt, Indent: Hanging 0.74 cm Flush left, Line spacing single, Space before 3 pt after 3 pt, Widow/orphan control, Keep lines together, Suppress line numbers, Outline numbered, Tabs: 0.74 cm

Microline: Normal + Font: 1 pt, Font color: White

Normal: Font: Arial, 10 pt, English (Australia), Kern at 10 pt, Flush left, Line spacing single, Widow/orphan control, Keep lines together, Suppress line numbers

Output: Default Paragraph Font + Font: Verdana, 9 pt, Underline color: Auto, No Proofing, Font color: Auto, No effect, Pattern: Clear

Page Number: Default Paragraph Font + Font: Arial, Bold, Underline color: Auto, No Proofing, Font color: Auto, No effect, Pattern: Clear

Subtitle: Title + Font: 18 pt, Space before 12 pt, Keep lines together

Terminal Screen: Generic + Font: Courier, 8 pt, No Proofing, Indent: Left 0.55 cm Right 0.55 cm, Space before 1 pt after 0 pt, Border: Top(Single solid line, Auto, 1 pt Line width), Bottom(Single solid line, Auto, 1 pt Line width), Left(Single solid line, Auto, 1 ...

TextBox: Generic + Font: Arial Narrow, Bold, Space before 0 pt after 0 pt, Hyphenate

TextBox C: TextBox + Centered

TextBox R: TextBox + Flush Right

Title: Generic + Font: Tahoma, 36 pt, Bold, Centered, Space before 72 pt after 12 pt, Not Keep lines together

TOC 1: Generic + Font: Verdana, 12 pt, Bold, No Proofing, Space before 18 pt, Keep with next, Not Keep lines together, Tabs: 0 cm, 14.64 cm right flush ...

TOC 2: TOC 1 + Font: 10 pt, Not Bold, Proof Text, Space before 3 pt after 0 pt, Not Keep with next, Keep lines together, Tabs:Not at 0 cm, 14.64 cm

TOC 3: TOC 2 + Indent: Left 0.74 cm

TOC 4: TOC 3 + Indent: Left 1.48 cm, Space after 3 pt

TOC 5: TOC 2 + Space after 3 pt

TOC 6: TOC 5 +

TOC 7: TOC 5 +

TOC 8: TOC 5 +

Version: Subtitle + Font: 14 pt, Not Bold, Space before 6 pt after 3 pt

PUBLISH TYPE: README   Body Text: Generic + Font: Arial, Hyphenate, Outline numbered, Tabs: 0 cm

Body Text C: Generic + Font: Arial, Centered, Hyphenate

Body Text R: Generic + Font: Arial, Flush Right, Hyphenate

Code: Default Paragraph Font + Font: Courier New, 10 pt, Underline color: Auto, No Proofing, Raised 1 pt, Font color: Auto, No effect, Pattern: Clear

Copyright: Generic + Font: Arial, 7 pt, Centered, Space before 0 pt after 0 pt, Hyphenate

Default Paragraph Font: The font of the underlying paragraph style + English (Australia)

Emphasis: Default Paragraph Font + Font: Bold, Not Italic, Underline color: Auto, Font color: Auto, No effect, Pattern: Clear

FollowedHyperlink: Default Paragraph Font + Font: Not Italic, Underline, Underline color: Auto, No Proofing, Font color: Gray-50%, No effect, Pattern: Clear

Footer: Header +

Generic: Font: Times New Roman, 10 pt, English (Australia), Kern at 10 pt, Flush left, Line spacing single, Space before 3 pt after 3 pt, Widow/orphan control, Keep lines together, Suppress line numbers, Don't hyphenate

Glossary: Default Paragraph Font + Underline color: Auto, Font color: Auto, No effect, Pattern: Clear

Header: Generic + Font: Arial, Tabs: 7.3 cm centered, 14.64 cm right flush

Heading 1: Heading 4 + Font: 15 pt, Space before 18 pt after 9 pt, Level 1, Numbered, Tabs: 0 cm

Heading 1 No TOC: Generic + Font: Verdana, 15 pt, Bold, Space before 18 pt after 9 pt, Keep with next, Not Keep lines together

Heading 2: Heading 4 + Font: 12 pt, Space before 18 pt, Level 2

Heading 2 No TOC: Generic + Font: Verdana, 12 pt, Bold, Space before 18 pt, Keep with next, Not Keep lines together

Heading 3: Heading 4 + Space before 18 pt, Level 3

Heading 4: Generic + Font: Verdana, Bold, Space before 6 pt, Keep with next, Not Keep lines together, Level 4

Heading 5: Heading 4 + Space before 3 pt after 6 pt, Level 5

Heading 6: Heading 4 + Space before 3 pt after 6 pt, Level 6

Heading 7: Heading 4 + Space before 3 pt after 6 pt, Level 7

Heading 8: Heading 4 + Space before 3 pt after 6 pt, Level 8

Heading 9: Heading 4 + Space before 3 pt after 6 pt, Level 9

Heading-table-centred: Heading-table-left + Centered

Heading-table-left: Generic + Font: Arial Narrow, 13 pt, Bold, Hyphenate

Heading-table-right: Heading-table-left + Flush Right

Hyperlink: Default Paragraph Font + Font: Not Italic, Underline, Underline color: Auto, No Proofing, Font color: Blue, No effect, Pattern: Clear

Index 1: Generic + Font: Arial, Hyphenate

Index 2: Generic + Font: Arial, Indent: Left 0.74 cm First 0.74 cm, Hyphenate

Index 3: Generic + Font: Arial, Indent: Left 1.48 cm First 1.48 cm, Hyphenate

Input: Default Paragraph Font + Font: Tahoma, 9 pt, Bold, Underline color: Auto, No Proofing, Font color: Auto, No effect, Pattern: Clear

KeyPress: Default Paragraph Font + Font: Tahoma, 9 pt, Bold, Underline color: Auto, Not Small caps, All caps, No Proofing, Font color: Auto, No effect, Pattern: Clear

List Bullet: Font: Arial, 10 pt, English (Australia), Kern at 10 pt, Indent: Hanging 0.74 cm Flush left, Line spacing single, Space before 3 pt after 3 pt, Widow/orphan control, Keep lines together, Suppress line numbers, Outline numbered, Tabs: 0.74 cm

List Number: Font: Arial, 10 pt, English (Australia), Kern at 10 pt, Indent: Hanging 0.74 cm Flush left, Line spacing single, Space before 3 pt after 3 pt, Widow/orphan control, Keep lines together, Suppress line numbers, Outline numbered, Tabs: 0.74 cm

List Number Outline: Font: Arial, 10 pt, English (Australia), Kern at 10 pt, Indent: Hanging 0.74 cm Flush left, Line spacing single, Space before 3 pt after 3 pt, Widow/orphan control, Keep lines together, Suppress line numbers, Outline numbered, Tabs: 0.74 cm

Microline: Normal + Font: 1 pt, Font color: White

Normal: Font: Arial, 10 pt, English (Australia), Kern at 10 pt, Flush left, Line spacing single, Widow/orphan control, Keep lines together, Suppress line numbers

Output: Default Paragraph Font + Font: Verdana, 9 pt, Underline color: Auto, No Proofing, Font color: Auto, No effect, Pattern: Clear

Page Number: Default Paragraph Font + Font: Arial, Bold, Underline color: Auto, No Proofing, Font color: Auto, No effect, Pattern: Clear

Subtitle: Title + Keep lines together

Terminal Screen: Generic + Font: Courier, 8 pt, No Proofing, Indent: Left 0.55 cm Right 0.55 cm, Space before 1 pt after 0 pt, Border: Top(Single solid line, Auto, 1 pt Line width), Bottom(Single solid line, Auto, 1 pt Line width), Left(Single solid line, Auto, 1 ...

TextBox: Generic + Font: Arial Narrow, Bold, Space before 0 pt after 0 pt, Hyphenate

TextBox C: TextBox + Centered

TextBox R: TextBox + Flush Right

Title: Generic + Font: Tahoma, 15 pt, Bold, Centered, Space before 0 pt after 0 pt, Not Keep lines together

TOC 1: Generic + Font: Verdana, 12 pt, Bold, No Proofing, Keep with next, Not Keep lines together, Tabs: 0 cm, 14.64 cm right flush ...

TOC 2: TOC 1 + Font: 10 pt, Not Bold, Proof Text, Indent: Left 0.74 cm, Space before 0 pt after 0 pt, Not Keep with next, Keep lines together, Tabs:Not at 0 cm, 14.64 cm

TOC 3: TOC 2 + Indent: Left 1.48 cm

TOC 4: TOC 3 + Space before 3 pt after 3 pt

TOC 5: TOC 2 + Indent: Left 0 cm, Space before 3 pt after 3 pt

TOC 6: TOC 5 +

TOC 7: TOC 5 +

TOC 8: TOC 5 +

Version: Subtitle + Font: 10 pt, Not Bold, Space after 3 pt

Deleting Unused Styles

I frequently edit books that are compilations of articles by various authors. Some know how to use Word pretty well; others don't have a clue. Those in the latter category either don't use paragraph styles or create styles that aren't needed. After I've fixed and consistently applied the styles I need, I like to get rid of the other unused styles the authors have created. The following macro seems to do the job quite well:

```
Sub DeleteUnusedStyles()
For Each sty In ActiveDocument.Styles
If sty.BuiltIn = False Then
If sty.InUse = False Then
sty.Delete
Else
Selection.HomeKey Unit:=wdStory
Selection.Find.ClearFormatting
Selection.Find.Style = ActiveDocument.Styles(sty)
With Selection.Find
.Text = ""
.Replacement.Text = ""
.Forward = True
.Wrap = wdFindStop
.Format = True
.MatchCase = False
.MatchWholeWord = False
.MatchWildcards = False
.MatchSoundsLike = False
.MatchAllWordForms = False
End With
Selection.Find.Execute
If Selection.Find.Found = False Then sty.Delete
End If
End If
Next sty
Selection.HomeKey Unit:=wdStory
End Sub
```

You'd think the macro could be a lot shorter:

```
For Each sty In ActiveDocument.Styles
If sty.BuiltIn = False Then 'Ignore built-in styles
If sty.InUse = False Then sty.Delete
End If
Next sty
```

But Microsoft Word, ever uncooperative, considers any style that has *ever* been used in a document to be "in use," even if the text formatted by that style has long since been deleted. That means a style can be "in use" even if it's not applied to text anywhere in the document. So, to see if a style is *really* in use, we have to search for text using that style. If no such text is found, then we know that the style really isn't in use and can be deleted.

Note that the macro completely ignores Word's built-in styles, since these *can't* be deleted.

Style Macros

While I was writing the previous article, I also wrote a couple of other style macros.

The first macro, ListCustomStyles, lists (at the end of the document) any custom styles in that document. If you need to know what weird styles your client is using, this macro will tell you what they are.

The second macro, ListStylesInUse, lists (at the end of the document) any style being used in that document.

```
Sub ListCustomStyles()
For Each sty In ActiveDocument.Styles
If sty.BuiltIn = False Then
Selection.EndKey Unit:=wdStory
Selection.InsertAfter Text:=sty.NameLocal
Selection.InsertParagraphAfter
End If
Next sty
End Sub


Sub ListStylesInUse()
For Each sty In ActiveDocument.Styles
If sty.InUse = True Then
Selection.HomeKey Unit:=wdStory
Selection.Find.ClearFormatting
Selection.Find.Style = ActiveDocument.Styles(sty)
With Selection.Find
.Text = ""
.Replacement.Text = ""
.Forward = True
.Wrap = wdFindStop
.Format = True
.MatchCase = False
.MatchWholeWord = False
.MatchWildcards = False
.MatchSoundsLike = False
.MatchAllWordForms = False
End With
Selection.Find.Execute
If Selection.Find.Found = True Then
Selection.EndKey Unit:=wdStory
Selection.InsertAfter Text:=sty.NameLocal
Selection.InsertParagraphAfter
End If
End If
Next sty
End Sub
```

Readers Write

Donna Payne:

I have a variation of the list styles in use macro. This is from my company's latest book, *Word 2003 for Law Firms*.

```
Sub DisplayAllStylesInUseAtInsertionPoint()
Dim oStyle As Style
Dim oRange As Range
Set oRange = Selection.Range
oRange.Collapse wdCollapseStart
For Each oStyle In ActiveDocument.Styles
If oStyle.InUse Then
oRange.InsertAfter oStyle.NameLocal
''' Some Styles cannot be displayed
''' in particular contexts
On Error Resume Next
oRange.Style = oStyle.NameLocal
If Err.Number <> 0 Then
oRange.InsertAfter " (Style Not Displayed)"
End If
On Error GoTo 0
oRange.InsertParagraphAfter
oRange.Collapse wdCollapseEnd
End If
Next oStyle
End Sub
```

Character Styles Macro

Most Microsoft Word users who need to use bold or italic just press CTRL + B or CTRL + I and go blithely on their way, not thinking any more about it. But at some point, they'll run into problems. For example, their directly applied formatting may disappear when they apply a paragraph style over the top of it. (You can read more about this in "Disappearing Character Formatting.") Another example is that sometimes directly applied formatting simply refuses to be found with Word's Find feature. I don't know why that is, but I've seen it time after time.

The solution to such problems is to avoid using directly applied character formatting entirely. Instead, use character *styles* formatted as bold or italic. Unfortunately, doing so isn't nearly as easy as using plain old character formatting—until now. I'm providing a macro that will create the character style you need and then toggle between bold and roman, italic and roman, or other formatting using Word's built-in keyboard shortcuts and toolbar buttons. Pretty slick! Here's the macro for italic:

```
Dim Found, myStyle
Found = False
For Each myStyle In ActiveDocument.Styles
If myStyle.NameLocal = "Italic" Then
Found = True
Exit For
End If
Next
If Found = False Then
ActiveDocument.Styles.Add _
Name:="Italic", _
Type:=wdStyleTypeCharacter
ActiveDocument.Styles("Italic").BaseStyle = _
"Default Paragraph Font"
ActiveDocument.Styles("Italic").Font.Italic = True
End If
mySel = Selection.Font.Italic
If mySel = wdUndefined Or mySel = False Then
Selection.Style = "Italic"
Else
Selection.Style = "Default Paragraph Font"
End If
```

The first part of the macro (from "For Each" to "Next") checks to see if the character style (in this case named "Italic") already exists. If it does, the macro leaves it alone, which means you can create and format your character styles any way you like so they will work with this macro. If the character style *doesn't* exist, the macro creates it with the appropriate formatting (in this case, italic—note the line that says "ActiveDocu-ment.Styles("Italic").Font.Italic = True").

The second part of the macro checks to see if any part of the selection (which may be selected text or simply the text at the cursor position) is already formatted as italic. If it's not (or if part of it is), the macro applies the Italic character style. If the selection is already italic, the macro applies the Default Paragraph Font to make the selection roman.

You've probably already figured out that you can modify the macro to take care of bold, underlining, or other kinds of formatting. To do so, you'll need to change "Italic" to "Bold" (or whatever) wherever it appears in these six lines of the macro:

```
If myStyle.NameLocal = "Italic" Then
Name:="Italic", _
ActiveDocument.Styles("Italic").BaseStyle = _
ActiveDocument.Styles("Italic").Font.Italic = True
mySel = Selection.Font.Italic
Selection.Style = "Italic"
```

Note that in the following line, you'll have to change it twice:

```
ActiveDocument.Styles("Italic").Font.Italic = True
```

In making your changes, you can use Bold, Italic, Underline, SmallCaps, AllCaps, Superscript, Subscript, Strikethrough, Hidden, Outline, or Shadow. (A few other formats are also available; if you're interested, see the "Properties" listing for "Font Object" in Word's Visual Basic Help file.)

There's one more line you might be interested in modifying:

```
"Default Paragraph Font"
```

You can change this line to the name of an actual font you want to use (for example, "Baskerville"). This is useful if you want to specify the name of a true italic font to provide italic formatting or to get fancy in other ways.

To get the macro to work when you press one of Word's built-in keyboard commands (such as CTRL + I) or toolbar buttons, simply give the macro the same name as the Word command. For example, if you name the macro "Italic," like this—

```
Sub Italic()
```

—then Word will happily treat it just as if it were the built-in Italic command! For your convenience, the names of Word's built-in character formatting commands are Bold, Italic, Underline, SmallCaps, AllCaps, Superscript, Subscript, Strikethrough, Hidden, Outline, and Shadow.

After you've used the macro to apply formatting to some text, you'll see the name of the character style (such as "Italic") in the Styles list on the Formatting toolbar.

Thanks to Steve Hudson for VBA advice.

Readers Write

TERRI SVILAR:

My question has to do with publishing a document created in Word that contains color. Is there a way to separate the color from the text? I work at a small community college, and every semester we publish a course schedule. Most of the text is not highlighted, but there are certain entries that are highlighted with a light yellow so that students can easily find them.

It takes the person who gets this ready to be sent to the publisher a considerable amount of time to convert from Word to a format the printers can use. What takes her the most time is the highlighting, and then sometimes the highlighting doesn't match the printed words.

I RESPONDED: The best way to approach this, in my opinion, is to use character styles to format the words that need to be in color. If you don't know about character styles, Word's Help file will tell you about them. You could create a character style named something like "Highlight" and apply it to the words in question. Then, when the file goes to the printer, it can be imported into QuarkXPress (or some other typesetting program), and the character styles can be formatted in color as needed in the typesetting program.

If your files currently use Word's built-in highlighting rather than character styles, you can use Word's Find and Replace feature to find highlighting and replace it with your character style.

Word's Style Area

If you use styles to format text in Microsoft Word (which you should), the style of the currently selected paragraph is displayed in the Style dropdown list on the Formatting toolbar. To see what style is applied to a paragraph, you can click the paragraph and look at the list on the toolbar.

Wouldn't it be nice, though, if you could see all of the styles applied to all of the paragraphs on your screen all at the same time? Well, you can. You just have to display Word's Style Area. Here's how:

1. Open a document that contains a bunch of styled text.
2. Make sure your document is displayed in Normal view (click View > Normal). The Style Area isn't accessible in Print Layout (Page) view (but it is in Outline view).
3. Click the "Tools" menu.
4. Click "Options."
5. Click the "View" tab.
6. In the box labeled "Style area width," enter 1 inch or the equivalent.
7. Click the "OK" button.

Now, on the left side of your screen, you'll see the Style Area. In the Style Area, to the left of the first line of each paragraph, you'll see the name of the paragraph's style. Pretty slick!

You can change the size of the Style Area under Tools > Options > View, or simply by using your mouse to move the vertical line between the Style Area and the body of your document. If you've got lots of long style names, make it bigger.

Need to modify one of the styles listed in the Style Area? Just double-click it to open the Style dialog.

Shifting Styles

Scene 1: You go through your document, fine-tuning its style formatting to the peak of perfection. Then you carefully save your document for posterity.

Scene 2: A week later, you open your document. What the . . . ? All of your styles have shifted back to their original formatting. You'll have to do all of that work over again! And how can you be sure it will stick?

Here's the secret:

1. Open the document.
2. Click "Tools > Templates and Add-Ins."
3. *Remove* that dadburned checkmark in the box labeled "Automatically update document styles."
4. Resave your document.

The next time you open the document, your exquisite style formatting will remain intact.

So what's the point of the "Automatically update document styles" feature? Well, let's say that your boss just loves to tinker with the look of your company's forms and stationery, mandating Helvetica one week and Comic Sans the next. If you turn on "Automatically update document styles" for every company document you create, changing the formatting is a snap. Just open the template on which the documents are based, modify the styles, and resave the template. The next time you open one of those documents, its styles will automatically update to match those of the template.

It's a slick feature, as long as you know when—and when not—to use it. And now you do!

Shifting Styles, Part 2

Here's the scenario: You've just opened a new document from a client, and you italicize the first paragraph, which is a short quotation introducing the chapter. But suddenly *all* of the chapter text is italicized. What in the world is going on?

You've just bumped into Word's "Automatically update" feature for styles. (This is different from the "Automatically update document styles" feature discussed previously.) If you don't know about the "Automatically update" feature, you can spend hours trying to adjust formatting, only to have everything in sight messed up beyond belief.

To turn the feature off, do this:

1. Click the "Format" menu.
2. Click "Style" (in Word 2002, that's "Styles and Formatting").
3. Click the style that's giving you fits (such as Heading 1). (In Word 2002, click the drop-down arrow to the right of the style in the Task Pane.)
4. Click "Modify."
5. Remove the checkmark from the box labeled "Automatically update."
6. Click the "OK" button.
7. If necessary, click the "Close" button.

Now, when you modify some formatting in your document, you'll change only the local selection and not everything that's formatted in the same style. But really, you should avoid using directly applied formatting anyway. Using paragraph and character styles is much more efficient—the True Way—and avoids a multitude of problems.

So what's the point of the "Automatically update" feature? It allows you to modify styles without drilling down, down, down through the Styles dialog. Well hey, that's good! It means you can change formatting directly, see the result immediately, and have the styles updated automatically to reflect that formatting. Pretty neat!

So here's my recommendation:

1. If you're *designing* a document, use the "Automatically update" feature with a bunch of junk text to set your styles exactly the way you want them (be sure to select the whole paragraph before changing the format). Once you've got them set, turn off "Automatically update." Then copy the styles to your real document, or save the junk document as a template that you attach to your real document. You can learn more about this in "Attaching Templates to Documents."
2. If you're *writing* or *editing* a document, make sure the "Automatically update" feature is turned off. You'll have a happier day.

Readers Write

In the article, I suggested turning on Word's "Automatically update" styles feature while designing a document but turning the feature off while editing. If you've got lots of styles, however, this can get pretty tedious. Gary Frieder, a Microsoft Word MVP at Woody's Lounge (http://www.wopr.com) created a macro to turn off updating for all styles, and Bill Rubidge edited the macro to turn on updating.

```
'MACRO THAT CRAWLS ALL THE STYLES AND TURNS AUTO-UPDATE ON
Public Sub TurnOnAutomaticallyUpdate()
' TurnOnAutomaticallyUpdate Macro
' Created by Gary Frieder, edited by Bill Rubidge to turn on,
not off
Dim aSty As Style
For Each aSty In ActiveDocument.Styles
If aSty.Type = wdStyleTypeParagraph Then
aSty.AutomaticallyUpdate = True
End If
Next aSty
End Sub
```

```
'MACRO THAT CRAWLS ALL THE STYLES AND TURNS AUTO-UPDATE OFF
Public Sub RemoveAutomaticallyUpdate()
' RemoveAutomaticallyUpdate Macro
' Created by Gary Frieder
Dim aSty As Style
For Each aSty In ActiveDocument.Styles
If aSty.Type = wdStyleTypeParagraph Then
aSty.AutomaticallyUpdate = False
End If
Next aSty
End Sub
```

RHANA PIKE:

I was interested to read the tip on automatic updating of styles. A related issue is the box that appears sometimes when I try to apply a style to a paragraph: it says something like "Update the style to match selection?" (I can't get it to appear now). Is there a way of getting rid of this or applying a default? I set styles through the menu and never want to update the style to match the selection.

I REPLIED: When you apply direct formatting to a paragraph (such as formatting it in bold with CTRL + B), and then immediately click the paragraph style (such as Heading 1) in the Styles list on the Formatting toolbar, Word asks if you want to:

1. Update the style to reflect recent changes, or
2. Reapply the formatting of the style to the selection.

If you click option 1, Word will modify the style to match the manual formatting you've applied to the paragraph. This is a quick way to modify styles.

If you click option 2, Word will override all of that lovely manual formatting you've just done and reapply the existing formatting of the style.

Is there a way to get rid of these options and just apply the style? The only way I know of is not to click the Styles list after applying formatting directly—or, better yet, to avoid using directly applied formatting altogether.

Shifting Styles, Part 3

You're working away, editing a client's document, and decide to modify the Heading 1 style to use a Goudy typeface. Whoa! Now the Heading 2 and Heading 3 styles are in Goudy as well. What's going on? What's going on is that your client has made the Heading 2 and Heading 3 styles "based on" the Heading 1 style. If you don't know how this works, you'll be scratching your head over the changing formats. If you *do* know how it works, you can use it to ensure consistent formatting throughout a document.

Let's say you want all of your headings set in Baskerville. You could go through and set Heading 1, Heading 2, Heading 3, Heading 4, Heading 5, Heading 6, Heading 7, Heading 8, and Heading 9 (whew!) all to use that font (in varying point sizes, say). But now what if you want to switch to Palatino? Do you really have to modify all of those styles again? Not if you originally based them all on Heading 1. If you did that, all you have to do is change the font for Heading 1, and all of your other heading styles will change as well. Here's how:

1. Click the "Format" menu.
2. Click "Style."
3. In the Styles list, click the style (Heading 2, for example) that you want to base on another style (such as Heading 1).
4. Click the "Modify" button.
5. In the "Based on" dropdown list, click the style on which you want to base the current style.
6. Click the "OK" button.
7. Click the "Close" button.

Now, whenever you modify the "parent" style (Heading 1), the "child" style (Heading 2) will be modified automatically. Please note, however, that any changes you make to the "child" style will override the attributes of the "parent" style. For example, if Heading 1 is set to 18 points, you can still modify Heading 2 (based on Heading 1) as 14 points. If you do that, though, you may wonder how to get rid of the override if you need to. Here's the secret: change the attribute in Heading 2 back to the way it's set in Heading 1 (14 points back to 18 points). The "child" style will simply pick up its attributes from the "parent style" once again.

This "based on" feature is extremely useful. You can use it to set up whole families of styles that are based on a "parent" style. For example, you might want to set up a family of heading styles, a family of body text styles, and a family of list styles, and then store them all in a special template. Just be sure to use a naming convention that makes it easy to remember which styles are the "parents." The easiest way to do this may be to use "1" to designate "parent" styles: Heading 1, Body Text 1, List 1, and so on. Then you can use other numbers (2, 3, 4) to indicate "child" styles.

Shifting Styles, Part 4

You're typing along, and suddenly the short line you entered a couple of paragraphs earlier has turned big and bold. Who does it think it is, anyway? When you investigate, you discover that the line has somehow been formatted with Word's Heading 1 style.

You've just discovered one of the wonders of Word's AutoFormat feature, which should be firmly beaten into submission before it takes over your whole document. If you want to see how it works, try this:

1. Click the "Format" menu.
2. Click "AutoFormat."
3. Click the "Options" button.
4. Click the tab labeled "AutoFormat As You Type."
5. Under "Apply as you type," put a check in the box labeled "Headings." If there's already a check there, you've found the source of your anguish.
6. Click the "OK" button.
7. Click the "Close" button.

Now, in a new document, do this:

1. Type "My Heading" (without the quotation marks), and be sure not to type any punctuation after it.
2. Hit the Enter key twice.

Wow, the text is now formatted with the Heading 1 style. You might think that's kind of neat, but what if you didn't *want* the text to be a heading? What if you were just typing a list of items without ending punctuation (which, by the way, seems to be the defining factor here)? Then you need to turn the feature off.

See, the whole issue is one of control. How much "help" do you want Word to give you? If you're editing, your answer may be "none," because editors need complete control over what's happening, and they can't have Word introducing changes that they may not even be aware of. When I'm editing, I allow one AutoFormat option—replace "straight quotes" with "smart quotes" as I type—and I watch it like a hawk.

If you turn off the AutoFormat option to apply headings as you type, and you *still* get automatic formatting, you may still have the last "AutoFormat As You Type" option turned on. It's labeled "Define styles based on your formatting," and the Tooltip Help explains its function: "Create new paragraph styles based on the manual formatting you apply in your documents. You can apply these styles in your document to save time and to give your documents a consistent 'look.'"

The idea that Word is creating new styles as I work just gives me the heebie-jeebies. This is one option I'm definitely going to keep turned off.

Frustrating Formatting

If you use Microsoft Word, I guarantee you've been frustrated by its formatting, especially if you edit someone else's documents. For example, you modify the Heading 1 style to use Palatino rather than Arial—but Arial it remains. What's going on here?

Consider my living room wall, which I daringly painted red. Then, coming to my senses, I painted it grayish green. But wait . . . What *was* I thinking? Finally, I covered it with an almond color that looked okay.

Microsoft Word's formatting works pretty much the same way. It's done in layers, like paint on a wall.

The underlying layer is the formatting of paragraph styles. For example, if you apply the Heading 1 paragraph style using Word's defaults, your text will be formatted in 16-point Arial bold. If you attach a new template to your document (and check the box labeled "Automatically Update Document Styles"), the formatting of Heading 1 will change to whatever is specified in the new template (18-point Baskerville italic, for example). Note that this doesn't change the style formatting in your Normal template. It just paints over that formatting *in your document.* And if you "detach" the new template, the formatting won't change back. Once the paint is on there, it's on there. Of course, you can always attach a *different* template or modify the styles in the document itself if you want to change the formatting yet again.

The next layer up is the formatting of character styles. You can use character styles to format text selections smaller than a paragraph. For example, you might use a character style called Book Title to format book titles in Times Roman italic. Like paragraph styles, character styles can be changed by attaching a different template or modifying the styles in the document itself.

Finally, on the topmost layer, your document could have directly applied formatting. That's what you get if you simply select some text and apply, say, 18-point Baskerville italic without using a style. In all but the simplest documents, this kind of formatting is of the devil. Why? Because you can't change it simply by modifying the underlying style—and that means you have no way to control it (or even identify it) *throughout* the document. So, if you modify the Heading 1 style to use Palatino rather than Arial—well, Arial it remains.

How can you avoid this problem in your documents?

1. Don't use directly applied formatting.
2. Use character styles to format text selections smaller than a paragraph.
3. Use paragraph styles to format everything else.
4. To change your formatting, modify the *style* that produces it.

But what if you're working on someone else's documents? You'll probably want to remove all that directly applied formatting and use styles instead. But that's a topic for another day.

Readers Write

YATEENDRA JOSHI:

A useful way to cross-check whether the specified formatting is being correctly implemented—at least the spacing part of it—is to check the At value in Word's status bar [at the bottom of the Word window]. We use a table that gives the correct value for different "zones" or positions: for example, if the cursor is in a header, the status line should show At 6mm; if in a footer, At 269mm; if in the first line of text following a chapter title, At 45mm and so on. Any departure from these values is a signal to check top and bottom margins, line spacing, and Spacing Before / After.

Removing Directly Applied Formatting

I previously discussed the evils of directly applied formatting but didn't explain how to get rid of it. I know what you're going to say: "Just press CTRL + A to select all and then press CTRL + SPACE." That will remove it, all right. The problem is, it will also remove italics, bold, and other formatting that you want to *keep*.

For example, let's say you're editing a scholarly tome with acres and acres of footnotes. Nearly every one of those notes is going to cite a book or journal of some kind—with the title of each publication in italics, like this:

> 39. G. B. Harrison, *The Profession of English* (New York: Anchor Books, 1967), p. 166.

But if you do the CTRL + SPACE thing, you're going to get this:

> 39. G. B. Harrison, The Profession of English (New York: Anchor Books, 1967), p. 166.

So what are you going to do? Go back and italicize everything by hand?
There *is* a better way. In general terms, here's the procedure:

1. Identify each kind of directly applied formatting you want to keep—italics, strikethrough, whatever. Maybe make a list.
2. Find and replace each kind of formatting with a unique code. For example, you might use |I| to indicate italic and |B| to indicate bold. (More on this in a minute.)
3. Press CTRL + A to select all and CTRL + SPACE to remove all directly applied formatting.
4. Find and replace your codes with the appropriate formatting.

Now let's get specific and say you're trying to preserve italics. Here's what you'd do:

1. Click Edit > Replace to open Word's Find and Replace dialog.
2. Leave the "Find What" box empty but press CTRL + I to specify italic formatting. The box will now say "Font: Italic" underneath.
3. In the "Replace With" box, enter this:

|I|^&|I|

That code in the middle, ^&, is the "Find What Text" wildcard, which tells Word to use whatever it *finds* (in this case, any italicized text) as the *replacement* between your italic codes. You can learn more about the "Find What Text" wildcard in "Replacing with Find What Text."

4. Click the "Replace All" button. All of your italicized text will now be marked with codes, like this:

39. G. B. Harrison, |I|The Profession of English|I| (New York: Anchor Books, 1967), p. 166.

(If you wanted to preserve other kinds of formatting, such as bold, you'd repeat steps 1 through 4 here, with different codes for each kind of formatting.)

5. Press CTRL + A to select all and CTRL + SPACE to remove directly applied formatting. Woo-hoo! Pretty scary, no? (You did keep a backup, right?)
6. Click Edit > Replace to open Word's Find and Replace dialog.
7. In the "Find What" box, enter the formatting codes and the * wildcard (in parentheses) to represent any text between the codes, like this:

|I|(*)|I|

8. Click the "No Formatting" button. The "Font: Italic" notation will go away.
9. In the "Replace With" box, enter this:

\1

That code tells Word to use any text it *finds* between italic codes as the *replacement* for the codes and the text between them. Clear as mud? You'll understand when you try it. You can learn more about the "Find What Expression" wildcard in "Using the Find What Expression Wildcard."

10. With your cursor still in the "Replace With" box, press CTRL + I to specify italic formatting. The box will now say "Font: Italic" underneath.
11. Put a check in the "Use wildcards" checkbox. You may need to click the "More" button before this is available.
12. Click the "Replace All" button. All of your italicized text will be restored to its former glory—and all of the directly applied formatting that you *didn't* want (such as 12-point Baskerville) will be gone!

If you need to do this kind of thing a lot, you can record the procedure in a macro that you can use over and over again. You can learn more about recording macros in "Macro Recording: The Basics." Or, if you'd like a macro that will clean up directly applied formatting (but preserve character formatting such as italic) in a whole folder full of documents at the same time, you might try my FileCleaner program.

Readers Write

Steve Dobney:

Instead of using the standard Paste command, use Paste Special then choose Unformatted Text. As you would expect, this pastes the copied text with no formatting (defaults to Normal style).

Copying and Pasting Styles

If you frequently use styles (which you should) to format your documents or specify text levels for typesetting, you're probably aware that you can press CTRL + SHIFT + S to activate the style list. (Then you can scroll through the list to get the style you need.)

You may not be aware, however, that you can easily copy and paste styles (both paragraph and character styles), just as you can copy and paste text. If you've never done this before, it will make you smile. Here's the procedure:

1. Put your cursor on some text formatted with the style you want to copy (Heading 1, for example).
2. Press CTRL + SHIFT + C (just like the keyboard shortcut for copying text, but with the SHIFT key added).
3. Move your cursor to (or select) the text you want to format with the style you just copied.
4. Press CTRL + SHIFT + V (just like the keyboard shortcut for pasting text, but with the SHIFT key added).

The text will be formatted with the style you copied.

Disappearing Character Formatting

Part of my editing process is applying paragraph styles (like Heading 1) to a manuscript. As I've done this, I've noticed an annoying bug: Applying the paragraph style often makes character formatting (such as italics) disappear. You can see this for yourself:

1. Create a new document in Word 97, 98, 2000, or 2001.
2. Type the words "This is" at the beginning of the document.
3. Italicize the word "This."
4. Apply the paragraph style for Heading 1.

Ouch! The italic formatting disappears. Word's Help file gives this "explanation": "Applying a style turns off bold, italic, or underlining.

"The format you apply by using a paragraph style or character style may change the existing character formatting of the text. For example, when you apply a built-in heading style such as Heading 1 to underlined text, the underlining disappears. This will not occur if you format the characters after you apply the style."

If I'm writing, fine. But if I'm editing, this is a nuisance.

Now try this:

1. Create a new document in Word 97, 98, 2000, or 2001 (2002 works a little differently).
2. Type the words "This is a test" at the beginning of the document.
3. Italicize the word "This."
4. Apply the paragraph style for Heading 1.

Well, look at that; the italic formatting is still there. What's going on here, anyway?

I think what's going on is that Word is trying (unsuccessfully) to be helpful, as the italics *sometimes* toggle off or on depending on the formatting of the paragraph style. For example, if you apply an italic Heading 2 to "*This* is" (the asterisks here represent italics), the character formatting of the text changes to "This *is*"—pretty cool! The problem is, the feature doesn't always work. If you try applying an italic Heading 2 to "This *is* a test," for example, the whole line goes italic. Ackk! Then reapplying a roman Heading 1 removes all italics from the line.

There is a way to keep Word from wiping out your character formatting: Use character styles rather than Word's built-in character formatting (such as italic). Here's how:

1. Click the "Tools" menu.
2. Click "Style" (or "Styles and Formatting").
3. Click the button labeled "New" or "New Style."

4. Give your new style a name, such as "Italic."

5. Under "Style Type," specify "Character."

6. If you'd like to add the style to your document's underlying template, put a check in the box labeled "Add to template."

7. To specify a shortcut key combination for your new style, click the "Shortcut Key" button. (If you're using 2002, you'll have to click the "Format" button before "Shortcut Key" is available.) I'd recommend using Word's built-in key combinations for these character styles—CTRL + I for italic, CTRL + B for bold, and so on. Then, whenever you use the key combinations, you'll get your custom character style rather than Word's character formatting. (To remove the style, select the text to which it was applied and press CTRL + SPACEBAR.)

8. Click the "Format" button.

9. Click "Font."

10. Click "Italic" (or whatever formatting you want to use). Please notice that you can also specify an actual italic font if you're interested in quality typesetting.

11. Click the "OK" button.

12. Click the "OK" button.

13. Click the "Close" button.

After you've formatted some text with your new character style, applying a paragraph style will no longer wipe it out. Hooray!

Glorious Color

In the past, I've recommended using your own template to apply to documents you're editing. This allows you to use a typeface that's easy to read on your monitor, offers plenty of differentiation between double and single quotation marks, and has a long em dash, a medium-sized en dash, and a short hyphen (so you can tell them apart). You can learn more about this in "Typefaces for Editing."

One difficulty I've encountered with my custom template is distinguishing between different heading levels. I like to know at a glance how a heading is styled, without having to look at the formatting toolbar or the "style area," which you can learn about in "Word's Style Area."

To get around the problem, I've usually formatted my Heading 1 style in 22-point type, my Heading 2 style in 18-point type, and my Heading 3 style in 14-point type, with Heading 1 and 2 centered and Heading 3 flush left. This works okay, but if I need to add Heading 4 and Heading 5 (which is sometimes necessary), I start running out of formatting.

But I've recently discovered a nice solution: color!

Why not make Heading 1 red?

And Heading 2 blue?

And Heading 3 green?

And Heading 4 orange?

And Heading 5 brown?

You get the picture! Some of the standard Microsoft Word colors stand out well on a white background and are easily distinguishable from each other. These are, in my opinion, red, blue, green, orange, brown, pink, sky blue, bright green, and dark yellow (one for each of Word's nine heading levels), but feel free to use whatever works well for you.

You might want to arrange the heading level colors in a way that is easy to remember. The order I used above works for me. I split the colors into groups of three: red, green, and blue (commonly known as RGB); orange, brown, and pink (which makes no sense except that I like orange better than brown, and brown better than pink); and finally (in order of sky, lawn, and dirt), sky blue, bright green, and dark yellow. But you could use the (approximate) order of the spectrum, or maybe some mnemonic device based on the first letter of each word.

Whatever system you choose, using color makes it easy to see and identify heading levels, and it also makes a manuscript much more fun to read!

Style Separator

Word 2002 and Word 2003 include a long-awaited feature: the Style Separator. The Style Separator is a special, hidden (and undocumented) paragraph mark. Rather than creating a paragraph *break,* however, it marks the spot where one paragraph style ends and another paragraph style begins—*all in the same paragraph.* That's right—starting with Word 2002, you can use two or more paragraph styles in the same paragraph.

Why should you care? Mainly because it gives you more control over what's included in a table of contents. Let's say you're editing a manuscript whose first chapter begins like this:

"Paris, City of Lights. After an excruciating ten-hour flight, I arrived at Charles de Gaulle International Airport, where my daughter was waiting with a large cardboard sign bearing the inscription 'Dad.'"

Since Word will create the table of contents from the Heading styles you've applied to your chapter headings (Insert > Reference [in Word 2002 and 2003] > Index and Tables > Table of Contents), you try applying the Heading 1 style to the paragraph. But that's no good, because you don't want the entire paragraph to show up in the table of contents. All you want is "Paris, City of Lights."

The workaround for this problem in earlier versions of Word was to break the paragraph in two:

"Paris, City of Lights."

"After an excruciating ten-hour flight, I arrived at Charles de Gaulle International Airport . . ."

Then, after applying the Heading style to the first paragraph, you would select its carriage return (paragraph mark) and format the return as Hidden text (Format > Font > Hidden). You might then have to insert a space to make everything look nice. And when you inserted the table of contents, sure enough, only the first bit would be included. Yes, you can still do that if you don't have Word 2002 or 2003.

If you do have Word 2002 or 2003, however, you can now use Word's built-in Style Separator instead of a hidden paragraph mark. First though, you'll have to drag it up from the storehouse of hidden Word commands and make it available on a menu, toolbar, or keyboard combination. The name you're looking for on the Commands list is InsertStyleSeparator. Okay, I'll make it easy for you:

1. Click Tools > Customize.
2. Click the Commands tab.
3. In the Categories list, click All Commands.
4. In the Commands list, scroll down to InsertStyleSeparator.
5. Drag InsertStyleSeparator to the Formatting toolbar.
6. Click the Close button.

To actually use the Style Separator, you'll still have to start with the paragraph split in two:

"Paris, City of Lights."

"After an excruciating ten-hour flight from Dallas/Fort Worth International Airport . . ."

Then follow this procedure:

1. Place your cursor anywhere in the text of the first paragraph.
2. Create a Style Separator (which will be inserted at the *end* of the current paragraph and not at your cursor position) by using your new toolbar button, menu item, or keyboard combination. The two paragraphs will magically become one, with the Style Separator between the two.
3. Select the text before the Style Separator and style it with the Heading style you want to use in the table of contents.

When you generate your table of contents, the text before the Style Separator will show up there, but not the text after it.

By the way, you can actually see the Style Separator (it looks like a regular paragraph mark with a thin dotted line around it). To do so:

1. Click Tools > Options.
2. Click the View tab and put a checkmark in the All checkbox under Formatting Marks.
3. Click the OK button.

Note that if you open your Style Separator document in an earlier version of Word (97, for example), your Style Separators will become nothing more than hidden paragraph marks. Hmmm. Maybe the Style Separator isn't so revolutionary after all.

Print What?

Recently a Microsoft Word user asked me, "Is there an easy way to print the names and descriptions of the styles I'm using in my document?" Fortunately, there is. Here's the procedure:

1. Click the File menu.
2. Click "Print."
3. Click the "Print what" box at the lower left of the Print dialog box.
4. On the list of items you can print, click "Styles."
5. Click "OK."

Microsoft Word will print out a nicely formatted list (names and descriptions) of the styles you're using in that document. If you try this, you'll notice that there are other items on the "Print what" list besides styles (and the document itself, of course). These include:

- AutoText entries. This will print your AutoText entries, including the AutoText name and the text itself.
- Comments (Annotations). This will print the comments in the document (including page number, reviewer's initials, and the text of the comment), which can be handy if you need to give a bunch of queries to an author or just want to review notes you've made to yourself.
- Document properties (Summary info). This will print the information in the document properties or summary info, such as title, subject, author, and so on.
- Key assignments. This will print the names, keyboard shortcuts, and descriptions of any custom key assignments you've made.

Print what? Almost anything you want.

Readers Write

AARON SHEPARD:

I came across a bad problem in Word 2004 for Mac. Unlike Windows versions and former Mac versions, this one antialiases all imported graphics, and will even change black-and-white line art to grayscale to do it. That means fuzzy charts and diagrams when printed. It's a scandal. The only way to avoid it is to insert art as EPS. On the Mac, that also enables you to place a CMYK graphic!

Eric Fletcher:

I am a big promoter of using only linked rather than embedded images. This not only keeps a Word document smaller but also leaves the source image unchanged. Moreover, if you have all linked images saved in a specific folder relative to the documents, you have the means to manage some otherwise complicated print issues.

For example, if I need to produce a publication for both screen viewing (or low-res print) and a high quality photosetter (offset press, for example), I prepare the images in the best quality for the latter and save them in a folder below where the Word documents are being saved (I use "art/highres"). I then copy the images "up" one level, and prepare the Word document with links to the named images within the "art" folder. This lets me print in the best quality possible for the photosetter, but can really bog down a lower resolution printer—and makes screen refresh irritating and unnecessarily slow.

So here's the trick: To prepare the lower-res version, I then use a batch function of an image editor to make copies of all of the high-res images in a more suitable resolution and save them to a different folder (I use "art/lowres") without changing their names. I then copy everything from this folder up into the "art" folder, replacing the high res versions. The links within the Word documents now point to lower-res versions of the same named images (i.e., a field like { INCLUDEPICTURE "art/c03f12migration.tif" \d } will point to whatever image is named "c03f12migration.tif" in the "art" folder, so Word will use that image when the page is recalculated for display or printing).

Using the same approach, I could have the batch routine in my image editor alter the images to retain the dimensions but remove all content (turn lightness to 100% for example) and resave to a third folder ("art/nores" maybe?). Copying these images up to replace the ones in my target "art" folder would then result in a document linking to "empty" images—and since the sizes would be the same, any text flow would not be affected. (This would mimic the placeholder behaviour Word provides through the Options View dialog.)

Word can do a lot, but it was never designed to be an image processor.

Understanding Styles in Templates

A hundred years ago when I switched from WordPerfect to Microsoft Word, there was one thing I just didn't understand. That thing was templates. What the heck were they, anyway? How was I supposed to use them? And what did they have to do with editing?

Part of my confusion came from the fact that Word templates have more than one function. In broad terms, they can be used to store macros, AutoText entries, and customized menus, toolbars, and keyboard shortcuts. But they can also be used to hold paragraph and character styles to be used in formatting other documents.

Webster's New Collegiate Dictionary defines "template" as a "pattern . . . used as a guide to the form of a piece being made"—a pretty good description of a template used for formatting in Microsoft Word.

In my opinion, the best way to see what that means is to play around with Word's Style Gallery for five minutes. Never heard of it? Try this:

1. Open a document you've been working on (make a backup first, just in case).
2. Click the "Format" menu at the top of your Word window.
3. In Word 2000 or 2001, click "Theme."
4. Click "Style Gallery."
5. In the "Preview" box (on the lower left), click "Document" (if it's not already selected).
6. In the "Template" window (on the upper left), click the name of a template.

Now, look at the "Preview of" window on the right. You'll see what your document would look like if you were using the template you selected in the "Template" window. For example, let's say your original document uses 12-point Times New Roman for its Normal text style. If you select the "Elegant Report" template in the "Template" window, the Normal text style will suddenly be displayed in 11-point Garamond. If you've used the Heading 1 style in your document, formatted as 16-point Arial bold, let's say, the text styled with Heading 1 will be displayed in 9-point Garamond bold. Quite a difference!

Now you see one of the main things that a template does: *It changes the formatting of all of the styles in a document.* It does that, however, only if the styles in the template are the ones actually *used* in the document, which is an excellent reason to use the same, standardized style names in every document you work on. For example, if you create a style named ChapHead for chapter headings in a certain document, that style definitely *won't* pick up the formatting from the Heading 1 style in the "Elegant Report" template.

Try clicking some other templates in the Style Gallery. Each template will change the look of your document in the "Preview of" window. If you want, you can click the "OK" button to copy the styles from the selected template into your document, which will actually change your document formatting. (You can't just "undo" this, by the way. You've got that backup, right?) Or, you can click the "Cancel" button to close the Style Gallery without changing your document.

As useful as it is, the Style Gallery isn't the *real* way to use templates. The real way, especially for editing and publishing, is to *attach* them to your documents. We'll talk about that next.

Attaching Templates to Documents

In the previous article, we used Microsoft Word's Style Gallery to understand one of the main reasons for using templates: to change the formatting of all of the styles in a document. Why would you want to change the formatting of all of the styles in a document? Let me suggest some reasons:

1. You're sick of editing in Weedpatch Ugly, which is the typeface your client has used. Why not (a) save your client's document as a template and then (b) go back to the original document and attach your own template that defines the styles in a typeface you like? When you're finished editing, you can simply attach the "client" template that you saved, which will restore your client's formatting in all of its hideous glory. For suggestions of typefaces that work well, see the article "Typefaces for Editing."
2. You've finished editing and you want to apply the final format to a document that's otherwise ready for printing. In the past you've saved certain elegantly designed documents as templates, so now you can attach one of those templates to your current document and create an instant masterpiece.
3. As the editor of an academic journal, you're pulling together a dozen papers from various scholars and want to give all the papers the same format. You attach your standard template, and voilà!

Note that for these scenarios to work, the documents in question must use styles that are also used in the templates you're going to attach. For example, if your document includes certain paragraphs formatted with the Heading 1 style, when you apply a *template* that uses the Heading 1 style, the formatting from the template will be copied to the headings in your document.

That is, it will if you've turned on the option to automatically update document styles. Here's the whole procedure:

1. Open the document to which you want to attach a template.
2. Click the "Tools" menu.
3. Click "Templates and Add-ins."
4. Click the "Attach" button.
5. Click the name of the template you want to attach.
6. Click the oddly-named "Open" button. (You'll now see the name and path of the template in the "Document template" box.)
7. Put a check in the box labeled "Automatically update document styles."
8. Click the "OK" button to attach the template to the current document and update the styles to match the formatting in the template.

I still haven't said why you should attach a template rather than use Word's Style Gallery to change your styles' formatting. Actually, the Style Gallery works just fine for that purpose. But attaching a template does more than just change the formatting of styles. It also makes certain items available in the document to which it is attached. Those items include AutoText entries, macros, and customized toolbars, menus, and key combinations—some very useful stuff! But that's a topic for another time.

Templates and Styles

It's midnight at the publishing house. All the cubicles are dark—except one in the back corner, where a frazzled production editor struggles to finish formatting a 700-page book that's due at press in eight short hours. Can't we do something to help?

As we've seen, Microsoft Word documents get their overall formatting from the templates attached to them. By changing a document's template, you automatically change the document's formatting. *Every* document is based on a template. If you don't attach one, Word uses the Normal template. The relationship looks like this:

Template —> Document

Styles and paragraphs have the same kind of relationship as templates and documents. Paragraphs get their overall formatting from the styles applied to them. By changing a paragraph's style, you automatically change the paragraph's formatting. *Every* paragraph is based on a style. If you don't apply one, Word uses the Normal style. The relationship looks like this:

Style —> Paragraph

Why does Word work like this? To give you greater and faster *control* over a document's formatting. Using templates and styles, you can instantly change the look of an entire document—or certain parts of a document, such as block quotations or headings.

Many people never even think about this. They'll go through an entire manuscript, manually formatting every single heading as Arial, 14-point, bold, small caps, 1-point condensed, center justified, exact line spacing, keep with next. It makes me absolutely crazy!

To get fast, consistent formatting throughout a manuscript, you'll need to do two things:

1. Attach a template that includes the styles you need with the formatting you want them to have. To learn more about this, see the previous two articles.
2. Consistently apply styles as needed. For example, you might use the Heading 1 style for part titles, Heading 2 for chapter titles, Heading 3 for subheads, and so on. You can read more about style levels in the documentation for my WordSetter program, here:

http://www.editorium.com/Wordset.htm/\#_Toc500857368

If parts of the manuscript still don't look right, they may have directly applied font and paragraph formatting (such as Arial, 14-point, bold, small caps, 1-point condensed, center justified, exact line spacing, keep with next). Directly applied paragraph formatting is easy to remove: just select the whole document (CTRL + A) and then press CTRL + Q. Unfortunately, directly applied font formatting isn't so easy to get rid of. Yes, you can select the whole document and press CTRL + SPACEBAR, but that will also remove all character formatting, such as italic, presenting a serious problem. The only solution I know of is my FileCleaner program's Standardize Font Formatting feature, which you can learn more about here:

http://www.editorium.com/Fileclnr.htm/\#_Toc500858918

Using templates and styles is the key to formatting that looks good and doesn't take all night to finish.

Now, go home and get some sleep.

Creating Custom Templates

Microsoft Word comes with several templates for creating reports, press releases, resumes, and other documents. These templates can come in handy, but, as subscriber David Ibbetson writes, "The best way to use templates is to make your own according to your tastes and needs. Built-in templates can be valuable as a source of ideas, and can sometimes be modified to meet your requirements. An off-the-shelf template is unlikely to be as satisfactory as one made-to-measure."

This is especially true of templates for editing and typesetting, which Microsoft's off-the-shelf templates simply aren't equipped to handle. Their main drawback is not having enough styles, especially for something as complicated as a book, which needs styles for everything from epigraphs to endnotes. If you'd like a template with lots of styles, please feel free to use, modify, and rename the highly generic Typespec template that comes with my Editor's ToolKit program.

The other drawback to Word's templates is that they don't provide enough variety. In my opinion, nearly every publication is worthy of its own design—one that fits its subject and style. For example, Moby Dick needs a different typeface (something wild and rough-hewn) than Paradise Lost (which calls for something dignified and classical). Book design is a little beyond the scope of this article, so you may want to consult such books as these:

> *The Elements of Typographic Style,* by Robert Bringhurst.
> *The Printed Word,* by David A. Kater and Richard Kater.
> *The Art of Desktop Publishing,* by Tony Bove, Cheryl Rhodes, and Wes Thomas.
> *Desktop Publishing with Word for Windows,* by Tom Lichty.
> *The Non-Designer's Design Book,* by Robin Williams.
> *The Non-Designer's Type Book,* by Robin Williams.

Besides the templates that you use for final formatting, you'll also need a template that you use with every document—but only while you're *editing* the document. That template should include all of the styles you'll use for final formatting (typesetting) but with typefaces, point sizes, and paragraph formatting that make editing easy. Currently, my favorite typeface for editing is Times New Roman, because its hyphens and dashes are so easily distinguishable from each other, as are its opening and closing curly quotation marks.

To create a custom template, follow this procedure:

1. Create a new document.
2. Paste in a bunch of text that you can play with.
3. Create and format the styles you'll need, experimenting on the pasted text (this will require time and care).

4. Delete the pasted text, leaving only the styles in your document.
5. Click the "File" menu.
6. Click "Save As."
7. In the "File name" box, give your template a name that will help you remember its purpose ("Editing.dot," "MobyDick.dot," or whatever meets your needs).
8. In the "Save as type" box, select "Document Template (*.dot)."
9. Click the "Save" button to save the template.

I recommend using the same style names in all of your templates, even though the styles will be formatted differently from template to template. Someday when you're converting hundreds of publications into a giant XML archive (or simply attaching a different template to a document), you'll be glad you did. I also recommend using Word's built-in heading styles (Heading 1 through Heading 9), which make it possible to navigate and rearrange whole sections of a document in Outline view.

Once you've created a template that you like, you can modify it as needed for other publishing projects, saving it with a new name for each one. After a while, you'll have a wide variety of templates designed specifically for *your* projects and needs.

Creating New Documents

In our past few articles, we've been talking about templates—attaching them, creating them, and so on. There's still one area we haven't talked about: creating *new* documents based on existing templates. If you're an editor, you may be thinking, "I usually work on documents someone else has created." True enough. However, as an editor you probably also:

- send letters to clients.
- send invoices to clients.
- write jacket blurbs.
- write manuscript reviews.
- send out an occasional resume.

And so on. If you create such documents using templates that fit your needs, you'll save time and frustration, and you'll also look more professional. For example, I've created a letterhead template that includes the Editorium logo from my Web site, my business address, and a date field, and I've stored it in Microsoft Word's Templates folder. When I need to write a letter, I do this:

1. Click Word's "File" menu.
2. Click "New."
3. Click my letterhead template (Letterhead.dot).
4. Click the "OK" button.

Word creates a new document with the Editorium logo, business address, and the current date. All I have to do is type in the text of my letter. Slick! I've also modified Word's built-in invoice template and created templates for different kinds of writing projects. I seldom need to create a new document from scratch.

When you *attach* a template to an existing document (as explained in previous articles), the styles from the template will be copied to the new document. However, any *text* in the template will *not* be copied. You'll probably use this feature most for documents you're editing.

When you use a template to *create* a new document, any text in the template *will* be copied to the new document (along with styles). You'll probably use this feature most for documents you're writing.

For example, if you write rejection letters to authors, having some "boilerplate" text in a template will save you lots of time. Just create a new document based on your Rejection template, modify the document as needed (inserting the author's name and some specific comments, for example), and you're done!

Please note that if you create a document by pressing CTRL + N or clicking the "New" button (on the far left of the Standard toolbar), Microsoft Word won't let you select a template to use. It will simply create the new document based on your Normal template. Since that's the case, you should modify your Normal template to create the kind of document you need most often.

Templates Galore!

Debby English wrote: "In your article "Creating New Documents," you mentioned that you have modified Word's built-in invoice template. I would like to do the same but cannot find it in my Word template directory. Can you give me a clue about where it might be and what it's called? I'm running Word 2000."

I hadn't realized that the Invoice template doesn't come with Word 2000 (at least *I* sure can't find it). However, Microsoft has several free Invoice templates available for download here:

> http://search.officeupdate.microsoft.com/TemplateGallery/ct104.asp

If you're a freelance editor, you'll probably find the Services invoice (for billing by the hour) and the Simple invoice (for billing by the job) most useful.

If you're bidding on a job or writing a proposal, you'll find other helpful templates here:

> http://search.officeupdate.microsoft.com/TemplateGallery/ct103.asp

Need more? You'll find many other templates in Microsoft's Template Gallery:

> http://search.officeupdate.microsoft.com/TemplateGallery/default.asp

Microsoft isn't the only game in town, however. KMT Software, for example, has sample templates that you can download for free if you register with them (and, of course, templates that you can buy):

> http://www.kmt.com/

Baarns Consulting offers numerous templates and add-ins that can make your work easier:

> http://archive.baarns.com/Software/index4.asp

If you'd like to see a template with lots of styles for writing and editing (especially for technical books), O'Reilly & Associates provides a truly excellent one for its authors, although anyone who visits the O'Reilly site can download it:

> http://oreilly.com/oreilly/author/ch02.html\#tools

Whether you need a template for an invoice, a memo, or a complex editing job, one of these places should have exactly what you're looking for.

Author Tools Template

I'm constantly having to clean up files from authors. Most of them have no clue about how a manuscript should be structured or formatted. That's why I've created an Author Tools template—to help authors write, structure, and format their manuscripts in an easy, consistent way. (And, of course, to simplify my life—and possibly yours.) You can download the template (at no charge)—along with complete instructions for using it—here:

> http://www.editorium.com/ftp/AuthorTemplate.zip

Like the template? Feel free to share it. Pass it around! Give it away! The main point of the template is to give it to authors who need it. If you can get them to use it, it should help prevent the following problems:

- Inconsistently applied formatting.
- Unstyled text.
- Messed-up footnotes and endnotes.
- Inconsistent chapter (and other) numbering.

And that should make your work easier. It will also make writing easier and more productive for the authors with whom you work. You may even want to use it yourself. I know I'm going to.

Footnotes and Endnotes

Editing Notes in Microsoft Word

It's hard to beat Microsoft Word if you're editing a document with footnotes or endnotes. If you add or delete a note, the other notes renumber automatically (assuming the notes haven't been typed as body text and numbered manually), and the program provides a notes "pane" that allows you to edit all of your notes at once. (With WordPerfect, you have to view and edit one note at a time. Yechhh.) To use the notes pane most effectively, follow this procedure:

1. Make sure you're using Normal view rather than Page Layout view (click the View menu and then "Normal").
2. Open the notes pane (click the View menu and then "Footnotes").
3. Use your mouse to grab the top of the notes pane and move it almost to the top of your document window, giving you plenty of room to work. (If you move it too far, the notes pane will close.)

Now you can see and edit all of your notes at once. (To close the notes pane, click the "Close" button at the top of the pane.)

Here are some other tips for working with notes:

- Use Word's Go To feature (CTRL + G) to go to a specific note. This will work in document text and in the notes pane.
- Let Microsoft Word do the numbering for you. Some writers and editors do such weird things as use Word's automatic note reference numbers but manually type notes and note numbers at the bottom of the document rather than use the notes pane. I've also seen cases where an author, wanting to use a number followed by a period for note numbers, deleted and retyped each note number (with a period) in the notes pane, or inserted a period after the automatic note number. This is madness. Let Word do the job it was designed to do.
- Don't put headings into the notes pane. Some authors type things like "Notes to Chapter 3" at the top of the pane. It may look okay when you print it out, but it's actually a note without a note number, and it may cause file corruption and other problems. If you need to use such headings, put them at the bottom of your document text.
- You can convert endnotes to footnotes or vice versa by clicking the Insert menu and then clicking "Footnote," "Options," and "Convert."
- If you're working with revision marking, or tracking, turned on, you can delete a note reference number from the document text, but the note itself will still show up in the notes pane, and your other note reference numbers won't renumber correctly. This appears to be a bug in Microsoft Word. The only remedy I've found

is to accept revisions by clicking the Tools menu, then "Revisions," and then "Accept All." (You can also accept a single revision by clicking "Review" rather than "Accept All.")

- If you're editing a document with manually typed notes rather than automatically numbered notes, you can turn them into automatically numbered notes with my NoteStripper program. Then you won't have to renumber the notes by hand when you're finished editing.

- If you need to turn automatically numbered notes into regular numbered text (perhaps for use in QuarkXPress or PageMaker), my NoteStripper program will do that as well. It also includes other tools to make working with notes a snap.

Editing Notes and Text Side by Side

Many of the books I edit in Word are loaded with footnotes, and I've often wished I had a way to see notes and text at the same time while scrolling through them independently. Comes the dawn! It's easy:

1. Open your footnote-laden document.
2. Make sure you're looking at the document in Normal view (View > Normal.)
3. Open your document in a new window by clicking Window > New Window. You'll now have two instances of your document open. Any change you make in one will be reflected in the other, but you can scroll through them independently.
4. Arrange and size your two windows so they're displayed on your screen side by side. (If you have my Editor's ToolKit program, click Windows > Arrange Documents to do this automatically.)
5. In one of the windows (I like the one on the right) open the Notes pane so you can see your notes (View > Footnotes).
6. Use your mouse to grab the divider bar between the Notes pane and the body text. Drag the bar to within about half an inch of the top of your Word window. (If you go too far, the Notes pane will close.) Now most of that window will be taken up by your notes.
7. Use CTRL + SHIFT + F6 to jump back and forth between the two windows while scrolling independently through them to your heart's content.

Now you can see and edit your notes and text at the same time.

Fixing Bad Notes

A few years ago I received the electronic manuscript of a book I had to edit—a collection of talks by various scholars at a symposium. Looking through the first talk, I noticed that the footnotes were a mess. The author had used Word's automatically numbering notes, sure enough, but then he'd typed a period after each automatically numbered superscript note number. What *was* he thinking? Those periods after the superscripts sure looked weird. How could I get rid of them? A wildcard search! Here's the procedure:

1. Switch to Normal view (View > Normal) if you're not already there.
2. Open the notes pane (View > Footnotes).
3. With your cursor at the top of the notes pane, click Edit > Replace.
4. In the "Find What" box, enter this:

    (^02).

The parentheses consititute a wildcard "group" containing the ASCII code for automatic note reference numbers. And, of course, they're followed by a period. You can learn more in "Wildcard Grouping," "Searching with Character Codes," "Searching with Microsoft Word's Built-in Codes," and "Searching with Numeric Character Codes."

Why not just use ^f to find the footnote numbers? Because the wildcard search engine will give you an error message if you try.

6. In the "Replace With box, enter this:

    \1

That's the "Find What Expression" wildcard, and it represents whatever was found with (^02)—in other words, a note number. But we've excluded the period since we want periods to go away.

1. Put a check in the "Use wildcards" checkbox. (You may need to click the "More" button before this is available.)
2. Click the "Replace All" button.

In my bad, bad document, that did the trick.

I opened the next chapter and looked at the notes first thing. Wow, messier still. Incredibly, this author had used Word's automatically numbered footnotes to create the note reference numbers in the text, but then she'd typed her notes after the body text, leaving the footnotes pane completely empty (except for the now-meaningless note numbers). Good grief! How was I supposed to fix that? Well, at least the note text was intact at the end of the document. Now I had to replace those automatic reference numbers with superscript text numbers. Time to write a macro!

```
Selection.Find.ClearFormatting
With Selection.Find
.Text = "^02"
.Replacement.Text = ""
.Forward = True
.Wrap = wdFindContinue
.Format = False
.MatchCase = False
.MatchWholeWord = False
.MatchWildcards = False
.MatchSoundsLike = False
.MatchAllWordForms = False
End With
Selection.Find.Execute
Do While Selection.Find.Found
i = i + 1
Selection.TypeText Text:=Str$(i)
Selection.Find.Execute
Loop
```

You may recognize this macro as a "repeating macro," as described in the article "Repeating Macros." The macro finds an automatic footnote reference number (^02), increments a plain old number in the computer's memory (i = i + 1), and then types over the top of the reference number with the incremented number (Selection.TypeText Text:=Str$(i)). *Don't* use this macro on documents that have properly working notes. It will delete the notes (and thus the note text), leaving only superscript numbers in their place.

Running the macro took care of my problem but left me with another: how to turn those text notes into automatically numbered ones so I didn't have to manually renumber as I edited the piece. I could have created a bunch of new footnotes by hand, pasting the note text into each one—if I'd wanted to be inefficient. Luckily, there's a better solution: the "Text to Notes" feature of my trusty NoteStripper program, which I used.

Gritting my teeth, I opened the third article and looked at the notes. Yes, also messed up. This guy had used Word's automatic notes feature but then opened the footnotes pane, *deleted* the note number (a quick invitation to file corruption), and *manually typed in* note numbers and periods. Grrrr. *Now* what? This one needed drastic measures. I selected all of the notes in the footnotes pane, copied them (they were nothing but text, so why not?), and pasted them at the end of the document. Then I used that macro again to turn the note reference numbers into superscript text. Finally, I used NoteStripper's "Text to Notes" feature to turn the text notes into automatically numbering ones.

And the rest of the articles? About a third of them used notes correctly. The rest were a mess, just like the first three. If you're ever faced with this kind of stuff, maybe this article will help.

Restoring Missing Notes

After learning how to fix messed-up notes, I ran into a new variety of "messed-upness" that I thought you might like to know about. If you want to see the problem in action, you can replicate it. For starters, do this:

1. Open a document and switch to Normal view (View > Normal).
2. Insert a footnote (Insert > Reference > Footnote).
3. Type a little text into your nice, new footnote.
4. Repeat steps 2 and 3 until you have, oh, three or four notes in your document.

Now, let's say you were a clueless author who wanted to delete a footnote. What would you do? Delete the note number in body text? Bzzzt. Wrong. That's what you'd do if you knew what you were doing. A clueless author would do what I saw recently: Open the Notes pane (View > Footnotes), select a note, and hit the DELETE key.

Go ahead, try it.

If you selected the entire footnote, including the final carriage return, you should have seen this message:

Microsoft Office Word Err=1156
This is not a valid action for footnotes.

Word is upset because you tried to delete that final carriage return, which isn't a normal carriage return but a special note carriage return that can't be deleted. (Why the error message doesn't say something straightforward like "You can't delete the final carriage return in a note; please delete the note in the body of your document" is known only to some programmer at Microsoft.) At any rate, if you want to delete a note, you must do so in the body of your document, which will automatically delete the note including its carriage return.

But if you're a clueless author, what will you do? You'll go to the Notes pane and delete everything *except* the last carriage return. That will leave your notes looking like this:

[1] Text of note 1.¶
[2] Text of note 2.¶
¶
[4] Text of note 4.¶

Wait a minute. Where's note 3? Our author deleted it, of course, leaving nothing but its undeletable carriage return (¶). So, there's your clue that this problem exists: a missing note number with a carriage return in its place. (If you want to see the carriage returns, click the Show/Hide [¶] button on Word's Standard toolbar.)

Okay, enough griping—and my apologies to any authors or editors I've offended. Here's how to fix the problem:

1. Select and copy the note number of some *other* note. In this case, 4 would do nicely.
2. Move your cursor to the spot where the number for note 3 should be—in other words, in front of the orphaned carriage return.
3. Paste the note number at that spot.

Surprise! Rather than getting another note number 4, you get note number 3—exactly what you needed. What you pasted isn't a number but a magic code that generates note numbers in sequence. Thus, note 3.

Now you can type some text after the new note number, if you like, or you can go into the body of your document and delete the note properly (you could also do that without first fixing the note number). Then make a friendly phone call to your author and politely explain how to delete notes in Word.

Restoring Superscript to Note Numbers

I get manuscripts with all kinds of weird formatting, but recently I got one from which all formatting had been removed. That might have been all right, but the note reference numbers were no longer superscript; they all looked something like this.42 I wasn't about to fix all those by hand, so I came up with this solution, which I hope you'll find as useful as I did:

1. Back up your documents, just in case.
2. Call up Word's Replace dialog (Edit > Replace).
3. In the "Find What" box, enter this:

    ([! 0123456789,:$\(])([0-9]{1,})

4. In the "Replace With" box, enter this:

    \1<V>\2</V>

5. Click the "More" button if it's available.
6. Put a check in the "Use wildcards" checkbox.
7. Click the "Replace All" button.
8. In the "Find What" box, enter this:

    <V>(*)</V>

9. In the "Replace With" box, enter this (formatted as superscript):

    \1

10. Click the "Replace All" button.

All of your note numbers should now be in glorious superscript.
For more infomation, see "Two-Step Searching."

Readers Write

RICHARD O'REGAN:

I have another of my long legal books to do. In this one the author, preparing his work in Word for Windows, has been inconsistent about how he punctuates at the footnote reference numbers. Sometimes he puts his comma or the period after the footnote reference number and sometimes he puts it before.

I want the comma or period to precede the reference number. I can't do it with search and replace because you can't put the footnote reference (^f) in the replace box.

I REPLIED: You can do it with a not-so-simple find-and-replace.

In the Find What box, put this:

(^02)([.\!\?])

The ^02 will find the note reference numbers. The characters in square brackets will find the closing punctuation you want to transpose. If you like, you can add other punctuation, such as commas, colons, and semicolons:

(^02)([.\!\?,:;])

The backslash on the ! and ? are necessary to tell Word that you're using them as characters and not as wildcards. The parentheses group the items so that you can switch them around in the Replace With box, which should have this in it:

\2\1

That tells Word to put the second group (the punctuation) first, and the first group (the footnote number) last. Doesn't the Bible say something about that?

Finally, you'll need to put a checkmark in the "Use wildcards" checkbox (you may need to click the "More" button before the checkbox is available).

Editing Notes Alphabetically

One of my editing projects a few years ago was just loaded with notes—4,028 of them to be exact. And boy, were they a mess—a garbled collection of inconsistency and error. They looked something like this:

Jones, Sunlit Land, 24.
Era of Sand, Jan. 1953, 59.
Today's News, April 17, 1965, 3.
Jones, Sunlit land, 33.
Era of Sandy, January 1953 20.
Jones, Sunlit Land, 78.

As I worked through them, I kept wishing I had a way to sort them alphabetically, so they'd look like this:

Era of Sand, Jan. 1953, 59.
Era of Sandy, January 1953 20.
Jones, Sunlit Land, 24.
Jones, Sunlit land, 33.
Jones, Sunlit Land, 78.
Today's News, April 17, 1965, 3.

Then I could easily compare notes that cited the same source and make sure everything was consistent. But how? Suddenly the solution struck me. (No, it didn't hurt.) I could put the notes into a sortable table. Since the notes were embedded, automatically numbering ones, I'd need my trusty NoteStripper program to strip them out as text. (If they had already been text at the end of the document, I could have put them into a table without first using NoteStripper.) Here's the procedure:

1. *Back up your document* in case something goes wrong.
2. If you've been working with Revision Tracking turned on, turn it off and make all revisions permanent. Otherwise, you'll run into problems with a bug that refuses to actually delete notes when Revision Tracking is on.
3. If you're not already working in Normal view, make the switch (View > Normal).
4. Open the notes pane (View > Footnotes).
5. With your cursor at the top of the notes pane, click "Edit > Replace."
6. In the "Find What" box, enter "[\^013]([!^02])" (carriage returns not preceded by a note number; don't include the quotation marks). Yes, this will work on a Macintosh.
7. In the "Replace With" box, enter "@@@\1" (again, without the quotation marks).

8. Put a check in the "Use wildcards" checkbox. (You may have to click the "More" button to make this available.)
9. Click "OK" to make the replacements. Now all of your notes are (temporarily) just one paragraph long.
10. Use my NoteStripper program to strip notes to text. For note number format, select "Number with period and tab." When you're finished, all of your notes will be (unembedded) text at the bottom of your document.
11. Select all of the notes.
12. Click "Table" and then "Convert Text to Table." Set "Number of Columns" to 2. Set "Separate Text At" to tabs.
13. Click the "OK" button.

You should now have a table full of numbers and their corresponding notes. To sort the table alphabetically:

1. Your table should still be selected from step 13, above. If you've moved your cursor so it's no longer selected, put your cursor in the table and select the table (Table > Select Table). *Don't skip this step.* (I'll explain more below).
2. Click "Table" and then "Sort Text."
3. In the "Sort By" box, select "Column 2," which is the column holding your note text.
4. In the "Type" box, select "Text."
5. Click "Ascending" and "No Header Row."
6. Click the "OK" button.

Now your notes should be sorted alphabetically, and you can edit to your heart's content. (If your paragraph formatting is double spaced, you may want to change it to single spaced.) This is a pretty efficient way to work. You can easily spot typos or discrepancies in citations just by looking at the length of the lines:

10142 Jones, Sunlit Land, 24.
11773 Jones, Sunlit land, 33.
10044 Jones, Sunlit Land, 78.

You'll probably notice that the second line is a little shorter than the other two, so you know something is off. Ah, there it is—that lowercased l on "land" should be capped.
You can also sort your notes numerically, if you want to look at them from that angle:

1. Put your cursor in the table and select the table (Table > Select Table). *Don't skip this step.* (I'll explain more below).
2. Click "Table" and then "Sort Text."
3. In the "Sort By" box, select "Column 1," which is the column holding your note numbers.
4. In the "Type" box, select "Number." (If you select "Text," your note numbers won't sort properly.)

5. Click "Ascending" and "No Header Row."
6. Click the "OK" button.

You can switch back and forth between alphabetical and numerical order as needed. Just be careful *not* to sort one column at a time (or change any of the note numbers— avoid globally finding and replacing numbers as you edit). If you do, you'll lose the correspondence between note numbers and their notes, which would be very, very bad. (Hence my emphasis on selecting the whole table before sorting. You kept that backup, right?) One way to avoid this entirely is to select the first column and format it as hidden, but then, before reembedding your notes (as explained below), you'll need to select the table and turn off the hidden formatting. Also, don't delete the @@@ markers that indicate paragraph breaks; you'll need them later to restore the breaks.

After you've finished editing your notes, you'll need NoteStripper again to get them back into your document as embedded, automatically numbered notes. Here's the procedure:

1. Select the table of numbers and (now-edited) notes (Table > Select Table).
2. Turn the table back to text (Table > Convert Table to Text; Separate Text with Tabs), which will give you a number and a tab preceding each note.
3. Use NoteStripper's "Text to Notes" feature to turn the text notes into embedded ones (see the documentation for instructions).
4. Open the notes pane (View > Footnotes).
5. Find "@@@" and replace with "^p" to restore your carriage returns.

That's it! If you're ever faced with a bunch of notes that need to be wrestled into submission, maybe this technique will help you as much as it did me. If your notes are simply text to begin with (not embedded), you can use the technique without NoteStripper.

Cross-Referencing Notes

If you're like me, you love Microsoft Word's note feature—in particular, being able to insert or delete a footnote or endnote and have all of the subsequent notes renumber automatically. Have you ever wondered, though, how to create a note reference number that refers to a note that already exists?

For example, let's say the following text is a Word document with notes (indicated with superscripted numbers):

Lorem ipsum dolor sit amet,[1] consectetuer adipiscing elit, sed diam nonummy[2] nibh euismod tincidunt ut laoreet dolore magna aliquam erat volutpat.[3]

[1] Ut wisi enim ad minim veniam.

[2] Duis autem vel eum iriure dolor in hendrerit in vulputate.

[3] Delenit augue duis dolore te feugait nulla facilisi.

We have a reference number for note 1 after "amet," but let's say we want to refer to note 1 again, this time after "elit," like this:

Lorem ipsum dolor sit amet,[1] consectetuer adipiscing elit,[1] sed diam nonummy[2] nibh euismod tincidunt ut laoreet dolore magna aliquam erat volutpat.[3]

[1] Ut wisi enim ad minim veniam.

[2] Duis autem vel eum iriure dolor in hendrerit in vulputate.

[3] Delenit augue duis dolore te feugait nulla facilisi.

Is that even possible in Word? Yes, it is, and it's called cross-referencing a note. The procedure is basically the same for footnotes or endnotes, although here I'll use footnotes for the example. Here's how to do it:

1. Open a document that has footnotes.
2. Put your cursor in your text where you want to cross-reference an existing note.
3. Click the "Insert" menu.
4. Click "Cross-reference."
5. Click the "Reference type" drop-down list.
6. Click "Footnote" in the list.
7. Click the "Insert reference to:" list.
8. Click "Footnote number (formatted)"—probably the last item in the list.
9. In the "For which footnote:" list, click the number of the footnote you want to cross-reference.
10. Click the "Insert" button.

These instructions sound more complicated than the procedure actually is—it's fairly easy. Be careful, though. If you insert a new note before your original note, the cross-referenced note won't change automatically. For example, here's our document with the cross-referenced note 1:

Lorem ipsum dolor sit amet,[1] consectetuer adipiscing elit,[1] sed diam nonummy[2] nibh euismod tincidunt ut laoreet dolore magna aliquam erat volutpat.[3]
[1] Ut wisi enim ad minim veniam.
[2] Duis autem vel eum iriure dolor in hendrerit in vulputate.
[3] Delenit augue duis dolore te feugait nulla facilisi.

Now, if we insert a new note after "ipsum," our original note 1 reference number will change to "2," but our cross-referenced note number after "elit" will remain as "1":

Lorem ipsum[1] dolor sit amet,[2] consectetuer adipiscing elit,[1] sed diam nonummy[3] nibh euismod tincidunt ut laoreet dolore magna aliquam erat volutpat.[4]
[1] Accumsan et iusto odio dignissim.
[2] Ut wisi enim ad minim veniam.
[3] Duis autem vel eum iriure dolor in hendrerit in vulputate.
[4] Delenit augue duis dolore te feugait nulla facilisi.

Why? Because the cross-referenced note number is what Microsoft calls a "field," and fields don't update automatically. To update the field (the cross-referenced note number), select it and press the F9 key. The document will then look like this, with the number after "elit" updated to a "2":

Lorem ipsum[1] dolor sit amet,[2] consectetuer adipiscing elit,[2] sed diam nonummy[3] nibh euismod tincidunt ut laoreet dolore magna aliquam erat volutpat.[4]
[1] Accumsan et iusto odio dignissim.
[2] Ut wisi enim ad minim veniam.
[3] Duis autem vel eum iriure dolor in hendrerit in vulputate.
[4] Delenit augue duis dolore te feugait nulla facilisi.

If you want to update all of the fields in your document (if you've got lots of cross-referenced note numbers, for example), select all (Edit > Select All) and then press F9. You can also set fields to update when you print by clicking Tools > Options > Print and putting a checkmark in the box labeled "Update fields."

Incidentally, these cross-referenced notes work beautifully with the "Notes to Text" feature of my NoteStripper program and, after being stripped, with my QuarkConverter program.

Endnote Headings

Many of the books I work on have endnotes—notes at the back of the book—with the note numbering starting over at 1 for each chapter. To keep things clear, I like to separate the notes with headings, like this:

> *Notes to Chapter 1*
> [1] Here's the first note.
> [2] Here's the second note.
> [3] Here's the third note.
> *Notes to Chapter 2*
> [1] Here's the first note.
> [2] Here's the second note.
> [3] Here's the third note.

And so on.

Unfortunately, Microsoft Word doesn't include a good way to do this. Undeterred, many of the authors I work with open the Notes Pane (click View > Normal; then click View > Footnotes) and just type in the headings as needed. What's wrong with that? It depends on how it's done. Let's say we have a bunch of notes that look like this:

> [1] Here's the first note in chapter 2.¶
> [2] Here's the second note in chapter 2.¶
> [3] Here's the last note in chapter 2.¶
> [1] Here's the first note in chapter 3.¶
> [2] Here's the second note in chapter 3.¶
> [3] Here's the last note in chapter 3.¶

Here, a pilcrow (¶) represents the final, magic, undeletable carriage return for each note. You can learn more in "Restoring Missing Notes."

Many authors put their cursor in front of the first note in chapter 3, hit ENTER, and type their heading, like this:

> [1] Here's the first note in chapter 2.¶
> [2] Here's the second note in chapter 2.¶
> [3] Here's the last note in chapter 2.¶
> *Notes to Chapter 3*
> [1] Here's the first note in chapter 3.¶
> [2] Here's the second note in chapter 3.¶
> [3] Here's the last note in chapter 3.¶

This is a problem, because it means there's a note in the Notes Pane that isn't really a note (it has no note number and doesn't end with a magic carriage return), which leads to document corruption. See "Restoring Missing Notes" for more information.

So what's an author (or editor) to do? Make the heading *part* of the preceding note. Done correctly, our example above would look like this:

[1] Here's the first note in chapter 2.¶

[2] Here's the second note in chapter 2.¶

[3] Here's the last note in chapter 2.

Notes to Chapter 3¶

[1] Here's the first note in chapter 3.¶

[2] Here's the second note in chapter 3.¶

[3] Here's the last note in chapter 3.¶

That's counterintuitive, because it requires the heading for chapter 3 to be part of the last note for chapter 2. But, in my experience, that's what needs to be done.

Note that since the heading is still a separate paragraph, it can be formatted with a heading style so it *looks* like a heading and not like part of the note text.

At this point you may be saying, "What about the heading for chapter 1? There's no previous note that can include it."

Simple answer: Type the heading at the end of your body text. Don't put it in the Notes Pane at all.

Thanks to Jay Parry for suggesting this topic.

The Notes That Wouldn't Die

Editors who use Microsoft Word's revision-tracking feature in documents with footnotes (or endnotes) have often complained of an annoyance: If you delete a note (which you should do only by deleting the reference mark in the text), the reference mark is struck out, but the *text* of the note itself is *not* struck out. This can be really confusing to clients who want to review your work:

"I thought we agreed to delete note 47."

"Right! I did delete it."

"Then why is it still there?"

Why Microsoft hasn't fixed this problem in, lo, these many years is beyond me. But since they haven't, I thought it might be possible to create a macro that would do the job. So here it is:

```
Sub NoteMarker()
Dim NumNotes
Dim RevType
Dim n
On Error Resume Next
'Set tracking to on
ActiveDocument.TrackRevisions = True
'Count the notes
NumNotes = ActiveDocument.Footnotes.Count
'Select each note reference and see if it's been deleted
For n = 1 To NumNotes
RevType = "" 'This must be reset each time through
ActiveDocument.Footnotes(n).Reference.Select
RevType = Selection.Range.Revisions.Item(1).Type
If RevType = wdRevisionDelete Then
ActiveDocument.Footnotes(n).Range.Delete 'Delete the note's text
End If
Next n
End Sub
```

You should run the macro on a document only *after* you've finished editing the document and have already deleted note references as needed. Why? Because the macro looks at each note reference in your document. If the reference has been deleted, the macro also marks the corresponding note text as deleted.

Enjoy! (But enjoy responsibly! Always back up your work before running a macro.)

Readers Write

GEOFF HART:

You wrote: "Editors who use Microsoft Word's revision-tracking feature in documents with footnotes (or endnotes) have often complained of an annoyance: If you delete a note (which you should do only by deleting the reference mark in the text), the reference mark is struck out, but the *text* of the note itself is *not* struck out. . . . Why Microsoft hasn't fixed this problem in, lo, these many years is beyond me."

The exact same thing occurs with comment markers and the associated text, and it's driven many an author to premature baldness due to frustrated hair-pulling. (I used to have to explain this to one of my pet authors pretty much every manuscript we worked on together, at least twice per year.) From that perspective (that is, based on the number of people it confuses), it's a bad design choice.

Seen from another perspective, however, this is actually a *good* design feature: When you delete a comment or note marker using revision tracking, the meaning is clear: "delete this marker *and* all the associated text." But if deleting the marker automatically removed the text, and the author decided that (contrary to the editor's advice) they wanted to retain the footnote, then there would be no easy way to recover the footnote text. Given Word's byzantine file format, possibly even no way at all to get it back. Seen in this light, Microsoft wisely decided to delete the marker but retain the text—at least until you accept the deletion. At that point, text and marker both do what they're supposed to do: go away.

So why not use the strikethrough format to mark all the note's or comment's text to show that it's been deleted? Because sometimes one or more edits may have been inserted in the note or comment text. If Word marked both the original text and any inserted text as deleted, you wouldn't be able to distinguish those edits from the original text: both would be marked as deleted. Leaving the original format untouched lets the author see what was done without having to use the Reviewing toolbar to work through the note or comment, one change at a time, accepting or rejecting each change individually without knowing when to stop.

In Word X, the note is marked for deletion, but the text is left in whatever state it was in before you deleted the marker. That's a good thing in my eyes, not a bug or oversight.

If you delete a note or comment marker by intent or by accident, a single keystroke would (invisibly) delete the entire content of that footnote, which can run many paragraphs or even pages in length. (You wouldn't believe some of the footnotes I've seen.) It's very easy to miss a single-character deletion, particularly if you're working (like many of us do) in Normal view, where the footnote text is invisible unless you open the Footnote pane. This is also (not coincidentally) why it takes two presses of the delete key to mark a footnote or comment for deletion: a clever safety feature. Of course, it doesn't protect you against deleting markers by block-selecting the text that contains them.

This problem doesn't exist for regular text, or at least is less likely to become fatal, because the deletion is much more obvious: if you inadvertently select an entire paragraph and press the Delete key, you'll see an entire paragraph formatted as strikethrough. That change is sufficiently dramatic that you have time to undo the change by CTRL + Z(apping) it.

There's probably a clever way to make the feature work better (i.e., to delete both the marker and the text without losing any embedded edits), but it would take a bit of thought to figure out how this might work. The current awkward situation is a tradeoff between non-transparency and protecting users from errors.

The Notes That Wouldn't Die, Part 2

The previous article included a macro for editors who use Microsoft Word's revision-tracking feature in documents with footnotes. The macro was designed to strike out the text of deleted notes—but only at the *end* of the editing process, after the editor has deleted any unnecessary note references. So then I started thinking: "Why not make a macro that strikes out the note text *each time* a note reference is deleted?"

So here it is:

```
Sub FootnoteDelete()
If Selection.Information(wdReferenceOfType) = 1 Then 'Footnote
If Selection.Type = 1 Then 'Text is not selected
Selection.MoveRight Unit:=wdCharacter, Count:=1, Extend:=wdExtend
End If
If ActiveDocument.TrackRevisions = True Then
Selection.Footnotes(1).Range.Delete 'Delete the note's text
Selection.Delete 'Delete the note reference
End If
End If
End Sub
```

The macro works by checking to see if your cursor immediately precedes a footnote reference. If it does, the macro selects the reference.

Next, the macro checks to see if revision tracking is turned on. If it is, it deletes the *note text* for the currently selected footnote reference. Then it deletes the reference itself. In both cases, the text is struck out as a revision rather than removed completely.

If your cursor doesn't precede a footnote reference, or if you haven't selected text including a footnote reference, the macro does nothing. (Handy!)

If text is already selected, the macro checks to see if the selection includes a footnote reference. If it does, the macro proceeds to carry out its work. Please note, however, that if you've selected text that includes *more than one* footnote reference, the macro will delete only the note text of the first footnote in the selection. Moral: Don't try to use the macro to delete more than one note at a time.

For ease of use, you may want to map this macro to a key combination. I recommend the Insert key, which sits just above your Delete key and usually just causes problems, at least for me. Then if you need to delete a note while revision tracking is turned on, press the Insert key. Both the note reference and the note text will be marked as deleted.

If you need a macro for endnotes rather than footnotes, here you go:

```
Sub EndnoteDelete()
If Selection.Information(wdReferenceOfType) = 2 Then 'Endnote
If Selection.Type = 1 Then 'Text is not selected
```

```
Selection.MoveRight Unit:=wdCharacter, Count:=1, Extend:=wdExtend
End If
If ActiveDocument.TrackRevisions = True Then
Selection.Endnotes(1).Range.Delete 'Delete the note's text
Selection.Delete 'Delete the note reference
End If
End If
End Sub
```

If you need a macro for both footnotes and endnotes, you can just cobble the two macros together (apologies to Steve Hudson, who would want me to do better):

```
Sub NoteDelete()
If Selection.Information(wdReferenceOfType) = 1 Then 'Footnote
If Selection.Type = 1 Then 'Text is not selected
Selection.MoveRight Unit:=wdCharacter, Count:=1, Extend:=wdExtend
End If
If ActiveDocument.TrackRevisions = True Then
Selection.Footnotes(1).Range.Delete 'Delete the note's text
Selection.Delete 'Delete the note reference
End If
End If
If Selection.Information(wdReferenceOfType) = 2 Then 'Endnote
If Selection.Type = 1 Then 'Text is not selected
Selection.MoveRight Unit:=wdCharacter, Count:=1, Extend:=wdExtend
End If
If ActiveDocument.TrackRevisions = True Then
Selection.Endnotes(1).Range.Delete 'Delete the note's text
Selection.Delete 'Delete the note reference
End If
End If
End Sub
```

Readers Write

HILARY POWERS:

Today's chore involved reviewing embedded endnotes and deciding what if anything needs preservation out of them, then deleting them from the text entirely—without tracking the deletion, even though the rest of the edit is tracked. That rapidly got so frustrating that I recorded a macro that allows me to kill a note by placing the insertion point to the left of the note number and pressing a hot key.

Then I discovered all sorts of other uses for the same macro—things that have been irritating me for years, at a level too low to bother doing anything about it, like removing extra tab characters and punctuation that the author won't care about. Sometimes something is so obvious it's utterly hidden. . . .

The following code will delete any one character (an embedded note number is one character, no matter how many digits it has)—without tracking it if you're tracking everything else, and with tracking if you're not.

```
Sub DelOne()
'Macro recorded 9/26/2004 by Hilary Powers
ActiveDocument.TrackRevisions = Not ActiveDocument.TrackRevisions
Selection.MoveRight Unit:=wdCharacter, Count:=1, Extend:=wdExtend
Selection.Delete Unit:=wdCharacter, Count:=1
ActiveDocument.TrackRevisions = Not ActiveDocument.TrackRevisions
End Sub
```

It doesn't matter how old an edit dog I get to be, there are always new tricks!

Notes to Bibliography

I'm often faced with the task of creating a bibliography for a book I'm editing, but I hate typing in all those entries from scratch. Lazy fellow that I am, I've figured out an automated way to turn parenthetical notes into bibliography entries. It's longish, but it sure beats doing it by hand. You may need to modify the procedure a bit to fit your own needs. Still, this article will give you the general idea.

Let's say we've got a document full of parenthetical notes, like this one:

(Jack M. Lyon, *Total Word Domination* [PocketPCPress, 2001], 121.)

The first thing we need to do is get all the notes out of there so we can turn them into bibliography entries, like this:

Lyon, Jack M. *Total Word Domination.* PocketPCPress, 2001.

If you need to do this with lots of documents, you'll definitely want to look at my Puller program. If you only need to do this with a document or two, you can use this sneaky little method:

1. *Back up your documents* in case anything goes wrong. There, you've been warned.
2. Click Tools > Replace.
3. In the Find What box, enter this:

\(*\)

4. With your cursor still in the Find What box, click the No Formatting button to remove any formatting that may be applied to the box.
5. In the Replace With box, enter this:

^&

6. With your cursor still in the Replace With box, click the No Formatting button to remove any formatting that may be applied to the box.
7. Click the Format button (you may have to click the More button before it's available) and then Font.
8. Under Effects, put a check in the box of an effect you *know* is not in your document. Shadow should do nicely. You should avoid using italic or bold, which probably *are* used in your document.

9. Click the OK button. The Replace With box should now be labeled as "Shadow."
10. Put a check in the "Use wildcards" checkbox.
11. Click Replace All.

All of your parenthetical notes will now be shadowed. Isn't that exciting?

Now get rid of everything in your document that's not shadowed, leaving only the parenthetical notes:

1. Click Tools > Replace.
2. Clear any text from the Find What box.
3. Click the Format button and then Font.
4. Make sure the check in the box next to Shadow is *blank*—no checkmark, either black or gray.
5. Click the OK button. The Find What box should now be labeled as "Not Shadow."
6. Clear any text from the Replace With box.
7. With your cursor still in the Replace With box, click the No Formatting button to remove the formatting applied to the box.
8. Remove the check from the "Use wildcards" checkbox.
9. Click "Replace All."

Wow, the only thing left in your document is a bunch of shadowed text in parentheses. You want each note to be followed by a carriage return, so if some of them aren't, you may need to put some in:

1. Click Tools > Replace.
2. With your cursor in the Find What box, click the No Formatting button to remove the formatting applied to the box.
3. In the Find What box, enter this:

)

4. In the Replace With box, enter this:

)^p

5. Click "Replace All."

Now you may need to get rid of double returns:

1. Click Tools > Replace.
2. In the Find What box, enter this:

^p^p

3. In the Replace With box, enter this:

^p

4. Click "Replace All."

If you think all of this is too much work, you really should check out my Puller program. What's next? Well, for starters, let's get rid of our opening and closing parentheses:

1. Delete the parenthesis at the beginning of your first note and the end of your last note.
2. In the Find What box, enter this:

)^p(

3. In the Replace With box, enter this:

    ^p

4. Click "Replace All."

Now let's get those names transposed:

1. Click Tools > Replace.
2. With your cursor in the Find What box, click the No Formatting button to remove any formatting that may be applied to the box.
3. In the Find What box, enter this:

    ,(*\))

4. In the Replace With box, enter this:

    ^t\1

5. Put a check in the "Use wildcards" checkbox.
6. Click "Replace All." There should now be a tab following each name in your document. Please note that if you've got "Jr.," "Sr.," "Ph.D.," and so on with some of those names, you'll need to get the tab *after* the suffixes and make sure your commas are right. Remember that you can use Find and Replace to help you with this.
7. Click Edit > Select All to select all the text in your document.
8. Click Table > Convert > Text to Table.
9. In the dialog box that appears, make sure "Number of columns" is set to 2 and "Separate text at" is set to Tabs.
10. Click the OK button. Your notes are now in two columns, with names in the first one and the bookish stuff in the second one.
11. Use your mouse to point at the top of the first column. A little black arrow should appear, pointing down.
12. Click the left mouse button to select the column.
13. Click Edit > Copy to copy the column.

14. Create a new blank document.

15. Click Edit > Paste. The name column should now be all by itself in the new document.

16. Put your cursor somewhere in column and click Table > Select > Table to select the column.

17. Click Table > Convert > Table to Text.

18. Under "Separate text with," select "Paragraph marks" and click the OK button. You've now got a list of names *not* in a table.

19. Download and install my free NameSwapper macro:

http://www.editorium.com/freebies.htm

20. Run the macro to transpose all those names to last name first. Pretty slick, no? Don't go sorting names or deleting duplicates just yet.

21. You guessed it, click Edit > Select All to select all those transposed names.

22. Click Table > Convert > Text to Table.

23. In the dialog box that appears, make sure "Number of columns" is set to 1 and "Separate text at" is set to Paragraphs.

24. Click the OK button. Your names are now back in a column.

25. Put your cursor somewhere in the column and click Table > Select > Table to select it.

26. Click Edit > Copy to copy the column.

27. Switch back to your main document.

28. Use your mouse to point at the top of the first column. That little black arrow should appear again.

29. Click the left mouse button to select the column.

30. Click Edit > Paste Cells to replace the column with your new one full of nicely transposed names.

Wow, thirty steps! That may be a record. I sure hope I got them all right.
Now let's de-table-fy the notes:

1. Put your cursor somewhere in the table and click Table > Select > Table to select it.

2. Click Table > Convert > Table to Text.

3. Under "Separate text with," select "Other" and put some weird character in the little box. I like to use the tilde character (˜), which you'll find on the upper left of your keyboard. Click the OK button to get rid of the table cells and hook your names back up with their notes.

Easy sledding from here, so I won't outline the rest of the steps in detail, but here's the basic procedure:

1. Remove the check from the "Use wildcards" checkbox.

2. Find the tildes and replace them with nothing.

3. Find all occurrences of a space followed by an opening bracket ([) and replace them with a period followed by a space (.).

4. Get rid of the closing brackets and page numbers by doing a wildcard search for this (yes, this will work on a Macintosh)—

\]*[\^013]

—and replacing it with this (note the period):

.^p

5. Replace Shadow with Not Shadow.

6. Sort the notes alphabetically and get rid of duplicates, using the automated techniques explained in "Working with Lists."

7. Go to the top of your document and type "Bibliography." You'll probably need to do some cleanup, but basically you're done. Now, wasn't that easier than typing all those entries by hand?

Special Characters

What's That Character?

Here's the scenario: You open a giant document from a client and start looking through it. But what's this? The same odd character at the beginning of every paragraph. Must be some kind of file translation error. Odder still, Microsoft Word won't let you paste the character into its Find and Replace dialog, so how are you going to get rid of them all? By hand? Horrors!

If you knew the character's numeric code, you could search for it, as explained in "Searching with Numeric Character Codes."

But this character isn't on the usual list. How can you find out its numeric code? By using my trusty NextCharacter macro:

```
Dim NextChar$
NextChar$ = Str(Asc(WordBasic.[Selection$]()))
WordBasic.MsgBox _
"The code for the next character is " + NextChar$ + ".", _
"Next Character"
```

After you run the macro, a message box will appear on your screen with the numeric code you need.

Identifying Unicode Character Numbers

Sometimes to find or replace a Unicode character in Microsoft Word, you need the character's number, as explained in "Finding and Replacing Unicode Characters." If you know the name of the character, you can probably look up its Unicode number at Alan Wood's Unicode Resources site:

http://www.alanwood.net/unicode/search.html

But what if you don't know its name? Isn't there a way to find out the number of a Unicode character that's used in your Word document?

Fortunately, there is. Alan Wood has provided a terrific macro for that purpose, and you can get the macro here:

http://www.alanwood.net/unicode/utilities_editors.html

You may have to scroll down a little (past the first, short macro) to find the macro, which is introduced by the following text: "The following macro will attempt to identify a single character that you have selected, and display its Unicode decimal character reference."

I'd recommend that you put the macro on a menu, toolbar button, or keyboard combination for easy access.

Please note that you must select a character before running the macro. By the way, the macro also identifies ANSI numbers, which makes it a good substitute for the macro in "What's That Character?"

Converting Unicode Characters

Earlier, I explained how to find and replace Unicode characters, which I'm seeing more and more in electronic manuscripts that come into my hands for editing. The problem is that many shops do typesetting in QuarkXPress, which, at least as of version 5.0, won't import Unicode characters. (This is also true of several other typesetting programs.) For manuscripts using lots of Hebrew, Greek, or other special characters, this is a real problem.

For several weeks, I had no solution. Then, late one night, I was thinking about how to create a Word add-in that would search for formatting and replace it with user-defined tags. That's when it struck me: You can't search for all Unicode characters at once and replace them with something else, since there are thousands of them. But if you know which Unicode characters are being used in a document, you can certainly find and replace them with a combination of characters and tags that are meaningful in QuarkXPress.

To understand this, you have to know how special characters, such as Greek, are handled in QuarkXPress. They're just regular alphanumeric characters formatted in a special font. For example, to get alpha, beta, and gamma in QuarkXPress, you'd typically type a, b, and c and then format those characters with a Greek font:

a produces alpha
b produces beta
c produces gamma

So what you have to do in Microsoft Word is find a Unicode alpha and replace it with the letter a, tagged with an XPress Tag that indicates a Greek character style sheet in QuarkXPress. Here's how:

1. In Word, click the "Edit" menu.
2. Click "Replace."
3. In the "Find What" box, enter the following string, which tells Word to search for the Unicode character alpha:

   ^u945

For more information, see "Finding and Replacing Unicode Characters."
4. In the "Replace With" box, enter the character (a for alpha) and the surrounding XPress Tags you'll use to tell QuarkXPress to format the character with Greek:

   <@Greek>a<@$p>

By the way, that's the standard format for XPress Tags that will create a character style sheet in QuarkXPress. The name "Greek" is arbitrary; call the style sheet whatever you'd like.

Now, to import the file into QuarkXPress:

1. In Word, save the file as a text document.
2. Create a new document (or open an existing one) in QuarkXPress.
3. Place your cursor into the document's text box where you want the text to begin.
4. Click the "File" menu.
5. Click "Import Text" (in older versions, click "Get Text").
6. Click "Interpret XPress Tags" (in older versions, put a check in the box labeled "Include Style Sheets.")
7. Find and click the XPressTag file (the text file).
8. Click OK (in older versions, click the "Open" button).

But remember: For this to work, your XPress Tags file *must* include the version tag as the first thing in the document. The tag should look something like this:

    <v7.31><e0>

To find out what the tag actually is for your version of QuarkXPress, export a document ("Save Text" or "Export Text") as an XPressTag file from QuarkXPress. Then open the that file into Microsoft Word. You'll see the version code at the top of the document.

You can type the code manually into an XPress Tags document, but a better solution is to enter the code into the QuarkConverter dialog (in the box on the lower right labeled "Quark version tag"). For more information, see the documentation for QuarkConverter.

At this point, the file will be imported into QuarkXPress, and the XPress Tags you used will be imported as a character style sheet named "Greek." Now, in QuarkXPress, edit the character style sheet to use your Greek font. Presto! The character that used to be a Unicode alpha in Word will once again become an alpha in QuarkXPress.

For this to work, you have to know three things:

1. The Unicode numbers for the characters you want to convert. You can look up such numbers here:

   http://www.alanwood.net/unicode/search.html

2. The font (such as Greek) you'll be using to produce special characters in QuarkX-Press.
3. The "ordinary" character (such as "a") that the font uses to produce each special character (such as alpha).

Then you can record a macro in which you find and replace each Unicode character with the ordinary character surrounded by the XPress Tags. Then, the next time you need to convert a bunch of Greek or Hebrew, just run the macro.

Of course, recording such a macro—or a series of them for different languages—is error-prone and tedious. A better solution is to use my MegaReplacer program, for which you can create a script that looks like this, with the Unicode numbers on the left (of the pipe symbols) and the XPress Tags and characters on the right:

```
^u945<@Greek>a<@$p>
^u946|<@Greek>b<@$p>
^u947|<@Greek>c<@$p>
```

MegaReplacer also has the advantage of batch processing, so you can run the script on a whole folder full of documents. And, of course, the scripts are easy to change as needed.

You might also want to use my QuarkConverter program to automatically insert additional XPress Tags for style and character formatting.

However you decide to work, you now have a way to convert Unicode characters to special characters for QuarkXPress or any other typesetting program that uses tags.

Readers Write

Melissa Bogen:

I read with interest your recent article on converting Unicode characters to QuarkXPress Tags. Is there a resource you can suggest where I can see a complete list of XPress Tags?

I replied: There's a particularly well-done list here, in PDF form:

http://www.macworld.com/downloads/magazine/XPressTagsList.pdf

Ellipses

In the documentation for my FileCleaner program, I say, "Authors have numerous ways of typing ellipses. Some use the horrid little ellipses 'character' available in some symbol fonts. Others type three periods in a row with no spacing in between. And there are many other variations."

So is there a *right* way to display ellipses in Microsoft Word? Yes, there is: any way that communicates clearly and looks good. In my opinion, that excludes the ellipses character (...), which Microsoft calls a "horizontal ellipsis" (PC character 133; Mac character 201; Unicode character 2026: press ALT + CTRL + . on a PC or OPTION + ; on a Mac). Let me explain my loathing of this little beast.

First, it doesn't communicate clearly. If it appears between two bits of text, like this...it's really too short to convey the idea that something has been left out (ellipses often indicate omission) or that the reader should pause. You can add a space on either side ... but then what's the point of using the character?

Second, it doesn't look good. It's tiny and ugly, like flyspecks on a wall. If you try to remedy that by putting spaces on the sides, those spaces don't match the spacing between the dots, so the whole thing looks funny. Also, sometimes you'll need to use ellipses with a period. But in many typefaces, the period isn't the same size as the ellipses dots, and there's no way to get the spacing after the period to match the spacing between the dots....Finally, since spacing in the ellipses character is fixed, it won't justify with the spaces in the rest of your text.

Besides, the character didn't exist in the days of setting type by hand. It's a capitulation to "desktop publishing" and has no place in fine typography.

How, then, should ellipses be created in Microsoft Word? One way is to type a straightforward succession of spaces and periods. . . . The meaning is clear, and they look fine. I'd recommend that you use nonbreaking spaces around the middle dot of the ellipses so they won't break at the end of a line, like this. .

. . but go neatly to the beginning of the next line, like this.

. . . To illustrate, the ellipses should be entered like this (<r> indicates a regular space and <n> indicates a nonbreaking space):

    <r>.<n>.<n>.<r>

To enter a nonbreaking space, press CTRL + SHIFT + SPACEBAR, which is nearly as easy as hitting the spacebar alone. In fact, why not record the whole sequence of characters as a macro and then assign the macro to a keyboard shortcut?

Some typographers argue that a standard space is too wide to use in ellipses. If you agree, you can use a thin space, which is sometimes defined as half the width of a standard space. In the next article, I'll explain how to get one.

Readers Write

Yateendra Joshi:

Most often, ellipses stand for omitted matter, and the dots will represent it even better if they do not sit on the line but are raised a bit, say to the centre of the letter x (lowercase eks). The extent to which the dots should be raised will depend on the font (raising by 2 points works best with 11-point Georgia). The sequence is therefore to type the dots as you explain, then select them, and raise them by Format > Font > Character Spacing > Position > Raised By followed by typing in the appropriate value. It helps to see the text enlarged by 500%.

Spaces

Microsoft Word comes with four kinds of spaces:

• word spaces
• nonbreaking spaces
• em spaces
• en spaces

The word space is just the ordinary space used between words—the kind you insert with the spacebar. Its main strength is its variable size, which is especially important with justified type. Microsoft Word ordinarily expands word spaces to make justification work, but you can also get it to compress them. For more information, see "Compressed Word Spacing."

The nonbreaking space, unlike the word space, won't break at the end of a line. It's often used to link proper names (so that "J.R.R." stays on the same line as "Tolkien"), as well as percentages ("98 percent"), page numbers ("page 3"), and ellipses (as explained in "Ellipses.")

Keep in mind, however, that the nonbreaking space is unlike the word space in another way: its size is fixed (relative to the current point size). In certain typefaces, with justified type, that fixed size may make ellipses look unevenly spaced, so be careful. To enter a nonbreaking space, click Insert > Symbol > Special Characters > Nonbreaking Space. Or just press SHIFT + CTRL + SPACE. For more ways to use nonbreaking spaces, see below.

The em space is as wide as an em, which is a linear measure equal to the point size. For example, in 12-point type, an em is 12 points wide. In traditional typesetting, an em space was used as fixed-width indentation at the beginning of a paragraph. Nowadays we usually specify first line indent as part of paragraph formatting. But if you insist on using an em space, you can get one by clicking Insert > Symbol > Special Characters > Em Space.

The en space is half as wide as an em space. For example, in 12-point type, an en space is 6 points wide. It's basically the same thing as a figure space, and it's used in aligning lists of figures, or numbers. For example, in a list like this—

8. Lorem ipsum.
9. Dolor sit amet.
10. Consectetuer adipiscing elit.

—the periods and terminal figures all line up because the space in front of 8 and 9 is the same width (one en) as the 1 in the number 10. That's right; in professional typefaces, all of the "lining figures" (numbers used in lists) are also one en wide. (Those old typesetters knew what they were doing.) In Microsoft Word you can achieve the same effect with tabs, but if you really want to use an en space, click Insert > Symbol > Special Characters > En Space.

In traditional typesetting, there are several other kinds of spaces, including (getting progressively fatter) the zero-width space, the hair space, the thin space, and the three-to-em space.

As its name indicates, the zero-width space has no width; you can't even see it. Nevertheless, it will break at the end of a line, which comes in handy when you've got a long string of characters that you *do* want to break but that otherwise wouldn't. For example, you might have some words joined by an em dash—like this. Ordinarily Microsoft Word won't break on the left side of the dash, which can make for some ugly typography if you've got long words and narrow columns. To remedy the problem, put a zero-width space in front of the dash. How? Microsoft Word doesn't include one, so you'll have to make your own:

1. Insert an em space (since we want the size to be fixed relative to the current point size).
2. Select the space.
3. Set the space's point size to 1. (We'd set it to 0, but Word won't allow it. Still, 1 works pretty well, although you *can* see it, which means you'd better balance it with another one on the right side of the dash.)

The hair space is also sometimes used, for aesthetic purposes, on both sides of an em dash. I've also seen it used between the letter f and a closing quotation mark or other characters that look crowded together. Again, you'll have to make your own:

1. Insert an em space (since we want the size to be fixed relative to the current point size).
2. Select the space.
3. Set the space's point size to 1/10 of the current size, or as close to it as you can manage. Remember that you can type in .5 (4.5, 5.5, etc.) to bump up the size by half a point. If you need to make the hair space smaller than 1/10 of the current point size, feel free; many typographers do.

Then there's the thin space, which some typographers (French ones, for example) use after certain punctuation marks, such as the colon. It's also used to set off the first two numbers of years that are more than four numbers long: 10 000 B.C. (Remember, commas shouldn't be used in dates.) I've also seen it used between ellipses. To make a thin space:

1. Insert an em space (since we want the size to be fixed relative to the current point size).
2. Select the space.
3. Set the space's point size to 1/5 of the current size, or as close to it as you can manage. Remember that you can type in .5 (4.5, 5.5, etc.) to bump up the size by half a point. Some typographers define a thin space as half the size of a standard word space.

The three-to-em space, as you've probably surmised, is as wide as a third of the current point size. For a size of 12, that would be 4. The Chicago Manual of Style says to use this space between ellipses, which is okay with me. By now, you know how to make one.

There ought to be a better solution than making spaces by hand—PageMaker and QuarkXPress come to mind. But if you must work in Word, there is another way. It's dark and dangerous, and its name is Unicode. But that's a subject for another day.

By the way, I'm not saying you should actually *use* all these spaces in your day-to-day work. I'd use them only if I had to approximate fine typography in Microsoft Word, which is possible but certainly not easy. If you ever need to do that, maybe these spaces will help.

Readers Write

Lou Burgoyne:

Places to use nonbreaking spaces:
Phone Numbers, Addresses. Also use non-breaking hyphens.

Martin:

Nonbreaking spaces are useful after Mr or Mrs.

Anne K. Bailey:

I use the nonbreaking space so often that I've got it mapped to my keyboard (alt s) so I can insert it without having to think about it (at least when using Word). I *always* use it in the following situations (I'll use a tilde to represent the nonbreaking space):

- Between a first name and a middle initial (Anne˜K. Bailey)
- Between the two parts of certain last names (Vincent Van˜Gogh)
- Between the month and the day (September˜11, 2001)
- Between the word "percent" and the number (75˜percent)
- Between the word "page" and the number (page˜42)
- Between the word "age" and the number (age˜65)
- Between a number and the word it modifies (15˜days) (three˜times) (18˜years old) (six˜miles) (12˜inches)
- Between two parts of most compound words (pay˜grade) (New˜York)
- Between the time and "a.m." or "p.m." (7:00˜a.m.)

In addition, I often use a nonbreaking space to force line endings. I've seen people insert a hard return in the middle of a paragraph to force the line endings to look "right." However, my preference is to use a nonbreaking space to force a particular word to the next line. That way, if the text is later edited and the line endings change, the nonbreaking space won't necessarily have to be removed, but a hard return would definitely have to be found and deleted.

(I would have used a nonbreaking space between the words "hard" and "return" in the previous paragraph.)

STEVE HUDSON:

I never use the nonbreaking space. My designer and I both agree that the examples we have seen it suggested to use don't actually add much to the readability and do interfere with justification. The main two examples are 75 percent and Dr Bob. To fully demonstrate the futility of the percent, what if one wrote seventy five percent, all with hard spacing? You could have half a line in nothing flat.

STEVE HUDSON:

The following macros use Unicode to set zero-width spaces around various characters and character combinations (/, :/, and so on) to make sure they will break at the end of a line. Notice that you can modify the characters specified in Sub FixWordWrap to suit your own needs. (For example, you could use ^+ for an em dash.)

```
Sub FixWordWrap()
FixSymbolWordWrap "/{1,2}"
FixSymbolWordWrap ":/{1,2}"
FixSymbolWordWrap "[\\]{1,2}"
FixSymbolWordWrap ":[\\]{1,2}"
FixSymbolWordWrap "_"
End Sub


Private Sub FixSymbolWordWrap(Symbol As String)
' inserts a zero-width space after the symbol if text either
side
Dim R As Range
Dim ZeroSpace As String
ZeroSpace = ChrW(8203)
On Error Resume Next
Const Pre As String = "([a-zA-Z0-9]"
Const Suf As String = ")([a-zA-Z0-9])"
Set R = ActiveDocument.Range
With R.Find
.MatchWildcards = True
.Text = Pre & Symbol & Suf
.Replacement.Text = "\1" & ZeroSpace & "\2"
.Execute Replace:=wdReplaceAll
End With
End Sub
```

This macro will remove the zero-width spaces if you change your mind:

```
Sub UnFixWordWrap()
Dim R As Range
Set R = ActiveDocument.Range
```

```
With R.Find
.Text = ChrW(8203)
.Replacement.Text = ""
.Execute Replace:=wdReplaceAll
End With
End Sub
```

DAVID M VARNER:

In the course of organizing some recent revisions, some text in one of the documents required a strikethrough. It occurred to me that strikethroughs other than a horizontal line would be handy, slashes perhaps, depending on the situation. My question is this: Is there a way in MS Word to overstrike any character with any other character? This is one thing you can do using a typewriter that you can't, as far as I know, do on a computer."

I REPLIED: There is a way to overstrike characters. You can condense the spacing between the characters to the point that the characters overlap. Here's how:

1. Type the two characters, such as "/e".
2. Select the two characters.
3. Click "Format > Font."
4. Click the "Character Spacing" tab.
5. In the "Spacing" list, select "Condensed."
6. In the "By" list, click the arrows until you've got the characters the way you want them. You can see a preview at the bottom of the dialog box.
7. Click the "OK" button.

KAREN L. BOJDA AND YEHUDA YOEL ZIMMERMAN:

To overstrike two or more characters (say, the / and e of your example), you can also use an "equation" field with the overstrike switch, \O:

   {EQ \O(/,e)}

This can be inserted with the Insert > Fields . . . command. The overstrike field does have the advantage that its formatting can't be accidentally removed, but the overstruck (overstricken?) characters produced this way are more or less centered. Your condensed-text method allows finer control over the extent of overlap. Plus your method allows overstriking a backslash, which mucks up a field.

Tools

Spell Checkers? We Don't Need No Stinkin' Spel Checkrs!

Maybe you've seen that funny little poem about spell checkers that occasionally makes its way around the Internet. It comes in various versions, but the first and last stanzas usually go something like this:

I have a spelling checker
That came with my PC.
It clearly marks four my revue
Mistakes I cannot sea.
I ran this poem threw it.
I'm sure your pleased two no
Its letter perfect awl the weigh;
My checker tolled me sew.

Editors like the poem because it points out an important fact: A spell checker can't catch words that are improperly used but spelled correctly. However, editors should not overlook another important fact: A spell checker *can* catch words spelled incorrectly—so why not use it to do that? Maybe we'd feel better about doing so if we thought of it not as a spell checker but as a typo catcher.

I usually use my "typo catcher" twice on a document: once before editing and once after editing. The first time through catches typos the author has overlooked. The second time through catches typos I may have inadvertently introduced while editing. It's a great system for two reasons:

1. It catches errors I might have missed, especially if I'm hurrying to meet a deadline (always).
2. It saves me time (the time I'd have had to spend finding and fixing those typos manually).

The second reason is so important that it deserves further comment: One of the main reasons for editing on the computer is to *save time.* That means you should learn to use the tools your word processor provides—including your spell checker. Doing so is an investment that will pay dividends every day of your working life.

GEOFF HART:

I've had a problem problem for some time with illegibly small type in the Word spellchecker, on both the Mac and the PC. The text displayed in the spellchecker is generally small but readable, but every now and then it decreases to an illegibly small size if the author has used a small font for their body text: you can't zoom in on the text in the dialog and zooming in on the text before you open the spellchecker doesn't help at all, there's no preference (Mac) or option (PC) setting to set this type size directly, and no amount of exploring in the bowels of Word has revealed an obvious solution.

Hilary Powers pointed me in the right direction to find a workable but very kludgy solution: turn off change tracking, increase the font size everywhere by several notches, turn on change tracking, do the spellcheck, turn off change tracking, decrease the font size back to its original, then turn on change tracking again. Are we out of breath yet?

The key trick is that you can't manually change the font size from the Font menu or from the toolbar: doing so loses all the font-size information that the author applied manually or by means of styles, and removing the font size change via the "remove manually applied formatting" shortcut (COMMAND + SHIFT + Z on the Mac, CTRL + Spacebar on the PC) loses you italics and boldface, among other things. Not acceptable.

The solution? First, "select all" the text: COMMAND + A on the Mac, CTRL + A on the PC. Next, hold down COMMAND + SHIFT (CTRL + SHIFT on the PC) then press the < or > keys. Each press (respectively) decreases and increases the font size _to the next size listed in Word's default list of font sizes_. If you press the > keyboard shortcut three or four times to enlarge the text, all the text will become legible in the spellchecker. When you're done, "select all" once again, then use the < keyboard shortcut the exact same number of times to restore the text to its original size.

Hilary also suggested another option, which works much more effectively: use the built-in "accessibility" features of the operating system. These features are designed to help computer users with visual or other disabilities to use their computer much more easily. As these settings affect the performance and behavior of the entire operating system, they also work in any program—even Word.

Here's how to solve the dialog box problem on the Mac using OS-X (I'm sure some kind Windows user can provide corresponding Windows details):

1. Open System Preferences (under the Apple menu).
2. Under the "System" heading, select "Universal Access".
3. Click the LARGE button labeled "Turn on zoom". Close the dialog box.
4. Until you return to this dialog box to turn off this setting (by clicking the LARGE button labeled "Turn off zoom"), you can zoom in an out while using any program: COMMAND + OPTION + = (equals sign) to enlarge the display; COMMAND + OPTION + [-] (the minus sign) to zoom back out again. Mnemonic: above the equals sign is the + sign (+ = increase); the "minus" sign means "decrease".

Works quite nicely, though it's not nearly as elegant a solution as being able to set the font size preferences directly in Word.

Exclude Dictionary

You've just sent a freshly edited manuscript back to your client, but you decide to glance through it one last time. Acck! What's this? "Our company has been highly visible in the pubic arena . . ." How did *that* get through?

It got through because you don't have an exclude dictionary in Microsoft Word. An exclude dictionary is a spell-check dictionary with words that are spelled correctly but that you want to verify during a spell check. If you're editing or writing, you *need* one of these. Here's how to set one up:

1. Create a new document.
2. Type the words (like "pubic") that you want to include (that is, that you want to *exclude* from the spell-checker's list of correctly spelled words).
3. Press the "Enter" key after each word, including the last one.
4. Click the "File" menu.
5. Click "Save As."
6. Navigate to the folder that contains the spell-checker's main dictionary.

In Windows 95, 98, or Millennium Edition (Me), the folder is C:\Windows\Application Data\Microsoft\Proof.

In Windows 95, 98, or Me with profiles enabled, or in Windows NT 4.0, the folder is C:\Windows\Profiles\Username\Application Data\Microsoft\Proof.

In Windows 2000 or XP, the folder is C:\Documents and Settings\Username\Application Data\Microsoft\Proof.

On a Macintosh, the folder is probably HD:Microsoft Office 2001[or whatever]:Shared Applications:Proofing Tools or HD:System Folder:Preferences:Microsoft.

If you don't save the file to the right folder, your exclude dictionary won't work.

7. In the "Save as type" box, click "Text Only" or "Plain Text."
8. In the "File name" box, type the name for your exclude dictionary. This should be the same name as your main language dictionary but with an ".exc" extension. For example, the English (United States) dictionary in Word 2000 and 2002 is Mssp3en.lex, so the exclude dictionary should be Mssp3en.exc. (In Word 97, the dictionary is named Mssp2_en.lex.) Make sure ".txt" isn't appended to the filename extension (you may need to put quotation marks around the filename to be sure).
9. Click "Save."
10. If the File Conversion dialog box appears, select the options you want to use.
11. Click "OK."
12. Close the document.
13. Close and then restart Microsoft Word.

The next time you do a spell check, the words in your exclude dictionary will be flagged as misspelled, allowing you to review them and avoid future embarrassment. If the exclude dictionary doesn't work, see Word's Help file or go here for possible solutions:

http://support.microsoft.com/default.aspx?scid=kb;EN-US;Q211639

Readers Write

APRIL KARYS:

In creating an exclude dictionary, as I did following your excellent directions, I found out that those of us running on a Mac platform using Word 2001 must save the document not in "text only" or "plain text," but in "speller exclude dictionary." Saving in plain text won't work. [This is also true in Word 98.]

TODD A. MANZA:

I've gotten together my exclusion dictionary list, and I followed your Editorium instructions for saving and placing it, but it seems not to be working. (Yes, I did close Word after each test.) Microsoft's online help gives basically the same information as yours; both end with Word 2000, but I wouldn't think that matters.

After following the instructions and saving as mssp3en.exc in

username\application data\microsoft\proof

and seeing that it didn't work, I searched my hard drive for the mssp3en.lex file and found it in:

c:\program\common files\microsoft shared\proof

So I saved my dictionary there, plain text, same routine, just a different location. Thought I was pretty smart, but unfortunately saving the file there didn't do any good.

Next I tried creating a new custom dictionary through Word's Options\spelling\custom dictionaries, saving with the same name (mssp3en.exc). I added a couple of words manually and closed out (after checking the box to enable), but even *that* didn't work.

Finally, I closed *all* Office programs, including Outlook (which was open, of course, when I was writing to you), since the dictionaries are apparently shared. Then, in Word, I saw one of my excluded words appear with redline!

RICH SHATTENBERG:

I live in the country of Madagascar. There is no Word spell checker for the Malagasy language, or at least I have not yet been able to find one. I have made a custom dictionary with about 7,000 words to do spell checks in Malagasy. However, here is the challenge.

The word *mandeha* means "to go" (present tense), *Nandeha* is past tense, and *handeha* is future tense. For the custom dictionary, I have to enter all three words. I have not yet been able to find wildcard symbols to use in the custom dictionary.

For example, is there a way of telling the custom dictionary to accept the word *andeha* if there is either an "m" or "n" or "h" in front of the word? This would mean I only have to make one entry for the three words.

STEVE HUDSON SENT THE DEFINITIVE REPLY: No wildcards in dictionary entries. Badda badda boom.

Exclude Dictionary Entries

The previous article discussed Microsoft Word's exclude dictionary, which is a list of words that are spelled correctly but that you still want to verify during a spell check. I also asked readers to submit words to include in an exclude dictionary. Thanks to Carolann Barrett, Steve Hudson, Sandee Lannen, Cher Paul, and Hilary Powers for the following list:

asses/assets
cavalry/calvary
curser/cursor
gray/grey
hare/hair
hone (to check whether it was used correctly or if it was meant to be "home in")
impotent/important
loose/lose
mange/manage
manger/manager
mangers/managers
martial/marital
sale/sell
stationary/stationery
their/there
valance/valence

The list suggests other possibilities:

• Commonly confused words, such as "discrete" and "discreet." You'll find a good list here:

    http://rinkworks.com/words/confused.shtml

• British/Canadian/American spellings (depending on your language settings).
• Words you love to hate: "impact," "paradigm," "empower," and so on. Make your own list.
• Words that readers might find offensive. I'm not suggesting that you bowdlerize the manuscripts that pass through your hands; I'm suggesting that there are plenty of words you wouldn't want to let through *accidentally*:

words that are usually considered profane or obscene
racial epithets

certain "politically incorrect" words
words that are usually avoided (for whatever reason) in your area of expertise
words for body parts and biological functions

And so on. This may not be the most pleasant list you'll ever compile, but it may save you from embarrassment, unemployment, or even litigation. Of course, you might want to explain to your employer the purpose of the list, which might also save you from embarrassment, unemployment, or litigation if someone finds it on your computer. If I were your employer, I'd be happy to know that "public" will never, ever show up as "pubic."

One final point: Don't rely on Microsoft Word to catch everything. Your editorial mind is the ultimate exclude dictionary.

Conditional Text

Conditional text is text that you want to appear only in a certain situation. For example, let's say you're using Microsoft Word to write two brochures for the new WidgetMaster 2000. One brochure is a sales piece; the other explains the product's technical specifications. However, certain sections of both brochures contain exactly the same information.

The brochures are going to go through several rounds of client approval, and you're not excited about having to make the same corrections in both. Of course, you could make the corrections in one and then copy the corrected sections into the other. But if you're like me, you'd start to wonder if you'd been consistent about it, and at some point you'd get confused about which version was really correct. Fussing around with different versions is a pain.

Instead of working with two versions, consider using conditional text—courtesy of our old friend, Hidden formatting. (See "Hidden Articles" and "More Hidden Secrets."

Using conditional text, you can write and correct just one document, hiding or revealing the conditional sections as needed. Here's how:

1. Create the styles for the sections that are the same in both brochures: CommonHeading, CommonBody, and so on. (Or just use your usual styles.)
2. Create the styles for the sales section: SalesHeading, SalesBody, and so on.
3. Create the styles for the technical section: TechHeading, TechBody, and so on.
4. Base all of the styles *for each kind of section* on one main style. For example, you might base the SalesHeading style on the SalesBody style, and the TechHeading style on the TechBody style.

Now write the brochure, using the styles to format the common, sales, and technical sections.

When you're ready to print one of the brochure versions (the sales version, for example), set the main style for the technical section (TechBody) to Hidden, as explained in "More Hidden Secrets."

All of the text for the technical section will disappear, leaving visible only the common and sales sections. There's your sales brochure!

When you're ready to print the technical brochure, remove the Hidden formatting from the main technical style (TechBody) and set it for the main sales style (SalesBody). All of the text for the sales section will disappear, leaving visible only the common and technical sections. There's your technical brochure!

This may not be as sophisticated as the conditional text feature in dedicated composition programs, such as FrameMaker. But somewhere, sometime, maybe it will help you get the job done.

Editioning Software

Microsoft Word guru Steve Hudson has sent me many an interesting thing. Here, I'd like to introduce you to his "Editioning" macro, which allows you to use true conditional text in Microsoft Word. Conditional text is the thing to use if you need to change a document in different ways for different audiences. I've written before about using Word's Hidden formatting to create conditional text (see "Conditional Text.")

Steve, however, has taken the idea to greater heights of power and usability. For your convenience, I've placed his template (with its accompanying toolbar and macro) on my Web site, and you can download it here:

http://www.editorium.com/ftp/editioning.zip

After you've unzipped the template, you'll need to load it as a global template or add-in, which you can learn more about in "Macros in Add-in Templates" and "Adding a Template Automatically."

Finally, here's how to use the program:

1. Open or create a document that will be your source document for the various versions you want to create, and be sure to keep a backup of this document.
2. Use Microsoft Word's Highlighter feature (available on the Formatting toolbar) to highlight the text that will appear only in the various versions you'll be producing. For example, let's say you're writing the documentation for a computer program that will be produced in three versions: basic, intermediate, and advanced. Some of the documentation will apply to all three versions, but some of it won't. For example, the advanced version will have features not available in the basic version, and you don't want the documentation for those features to show up in the basic documentation. So let's say that you highlight the information that applies only to the basic version in yellow, the intermediate in blue, and the advanced in red. Save this document with a new name, such as "Single Source."
3. With the Editioning template loaded, you'll see a new Editioning toolbar on your screen. Click the Editioning button to start the program.
4. In the "Color" box, on the right, click one of the colors you want to use, such as yellow.
5. In the "Description" box, on the bottom, type in a description of what that color represents, such as "Basic."
6. Click the "New" button to add the color and its description to the "Current List of Editions" box. (You can also click the "Delete" button to delete them.)
7. Repeat steps 4 through 6 for each color you want to use.

8. In the "Current List of Editions" box, click the color/description for the type of document you want to produce. For example, if you wanted to create the basic documentation, you'd click "Yellow Basic."
9. Click the "Publish" button.
10. Click the "Exit" button to close the program. (It will remember your definitions for the next time you use it.)

Now, in the document on your screen, all of your *unhighlighted* text will be preserved (since you want to use it in all of your versions), and the text that was highlighted in the color you selected (yellow) will also be preserved (but now unhighlighted). Text that was highlighted in other colors (blue and red) will be removed. So, you now have the basic version of your software documentation! Be sure to save it with a new name (such as "Basic Documentation"), and be careful not to save it over the top of your previously marked-up file.

That's it! Rinse and repeat for your other versions. Many thanks to Steve for making this program available.

Merriam-Webster's Collegiate Dictionary and Thesaurus on CD-ROM

If you haven't yet read the *New York Times* editorial by Mark Goldblatt on the bowdlerization of Microsoft Word's thesaurus, you owe it to yourself to do so:

http://www.nytimes.com/2001/10/23/opinion/23GOLD.html

Goldblatt chronicles his discovery that Microsoft has, astonishingly, removed "offensive" terms from Microsoft Word 2000's thesaurus—including such words as "fool," "idiot," and "nitwit." So can this milquetoast collection still be called a thesaurus? Not anymore.

But I don't care, because even before I found out about this idiotic (oops!) turn of events, I bought Merriam-Webster's Collegiate Dictionary and Thesaurus on CD-ROM. You can learn more about the program here:

http://www.merriam-webster.com/cgi-bin/book.pl?elecc11.htm\&7

The Merriam-Webster Web site describes this little marvel as "the complete Collegiate Dictionary, Tenth Edition, and Collegiate Thesaurus in a fully searchable electronic format [that] delivers accurate, up-to-date language information." The price? Just $14.95. (I'm not making any money from this, by the way. I just like the product.) The program can be used "while word processing, composing e-mail, preparing presentations, surfing the Web, browsing CD-ROMs, or designing spreadsheets." But to me the most important thing is that it can be used from *inside* Microsoft Word. It comes with a Word macro that you can assign to a menu or key combination. Then you can put your cursor on a word you want to look up and run the macro. The Merriam-Webster dictionary (or thesaurus) will open for your use.

Amazing! Astonishing! Astounding! Marvelous! Miraculous! Staggering! Stupendous! And not bowdlerized.

Readers Write

MARK POOL:

I think you and your readers might be interested to know that Merriam-Webster now has a free toolbar. To read all about it and/or download it go to:

http://www.merriam-webster.com/downloads/index.htm

Typesetting

Typesetting with Microsoft Word

So, you've got a client (or a boss) who wants you to create a *finished* document in Microsoft Word. In other words, you get to do typesetting—in a program that isn't really designed for typesetting.[1] Here are some tips you might find useful:

1. Consult Word's Help file or, better yet, a good reference book to learn about Word's Page Setup, Section Layout, and Heading features. Then use those features to set up different sections of your document in the way you need them—for example, you can use roman numerals for page numbers in front matter and have different running heads in different chapters.

2. Attach a good-looking template to your document by clicking "Tools > Templates and Add-ins > Attach," being sure to check the box labeled "Automatically update document styles." For this to work, you'll need to format your document with paragraph styles that have the same names as those in the template. You can create your own template, use one of Word's built-in templates, or use a template from one of the sources mentioned in "Templates Galore!"

3. Turn hyphenation on by clicking the "Tools" menu, clicking "Language," and then clicking "Hyphenation." Put a check in the box labeled "Automatically hyphenate document." Set the hyphenation zone to about half an inch or the equivalent. (You may need to experiment with this.) Limit consecutive hyphens to 3 or 4. (The more consecutive hyphens you allow, the better Word can adjust justified text—but you'll also get more word breaks.)

4. Make sure that styles allow hyphenation to occur. For each paragraph style, click "Format > Style > Modify > Format > Paragraph > Line and Page Breaks" and make sure the box labeled "Don't hyphenate" is empty. Also, make sure the box labeled "Widow/Orphan Control" is checked.

5. Turn on kerning for all text. For each paragraph style, click "Format > Style > Modify > Format > Font > Character Spacing" and make sure the box labeled "Kerning for Fonts" is checked and the box labeled "Points and Above" has a value equal to the smallest point size in the document (usually 8 points). This is probably overkill, but that's okay.

6. Set line spacing to an exact point size. For each paragraph style, click "Format > Style > Modify > Format > Paragraph > Indents and Spacing > Line Spacing" and set line spacing to an "exact" amount. This should be about 120 percent of the character point size. If your character point size is 10, for instance, you should probably set your line spacing to 12 points.

---

1. This book was typeset using the LaTeX composition system: http://www.latex-project.org/

7. Adjust all of your styles to fit your design. This even includes such styles as Footer, Header, Footnote Reference, and Page Number, which should not be left with their default formatting. For example, if you're setting body text in Garamond, you should set your footnote references in Garamond as well.

8. Using "File > Page Setup," set your right and left margins to create an easily readable line length. One rule of thumb is that lines in body text should be roughly as long as an alphabet and a half in the current font and point size, like this:

abcdefghijklmnopqrstuvwxyzabcdefghijklm

That may not seem long enough, but go look at several of the well-designed books on your shelf. You'll be surprised at how short the lines are. If you want to use a longer line, you should also increase your line spacing so the reader's eye can "track" more easily from the end of one line to the beginning of another.

9. Click the Tools menu (Edit on a Macintosh), click "Options" (Preferences on a Macintosh), click the "Compatibility" tab, and put a check next to these options:

- "Do full justification like WordPerfect 6.x for Windows." (Or better yet, use my WordSetter program to adjust word spacing to your own liking.)
- "Don't add extra space for raised/lowered characters."
- "Don't center 'exact line height' lines."
- "Don't expand character spaces on the line ending SHIFT + Return."
- "Suppress 'Space Before' after a hard page or column break."

At this point, your text should look pretty good, but you can make it even better by applying the principles described in such books as these:

Desktop Publishing with Word for Windows, by Tom Lichty.
The Printed Word, by David A. Kater and Richard Kater.
The Elements of Typographic Style, by Robert Bringhurst
The Art of Desktop Publishing, by Tony Bove, Cheryl Rhodes, and Wes Thomas.
The Non-Designer's Design Book, by Robin Williams.
The Non-Designer's Type Book, by Robin Williams.
The Mac Is Not a Typewriter, by Robin Williams (for beginners only)
The PC Is Not a Typewriter, by Robin Williams (for beginners only).

Content vs. Presentation

Several years ago I created a program called SpaceCadet that creates typographic spaces by changing a space's point size relative to the surrounding text. But why is that a good idea? If you save a document with such spaces in almost any other format—HTML, XML, or even ASCII—you'll have problems. That hair space you so carefully placed in front of those closing quotation marks will turn into a full-fledged *space*—with no "thin" about it. So why use special characters and formatting? To enhance the *presentation* of a document's content. Presentation is what the document looks like. It includes such things as typeface, point size, kerning, and all the other paraphernalia of the typesetter's art.

Content, on the other hand, is a document's text—and its structure: paragraphs, block quotations, headings—the kind of thing you should designate with paragraph styles. In fact, the whole point of a paragraph style is what it represents—not what it looks like. The fact that your heading style is named "Chapter Head" is what matters. The fact that it's currently formatted as Baskerville 16-point bold is immaterial as far as content goes.

In today's publishing environment the distinction between content and presentation is especially important, because your Word document may end up as a Web page, a Help file, an electronic book, or some other kind of presentation document that hasn't been invented yet—each with different formatting than the others. For that reason, you need to keep your Word documents free from such tinkering as artificially created thin spaces.

But there is an exception. If your Word file *itself* will be the presentation document (to be printed or displayed in Word), then go ahead and put in those thin spaces, optional hyphens, and so on—whatever will make the document look good. Be aware, however, that this *is* a presentation document—a final product. So be sure to keep a backup of your *content* document safely in a separate file. Then, when it's time to create that Web page, you won't have to spend hours cleaning up the manual tweaking you did in your presentation document. Just open the content document and off you go.

Editors need to be concerned with both content and presentation. As a book editor, I look almost exclusively at content when editing a manuscript. I usually don't even know what typeface the designer will use. But after the book has been typeset, I look almost exclusively at presentation—widows, orphans, line breaks, and so on. The difference is that the manuscript is a content document. The galleys are a presentation document. And that distinction should be kept firmly in mind.

I do not know which to prefer,
The beauty of inflections
Or the beauty of innuendoes,
The blackbird whistling
Or just after.
                    —Wallace Stevens

Microsoft Word's Layout Features

Microsoft Word includes a number of layout features that you'll need if you're doing serious typesetting or desktop publishing. They're not always easy to get to, however, or to understand. For various reasons, Microsoft has strung them all over the place, under File, View, Insert, Format, and Tools. Good grief! I recommend that you use Word's Customize feature (Tools/Customize) to put them all in one place on a new menu or toolbar where you can easily find and use them together.

Basically, these features are related to document sections or to the document as a whole. I've listed some of the most important ones below, with the command name following the descriptive name (so you'll know what commands to use if you want to create your own menu or toolbar):

Templates and Add-ins (FileTemplates)
Style Gallery (FormatStyleGallery)
Style (FormatStyle)
Page Setup (FilePageSetup)
Hyphenation (ToolsHyphenation)
Insert Break (InsertBreak)
Section Layout (FormatSectionLayout)
Header (ViewHeader)
Page Numbers (InsertPageNumbers)
Columns (FormatColumns)
Note Options (NoteOptions)

Once you've brought these far-flung cousins together, you'll be surprised at how easy it is to set up a document so that it looks and works right.

Feeling lazy? My WordSetter program puts all of these features together under a new Layout menu and on a Document Formatting toolbar for easy access. It also provides other new features for section and document formatting, including:

- Crop marks
- Adjustable word spacing (tracking)
- Thin spaces
- Automatic styling for block quotations, lists, and poetry
- Ligatures (Macintosh only)

Typesetting Tips for Word

I can't leave the topic of typesetting without explaining some of the things I learned on the last book I typeset—in Microsoft Word. The book had more than 400 pages and several hundred footnotes, and Word would have handled it better if I'd been more particular about the following:

1. Pull all the chapters together into a single document.
2. Set up pages as explained in "Setting Up Book Pages."
3. Set up text block and margins as explained in "Calculating Page Margins" and "Adjusting Line Spacing and Margins."
4. Set up running heads and footers as explained in "Setting Up Headers and Footers."
5. But while you're doing that, please consider this additional advice:
6. Insert a "Next page" section break for *each page* that requires a different kind of running head or folio (including *no* running head or folio) than the previous section (Insert > Break > Next page). In the front matter, that's quite a few section breaks. Each chapter should also be a separate section (be preceded by a section break). All of these section breaks should be of the "Next page" variety. If you use an "Even page" or "Odd page" section break, Word will try to take control, in its usual "helpful" way, and you don't want that to happen.
7. After inserting a section break, *always* turn off "Link to previous" for both header *and* footer (View > Header and footer > Link to previous [fourth icon from the left]). To move from header to footer, click the "Switch between header and footer" button (third icon from the left). Again, turn off "Link to previous." That means you'll need to insert folios (page numbers) and running heads separately for each section. It's a pain, but it's the only way to make sure Word does exactly what you want it to.
8. Set up the layout for each section by clicking File > Page Setup > Layout. "Section start" should always be "New page." If you need to make sure a chapter starts on an odd page, you may have to insert an additional break. Under "Headers and footers," check both "Different odd and even" and "Different first page." Under "Preview," set "Apply to" as "This section." Then click OK.
9. To insert page numbers, go to the beginning of your document (CTRL + HOME). Click View > Header and footer. If you want folios in the header, click the # icon. To specify arabic or roman numbers and what number to start with in the current section, click the "Format page number" icon (third from the left). If you want folios in the footer instead, first click the "Switch between header and footer" button.
10. To go to the next header (or footer), click the "Show next" button (icon on the far right). Very handy. Use this button to jump from header to header and footer to

footer. If you followed the instructions in step 2, you'll have three separate headers and three separate footers in each chapter. After you've played around with this, along with the "Show previous" button, you'll understand what's going on here.

11. After doing the steps above, turn off automatic repagination. If you don't, Word will sometimes repaginate your whole document on even minor changes, which will eventually make you feel like throwing your computer out the window—even more than you do now. To turn off repagination, switch to Normal View (View > Normal). Click Tools > Options > General and clear the Background Repagination box. Word will now (mostly) refrain from repaginating unless you print, switch to Print Preview or Print Layout view, compile a table of contents or index, or do a word count. If necessary, you can reenable automatic repagination by rechecking the Background Repagination box.

12. If for some reason you need to *delete* a section break, *carefully* check nearby headers and footers to make sure something didn't go wacko.

13. After you think you have everything the way you want it, you can check your layout in spreads as explained in "Two Up."

If these tips help you avoid some of the pitfalls into which I pitfell, writing this article will have been well worth the trouble.

Feathering Text

Microsoft Word has no way to justify lines vertically (also known as "feathering"). It is possible to vertically justify space between paragraphs under File > Page Setup > Layout > Vertical Alignment, but that's of little use in serious typography. Since vertical justification actually changes the specified leading between lines, it's seldom "justified" (sorry, couldn't resist) as a way to keep page bottoms even. Sometimes, however, there simply is no other solution, which is why vertical justification is available in dedicated typesetting programs like QuarkXPress. But what if you're working in Word? Macros to the rescue! Here are two macros that will adjust the line spacing of selected paragraphs by .05 points each time one of the macros is run.

The first macro decreases leading:

```
Sub LeadingDecrease()
Dim CurrLineSpace
CurrLineSpace = Selection.ParagraphFormat.LineSpacing
With Selection.ParagraphFormat
.LineSpacingRule = wdLineSpaceExactly
.LineSpacing = CurrLineSpace - 0.05
End With
End Sub
```

The second macro increases leading:

```
Sub LeadingIncrease()
Dim CurrLineSpace
CurrLineSpace = Selection.ParagraphFormat.LineSpacing
With Selection.ParagraphFormat
.LineSpacingRule = wdLineSpaceExactly
.LineSpacing = CurrLineSpace + 0.05
End With
End Sub
```

The best way to use these macros is to hook them up to a couple of keyboard shortcuts. CTRL + SHIFT + comma and CTRL + SHIFT + period are good choices because the comma and period keys are also marked with < and >, which could be thought of as "less" (decrease) and "more" (increase).

To use one of the macros, select the text you want to feather. Then run the macro over and over until the type looks the way you want it to. Most of the time, you'll probably select a whole page at once, since the difference in leading between two adjacent paragraphs could be quite noticeable. (The change in leading will affect an *entire* paragraph, not just a part of a paragraph that you have selected.) If you have a choice, I'd recommend sticking to the more traditional methods described previously. But if you really need to feather text in Word, now you can.

Adjusting Word Spacing

A previous article included macros for condensing or expanding line spacing (leading) in selected paragraphs. If you're trying to eliminate widows and orphans, however, it's often better to condense or expand word spacing and leave leading alone. In Microsoft Word, you can easily condense or expand *character* spacing (Format > Font > Character Spacing > Spacing). But to adjust *word* spacing, you have to individually select spaces between words and then individually condense or expand them. Too much work! But a macro could do it for you.

Here are two macros, one to condense word spacing and one to expand it. The best way to use these macros is to hook them up to a couple of keyboard shortcuts. CTRL + comma and CTRL + period are good choices because the comma and period keys are also marked with < and >, which could be thought of as "less" (decrease) and "more" (increase).

To use one of the macros, select the text whose word spacing you want to condense or expand. Then run the macro over and over until the type looks the way you want it to. Each time you run it, word spacing for the selected text will be adjusted by 0.05 of a point, and you'll see the current adjustment (in points) in the lower left corner of your Word window.

Remember that if you type something to the right of one of your adjusted spaces, whatever you type will also be adjusted. To prevent that from happening, press CTRL + SPACE before typing.

And now, here are the macros, which I hope you'll find useful:

```
Sub CondenseWordSpacing()
Dim CurrentFontSpacing$
Dim CurrentFontSpacing_
'See if text is selected
If WordBasic.GetSelStartPos() <> _
WordBasic.GetSelEndPos() Then
WordBasic.EditBookmark "tmp0"
Else
GoTo EndMacro
End If
'Go to first space in selection
WordBasic.EditFindClearFormatting
WordBasic.EditReplaceClearFormatting
WordBasic.EditFind Find:="^w"
If WordBasic.EditFindFound() = 0 _
Then GoTo EndMacro
'Calculate new size for space
Dim dlgFont As Object
Set dlgFont = _
```

```
WordBasic.DialogRecord.FormatFont(False)
WordBasic.CurValues.FormatFont dlgFont
CurrentFontSpacing$ = dlgFont.Spacing
CurrentFontSpacing_ = _
WordBasic.Val(CurrentFontSpacing$) - 0.05
CurrentFontSpacing$ = _
WordBasic.[LTrim$](Str(CurrentFontSpacing_)) _
+ " pt"
'Apply new size to spaces in selected text
WordBasic.WW7_EditGoTo "tmp0"
WordBasic.EditBookmark "tmp0", Delete:=1
WordBasic.EditFindClearFormatting
WordBasic.EditReplaceClearFormatting
WordBasic.EditReplaceFont _
Spacing:=CurrentFontSpacing$
WordBasic.EditReplace _
Find:="^w", Replace:="^&", ReplaceAll:=1, Format:=1
WordBasic.PrintStatusBar "Spaces adjusted by " + _
CurrentFontSpacing$ + "."
EndMacro:
End Sub


Sub ExpandWordSpacing()
Dim CurrentFontSpacing$
Dim CurrentFontSpacing_
'See if text is selected
If WordBasic.GetSelStartPos() <> _
WordBasic.GetSelEndPos() Then
WordBasic.EditBookmark "tmp0"
Else
GoTo EndMacro
End If
'Go to first space in selection
WordBasic.EditFindClearFormatting
WordBasic.EditReplaceClearFormatting
WordBasic.EditFind Find:="^w"
If WordBasic.EditFindFound() = 0 _
Then GoTo EndMacro
'Calculate new size for space
Dim dlgFont As Object
Set dlgFont = _
WordBasic.DialogRecord.FormatFont(False)
WordBasic.CurValues.FormatFont dlgFont
CurrentFontSpacing$ = dlgFont.Spacing
CurrentFontSpacing_ = _
WordBasic.Val(CurrentFontSpacing$) + 0.05
CurrentFontSpacing$ = _
WordBasic.[LTrim$](Str(CurrentFontSpacing_)) _
+ " pt"
'Apply new size to spaces in selected text
WordBasic.WW7_EditGoTo "tmp0"
WordBasic.EditBookmark "tmp0", Delete:=1
WordBasic.EditFindClearFormatting
```

```
WordBasic.EditReplaceClearFormatting
WordBasic.EditReplaceFont _
Spacing:=CurrentFontSpacing$
WordBasic.EditReplace _
Find:="^w", Replace:="^&", ReplaceAll:=1, Format:=1
WordBasic.PrintStatusBar "Spaces adjusted by " + _
CurrentFontSpacing$ + "."
EndMacro:
End Sub
```

Adjusting Line Spacing and Margins

I'm getting ready to typeset another book in Microsoft Word (yes, it can be done, and very nicely, too). My last one turned out quite well, but the design called for ragged page bottoms (to accommodate Word's idiosyncrasies), and I wanted to see if page bottoms and line spacing could be set uniformly in Word. I learned that they can, and I'm passing the secret on to you.

The secret is to do typesetting in the traditional way, with fixed line spacing (Formatting > Paragraph > Indents and Spacing > Line spacing: Exactly) and a text block calculated as a multiple of that spacing. The problem is that in a word processor, it's possible to set page margins (and thus the size of the text block) that have no relation at all to line spacing. In traditional typesetting, the size of the text block is *defined* by line spacing. And that's how it should be in a word processor, too.

For example, let's say we're setting body text as 10/12—10-point type with 12-point leading (line spacing). Let's also say a standard page has 35 lines. That means we should calculate our top and bottom margins to give us a text block of 420 points (12 * 35).

If we're working with 8.5 by 11 paper (U.S. standard), we have to calculate 11 inches times 72 points (72 points per inch, remember) equals 792 points, minus 420 points equals 372 points, divided by 2 (we have both a top and a bottom margin) equals 186 points. So we should set our top margin to 186 points and our bottom margin to 186 points (if we want to center the block on the page). And that will give us a text block of 420 points, which is 35 lines of type on 12 points of leading—to bring us back to where we started. If you're mathematically inclined, that's ((11 * 72) - (35 * 12))/2. So here's the formula:

Margin = ((Paper length in units * Points per unit) - (Lines * Leading point size))/2

You'll find more on calculating page size and text block (without even a *mention* of leading!) in "Calculating Page Margins."

When you set up your margins and line spacing in this way, you'll find that page bottoms and lines of type align very well indeed. "But what about headings?" you ask. "And block quotations? Won't they mess things up?" Good question.

Robert Bringhurst, in his book *The Elements of Typographic Style* (p. 38), explains:

"Headings, subheads, block quotations, footnotes, illustrations, captions and other intrusions into the text create syncopations and variations against the base rhythm of regularly leaded lines. These variations can and should add life to the page, but the main text should also return after each variation precisely on beat and in phase. This means that the total amount of vertical space consumed by each departure from the main text should be an even multiple of the basic leading. If the main text runs 11/13, intrusions to the text should equal some multiple of 13 points: 26, 39, 52, 65, 78, 91, 104 and so on. . . .

"If you happen to be setting a text 11/13, subhead possibilities include the following:

"• subheads in 11/13 small caps, with 13 pt above the head and 13 pt below;

"• subheads in 11/13 bold u&lc (upper and lower case), with 8 pt above the head and 5 pt below, since 8 + 5 = 13;

"• subheads in 11/13 caps with 26 pt above and 13 pt below;

"• one-line subheads in 14/13 italic u&lc, with 16 pt above the head and 10 pt below."

Setting type up in this way requires careful forethought and calculation, but the result is wonderful to behold.

But what if your design calls for 13 points of lead in body text and 12 points of lead in block quotations? Bringhurst explains:

"Suppose your main text is 11/13 and a five-line block quotation set to 10/12 intervenes. The depth of the quotation is 5 x 12 = 60. This must be bulked up to a multiple of 13 to bring the text back into phase. The nearest multiple of 13 is 5 x 13 = 65. The remaining space is 65 - 60 = 5, and 5/2 = 2.5, which is not enough. Adding 2.5 points before and after the quotation will not give adequate separation. The next multiple of 13 is 6 x 13 = 78, which is better: 78 - 60 = 18, and 18/2 = 9. Add 9 pt lead before and after the quotation and the text will realign."

See, I told you we'd be doing this the traditional way.

What about widow and orphan control? Word can do that automatically (Format > Paragraph > Line and Page Breaks > Widow/Orphan control), but it will throw off your beautifully aligned pages.

Bringhurst again:

"Balance facing pages not by adding extra lead or puffing up the word space, but by exporting or importing single lines to and from the preceding or following spreads. The same technique is used to avoid widows, and to extend or shorten any chapters that would otherwise end with a meager few lines on the final page. But this balancing should be performed with a gentle hand. In the end, no spread of continuous text should have to run more than a single line short or a single line long."

In other words, a little editing may be in store. You may have to remove a few words here, add a few there, and maybe break or join existing paragraphs. Remember when we used to do that?

We don't do it anymore because today's major typesetting programs (QuarkXPress, InDesign, FrameMaker, and Ventura) can use vertical justification (feathering) to align the bottoms of pages. The problem is that then 13 points of leading isn't really 13 points; it's 13.5 or 14 or something else altogether—definitely *not* traditional typesetting. In some publications, you can actually see how "spacey" the lines have become, and it doesn't make for beautiful typography. Nevertheless, I sometimes wish Word had that ability. Until it does, we're basically limited to setting type the old-fashioned way. And I'm not so sure that's a bad thing.

Readers Write

Anne-Marie Concepcion:

I've been meaning to whine to you about the following passage you wrote about leading in Word:

"'In the end, no spread of continuous text should have to run more than a single line short or a single line long.' In other words, a little editing may be in store. You may have to remove a few words here, add a few there, and maybe break or join existing paragraphs. Remember when we used to do that?

"We don't do it anymore because today's major typesetting programs (QuarkXPress, InDesign, FrameMaker, and Ventura) can use vertical justification (feathering) to align the bottoms of pages. The problem is that then 13 points of leading isn't really 13 points; it's 13.5 or 14 or something else altogether—definitely *not* traditional typesetting. In some publications, you can actually see how "spacey" the lines have become, and it doesn't make for beautiful typography. Nevertheless, I sometimes wish Word had that ability. Until it does, we're basically limited to setting type the old-fashioned way. And I'm not so sure that's a bad thing."

My whine has to do with the fact that I have *never* encountered any professional graphic designer use vertical justification in this way—to even out bottom lines of text in pages. I think people who use these programs you list—likely working designers—are more aware than anyone how horrid it would look to have two pages of the same continuous story carry different leading! [Note: The designers and typesetters at the publishing house where I used to work routinely use vertical justification.]

(Besides which, when you use vertical justification, that feature first adds/removes spacing between paragraphs; then, as a last resort, it changes the leading value.)

Designers do the math (leading/space above for each style sheet in even increments) you cite routinely to get leading equalized across pages and columns, and/or they use the layout program's "Lock to Baseline Grid" feature to help enforce it.

With this feature, you set a baseline starting point and increment amount (starting point = top margin, increment = body text leading) in the program's preferences. The program forces all text's baselines to grid positions, overriding any leading you set manually or in style sheets.

Normally this is used for publications like magazines, books, journals, and newspapers, where baselines need to line up across the page/spread and the bottom line needs to sit at the bottom across the board.

For less formal publications like brochures and some newsletters, the designer doesn't employ Lock to Baseline Grid. Different stories on a page may have different leading—captions, body text, space above subheads, sidebars, callouts, etc. But they still make sure that a single story carries the same leading for its body text throughout.

The Vertical Justification feature is actually seldom used. When it *is* used, it's mainly for standalone stories—for example, a sidebar that's the same height as the story columns it accompanies. It would be a quick and dirty way to get the text to "fill up" the vertical space—again, mainly employing space in between paragraphs, not leading.

STEVE HUDSON:

I use a simplified system for typesetting. You might like it, so I'll describe it.

I start out roughly like you. However, I try to set all text blocks to be a multiple of a smaller figure. I find that supporting multiples of 3 works well.

Then I define special paragraph styles with the following line spacing:

Microline 1 pt
Thin Lead 3 pt
Fat lead 6 pt

I then insert these paragraphs as required to add spacing instead of fiddling with paragraph and line spacing. All Styles are white font, no space before or after, and use the same font (but not typeface) as the common body text.

Finally, I make a similar style that matches body text exactly, for example, line lead 10pt, 3 before and 3 after.

Why? Well, I can strip them out easily enough, or even just find the next one, for repurposing the document. If they are only there for strict typography, I say *identify* them as such. This also exactly mimics the lead strips used in traditional typesetting, so it is easier to translate existing works on typography into Word methodologies.

Calculating Page Margins

In past articles, I've discussed various aspects of typesetting in Microsoft Word. One item I haven't addressed is how to calculate page margins *for publication,* which is not the same as just clicking File > Page Setup and putting in some numbers. If you needed to set up page margins for a printed book, for example, you'd need to set your margins to accommodate the size of your page and the text block on your page. This is not the same as *paper* size, which we'll say is 8.5 by 11 inches, a U.S. standard.

Let's say you want your *page* size (the size of your book) to be 7.5 by 9 inches. Here's what you'd do:

1. Calculate the margins you'd need to set to obtain the trimmed page size. (If you were using crop marks, this would be the measurement between them and the edge of the paper.)

- For the side margins, 8.5 minus 7.5 equals 1 inch. Divide that inch in half because, by golly, you have two side margins. That gives you a margin of .5 inch on each side of the page.
- For the top and bottom margins, 11 minus 9 equals 2 inches, divided in half equals a 1-inch margin for top and bottom.

2. Calculate the space from the edges of your *text block* to the top, bottom, and sides of your page. For convenience, let's say you're going to have 1 inch all around, but you could make those measurements anything you wanted. If it's 1 inch, then you'd just add 1 inch to the side margins, making 1.5 inches for each, and 1 inch to the top and bottom margins, making 2 inches for each.

3. Finally, click File > Page Setup and set your margins according to your calculations: side margins should be 1.5 inches, and top and bottom margins should be 2 inches.

Now when you type in your text, you'll get a text block of, let's see, 8.5 - (1.5 + 1.5) = 5.5 inches wide, and 11 - (2 + 2) = 7 inches high.

Basically, that gives us a box within a box within a box.

The smallest box, in the middle, is the text block, 5.5 by 7 inches.

The box out from that is the trimmed page size, 7.5 by 9 inches.

And the outside box, of course, is the paper size, 8.5 by 11 inches.

You can adjust the position of header and footer on the page by modifying their paragraph style to include space before and after as needed.

If you need to add crop marks, you should check out my WordSetter program, which will create them for you—yes, even in Microsoft Word!

Thanks to Dorian Cougias for suggesting this topic.

Readers Write

THOMAS C DIXON:

I edited a book recently that showed two book pages per screen, with the pages numbered consecutively. I've read your article on page sizing, etc., but can't get this effect. How is it achieved?

I RESPONDED: You can achieve what you're describing like this:

1. Click File > Page Setup.
2. Click the Margins tab.
3. Set Orientation to Landscape.
4. Set your document (under Multiple Pages in Word 2002) to 2 pages per sheet.
5. Apply to whole document.
6. Click OK.
7. Click View > Zoom.
8. Click Many Pages.
9. Select two pages.
10. Click OK.

Setting Up Headers and Footers

After you've set up the pages of your book, you'll need to set up headers and footers. Using Microsoft Word, you might think you'd find headers and footers under the Insert menu. Not so; they're under View. Why? Because your document *already* includes headers and footers. *Every* Word document does. But they're empty until you put something in them. Here's how:

1. Click View > Header and Footer. You'll now find your cursor in the Header pane, with a nice little toolbar that lets you do various things:

Insert Page Number
Insert Number of Pages (so you can create a footer like "Page 7 of 123")
Format Page Number (1, 2, 3; a, b, c; i, ii, iii; and so on. Include chapter number [1-1; 1-A]. Continue from previous section [neat!] or specify a starting number.)
Insert Date (useful for creating slug lines)
Insert Time (ditto)
[Activate] Page Setup (handy!)
Show/Hide Document Text (to keep things uncluttered while creating headers and footers)
[Set header and footer to] Same as Previous [section] (in case you're using columns, for example, in one of your chapters; I almost always turn this off)
Switch between Header and Footer
Show Previous [header or footer]
Show Next [header or footer]
Close Header and Footer

2. Skip the header of your first page (labeled "First Page Header"), which will be the opening page of your chapter and thus doesn't need a running head. To do so, click the button to Switch between Header and Footer.
3. You're now in the footer (labeled "First Page Footer") of your chapter's opening page. Do you want a page number? I do. To get one, click the Insert Page Number button. (If this were front matter, you could click the Format Page Number button and set your numbering to use Roman numerals.) I *don't* recommend creating a page number with Insert > Page Number, because it puts the page number into a frame.
4. Decide whether you want the page number on the left, center, or right of your page and make it so. The easiest way to do this—and the most heretical, since it doesn't use styles—is to click Format > Paragraph > Alignment and pick your pleasure.

5. Move to the next page by clicking the Show Next button. This will take you to the next page's footer (labeled "Even Page Footer"). Since we previously set up our document to have different first, left, and right pages, you'll need to insert another page number here; it won't just continue the numbering from the first page. Again, format the number as left, center, or right. Since this is an even (and therefore left, or verso) page, you may want to put the page number on the left.

6. Repeat step 5 for the footer on the next page, which will be a right-hand (recto) page. You may want to put the page number on the right.

7. Move to the previous page's header (verso; labeled "Even Page Header") by clicking the Show Previous button and then the button to Switch between Header and Footer. Type the text of your header into the Header pane. In book publishing, items that are more inclusive go on the left; items that are less inclusive go on the right. A few options:

Left	Right
Author Name	Book Title
Author Name	Part Title
Author Name	Chapter Title
Book Title	Part Title
Book Title	Chapter Title
Part Title	Chapter Title

8. Again, the easiest way to put the running head on the left, center, or right of the page is to click Format > Paragraph > Alignment. Since this is an even page, you may want to put the running head on the left.

9. Move to the next page's header (recto) by clicking the Show Next button. Type the text of your header into the Header pane. Since this is an odd page, you may want to put the running head on the right.

10. Set the font and point size for your running heads and page numbers by modifying their styles under Format > Style. You want them to match the rest of your text, right? While you're in there, make sure they're not set up with an automatic first-line paragraph indent, which will make them look funny on the page.

11. Adjust the space between headers, text blocks, and footers by clicking the Page Setup button and the Margins tab. Then set the distance "From edge" (of the paper) of the header and footer. This may take some experimentation to get right, but when you're finished, your pages should look pretty good.

12. Click the Close button to get back to your document text.

To see your handiwork, click View > Print Layout and set View > Zoom to Whole Page. Wow! (Note that your folios [page numbers] and running heads are automatically repeated on successive pages.)

You'll need to repeat this whole procedure for each succeeding chapter, and if all of your chapters are in one document, you'll need to separate them with section breaks. More on that next.

Section Breaks

In this final installment of how to set up book pages for publishing, we look at section breaks in Microsoft Word. Section breaks let you do a number of things. The most important ones for our purposes are:

- Restart page numbers from section to section—between front matter and chapters, for example.
- Restart footnote and endnote numbers from chapter to chapter.
- Use different running heads from chapter to chapter.

Let's say you've got your whole book in one giant document. (Yes, that's how I like to work.) You'll now want to separate your chapters with section breaks. To do so:

1. If you're not already in Normal view, switch to it by clicking View > Normal. That will allow you to see the breaks you're going to insert.
2. Go to the first place you want to change page numbers, note numbers, and running heads. The first page of your preface will do nicely.
3. At the top of the page, insert a section break by clicking Insert > Break > Page break. Under "Section break types," select "Odd page" (if you want to go the traditional book-publishing route). Then click the OK button. Your document should now include a double-lined section break labeled "Section Break (Odd Page)." If you already had a manual page break there, get rid of it.
4. Repeat steps 2 and 3 at the beginning of each chapter in your book.

Microsoft, catering as usual to office workers rather than publishing professionals, has set up Word by default to have headers and footers from section to section be the "same as previous." That is, if you set up running heads in one section, they'll automatically continue into the next. But in book publishing you don't want them to be the same; you want them to be different.

One way to "unlink" them is to go to your second section (your preface, for example), click View > Header and Footer, and then click the "Same as previous" button on the Header and Footer toolbar. (To see which button is which, rest your mouse cursor over each button for a few seconds until the ToolTip appears.) Then repeat the procedure for each chapter (section) of your book. Failure to unlink headers and footers will eventually drive you mad.

An easier way to unlink them is to use the following macro:

```
Sub UnlinkHeadersFooters()
Dim curSection As Section, curHeader As HeaderFooter
For Each curSection In ActiveDocument.Sections
```

```
For Each curHeader In curSection.Headers
curHeader.LinkToPrevious = False
Next curHeader
For Each curHeader In curSection.Footers
curHeader.LinkToPrevious = False
Next curHeader
Next curSection
End Sub
```

Once the headers and footers are unlinked, you can set up headers, footers, and page numbers for *each section* as explained in "Setting Up Headers and Footers."

While you've got the Header and Footer toolbar available, click the Format Page Number button and tell Word how you want page numbering to work from the previous section to the current one. You can "continue from previous section" or "start at" a number you specify. If you're going from front matter (with Roman numerals) to a chapter (with Arabic numerals), "Start at" is the option you want to use.

And now for those note numbers:

1. Click Insert > Reference (in Word 2002+) > Footnote.
2. Select Footnote or Endnote as appropriate.
3. Click the Options button.

If you're using Footnotes, you can set note numbers to:

• Continuous (throughout the book—not recommended).
• Restart each section (chapter, that is; the traditional method).
• Restart each page (unorthodox but elegant).

With endnotes, only the first two options are available, since endnotes don't appear on each page.

Click the OK button to finish up.

Unlinking Headers and Footers

If you work much with headers and footers in Microsoft Word, you've probably noticed that when you insert a section break, it's automatically set to "Same as Previous." For many Word users, especially in the publishing world, this is an annoyance. If I'm creating a new chapter in a book, I want my headers to be *different* from those in the previous chapter, not the same. Ideally, there should be a way to set this (or not) as an option:

[] Automatically set headers and footers to "Same as Previous"

As far as I know, this option doesn't exist. But here's a macro that will go through a document's headers and footers and unlink them all:

```
Dim curSection As Section, curHeader As HeaderFooter
For Each curSection In ActiveDocument.Sections
For Each curHeader In curSection.Headers
curHeader.LinkToPrevious = False
Next curHeader
Next curSection
```

The macro won't set the option permanently, but at least you'll no longer need to unlink all of your headers and footers by hand.

Thanks to Susan Bullowa for suggesting this topic.

Inserting Unlinked Sections

Microsoft Word, in a broad sense, has two kinds of section breaks (Insert > Break):

1. The kind that starts a new page (which includes "Next page," "Even page," and "Odd page).
2. The kind that doesn't (which includes "Continuous").

The second kind is used for such things as inserting two-column text in the middle of single-column text, all on the same page, and it doesn't concern us here. What does concern us, as editors, is what happens when we insert a section break that starts a new page.

By default, Word "links" the headers and footers in the new section to those in the previous section. In other words, when you insert a section break, the headers and footers will be the same in the new section as in the old. If you're working as an office assistant and spend most of your time formatting letters and reports, that might be exactly what you want. But if you're a book editor, that's probably *not* what you want. You probably want each section (that is, each *chapter*) to have its own headers and footers, as explained in "Setting Up Headers and Footers."

In a previous article ("Unlinking Headers and Footers") I supplied a macro that would unlink *all* headers and footers en masse. But wouldn't it be nice to be able to simply insert an *unlinked* section break? Here's a macro that will do just that, using a break of the "Next page" variety:

```
Sub InsertUnlinkedNextpageSection()
Selection.InsertBreak Type:=wdSectionBreakNextPage
If ActiveWindow.View.SplitSpecial <> wdPaneNone Then
ActiveWindow.Panes(2).Close
End If
If ActiveWindow.ActivePane.View.Type = wdNormalView Or
ActiveWindow. _
ActivePane.View.Type = wdOutlineView Then
ActiveWindow.ActivePane.View.Type = wdPrintView
End If
ActiveWindow.ActivePane.View.SeekView = wdSeekCurrentPageHeader
Selection.HeaderFooter.LinkToPrevious = Not Selection.HeaderFooter. _
LinkToPrevious
ActiveWindow.ActivePane.View.SeekView = wdSeekMainDocument
End Sub
```

Note that you can modify the macro to insert an odd-page section break or an even-page section break, which are particularly useful in book publishing. To do so, change this line—

```
Selection.InsertBreak Type:=wdSectionBreakNextPage
```

to this—

```
Selection.InsertBreak Type:=wdSectionBreakOddPage
```

or this—

```
Selection.InsertBreak Type:=wdSectionBreakEvenPage
```

For ease of use, I'd recommend that you hook the macro to a menu, toolbar button, or keyboard shortcut. Then, the next time you insert a section break (using the macro, of course), it will be automatically unlinked!

Ligatures in Microsoft Word

Ligatures, in case you didn't know, are letters that have been mashed together as one character. Why would anyone want that? For aesthetic reasons. (Yes, there is an ae ligature for words like "æsthetic.") The ligatures used most often are fi and fl, accompanied by their friends ff, ffi, and ffl. That's because these letter combinations really do look ugly in many fonts, with the dot on the i running into the top of the preceding f, and so on. You can set ligatures automatically in dedicated typesetting programs like QuarkXPress and InDesign. In Microsoft Word, it's not so simple, but it is possible. Here's how:

1. Have a font that includes ligatures. (You probably already have several.)
2. In Microsoft Word, click "Insert."
3. Click "Symbol."
4. On the "Symbols" tab, make sure there's a "Subset" dropdown list on the right. If there's not, pick a different font from the "Font" list on the left. (If you've got Palatino Linotype, you've hit the jackpot.)
5. Scroll down the "Subset" list until you find a subset called "Alphabetic Presentation Forms." Or, easier still, click in the list and then press the "A" key on your keyboard until you come to "Alphabetic Presentation Forms."
6. Somewhere in the characters displayed will be some ligatures, probably fi and fl but maybe others as well. Click one of them, click "Insert," and then click "Close."

You should now have a ligature in your document—in Microsoft Word, of all places! Of course, you'll want to use ligatures from a font that you're using for the rest of your document so that everything matches up nice and pretty. You'll probably be surprised at how good the ligatures look.

I doubt that you'll want to insert all those ligatures by hand in an existing document. Instead, you can insert them using Word's Find and Replace feature. For example, you can find "fi" and replace it with the fi ligature character. If the ffi and ffl ligatures are available, you should find and replace those character combinations *before* doing fi, fl, and ff. Otherwise, the fi, fl, and ff in the ffi and ffl letter combinations will be replaced with the fi, fl, and ff ligatures—not good. (Try saying that last sentence three times really fast.) If the ffi and ffl ligatures are *not* available, you may not want to use fi and fl either, for the same reason. (If you like, you can record the whole Find and Replace procedure as a macro that you can use again on future projects.) If you need more information, see "Finding and Replacing Unicode Characters."

And now, a caution. Using ligatures will foul up spell-checking for the words in which they are used, because Word will see the words as misspelled. For that and other reasons, you should keep a backup of your original file as a source document and consider the file containing ligatures as a presentation document. You can learn more about this in "Content vs. Presentation."

Fractions

Using fractions has always been a challenge in Microsoft Word. A few (1/2, 1/4, and 3/4) have been readily available. But what about 1/3, 2/3, and other common ones?

Microsoft recommends creating additional fractions by using equation fields or the Equation Editor. You can learn more about these methods here:

http://support.microsoft.com/default.aspx?scid=kb;en-us;Q137734

Unfortunately, these methods are inadequate, for a couple of reasons:

1. They're ugly. The fractions they create are typographically unacceptable.
2. They're clunky. Using them is a chore, and they create fields or graphics, not actual text.

Fortunately, better methods are available.

Roll Your Own

The "roll your own" method consists of creating a fraction by hand, using a superscript number, a fraction bar, and a subscript number. Here's how it works:

1. Type the top number of your fraction (the dividend, if you're mathematically inclined).
2. Insert a fraction bar (which is different from [more slanted than] the virgule, diagonal, solidus, slash, or whatever you want to call that character below the question mark on your keyboard). To do this:

a. Click Insert > Symbol.
b. Click the Font list
c. Select "Symbol."
d. Find the number 4 on the top row and count down five squares. See the fraction bar? (ANSI 164.)
e. Click the square containing the fraction bar.
f. Click the "Insert" button.
g. Click the "Close" button.

4. Type the bottom number of your fraction (the divisor). Your fraction should now look like this: 2/3.
5. Select the top number and format it as superscript (Format > Font > Superscript).
6. Select the bottom number and format it as subscript (Format > Font > Subscript).

That's it! Not a bad-looking fraction, if you ask me. And once it exists, you can turn it into an Autocorrect or Autotext entry so you don't have to create it from scratch the next time you want to use it.

Unicode

Unicode fonts include *lots* of characters, including quite a few fractions. So why not use them? You can learn more about Unicode characters in the article "Unicode."

Here's the easiest way to insert Unicode fractions (if your fonts, operating system, and version of Word support it):

1. Click the Insert menu.
2. Click "Symbol."
3. In the Font list, select a Unicode font, which will display the Subsets list to the right of the Font list and have lots of subsets available (such as Latin-1, Spacing Modifier Letters, and so on).
4. In the Subset list, select "Number Forms."
5. Somewhere in the characters displayed, you should see some fractions. Click the one you want to use.
6. Click the "Insert" button.
7. Click the "Close" button.

There's your fraction. Again, you can turn it into an Autocorrect or Autotext entry for easy access.

If you like entering Unicode characters directly (using ALT + X), here are the Unicode numbers you'll need:

1/3: 2153
2/3: 2154
1/5: 2155
2/5: 2156
3/5: 2157
4/5: 2158
1/6: 2159
5/6: 215A
1/8: 215B
3/8: 215C
5/8: 215D
7/8: 215E

Thanks to Maggie Brown for suggesting this topic.

Fraction Macro

The previous article explained how to make your own typographical fractions in Microsoft Word. But if your document is full of plain-text fractions, like these—

1/3
2/3
5/8

—why not let a macro do the work? I owe my thanks to Wordmeister Steve Hudson for the idea. Steve would probably take a more elegant approach, but this macro will definitely work. Enjoy!

```
Selection.Find.ClearFormatting
Selection.Find.Replacement.ClearFormatting
With Selection.Find
.Text = "([0-9]@)/([0-9]@)"
.Replacement.Text = "sp|\1|sp|" + ChrW(8260) + "|sb|\2|sb|"
.Forward = True
.Wrap = wdFindContinue
.Format = False
.MatchCase = False
.MatchWholeWord = False
.MatchAllWordForms = False
.MatchSoundsLike = False
.MatchWildcards = True
End With
Selection.Find.Execute Replace:=wdReplaceAll
Selection.Find.ClearFormatting
Selection.Find.Replacement.ClearFormatting
With Selection.Find.Replacement.Font
.Superscript = True
.Subscript = False
End With
With Selection.Find
.Text = "|sp|([0-9]@)|sp|"
.Replacement.Text = "\1"
.Forward = True
.Wrap = wdFindContinue
.Format = True
.MatchCase = False
.MatchWholeWord = False
.MatchAllWordForms = False
.MatchSoundsLike = False
.MatchWildcards = True
End With
```

```
Selection.Find.Execute Replace:=wdReplaceAll
Selection.Find.ClearFormatting
Selection.Find.Replacement.ClearFormatting
With Selection.Find.Replacement.Font
.Superscript = False
.Subscript = True
End With
With Selection.Find
.Text = "|sb|([0-9]@)|sb|"
.Replacement.Text = "\1"
.Forward = True
.Wrap = wdFindContinue
.Format = True
.MatchCase = False
.MatchWholeWord = False
.MatchAllWordForms = False
.MatchSoundsLike = False
.MatchWildcards = True
End With
Selection.Find.Execute Replace:=wdReplaceAll
```

What's basically going on here is that Word uses a wildcard search to find all numbers that have a slash between them:

Find What:

([0-9]@)/([0-9]@)

Then it replaces those numbers with *themselves* surrounded by arbitrary codes denoting superscript (|sp|) and subscript (|sb|). It also replaces the slashes with the fraction bar character, Unicode number 8260:

Replace With:

"|sp|\1|sp|" + ChrW(8260) + "|sb|\2|sb|"

(If you were doing this by hand, you could insert the fraction bar into your document using Insert > Symbol [as explained in earlier], then copying it, and then pasting it into the Replace dialog's "Replace With" box. The result would look something like this:

|sp|\1|sp|/|sb|\2|sb|)

Finally, the macro uses parentheses to group the numbers so that after they and their surrounding codes are found, the numbers can be replaced by *themselves,* properly formatted and without the codes, using the "Find What Expression" wildcard:

Find What:

|sp|([0-9]@)|sp|

Replace With:

\1 [formatted as superscript]

Find What:

|sb|([0-9]@)|sb|

Replace With:

\1 [formatted as subscript]

You can learn more about wildcard searches in the "Find and Replace" section in this book.

Readers Write

BILL RUBIDGE:

The fraction macro is an excellent start, but I suspect many of your readers would need to add an additional search process at the beginning of the macro, to search for dates formatted with slashes and mark those so that they do not get converted to these fancy fractions.

Without much thought, I would imagine you would need to run a wildcard search for:

([0-9]{1,2})/([0-9]{1,2})/([0-9]{1,4})

(Note that the last item, the year, has space for up to four digits, being used a lot lately as we turn centuries.)

I would then (probably crudely) replace with \1DATESLASH\2DATESLASH\3DATESLASH

Then run the macro you provide, but add a final replace at the end to replace DATESLASH with / to get back my XX/XX/XX dates.

It's worth reminding readers that the most challenging part of writing any of these search and replace macros is making sure that you write your search criteria and/or mark out items that might otherwise be unintentionally replaced.

STEVE HUDSON:

[A previous article featured a macro to convert typed-in fractions (like 1/2) into typographically acceptable ones (like 1/2). In the article, I wrote, "I owe my thanks to Wordmeister Steve Hudson for the idea. Steve would probably take a more elegant approach, but this macro will definitely work." Well, by golly, Steve did create a beauty of a macro (the Fractionator) that even watches out for dates (4/10/2001, for example) and URLs and leaves them alone, while still creating beautiful fractions. Many thanks to Steve for this useful tool, and for his comments throughout the macro to explain what is going on.]

```
Private Const msgNoFraction As String = "No fractions found."
Private Const hitInfo As String = "Information"
Public Sub TextFormatAllFractions()
System.Cursor = wdCursorWait
```

```
    If FractionFormatting = 0 Then MsgBox msgNoFraction, , hitInfo
    System.Cursor = wdCursorNormal
    End Sub
    Public Function FractionFormatting(Optional Scope As Range) As
Long
    'returns the number of entries formatted
    'formats 123/456 with super and subscript
    'The Word Heretic
    Const Search As String = "[0-9]@^47[0-9]@"
    Dim Fractionator As String
    Dim Divisor As Range
    Dim Dividend As Range
    Dim Slash As Range
    Dim Finder As Range
    Dim TestStart As Range
    Dim TestEnd As Range
    Dim IsFraction As Boolean
    Dim StartChar As String
    Dim EndChar As String
    Const UrlText As String = "?%#_|$/"
    If Scope Is Nothing Then Set Scope =
    ActiveDocument.StoryRanges(wdMainTextStory)
    Fractionator = ChrW$(8260) 'unicode
    Set Finder = ActiveDocument.StoryRanges(wdMainTextStory)
    Finder.Collapse
    With Finder.Find
    .Text = Search
    'only search forwards
    .Forward = True
    .Wrap = wdFindStop
    .MatchWildcards = True
    While .Execute(replace:=wdReplaceNone)
    FractionFormatting = True
    Set Divisor = Finder.Duplicate
    Set Dividend = Finder.Duplicate
    'divisor is the bit at the end
    'so move start until we find a slash
    Divisor.MoveStartUntil cset:="/"
    'then move just past it
    Divisor.MoveStart unit:=wdCharacter, Count:=1
    ' now make sure we get the rest of the number
    ' (Word's Find wildcards feature sux)
    Divisor.MoveEndWhile cset:="0123456789"
    'dividend is the bit at the start
    'so start from the beginning
    Dividend.Collapse
    'include everything up to the slash
    Dividend.MoveEndUntil cset:="/"
    'The slash is right after our dividend
    Set Slash = Dividend.Duplicate
    'so start at the end
    Slash.Collapse wdCollapseEnd
    'and move forward 1!
```

```
Slash.MoveEnd unit:=wdCharacter, Count:=1
'Now, test if it is a fraction or part of a bigger formula.
'First, get the chars immediately before and after
Set TestStart = Dividend.Duplicate
TestStart.Collapse
TestStart.MoveStart unit:=wdCharacter, Count:=-1
Set TestEnd = Divisor.Duplicate
TestEnd.Collapse Direction:=wdCollapseEnd
TestEnd.MoveEnd unit:=wdCharacter, Count:=1
StartChar = TestStart.Text
EndChar = TestEnd.Text
IsFraction = True 'innocent until proven guilty
'Check if this is a field. Its probably a hyperlink or similar
'So don't process it
If Slash.Fields.Count > 0 Then IsFraction = False
'Test for some obvious false positives
If (LCase$(EndChar) >= "a" And LCase$(EndChar) <= "z") Or _
(LCase$(StartChar) >= "a" And LCase$(StartChar) <= "z") Or _
InStr(1, UrlText & ".", StartChar) > 0 Or _
InStr(1, UrlText, EndChar) > 0 Then IsFraction = False
If IsFraction Then
'set the styles at LAST!
Dividend.Font.Superscript = True
Divisor.Font.Subscript = True
Slash.Text = Fractionator
FractionFormatting = FractionFormatting + 1
End If
'Now, set the find range so we find
'the next fraction
Finder.Collapse wdCollapseEnd
Wend
End With
End Function
```

Compressed Word Spacing

If you've tried using Microsoft Word to produce decently justified text, you've seen the problem: Word justifies text by expanding rather than compressing space between words, which leads to "spacey" typesetting. That's why I created my WordSetter program, which lets you adjust word spacing according to your taste.

However, it turns out that you *can* make Word compress word spacing (although without adjustment) by changing a deeply buried option. Using this option *greatly* improves typographic quality. Here's how to set it:

1. Click the "Tools" menu ("Edit" in Word 2001).
2. Click "Options" ("Preferences" on a Macintosh).
3. Click the "Compatibility" tab.
4. Put a check next to the option labeled "Do full justification like WordPerfect 6.x for Windows."

Now, as you type in justified text (Format > Paragraph > Alignment > Justified), you'll see the word spacing compress automatically as it would in a dedicated typesetting program (or WordPerfect, of course). What joy! What rapture!

Microsoft's Knowledge Base describes the option like this:

"To achieve full justification, WordPerfect compresses the spaces between words while Word expands them. This often results in different line breaks and leads to different page breaks. To implement the WordPerfect justification method, select 'Do full justification like WordPerfect 6.x for Windows' in the Options list."

This option was created to preserve line formatting when opening a WordPerfect document in Word, but it's far more important than that. It actually makes it possible to do fairly decent typography in Microsoft Word. Evidently Microsoft missed this point (or didn't want to admit WordPerfect's superiority in this regard).

While you're looking at the "Compatibility" tab, put a check next to the option labeled "Don't expand character spaces on the line ending SHIFT + Return." Then if you break a line with a soft return (SHIFT+ENTER), the line will still be properly justified. Otherwise, the spaces in the first half of the broken line will expand broadly, justifying the line clear to the margin. Bad, bad, bad.

Even after you've set these options, justification may not look quite right on your screen, especially at the ends of lines, since Word doesn't render everything perfectly. When you print your document, however, you'll see the justified text in all its glory.

Word's Compatibility tab includes other options you might want to explore if you're doing typesetting with Word, including:

• Don't center "exact line height" lines

- Don't add extra space for raised/lowered characters
- Suppress "Space Before" after a hard page or column break

You can learn more about these and other options in the Microsoft Knowledge Base article here:

http://support.microsoft.com/support/kb/articles/Q288/7/92.ASP

There are other things you'll need to adjust if you want to do typesetting in Microsoft Word, but we'll leave those for another day.

I can't take credit for "discovering" the option to "Do full justification like WordPerfect 6.x for Windows." I learned about it from Woody's Office Watch, a great email newsletter about the quirks of Microsoft Office. Woody and friends can't take credit for it either, though; they learned about it from one of their subscribers, Dermod Quirke, to whom we are now all indebted. You can read their article (and sign up for the newsletter) here:

http://www.woodyswatch.com/office/archtemplate.asp?v6-n40

Readers Write

NANCY ADESS:

Another "Compatibility" item I've found extremely important, at least on the Mac, is to turn on "Use printer metrics to lay out document." Often when I get documents from others they are somehow wired to print double-spaced only, even if I change the spacing to single spaced on the screen. Turning on this compatibility option (tools>preferences>compatibility) restores control of line spacing to me. Even though I've set that option in my default template, that doesn't apply to imported documents and I need to turn it on for each one. Until I found that (I think with the help of a Microsoft tech) I was endlessly frustrated.

JIM CRONIN:

I heard about this compatibility setting elsewhere and thought it needed some easier method to both apply it and to know whether it was in effect in a document. So, I wrote the following macro and assigned it to a toolbar button. When you click the button, the Office Assistant appears. The checkbox in the balloon is empty if WP Justification is not "on" and it is selected when justification is "on". Give it a shot!

```
' WordPerfect_Justification Macro
' Macro created 10/22/01 by JimC
If Documents.Count < 1 Then GoTo ErrorHandler
With Assistant.NewBalloon
.Heading = "For better spacing in fully justified text..."
.Checkboxes(1).Text = "Make Word justify text like WordPerfect
does it."
```

```
.Button = msoButtonSetOK
With Assistant
.On = True
.Visible = True
.Animation = msoAnimationCheckingSomething
End With
If ActiveDocument.Compatibility(wdWPJustification) = True Then
.Checkboxes(1).Checked = True
.Show
Else
.Checkboxes(1).Checked = False
.Show
End If
If .Checkboxes(1).Checked Then
ActiveDocument.Compatibility(wdWPJustification) = True
Else
ActiveDocument.Compatibility(wdWPJustification) = False
End If
Assistant.Visible = False
End With
ErrorHandler: Exit Sub
End Sub
```

Checking Word Breaks

Automatic hyphenation in Microsoft Word is surprisingly good. Sometimes while working in Word I'll think, "That word break doesn't look right." Then I'll look it up in Webster's Collegiate. Most of the time I'm wrong and Word is right. Who'd a' thunk it?

Occasionally, however, Word gets it wrong. And that means it's still necessary to check all Word breaks. I've been doing this by manually scrolling through a document and watching for hyphenated words—not really a good use of time.

Thinking there must be a better way, I created the following macro, which, starting at the cursor position, finds and selects the next word that's broken over two lines.

For ease of use, I'd recommend that you hook the macro to a toolbar button or keyboard shortcut. Then you can quickly run the macro over and over again, and each time it will go to the next broken word until it reaches the end of the document. When you see a bad break, fix it (using CTRL + HYPHEN to insert a conditional hyphen). Then run the macro again.

```
Sub CheckWordBreaks()
Dim endmark1 As Integer
Dim endmark2 As Integer
CheckAgain:
If Selection.Type = wdSelectionIP And _
Selection.End = ActiveDocument.Content.End - 1 _
Then GoTo EndMacro
Selection.EndKey Unit:=wdLine
Selection.MoveLeft Unit:=wdWord, Count:=1
Selection.MoveRight Unit:=wdWord, Count:=1, _
Extend:=wdExtend
endmark1 = Selection.Range.Information _
(wdFirstCharacterLineNumber)
Selection.MoveRight Unit:=wdWord, Count:=1
Selection.MoveLeft Unit:=wdCharacter, Count:=1
endmark2 = Selection.Range.Information _
(wdFirstCharacterLineNumber)
If endmark1 <> endmark2 Then
Selection.MoveLeft Unit:=wdWord, Count:=1
Selection.MoveRight Unit:=wdWord, Count:=1, _
Extend:=wdExtend
GoTo EndMacro
End If
Selection.EndKey Unit:=wdLine
Selection.MoveRight Unit:=wdWord, Count:=1
GoTo CheckAgain
EndMacro:
End Sub
```

Don't Break That Word!

A few years ago I edited a long, scholarly tome that, for complex reasons, my co-workers and I decided to typeset in Microsoft Word, following the techniques discussed in the "Typesetting" section.

Our intrepid typesetter has been fairly content except for one thing: there seems to be no way to keep a word from breaking at the end of a line. Microsoft Word happily breaks "Je-sus" and "Bud-dha," for example, which we'd like to avoid. We could force a word down with a soft return, but that doesn't seem like a very elegant solution. Clever idea: how about putting an optional hyphen (CTRL + -) at the *beginning* of the word? That works, but it also *displays* a hyphen at the beginning of the word, which certainly won't do. Can the optional hyphen go at the end of the word? No, that doesn't work at all. So where might we find an answer?

Well, Unicode fonts include all kinds of interesting things. Would they, by chance, include a zero-width nonbreaking space? If we had one of those, we could insert it at the spot where we didn't want a break to occur. I went to Alan Wood's spectacular Unicode Resources site and searched for "zero-width nonbreaking space":

http://www.alanwood.net/unicode/search.html

There it was, not under general punctuation but as the last entry under Arabic Presentation Forms, of all things:

http://www.alanwood.net/unicode/arabic_presentation_forms_b.html

The Web site told me the decimal number (65279) and hex number (FEFF) of the character, so I fired up Word 2002 (XP) and entered the character by typing the hex number followed by ALT + x. With nonprinting characters showing, I could see the little beauty—it looked like a gray box inside a gray box. When nonprinting characters *weren't* showing, the character was invisible, since it had no width. And sure enough, when I put the character into a word and then pushed that word to the end of the line, the word refused to break. Success!

I sent a sample to Word guru Steve Hudson, who tested the idea in various ways and pronounced it good. Thanks, Steve! So now I share this little marvel with you. If you'd like to see the character in action (and get a sample of the character that you can copy and use in your own documents), you can download the following document to play around with:

http://www.editorium.com/ftp/nonbreaking.zip

After you download, unzip, and open the document, notice the automatically hyphenated "excellent" on the first line. Now add a character somewhere in the middle of the *second* line—enough to make the second "excellent" break. But it won't!

Incidentally, the character works in Word 2000 and later versions as long as you have Unicode fonts installed on your computer. You can learn more here:

http://www.alanwood.net/unicode/fonts.html

Please note that using this character within a word will mess up spell-checking for that word, so you might want to check spelling *before* inserting the character hither and yon. If you need to get rid of the characters, display nonprinting characters; then search for ˆu65279 and replace with nothing.

Readers Write

PATSY PRICE:

I too have been very frustrated when specific words insisted on breaking in Word 98 (Mac) whether I wanted them to or not. I tried everything I could think of, including inserting a nonbreaking hyphen before the word, but nothing worked. Then somebody on one of the lists I belong to made a suggestion that has worked for me so far: select the word and change the language to No Proofing [Tools > Language > Do not check spelling or grammar]. Even when the file is opened in Word 2000 PC the word doesn't hyphenate. [Patsy made the effort to track down the person who originally made the suggestion, Hélène Dion on the McEdit list. So thanks to Hélène for the tip and to Patsy for passing it on.]

BILL RUBIDGE:

Interesting zero-width action. In my case I wanted to break long URLs in a narrow text column. Unfortunately, I am still using Word 97, so I had to resort to a conditional hyphen solution, but I set the hyphen size to 1 point and colored it white to hide it.

In any case, my experience on that issue and your description of the one below made me think you could take your "Don't break that word" solution a step further. I never use hyphenation, so I don't have your issue, but I dislike short words ending up all by their lonesome as the final line of a paragraph. My solution is:

Search for:

([A-Za-z0-9,.$\?;:"""\)\!*]{1,8}) ([A-Za-z0-9,.$\?;:"""\)\!*]{1,8})[\ˆ013]

Replace with:

\1ˆs\2

This forces the last two words (up to eight characters long) to be on the last line together.

Your hyphenation problem seems similar, but I shudder at the thought of inserting the Unicode characters manually. Would it do the job for you to search for the end of a paragraph and then insert the nonbreaking zero-width space character between EVERY letter of the last word? This way, you could run this macro automatically for the whole document.

By the way, I found I had to do an additional undo search to take out these things where I knew that the item was part of a small column. For example, if the found item was in a table, I would undo the nonbreaking material, as the table columns might be too narrow for this to be appropriate.

Break That Word Here!

The previous article explained how to use a zero-width nonbreaking space to keep a word from breaking at the end of a line when hyphenation is turned on (Tools > Language > Hyphenation > Automatically hyphenate document). Fine as far as it goes. But what can you do to break a word at a place other than one Microsoft Word insists on using? For example, Word will happily break "convertible" as "converti-ble." Ugh. (See your favorite style manual for more information about how to break words properly; I prefer the *Chicago Manual of Style*.)

The solution is to insert an optional hyphen at any acceptable breaking points. In "convertible," for example, you could insert optional hyphens as follows: con-vert-ible. The optional hyphens will override word's automatic hyphenation and break the word at one of the points you've specified.

To get an optional hyphen, click Insert > Symbol > Special Characters > Optional hyphen. Or, easier yet, press CTRL + - (on a Macintosh press COMMAND + -).

In our shop, proofreaders check galleys for bad breaks, which are then corrected manually by our typesetters, who insert optional hyphens as needed (although usually in QuarkXPress rather than Word). Wouldn't it be nice if there was a way to insert optional hyphens automatically? As it turns out, there is—even in Microsoft Word.

Hyphenation Exception Dictionary

A few years ago, I worked on a long, complex book that had to be typeset in Microsoft Word. As I worked on the book, one problem quickly became apparent: Microsoft Word has no hyphenation exception dictionary. A hyphenation exception dictionary is a list of words that specifies how certain words should (or should not) be broken at the end of a line. For example, a really tiny hyphenation exception dictionary might include the following entries as words that shouldn't be broken at all:

people
little
create

It might also include the following words, with optional hyphens indicating breaking points:

con-vert-ible (not con-ver-ti-ble)
tan-gible (not tang-i-ble)
tri-angle (not trian-gle)

Microsoft Word will break all of those words badly.

Dedicated typesetting programs such as QuarkXPress will automatically check a hyphenation exception dictionary (if you've provided one) and break words accordingly. Microsoft Word won't, but there is a way around the problem. First, compile your hyphenation exception list. Then record a macro that finds each word on your list and replaces it with the same word including optional hyphens and zero-width nonbreaking spaces as needed. You can learn more about zero-width nonbreaking spaces in "Don't Break That Word!" And you can learn more about optional hyphens in "Break That Word Here!"

Using the words above, our list might look like this (I'm using a hyphen [-] to represent optional hyphens and a tilde [~] to represent a zero-width nonbreaking space):

peo~ple
lit~tle
cre~ate
con-vert-ible
tan-gible
tri-angle

So you'd find "people" and replace it with "peo~ple," "triangle" and replace it with "tri-angle," and so on. Then, when Word does its automatic hyphenation, the words will break in the way you've specified rather than in the (incorrect) way Microsoft Word uses by default (using, in my case, American English rules). It's not that Word does a bad job of hyphenation, mind you. It's actually pretty good. But even the best hyphenation algorithms need a little help.

A more elegant (and probably more reliable) way of preventing breaks is to mark the words in question so that they are not "proofed"—that is, so that they won't be checked for spelling, grammar, or (most important) hyphenation. To do that, select a word, click Tools > Language > Set Language, and put a check in the checkbox labeled "Do not check spelling or grammar." This has the advantage of not introducing an invisible character into the word, which will keep an unwanted space from showing up later if you use the document to create a Web page, an ebook, or whatever.

A better way than recording all of these words in a macro is to use my RazzmaTag program, which will run your hyphenation exception list on a whole folder full of documents at one time. It will also let you edit and add to your list as needed. I've prepared preliminary versions of such lists that you can download and play with. The one using the zero-width nonbreaking space is here (this list will work with MegaReplacer as well as RazzmaTag):

http://www.editorium.com/ftp/nonbreakinglist.zip

And the one marking the words so they won't be proofed is here (RazzmaTag only):

http://www.editorium.com/ftp/noproofinglist.zip

Rebecca Evans was kind enough to send me her list, which is available for download here:

http://www.editorium.com/ftp/Exceptionary.zip

Here are Rebecca's comments on the dictionary:

"This is the hyphenation exception dictionary I currently use with Ventura. Ventura lets me specify how many letters must appear before a hyphen at the beginning of a word and how many after at the end so some of the words show hyphenation points at places I would not actually allow.

"In Ventura, words in the exception dictionary shown without hyphenation points are words that Ventura is told not to hyphenate at all. I use this for words that hyphenate differently depending on usage, such as pro-ject and proj-ect. I also place unhyphenated words in here to prevent unfortunate breaks, such as anal-ist.

"The words in this exception list also don't include every possible hyphenation point because I use this list to force preferred hyphenation, such as dem-onstrate instead of demon-strate.

"Microsoft Word and Ventura mis-hyphenate differently, I would imagine, so many of these words may hyphenate properly in Word. In fact, I've been using this list for so long now (so many versions of Ventura) that many of these may actually hyphenate properly in Ventura."

Microsoft's Font Properties Extension

If you work a lot with fonts, you'll probably be interested in Microsoft's Font Properties Extension, which will run under Windows 95 or higher (sorry, Mac users).

The extension makes it possible to display information about a font's origin, copyright, and licensing; its hinting and smoothing; whether or not the font can be embedded in a document; and perhaps most important, the font's character set.

Microsoft notes that the extension also "includes version and date information" and "describes the font in terms of number of glyphs, number of kerning pairs, the possible existence of a euro symbol, and the presence of embedded bitmaps within the font."

It's a useful tool, and best of all, it's free. You can learn more here:

http://www.microsoft.com/typography/property/property.htm

Word to PDF

Ever find yourself needing to convert a Word document into PDF (Portable Document Format)? Adobe Acrobat, the program usually used to create PDF documents, is fairly expensive, so you may be interested in some cheaper or even free alternatives:

The free OpenOffice.org software is made specifically to work with Microsoft Word documents, and it allows you to save documents in PDF:

http://www.openoffice.org

PDF995 allows you to print as a PDF document from inside Microsoft Word. The program works well, but the free version does insist on displaying ads unless you pay the reasonable price to make it stop:

http://www.pdf995.com/

You can use the free Ghostscript program to create PDF files:

http://pages.cs.wisc.edu/~ghost/

And you'll find an excellent tutorial on how to do so here:

http://tinyurl.com/ma5h

In 2003, PC Magazine featured an article titled PDFing Cheap that reviewed a dozen alternatives to Adobe Acrobat for creating PDFs:

http://tinyurl.com/ma1v

Need other options? You'll find a bunch of Web sites that will convert Word documents to PDF. Just go to Google.com and search for "convert word to pdf free."

Finally, if you have a Macintosh running OS X, you'll find that the operating system itself includes the ability to create a PDF document through the print dialog box.

Press-Ready PDFs from Word

So I typeset the book in Microsoft Word, created a PDF using Ghostscript, and sent the PDF off to press. But the press didn't like it. "You didn't embed your fonts," they said. Well, I sure *thought* I'd embedded the fonts. To check, I followed this procedure:

1. Opened the PDF in the free Adobe Reader:

   http://www.adobe.com/products/acrobat/readstep2.html

2. Clicked File Document Properties.
3. Clicked the Fonts tab.

Sure enough, no fonts were listed. What did I do wrong?
I neglected to install the Acrobat Distiller PPD file. Basically, I didn't follow (or know about) Adobe's instructions here:
Windows:

   http://www.adobe.com/support/techdocs/328620.html

Macintosh:

   http://www.adobe.com/support/techdocs/328844.html

Those instructions are completely adequate to do what's needed. Just remember that you need to install both the universal PostScript printer driver *and* the Acrobat Distiller PPD file.
The instructions are intended to help you create a PostScript file suitable for use with Adobe's "Create Adobe PDF Online service":

   http://createpdf.adobe.com/index.pl/2737602610.5272?BP=NS6

But you don't have to use their service. Instead, you can use convert the PostScript file to PDF using the free Ghostscript and GSView programs:

   http://pages.cs.wisc.edu/~ghost/

After you've installed all this good stuff, creating a press-ready PDF is easy:

1. Open your typeset document in Word.
2. Click File Print.
3. Under Printer Name, select "Acrobat Distiller."
4. Click the Properties button.

5. Click the Advanced button.

6. Under Graphic:Print Quality, select the dpi (dots per inch) you were told to use by the service representative at the printing company you're using. This should probably be at least 2400 dpi. You should also ask about the other settings you should use, although I'm giving you the ones that worked for me under steps 7-9 and 18-20, below.

7. Under "TrueType Font," select "Download as Softfont."

8. Under PostScript Options:PostScript Output Option, select "Optimize for Portability."

9. Under PostScript Options:TrueType Font Download Option, select "Native True-Type."

10. Click the OK button.

11. Click the next OK button.

12. Click the next OK button to print your document as a PostScript file.

13. In the "Print to file dialog," under "Save as type," select "All Files(*.*)."

14. In the "File name" box, give your PostScript file a name ending with a ".ps" extension.

15. Click the OK button.

16. Open your newly created PostScript file in GSview.

17. In GSview, click File Convert.

18. Under "Device," select "pdfwrite."

19. Set "Resolution" to 720.

20. Click the Properties button and set EmbedAllFonts and SubsetFonts to true, set PDFSETTINGS to /prepress, and set MaxSubsetPct to 100. *Don't miss this step!*

21. Click "All pages" (assuming that's what you want in your PDF).

22. Click the OK button.

23. In the Output Filename dialog, provide a name for the PDF file you're about to create, being sure to give it a .pdf extension.

24. Click the Save button.

25. Watch the GSview button in your taskbar as it tells you the percentage complete. Be patient. Don't try to open the PDF until GSview has finished creating it.

26. Double-click the PDF to open it in Adobe Reader.

27. Check to see if your fonts are embedded, as explained at the beginning of this article.

Could I be missing something? Sure. I'm no expert when it comes to making PDFs. But these instructions work for me. If they don't work for you, don't be afraid to talk to the representative at your printing company, who should be glad to give you the help you need.

Proofreading

The Death of Proofreading

There you are, editing somebody's book in Microsoft Word.

If you were working 20 years ago, you'd be editing on paper. After you finished, a typesetter would retype the entire manuscript (including your changes) by hand and run out typeset galleys. Then you'd assign a proofreader to check the typesetter's work against your edited manuscript. But today, after being edited in Microsoft Word, the manuscript will *not* be retyped. In fact, it will *become* the typeset galleys. So what's the point of proofreading the galleys against the edited manuscript?

Using an electronically edited manuscript for typesetting is a good thing. It completely prevents all of the errors that would be introduced if a typesetter retyped it. But it also eliminates the opportunity to have someone comb through the text of a book *in a different way* from what the editor has done. Comparing galley proofs and manuscript point by point forces proofreaders to slow down, so they catch errors that editors overlook in a straight read-through.

If you've figured out the solution to this dilemma, I'd love to hear about it. In the meantime, what can you do as you edit electronically to prevent some of the errors a proofreader might catch in a copy-to-copy read-through?

1. Use your spell checker. As I've pointed out before, a spell checker won't catch correctly spelled words that are misused. It *will*, however, catch the most elusive of typos, and you should use it to full advantage for this purpose.
2. Use Microsoft Word's find-and-replace feature to standardize every inconsistent spelling, capitalization, and punctuation mark. You may want to use some of my programs (such as FileCleaner and MegaReplacer) to help automate this task. Please *don't* do it by scrolling through the file over and over again, hoping you'll somehow spot everything.
3. Mark typesetting spec levels with styles (such as Heading 1, Normal, and so on) to minimize the amount of formatting typesetters have to do by hand.

Does all of this electronic editing mean the death of proofreading?

Well, not quite.

The point of proofreading is to see if an error has occurred *at any point an error can be introduced* in the publishing process. So, in the old days, a proofreader basically checked every typeset character against the edited manuscript, because every time the typesetter's finger hit a key, there was a possibility for error.

Similarly, a proofreader checked every correction the typesetter made at galley stage, because for every correction there was also the possibility that the typesetter would introduce a new error.

In your electronic production process, you need to identify the places errors can be introduced. Then have a proofreader check those places. For example:

1. Try editing in Word with revision marks (tracking) turned on. Then have a proof-reader double-check your revisions to make sure *you* haven't introduced errors during your editing. You'll be surprised at how many things turn up.
2. Have a proofreader check corrections made by authors or reviewers (unless, as editor, you do this yourself).
3. After typesetting, have a proofreader check formatting, widows, orphans, and breaks—all of the things that typesetters still impose on a manuscript even though they no longer retype it. In fact, you should have a proofreader check the final output for every medium in which a document will be published: print, HTML, Microsoft Reader, Adobe Acrobat, and so on. Publishing in different formats is like Forrest Gump's box of chocolates: You never know what you're going to get.
4. Have a proofreader read slowly through the document looking for things you may have missed while editing. This isn't proofreading in the strict sense of the word, but I'm always glad to have a second pair of eyes review my work. Maybe you are too.

Readers Write

JAMES SPEAR:

As a technical writer, I typically find my self flying solo through the document creation process. Proofing my own work is a part of this process dominated by one major pit-fall—I read through certain errors, because I know what I intended to say. So, what I have actually put "on the page" doesn't always register.

Conversations with other tech writers have reinforced my suspicions that our brains have this marvelous ability to unconsciously interpret and correct errors as we read through our own work. This is fascinating stuff for a study of the human cognitive processes. But—it can become a major obstacle when you are working alone against a deadline.

I have adopted two techniques for tackling my proofreading dilemma. These are recruiting my sources as proofreaders and manually inserting/reviewing the table of contents.

In technical writing, I typically report information from engineers, technicians, and programmers. This process starts with interviewing these technical types, then concludes with writing the documents.

I am able to keep the technical people in the process as proofreaders, simply by asking. They are often extremely reliable proofreaders for spelling, punctuation, and grammar. I find that these people are generally glad to review documents that are based on information they have provided, under one condition. You have to dole things out in small chunks! If you ask someone to read through 5 or 10 pages, they will almost always say yes. If you ask someone to read 300 pages, you may gain a reputation as a nut case.

The other technique that I have adopted for solo-proofreading affects my approach to the table of contents.

I try to avoid using Word's automatic table of contents feature. I know this is contrary to the notion of using automatic word-processing features to save time. But—I have found that manually entering each entry into the table of contents forces me to look at each page of a document, individually.

Rather than just reading headings and typing them into the table of contents, I use the opportunity to read each page. This forces me to slow down and address each page. I find that this type of careful reading, in small chunks, produces the best proofreading results. Once I have entered an individual item in the table of contents, I use Word's Cross-reference feature to insert automatic page numbers for each entry.

Paperless Proofreading

I started in the publishing business as a proofreader, reading type set in hot metal on a Linotype machine. I'd compare the type against the edited manuscript and mark any discrepancies. Then back the type would go for corrections, with additional cycles of proofreading and corrections until the type was error free.

Now the Linotype machine is gone. My electronic text is imported into QuarkXPress, and the number of errors on galleys is vastly lower than in the old days when everything had to be rekeyed by hand. Proofreaders still look over the typeset galleys for errors the editor may have missed as well as widows, orphans, and bad line breaks. But then we're right back into the old correction cycle. Isn't there a way to make it go away?

It turns out that there is. I call it "paperless proofreading." The idea is that proofreading should be done on the edited Word document *before* typesetting takes place. Some of the advantages are:

- No paper is involved, eliminating printing costs, copying costs, postage costs, and time in transit.
- Editors can merge the proofread documents and then use Word's reviewing tools to jump quickly to each correction and accept or reject it. This decreases the time needed to reconcile galleys.
- The corrected manuscript goes directly into typesetting, eliminating the correction cycle after proofreading.

Disadvantages include:

- The author and proofreaders must have a computer, Microsoft Word, and the ability to send and receive email. However, if they don't have Microsoft Word, they can download and install the free OpenOffice.org software and use its Write module to make and track their corrections. You can learn more here:

  http://www.openoffice.org

- There will need to be a separate proofreading for typography (bad breaks, etc.) and an accompanying correction cycle after the galleys have been typeset.

If you'd like to try this method of proofreading, here are the steps you'll need to follow:

Preparing the Manuscript

1. Edit your manuscript in Microsoft Word.

2. When you're ready to send the manuscript out for proofreading, make any tracked revisions permanent (so you don't have to review them later along with the proofreaders' revisions). Then save the manuscript with a new name, such as "My Galleys.doc."

3. "Protect" the manuscript so the proofreaders can't change it without revisions being tracked. To do so, click Tools > Protect Document > Tracked changes. I'd recommend using a password here, but write it down so you don't forget it. You might want to use a password that's the same from job to job or even for all your editors. Just don't give the password to authors or proofreaders. Word will ask for the password twice. Click OK and then save the document.

4. Send the manuscript to your author and proofreaders as an email attachment. In the message, include your name, phone number, and proofreading deadline along with any special instructions. (Since they now have access to Word's Find and Replace feature, you should probably instruct them to *call you* before using the feature to make extensive changes. If you've already done a spell check, you might also mention that.) Part of your instructions should be to delete and insert whole words, not just modify existing words. That will make reviewing the changes much easier later on.

The author and proofreaders will need to save the document to their hard drive, open it in Word, make their corrections in Microsoft Word (*not* WordPerfect, which doesn't handle revision tracking well), save the document, and return the document as an email attachment.

Reviewing the Manuscript

1. After the proofreading has been done and sent back to you, save the documents from the author and the proofreaders to your hard drive, being careful to give each one a unique name so they don't overwrite each other ("My Galleys Author.doc," "My Galleys Proofer 1.doc," "My Galleys Proofer 2.doc").

2. Open the author's copy of the proofread document to be your reconciled version.

3. Make sure revisions are showing (Tools > Track Changes > Highlight changes on screen) and note the color of the revisions. After you've merged the other documents into this one, you may want to give revisions in that color more weight because they were made by the author.

4. Open the document and merge each of the others into it by clicking Tools > Merge Documents.

5. "Unprotect" the document by clicking Tools > Unprotect Document and entering the password.

6. Save the document with a new name, such as "My Galleys Reconciled.doc."

7. Review the corrections and accept or reject them as needed. There are two different tools you can use to do this:

- The Accept or Reject Changes dialog.
- The Reviewing toolbar.

If you have Word 2002, the Accept or Reject Changes dialog will not be available—unless you know the secret way to get it back: Click Tools > Macro > Macros > Macros in: > Word commands > ToolsReviewRevisions > Run. Note that you can put this little beauty on a menu or toolbar for easy access.

You can also move your mouse cursor over a correction to show who made it (as long as you've turned on Tools > Options > View > Screen Tips).

Using the Accept or Reject Changes Dialog

1. Click Tools > Track Changes > Accept or Reject Changes.
2. Click the Find button (or press F) to find the next correction.
3. Click the Accept button (or press A) to accept the correction. Click the Reject button (or press R) to reject it. Word will automatically go to the next correction. This has the advantage of speed but the disadvantage of not being able to review the text around the correction.

If you inadvertently reject a correction that you wanted to keep, click the Undo button to undo the rejection.

Using the Reviewing Toolbar

1. Click View > Toolbars > Reviewing. In the middle of the toolbar you'll notice two buttons with blue arrows on them, one pointing left and the other right. Click the button with the right-arrow to go to the next correction. Click the button with the left-arrow to go to the previous correction.
2. To the right of these two arrows are two more arrows, one with a checkmark and the other with an X. Click the one with the checkmark to accept the correction. Click the one with the X to reject (or stet) it. Word will *not* automatically go to the next correction. This is an advantage if you want to double-check the text around the correction but a disadvantage if you need to move quickly.

If you inadvertently reject a correction that you wanted to keep, press CTRL + Z to undo the rejection.

In Word 2002, you can limit your review to corrections by a certain reviewer. On the Reviewing toolbar, click Show. Then click "Reviewers" and clear the checkboxes except those next to the name of the reviewer whose changes you want to review.

After you've finished reviewing corrections, save the manuscript and send it to typesetting as usual.

Ah, but there'll still be a correction cycle because you'll want to review the typography in the typeset document. Well then, how about typesetting the document in Microsoft

Word *before* proofreading takes place? That would eliminate the correction cycle entirely! You can learn more about typesetting in Word in the "Typesetting" chapter.

Readers Write

ANNA MARSHALL:

I enjoyed very much your proofreading sequence. It's essentially what I use, aided by your Editor's ToolKit and FileCleaner tools.

One step you might add to your sequence is viewing the text differently by changing the background color, using columns, or employing one of the other methods listed in "New Views on Typos" and "Background Colors."

Although these methods don't completely substitute for a review of the printed document (for me), they get darn close.

Also, your sequence doesn't acknowledge the importance of interplay between text and images in the final document. I've never seen text stand with no changes once imported into a layout. Frustrating as it is to document managers and designers, the layout generally spotlights a need for minor text adjustments if not content adjustments (e.g., certain content commands more visual emphasis than intended).

Some designers I know import a rough draft of the text into the layout to nail text-design interplay issues up front, so that when final text comes through, it gets imported into a final layout, and there should be few surprises.

BRAD HURLEY:

Thanks for the paperless proofreading tips—I used the same procedure when working on magazine articles that were reviewed by several outside experts and editors.

Here's another tip that might be useful to some of your readers: Recently, I edited a government publication that was put through an unplanned multi-agency review after the report had already been laid out in Quark. The process lasted several months, and there were extensive revisions. I saved a ton of time and hassle by buying a copy of Quark CopyDesk, which allowed me to make direct edits to the text in the Quark file. No need to give the designer marked-up hard copies, and CopyDesk protects the layout so the artist needn't worry about the editor messing up the design. Furthermore, CopyDesk lets you easily extract the text as a Word file, which allowed me to track all the changes I'd made: I extracted the text from the original CopyDesk file, and then when the revisions were complete I asked the designer to send me a new CopyDesk file. I extracted the text from the new file into another Word document and used Word's "Compare Documents" feature to reveal the differences between the two versions.

For me the real value of CopyDesk wasn't so much fitting the copy to the layout, but being able to make text edits directly to the Quark file without having to fax marked-up copy or e-mailing a commented-up PDF to the graphic designer. It reduces the opportunity for error and saves a lot of time.

DAVE GAYMAN:

Beyond the automated means for proofreading that have been recently discussed, there's a final method that I absolutely must use—because my brain has a way of blithely seeing what I intend to say, rather than what's actually on the screen or page.

I have the computer read the file to me. Of course, to do this, your computer must have sound capabilities—but most computers do, these days—plus software that synthesizes human speech from text files.

This is the single-practitioner equivalent to the standard editing group procedure in which the newest member of the team is chained to a chair and forced to read to the proofreader.

For the PC, there are a number of text-to-speech options out there; I happen to use an old one, no longer available and no longer supported. Search for "text to speech" in your favorite Web search engine. Look for one that "reads" from the Windows clipboard, so that all you have to do is select text you want the computer to read to you, then hit CTRL+C or Edit > Copy. Avoid the ones that are designed specifically for medical use, as they typically have inflated prices, thanks in large part to medical insurance.

A second must-have option is the ability to control the speed of reading; you'll find that different speech engines (and different voices within each engine) provide different default speeds, and some defaults are too slow or too fast for optimum, follow-along reading.

If you have extra money lying around, and if the package you choose has optional voices, shell out for the high-end voices. Their sound and speech quality is much better than the standard ones.

Reviewing Revisions with the Keyboard

The previous article on paperless proofreading explained how to use Word's Reviewing toolbar to review revisions in a merged document. It's a great tool except for one thing: the need to locate and click those tiny toolbar buttons for every revision you want to find, accept, or reject. Wouldn't it be nice to use the same commands from the keyboard? Here's how:

1. Click Tools > Customize > Commands > Keyboard.
2. In the Categories window, find and click "All Commands."
3. In the Commands window, click "ToolsRevisionMarksNext."
4. Put your cursor in the box labeled "Press new shortcut key."
5. Press the keyboard combination you want to use. For example, for the "Next Change" command (ToolsRevisionMarksNext), you could use ALT + SHIFT + N.
6. Click the "Assign" button.
7. Repeat steps 1 through 6 for the following commands:

    ToolsRevisionMarksPrev ("Previous Change," ALT + SHIFT + P)
    ToolsRevisionMarksAccept ("Accept Change," ALT + SHIFT + A)
    ToolsRevisionMarksReject ("Reject Change," ALT + SHIFT + R)

9. Click the "Close" button.

Now by pressing the key combinations you specified, you'll be able to review, accept, and reject changes just as if you were using the toolbar buttons—but without the aggravation.

Accepting Changes by a Single Reviewer

Sometimes, in a document that's been reviewed by several people, it's nice to be able to accept all changes by a single reviewer—maybe the author or a proofreader whose judgment you trust. (Or maybe yourself!) In Word 2002 (XP) and later versions:

1. Click View > Toolbars > Reviewing to display the Reviewing toolbar.
2. On the toolbar, click Show > Reviewers.
3. Select the name of the reviewer whose changes you want to accept (and deselect any others that are checked).
4. Click the > Accept Change button (blue checkmark, middle of the toolbar).
5. Click Accept All Changes Shown.

In Word 97, 98, 2000, and 2001, it's not so easy; it requires a macro. This one, in fact:

```
Sub AcceptRevisionsByAuthor()
Dim aRevision, ThisAuthor As String
For Each aRevision In ActiveDocument.Revisions
ThisAuthor = aRevision.Author
If ThisAuthor = "Jack M. Lyon" Then
aRevision.Accept
End If
Next aRevision
End Sub
```

When you use the macro, of course, you'll want to replace "Jack M. Lyon" with the name of your choice.

If you want to accept changes for all reviewers *except* Jack M. Lyon, you can change this line—

```
If ThisAuthor = "Jack M. Lyon" Then
```

—to this:

```
If ThisAuthor <> "Jack M. Lyon" Then
```

You can also *reject* all the changes by a single reviewer. To do so, change this line—

```
aRevision.Accept
```

—to this:

```
aRevision.Reject
```

In Word 2002 and later, you can reject all changes by a single reviewer by clicking the Reject Change/Delete Comment button (to the right of the Accept Change button) and then clicking Reject All Changes Shown.

Thanks to Anna Marshall for requesting this article.

Compare Vs. Merge

If you do paperless proofreading, you've probably bumped into some of the same problems I've had with comparing documents (Tools > Track Changes > Compare Documents) and merging documents (Tools > Merge Documents). In particular, sometimes I'll go to compare two documents and get the following message:

> The new document already has changes. Word may ignore some existing changes. Compare anyway?

At other times I'll go to merge documents and get this cryptic notice:

> The merged documents contain unmarked changes. Do you want to merge up to the first untracked change?

If you've had similar problems, maybe you'd be interested in better understanding Compare and Merge.

On the surface, Compare and Merge look a lot alike. They're both ways to show the differences between documents, right? Wrong. Well, okay, the Compare feature *is* a way to do that—in documents that don't already include tracked revisions. Merge, however, is something completely different—a way to combine documents that *already* contain tracked revisions and that have previously been "protected" for that very purpose. Here's a breakdown of the two features:

> Compare's reason for living is to mark the differences between two documents.
> Merge's reason for living is to combine tracked changes from two or more copies of the same document.

> Compare expects that the documents are different (an original manuscript versus an edited manuscript, for example).
> Merge expects that the documents are identical except for tracked changes.

> Compare doesn't care where the documents came from.
> Merge expects that the documents came from two or more different people—in other words, that the documents were reviewed on different computers than the one on which they are being merged. (If you want to get really specific, Word checks the name of the person who last saved the file. This name is set under Tools > Options > User Information.)

Compare expects that the documents do *not* already include tracked revisions. (If they do, you'll get the error message mentioned earlier.)

Merge expects that the documents *do* include tracked revisions (although they don't have to).

Compare doesn't care whether the documents have been protected for revisions or not.

Merge expects that the documents *have* been protected for revisions. (If they're not, you may get the error message mentioned earlier.)

Here's the breakdown in table form:

	Compare	**Merge**
Combines revisions	No	Yes
Marks revisions	Yes	No
Documents identical	No	Yes
Different reviewers	No	Yes
Documents have revisions	No	Yes
Documents protected for re-visions	No	Yes

Use Compare when you have two different versions of the same unmarked document and want to see the differences between them.

Use Merge when you have reviewed documents that were originally identical and want to see the combined revisions from different reviewers.

New Views on Typos

Lyon's Law of Typos: On your first glance at a newly typeset document, you will immediately discover an error you missed while editing.

Why this maddening experience occurs is a mystery to me, but it's nevertheless true that when I see a document in a new form, I also spot "new" errors. If this is true for you, too, you can use Microsoft Word to turn it to your advantage. How? By changing the way you view a document in Microsoft Word.

Let's say you've already "finished" editing a document—you've made everything consistent, fixed errors of fact, run a spell-check, and so on. Ordinarily, you'd send it off to be typeset—*after* which you'd spot those additional typos. This time, however, why not try reading through the document again after changing the way it's displayed? You could try any of the following:

- If you've been working in Normal view, switch to Print Layout view (under the View menu)—or vice versa.
- Read the document in Outline view (under the View menu).
- Change the Zoom percentage to something radically bigger or smaller than what you've been using (View > Zoom).
- Attach a different template (using the same style names) to display your type in a different color and font. If you're going to do this, make sure you have a "real" template that you can attach later to restore the document's true formatting. You can learn more about this in "Attaching Templates to Documents."
- Switch to Draft font. You've never used Draft font? It shows text in a plain font with a minimum of formatting. Here's how to display it:

1. Click "View."
2. Click "Normal" (you must be in Normal view to use Draft font).
3. Click "Tools."
4. Click "Options."
5. Click the "View" tab.
6. Put a check in the box labeled "Draft font."
7. Click the "OK" button.

Word 2000's Draft font has a bug that prevents the display of bold and italic. But in other versions of Word, Draft font works fairly well and is definitely a different way to look at your documents.

Will using one of these methods eliminate typos in typesetting? Well, probably not. After all, Lyon's Law of Typos is a law. But another read-through in a different view should help catch some of those errors.

Readers Write

MARIE SHEAR:

Shear's Law of Typos, discovered by a widely unheralded writer and editor, specifies that the number of errors is directly proportional to the number of copies that have just been distributed and to the rank of the recipients.

NANCY NEWLIN:

Here's another technique I learned many years back that "tricks" the eyes into thinking they're seeing something new: print the document on something other than white paper— yellow, green, blue, etc. Then it all looks *new*. Works for me!

PRESTON EARLE:

Another effective way to spot typos is to read the document backwards.

DAVE ERICKSON:

Try reading aloud as a way to catch errors.

ED MILLIS

[Ed Millis asked for help with the final checking of a document, including, as he wrote, "ensur[ing] all tables and figures are numbered correctly and correspond to their text mention, mak[ing] sure every paragraph has the proper indent and reference (every (a) has a (b), and it's not (b) when it should be (2), and I didn't overlook any abbreviations."]

ERIC FLETCHER: I run into similar types of issues as described by your reader Ed Millis, but would never consider printing the document! IMHO, viewing it on the screen is not only less wasteful of paper, but with a few tweaks, you can focus specifically on the particular issue.

I would use Find & Replace's wildcard feature to highlight all elements contained within parentheses, then put the file in normal view (zoomed up quite large so I could lean back and do my review with mouse only . . .), use the Find dialog to find the first instance of a highlight, then use the downward pointing icon in the lower left of the vertical scrollbar to skip through and review all of the others.

For abbreviations, you can pull everything in all caps to a second document, then sort it and look for anomalies. Use Find with wildcards to look for the pattern "[A-Z]{2,5}" (to get all instances of 2-5 capital letters) but choose "Find All" instead of the normal Find. This will select all instances. Drop out of the dialog and CTRL + C to copy. Make a new document and Paste: you will have a complete set of all found items. When sorted, abbreviations that don't look right are easy to spot.

In fact, for this application, I typically set the abbreviations in their own character style so I can pull them for generating an acronym list. Some abbreviations don't follow the all caps rule ("SoS/E" is a recent example in a book I'm working on for example), but if I have a button to attach the style, it is easy to do as I encounter it. Then, later, I can pull anything tagged with the "abbreviation" style to help create the acronym list.

I have a little macro that helps me correct all other instances of a selection and set them in a character style. I needed it to set Latin names in a document where they needed to be ignored for spell check, but were inconsistently spelled and presented in the supplied content. For example, "tuberosa" was sometimes "tuberaso" but both needed to be tagged as my "Latin" style. As I review words that had been set in italics (Find, CTRL + I), and came across a word I had not yet set, I can select it and click my SetLatin button. The VBA code presents "tuberaso" (selected) in a dialog and lets me type in "tuberosa". When I click Okay, it uses the VBA Replace all to fix any other instances throughout the document. What makes this particularly helpful is that I have the "Latin" character style set in a temporary colour (say purple) so that as I progress through the document, terms I've dealt with show up distinctly because they are coloured. I then reset the colour to automatic within the style definition before I complete the job. Here's the code I use (it can be modified to fit other requirements):

[Note: Before using the macro, you must create a character style named "Latin." You should take seriously Eric's suggestion to modify the macro to fit other requirements; this macro could be a very useful tool for many purposes.]

```
Sub SetLatin()
' Proposes to replace the selected string
' with whatever you type in,
' and applies the Latin character style
' to each instance.
' Set up to deal with correcting
' all instances of italicized words
' in a scanned document (e.g., Latin names)
' because they can be both misinterpreted
' and need to be set in italics consistently.
Dim strReplacement As String
strReplacement = _
InputBox("Replace all instances of [" & _
Selection.Text & _
"] with whatever is entered below, " & _
"and also set each with the " & _
"Latin character style.", _
"Set all like this as Latin", _
Selection.Text)
If strReplacement <> "" Then
With ActiveDocument.Range.Find
.Text = Selection.Text
.MatchWholeWord = True
.Replacement.Text = strReplacement
.Replacement.Style = _
ActiveDocument.Styles("Latin")
.Execute Replace:=wdReplaceAll, _
```

```
Forward:=True, Wrap:=wdFindContinue
End With
End If
End Sub
```

The advantage of using code like this is that it doesn't change what you have set in the Find & Replace dialog. If I did it within the dialog, I'd need to remember to turn off the style the next time I used the dialog. I have several little chunks of code for such things, and it can really improve the efficiency of reviewing.

Incidentally, my temporary colour method can also be very handy for setting styles. If the main body styles area all defined to be based on, say, Body Text, I can set its colour to green. Then, as I tag the content by whatever method, the paragraphs with my styles attached will show up in green so I can concentrate on the non-green content. This is particularly useful if you use either Find & Replace to help tag, or use the "Select all instances" option available from the Styles and Formatting task pane. Either way enables you to assign styles "blindly," but with the colour, you can see what remains to be tagged manually as you review.

This is probably only peripherally relevant to Ed's question, but hopefully some of it will apply!

Background Colors

The previous article suggested various ways to change the view in Word as a way to pick up errors missed during a first editing pass. Unfortunately, I forgot to include one method that is both effective and easy to use—a feature called "Blue background, white text." Here's how to turn it on:

1. Click the "Tools" menu.
2. Click "Options."
3. Click the "General" tab.
4. Put a check in the box labeled "Blue background, white text."
5. Click the "OK" button.

That will display your document with white text on a blue background, just like the old WordPerfect 5.1 for DOS—definitely a new way to view your document. You may find that you actually prefer working with this feature turned on—it's certainly easy on the eyes. If so, when you're ready to give your document a second look for missed typos, just turn the feature off, reverting to black text on a white background.

If you want other background colors (bright green!), they're certainly available. Here's how to get them:

1. Click the "Format" menu.
2. Click "Background."
3. Click the color you want to use.

Note that using this feature overrides the blue background (but not the white text) of "Blue background, white text," if you have it turned on, so you'll probably want to turn it off before using a background color. Also, happily, background colors don't print; as the Help file notes, they're designed for "viewing documents only"—which is exactly what we want. (Background colors are also useful in creating Web pages, but that's another story.)

By the way, you may find that you like editing in some of the background colors. As I write this, I'm using the light green on the bottom row of standard colors—a nice change from Word's usual stark white. If the standard colors aren't enough, you can click "More Colors" and really get crazy. Furthermore, once you've set a color you like, you can save it in a template that you can attach to any document you like. Just be sure to reattach the regular template before sending the document out into the real world.

Thanks to Nancy Newlin, who inspired this article.

Readers Write

CHUCK TUCKER:

I don't know about your version of Word, but background colors (other than white on blue) only work in Normal view. They go away when you switch back to Print View.
I have a couple of other observations.

1. When I switch to Normal view with Tools\Options\View\ Style Area Width set greater than zero I get the usual display of styles along the left margin.
2. When I set a new background color in the Normal view the styles in the margin disappear (Area Width = 0)??
3. Switching back to Print Layout view gets rid of the background.
4. Switching back to Normal view omits the background color and returns the Styles in the margin.

Go figure?
However, if you simply use the standard "white on blue background" option, then the Styles margin display remains when switching back and forth.

Checking Page Proofs in Acrobat Reader

When a book is ready to go to press, publishers ususally create a PDF and send it to the printer. But before sending it off, they print it out on paper and review the pages to make sure that they're numbered correctly, that the running heads are right, and so on. All of this checking means turning those paper pages many, many times, and you know how much I dislike unnecessary work. Thinking there must be a better way, I turned my attention to the free Adobe Reader:

http://www.adobe.com/products/acrobat/readstep2.html

Guess what I found?

1. Open the press-ready PDF in Adobe Reader.
2. Click View > Fit Page to display a whole page at once.
3. Click View > Page Layout > Facing to display two whole pages at the same time.

Now press the PAGE DOWN key to see each set of pages at the same time, with the even pages on the left and the odd pages on the right. PAGE UP, of course, takes you up.

If you have the full Adobe Acrobat, you can add comments, highlighting, and other markup to the PDF file for any last few corrections that might need to be made:

http://www.adobe.com/products/acrobatstd/overview.html

But you can also do much of this in the free PDF Xchange Viewer, as discussed in the next article.

Using PDFs is a great, fast way to check page proofs—one I'll be using from now on.

Readers Write

ARNOLD HOWARD:

I used to edit a magazine. After laying out the articles, the art director sent me the pages in PDF format by email. I used the highlighter in Adobe Acrobat to circle mistakes, and the notes feature to explain the corrections. Then I loaded the proofed pages to the publisher's FTP site.

I added a "+" to the beginning of the file name for proofed files.

I never proofed from printed copies. PDF files were all I needed.

When proofing from a computer screen, I found it helpful to enlarge the pages so that a column filled the monitor. I could spot errors easier because that forced me to concentrate on one column at a time.

PDF-Xchange Viewer

In the publishing house where I used to work, we experimented with what I call "paperless proofreading" (for more information, see the article by that name).

We also talked about having proofreaders work from PDF files, but that would mean they'd need to get the full-fledged Adobe Acrobat software so they could annotate the text, pointing out errors for the typesetter to correct and inserting queries for the editor. Acrobat has some wonderful features, but at $299 it's a tad expensive for many proofreaders:

http://www.adobe.com/products/acrobatpro/acrobatstd.html

If only we'd known about the wonderful (and free!) PDF-XChange Viewer from Tracker Software Products:

http://www.docu-track.com/home/prod_user/pdfx_viewer/

It won't do everything that Acrobat does (for example, merge annotations from multiple PDF files), but it includes a wide range of PDF annotation tools. And that means you could send PDF galleys by email rather than sending paper galleys by postal mail. How much money would that save you? A 300-page book at 2.5 cents (or more) per page to print or photocopy comes to $7.50. If you make three copies (for two proofreaders and the author), that's $22.50. Add postage of, say, $4.60 X 3 = $13.80, for a grand total of $36.30:

http://postcalc.usps.gov/

If you want overnight delivery (deadlines, right?), you're looking at postage of about $65, for a grand total of $87. And that doesn't include mailing envelopes, time spent copying and mailing, or the time cost of losing at least two days in transit. How many books do you handle a year? Ouch!

So, would PDF proofreading work for you? If you'd like to find out, PDF-XChange Viewer could be the way to go.

http://www.docu-track.com/home/prod_user/pdfx_viewer/

Indexing

Indexing in the Dark

Microsoft Word uses what's known among professional indexers as "embedded indexing." That means the index entries are placed as codes in the text of the document being indexed. Then, later, the codes are used to generate the index automatically. (You can learn more about using Word's indexing features by searching for "Index" in Word's Help file.)

Embedded indexing offers one big advantage over traditional indexing: if your pagination changes (for whatever reason), you can easily regenerate the index with fresh, new page numbers for all the entries.

But embedded indexing also has a big *disadvantage* over traditional indexing: there's no way to see your entries in alphabetical order or even in one place, so it's like working in the dark. In books with many pages (the kind I tend to get), this is a real problem. For example, I may make an entry for "Gandhi, Mohandas" on page 300, not remembering my earlier entry for "Gandhi, Mahatma" on page 30. That means my index will need lots of editing after it's been generated.

You can alleviate the problem completely by using my DEXter indexing add-in. Or you can alleviate it somewhat by opening your document in two windows at once, scrolling to the bottom of the second window, generating your index, and using the index for reference as you create more entries in the first window. Here's the procedure:

1. Open the document you want to index.
2. Place your cursor in some text where you want to insert an index entry.
3. Click Insert > Index and Tables > Index > Mark Entry. (In Word 2002, click Insert > Reference > Index and Tables > Index > Mark Entry.)
4. Type in your main entry, a subentry, and any other information you want to include.
5. Click the Mark button. If you like, you can enter more index entries for the same text selection, clicking the Mark button for each one. When you're finished, click the Close button.
6. Repeat steps 2 through 5 to create a few additional entries.
7. Open your document in a new window by clicking Window > New Window.
8. Click Window > Arrange All to put one Window at the top of your screen and the other at the bottom. If you have my Editor's ToolKit program, click Windows > Arrange Documents to place the windows side by side—or arrange them that way by hand.
9. Place your cursor in the second window and press CTRL + END to go to the end of the document.
10. Click Insert > Index and Tables > Index > OK to generate the (unfinished) index. (In Word 2002, click Insert > Reference > Index and Tables > Index > OK.)
11. Place your cursor in the first window and insert some more index entries.

12. Go back to the second window and update the index (so you can see your new entries in place) by placing your cursor in the index, clicking the right mouse button, and clicking "Update Field." On a big book with lots of entries, this may take several seconds. (On my old, not-so-fast computer, a 500-page document with 2,400 entries took 45 seconds to update.)
13. Repeat steps 11 and 12 as needed.

This is far from being the perfect solution to the problems of embedded indexing, but at least it will keep you from having to work completely in the dark.

Page Down in Synch

Working on an index recently, I needed to ensure that pagination of the document I was indexing matched another document in which pagination had already been set. Because of the complexity of the material, I had to do this manually and visually, paging down in document 1, switching to document 2, paging down again, and then switching back to document 1. What a pain! It wasn't long before I found myself writing a macro to move down a page in both documents at once. Here it is, short but sweet:

```
Sub PageDownInSynch()
Documents(2).Activate
Selection.GoTo What:=wdGoToPage
Documents(1).Activate
Selection.GoTo What:=wdGoToPage
End Sub
```

For the macro to work, you must have two documents open in Word at the same time, and the process works best if you've sized and arranged the two documents vertically side by side. (My Editor's ToolKit program includes an "Arrange Documents" macro that will do that for you instantly and automatically.)

For best results, assign the macro to a keyboard combination so you can quickly run it over and over with the touch of a key.

Now you can page through your documents, adjusting pagination as needed with manual page breaks (CTRL + ENTER). You'll probably find other uses for the macro as well.

Note that in Word 2003 and later, you can accomplish the same thing under Window > Compare Side by Side.

Indexing with Page Breaks from Quark

I started indexing a book yesterday, and I wanted to work on the text of the document in electronic form, with page breaks that matched those of the galleys, which had already been typeset in QuarkXPress. After a little experimentation, I figured out the following procedure:

1. Ask the typesetter to provide a PDF file, exported from QuarkXPress.
2. Open the PDF using the free Acrobat Reader (probably already on your computer).
3. Click File > Save as Text and save the resulting file to the desktop.
5. Open the file in Microsoft Word. Wow! All of the page breaks are exactly where they're supposed to be (inserted as manual page breaks). Of course, formatting has been lost (since this is a text file), but for pure indexing purposes that doesn't matter.
6. Click File > Page Setup > Layout and set paper size to 22 by 22 inches. Why? So Word won't insert any automatic page breaks and thus throw off pagination.
7. Insert a section break (Insert > Break > Odd page) between the book's front matter and chapters to prepare for step 7.
8. Put the cursor in the front matter, click Insert > Page Numbers, click the Format button, and specify a number format of lowercase Roman numeral. Also specify that page numbering should start at page i. Then click OK and click OK again.
9. Put the cursor in the first chapter, after the section break, click Insert > Page Numbers, click the Format button, and specify a number format of lowercase Arabic numbers. Also specify that page numbering should start at page 1. Then click OK and click OK again.

Now, when the cursor is in the front matter, the far left side of Word's status bar will display the correct page number in Roman numerals. When the cursor is in the chapters, the far left side of Word's status bar will display the correct page number in Arabic numbers. And when the index is generated, the page numbers will be Roman or Arabic as required.

After I was finished with all this, I began indexing with pleasure. Now you can too.

Readers Write

STEVE HUDSON:

<Looks around nervously before whispering a few trade secrets.>

Ya know Jack over at the Editorium, right? Well he and I have two completely different approaches to indexing. Yet some of the fringe bits are compatible. However, we both get the job done.

He is making tools for helping hand-build an index. I am making tools for helping clean up a concordance approach. Neither does the job properly without a skilled hand guiding them.

That having been said, naturally I have a heretical stance on the whole thing. This is an abridged and appended version of a longer yack I had with a writer up in the mountains last weekend. She is working on cleaning up my Word Spellbook. I've barely started indexing because there is more dump left. This is also the exact same issue I face doing up development documentation: there is always more to add, and that added stuff needs to be indexed like the old stuff.

Quicker, Easier Indexing by Subtraction
or
How to Use a Concordance File and Still Produce a Decent Index
or
The Heretic's Hack 'n' Slash Method of Indexing

Note key terms on the way by indexing them. It's just as easy to mark all as to mark one. Keep on developing away. Time for a minor, internal release. Update yer dynamic index. Copy it to a new doc, flatten it with ctrl+shift+f9 and be clever with find and replace wildcards to blow away numbering, leaving terms ready for use in a concordance file. This then re-performs "mark all" on all your entries.

This works great for getting a good start together. First you review for addition. Get all new terms in there. Either index them all or add them to the concordance. Do this until you are satisfied all key terms have been identified. Search out used synonyms and either kill them or add them to the index. Etc. Hunter-gatherer mode.

Then you review by subtraction, accountancy-management style. If it ain't important, slash it from your budget. During your passes, you marked separate instances of your word stems:

Finding
Find
Finder
Found
Search
Searching

Time to rationalise, quickly. Use find and replace to do the dirty work for you el pronto! I am planning to help this part with a macro to do stem matching and an interface for hand-matching synonyms and keeping that information in select peer-shared databases. Technically speaking, you can insert HERETIC-NOT-nnnnn bookmarks with the same range as spurious concordance artefacts for future proofing, and auto-expand multiple similar references based on a sliding log scale of the distance of the inference—but that's a while off yet.

This leaves you with a poor index. Now you do the stuff that good "hand" indexers do as part of their addition process that you've missed, which is pretty simple by now.

Simply scan through the text looking at your index field placements. Forget the words themselves; we're beyond words now, we're being artistic.

Let's imagine that every major subject in the index is a colour. If it's a small range, it's a saturated strong colour; if it's a large range, it's pale. Synonyms are varying shades of that colour. This is badly implemented by a simple macro I wrote ages ago to highlight index entries. (Highlight doesn't have a custom color range.)

If I look at a document from a chapter perspective, I see a rainbow of the base colours with colour boundaries being clearly defined. I zoom in to section level. I see the base colour for that chapter and some interesting hues from cross-over colours where index entries straddle colour boundaries for their multiple relationships. Thickens the spectrum right out for that colour. Some sparkling of other colours is also starting to show.

I zoom in to topic level. Surprisingly at this level, from what we've seen above, the base hue is quite pale. A kaleidoscope of colours of all shades is present. Well, at least it *should* be, but it probably isn't if we've just finished the sluggo approach I outlined.

What you will have is lots of strong shades and no pale ones. So, we look at the patterns in front of us. Seas of white are either bad and need rectifying or they are long references or graphical content.

Pale shades should feature regularly and will generally be of the hue of the section. However, there should be patches of pale contrasting colour as well, otherwise our index is just a TOC and is useless. A tint of every colour should be represented, somehow, everywhere in a section.

If you see clusters of the strong colours, you need to smudge them and make them paler. Don't let areas of the same shade sit beside each other; make them paler and covering the whole area.

On a real-world level this means looking behind the words still for meta-concepts that flow from areas as well as ensuring your master : slave pairings are suitable and a good whack of 'em represented richly.

Indeed, it is possible even to try a network theory approach. The words themselves are scale free, but we don't index them all. Major word hubs are trivials. We try and deal with any minor hubs by clever document structures (TOC) rather than the index, yet still have power terms with many sub-entries. The index picks up the lesser nodes of interest. Log(references) x log(incidences) wouldn't be a straight line. References x incidences would be closer to a flat line. I'm sure there's an existing work that's been done on it somewhere.

Indexing with a Concordance

In the previous Readers Write section, Word expert Steve Hudson provided some tips about indexing with a concordance. If you don't know what that means, the idea is to make a list of terms that you want to include in your index. Then you feed that list to Microsoft Word, which creates an index entry every time one of those terms appears in your document. Purists say that's no way to create an index, and for most documents I tend to agree. There are times, however, when using a concordance is the only way to go.

Let's say you need to create a title index for a 200-page catalog of all the books published by your company. Why do you need an index? Because each book appears in several different sections (Title, Author, Subject, and so on). Let's also say each entry appears as a row in a table in each section. In the title section, it would look something like this:

Billy Budd Herman Melville $19.95

Creating the concordance is easy:

1. Click and then select the Title column (Table > Select > Column).
2. Copy the column (CTRL + C).
3. Create a new document (CTRL + N).
4. Paste the column into the new document (CTRL + V).
5. Click and select the column again (Table > Select > Column).
6. Convert the column to text (Table > Convert > Table to Text).

Hey, there's your concordance!
To use it:

1. Save it.
2. Switch to your catalog document.
3. Click Insert > Index and Tables > Index > AutoMark. (In Word 2002, click Insert > Reference > Index and Tables > Index > AutoMark.)
4. Navigate to your concordance file and click it to select it.
5. Click the Open button and wait while Word marks all of those index entries.
6. Generate your index as explained in the "Indexing in the Dark."

Or, if you insist, you can go through and create all those entries by hand. In cases like this, I'll take the concordance every time.

Thanks to Ron Strauss, a real indexer, for suggesting this topic.

Indexing with a Two-Column Concordance

Recent articles have discussed editing with a concordance, which may be confusing for some readers. Let me explain. In those articles, "concordance" really means "word list." It's simply a list of all the words in a document, and it can come in pretty handy in editing.

Experienced Word users know, however, that a concordance is also a list of words used to create an index. You can learn more in "Indexing with a Concordance."

That article explains how to use a one-column concordance, but it's also possible to use a two-column concordance to create an index in a Word document. Why would that be useful? Because it tells Word to index certain words and phrases differently than they appear in the text.

Let's say your text includes a sentence like this:

George Washington was the first president of the United States of America.

You can create a concordance entry that looks like this:

George Washington Washington, George

Then, when Word comes to the words "George Washington" in your document, it will create an index entry for "Washington, George." And it will do that for each instance of "George Washington" in your document.

To create a two-column concordance:

1. Create a new document (CTRL + N).
2. Click Table > Insert > Table.
3. Under "Number of columns," enter 2.
4. Under "Number of rows," enter 1.
5. Click the OK button to create your table.
6. In the table, enter your first term and its replacement. For example, in the first column you could enter "George Washington," and in the second column you could enter "Washington, George." (Don't include the quotation marks.)
7. Press the Tab key to create a new row.
8. Enter more terms and replacements and rows as needed.
9. Save your concordance.

When you're finished, create your index:

1. Switch to your document.
2. Click Insert > Index and Tables > Index > AutoMark. (In Word 2002 and later, click Insert > Reference > Index and Tables > Index > Mark Entry.)

3. Navigate to your concordance file and click it to select it.
4. Click the Open button and wait while Word marks all of those index entries.
5. Generate your index as explained in "Indexing in the Dark."

If you're a professional indexer, you probably avoid indexing in this way, although my DEXter and DEXembed programs can help a lot with creating embedded indexes in Word.

In the next article, however, I'll show you the perfect example of when to use a double-column concordance in preparing an index—and an automatic way to create it.

Thanks to Mark Taylor for suggesting this article.

Readers Write

MARK TAYLOR:

Using a concordance table allows you to index using an "alias." A table also allows you to index multiple instances of a word, regardless of capitalization. For example, you could find Delaware and DELAWARE in the same document, but both would be a separate entry because the concordance is case sensitive. Using a concordance table gives you a simple workaround to this problem. You could force the index to have both entries found under the heading Delaware, or under DELAWARE.

Indexing with a Two-Column Concordance, Part 2

In the previous article, I promised to show you the perfect example of when to use a double-column concordance in preparing an index, and an automatic way to create such a concordance. The perfect example is a poetry anthology, but almost any consistently structured compilation of articles or addresses will lend itself to this kind of indexing.

Let's say you've got that poetry anthology in front of you on the screen—"100 Poems to Brighten Your Day." As you look through the anthology, you notice a consistency in the way the poems are laid out:

> Title
> Author
> Poem

For example:

> Your Day
> Jack M. Lyon
> Roses are red;
> Violets are blue;
> This is a day
> especially for you.

How inspiring!

And of course, the anthology was edited by an astute editor (probably you) who used paragraph styles for each text level:

> Heading 1 (for the title)
> Heading 2 (for the author)
> Poem First Line (for the poem's first line)

Since this is a poetry anthology, you'll need to create at least three indexes:

> Index of Titles
> Index of Authors
> Index of First Lines

Let's start with the titles. Since they've been styled as Heading 1, you can easily pull them out to put them in a concordance:

1. Click Edit > Replace.

2. Make sure your cursor is in the Find What box.
3. Click the More button if it's available.
4. Click the Format button.
5. Click Style.
6. Scroll down to Heading 1 and select it.
7. Click the OK button.
8. Move your cursor to the Replace With box.
9. Enter "<^&>" (without the quotation marks). That code in the middle of the angle brackets, ^&, is the "Find What Text" code (see the "Find and Replace" chapter.)
10. Click the Replace All button.

All of your poem titles should now be enclosed in angle brackets:

<Your Day>

Now install my Puller program (use it free for 45 days), which makes it easy to pull delimited items into a separate document:

http://www.editorium.com/puller.htm

Use Puller to pull the items in angle brackets (the poem titles) into a separate file, which will look something like this:

<Your Day>
<The Birds Are Singing>
<Sunshine and Lollipops>
<A Smile for You>

Use Word's Replace feature to find "<" and replace it with nothing, then ">" and replace it with nothing, leaving just the list of titles:

Your Day
The Birds Are Singing
Sunshine and Lollipops
A Smile for You

Now put the titles into a table:

1. Click Edit > Select All.
2. Click Table > Convert > Text to Table.
3. In the dialog box, under "Separate text at," make sure "Paragraphs" is selected. Make sure "Number of columns" is set to 1.
4. Click the OK button.

Your titles will now be inside a single-column table. But this is supposed to be a double-column concordance. Why? You'll see. First, make it so:

1. Put your cursor inside the table.
2. Click Table > Select > Column.
3. Click Edit > Copy.
4. Put your cursor to the right of (and outside) the table's first row. (Just click there with your mouse and make sure nothing is selected. You should see just your regular, thin cursor to the right of the table's top row.)
5. Click Edit > Paste Columns.

There! Two columns! And you'll need two columns, because the second column tells Word how to index what's in the first column. For example, you're going to want to lose those initial articles:

The Birds Are Singing Birds Are Singing
A Smile for You Smile for You

Thus, in the finished index, the titles will look like this:

Birds Are Singing
Smile for You
Sunshine and Lollipops
Your Day

Here's an easy way to get rid of those initial articles:

1. Select the second column by putting your cursor into it and clicking Table > Select > Column.
2. Copy the column (Edit > Copy).
3. Create a new document (CTRL + N).
4. Paste the column into it (Edit > Paste).
5. Select the column in the new document.
6. Click Table > Convert > Table to Text.
7. Click the OK button.
8. For each article you want to get rid of ("The," "A," "An," and so on), search for a paragraph return followed by the article (^pThe) and replace it with a carriage return (^p). This will miss an article on the first item in your list, so you'll need to remove that one by hand.
9. Select your edited list.
10. Convert the list back to a table.
11. Copy the single-column table.
12. Switch back to your document with the double-column concordance.
13. Select the second column.
14. Paste the edited column over the selected column.
15. Save your concordance with a name like "Title Concordance."

Next, you'll need to make a concordance of authors. Just follow the instructions above, searching for Heading 2 rather than heading 1. You'll end up with a double-column table that looks like this:

Jack M. Lyon	Jack M. Lyon
Ima Happy	Ima Happy
Sonny Day	Sonny Day

What you really want, however, is a concordance that looks like this:

Jack M. Lyon	Lyon, Jack M.
Ima Happy	Happy, Ima
Sonny Day	Day, Sonny

The easiest way to get one is to follow steps 1 through 7 in the instructions immediately above. That will give you a list of names, not in a table, and you can use my free NameSwapper macro to transpose the names with last name first:

http://www.editorium.com/freebies.htm

To get your list of names back into the concordance, follow steps 9 through 14 above. Then save your concordance with a name like "Author Concordance."

You can repeat all of this for the index of first lines, although you may not need to change anything in that second column. Up to you!

When you're finished, create your index, using each concordance to automatically mark index entries:

1. Click Insert > Index and Tables > Index > AutoMark. (In Word 2002 and later, click Insert > Reference > Index and Tables > Index > Mark Entry.)
2. Navigate to your concordance file and click it to select it.
3. Click the Open button and wait while Word marks all of those index entries.
4. Generate your index as explained in "Indexing in the Dark."

If you're doing a poetry anthology, you'll probably also need an index of topics. Unfortunately, there's no good way to automate that. Instead, you'll need to use your indexer's brain. But maybe the techniques explained in this article will help when you do have items that can be indexed automatically.

Readers Write

PATRICK LaCOSSE:

Why bother going through the extra step of delimiting styled paragraphs with certain characters (i.e., "<>")? The style itself is sufficient. Here is an example to show what the logic might be:

```
Set d = ActiveDocument
Set a = Documents.Add
d.Activate
Selection.HomeKey Unit:=wdStory
With Selection.Find
.ClearFormatting
.Style = "Author" 'Change this to the style of your choice
.Text = "" 'Include specific text if you like
.Wrap = wdFindContinue
.Execute
While .Found
a.Range.InsertAfter Selection.Text
.Execute
Wend
End With
```

[Note: The simplicity of that macro is deceiving; it's an extremely useful tool.]

GEOFF HART:

[Editing and Microsoft Word expert Geoff Hart wrote to suggest that I might want to make a further clarification about what a concordance is. When I say concordance, I'm not talking about a back-of-the-book index, such as an index of topics in a poetry anthology or an index of subjects in a textbook. In my opinion, such an index can be created only by a human mind. As Geoff wrote:]

An indexer examines each occurrence of a word and communicates why that occurrence is important by providing context. For example, "Washington, George" (in a concordance) becomes "Washington, George—birth of, —death of, —election of" and so on in an index. Similarly, an indexer provides cross-references (e.g., President: see Washington), synonyms (Walstein: see Washington — here, a fictitious example assuming that George Walstein changed his name to George Washington to make it more likely he'd be elected <g>), and so on. The index is clearly more useful, but is also enormously more difficult to create.

I'm a half-decent indexer, but stand in awe of the real pros like Lori Lathrop, who provide an almost magical means of access to a large book. A concordance can help a professional indexer in their work, but it can't take the place of an index, and an amateur shouldn't even attempt this task without doing some study to learn how it's done. *The Chicago Manual of Style* provides a decent introduction to indexing."

NOTE: In the previous article, I mentioned two definitions for "concordance":

1. A list of all words in a document, to be used as an aid in editing.
2. A list of words used to create an index, as explained in today's article.
3. Geoff is suggesting one more definition:
4. A list of every word in a document and the *pages* on which that word appears.

This kind of concordance is most commonly seen in the back of certain editions of the Bible, making it possible for readers to look up any word used in the Bible and find the places in the text where that word is used. Again, let me emphasize that this is not the same as a back-of-the-book index. A concordance can be created by a computer; an index can be created only by a human mind.

Sorting Index Entries Letter by Letter

If you've used Microsoft Word's Index feature, you know that Word alphabetizes index entries word by word, like this:

New Deal
New World
Newborn
News release

Most indexers and publishers, however, prefer to sort index entries letter by letter, like this:

Newborn
New Deal
News release
New World

Is there a way to get Word to sort entries in this way? Yes—with some manual intervention. (If you've never used Word's indexing feature, you might want to read about it in Word Help before continuing.)

A typical Word index entry looks like this—

{XE "New Deal"}

—and it will sort in word-by-word order.

However, if you add a semicolon to the entry, followed by a letter-by-letter spelling (in other words, a spelling that omits the space between words), you can make the entry sort letter by letter. (In case you're wondering, this feature isn't documented in Word Help; you have to dig for it on Microsoft's Web site.)

The edited entry should look like this:

{XE "New Deal;NewDeal"}

So for our other examples above, the edited entries would look like this:

{XE "New World;NewWorld"}
{XE "Newborn"}
{XE "News release;Newsrelease"}

("Newborn" doesn't need editing, since it's already just one word.)

If we then have Word generate an index using those entries, they'll be sorted letter by letter, like this:

Newborn
New Deal
News release
New World

Neat!

But now I'm wondering: Is there an automated way to edit those index entries?

[Offstage, right: Loud clanks and clunks as your correspondent rifles through his toolbox.]

Hmmm. Here's something that *might* do the job. I'll try it and get back to you soon.

Automated Letter-by-Letter Index Sorting

Want to sort Word's index entries letter by letter in an automated way? Try wildcard Find and Replace. You can record this procedure as a macro for future use. Or, better yet, just use the prerecorded macro I've included at the end of this article. Work through the procedure if you want to know more about using complicated searches, or if you just want to see how my devious little mind works. (There's probably a better way to do all this using Visual Basic for Applications, but that's a subject for another day.)

1. Make sure your index entries are visible by showing hidden text (Tools > Options > View > Hidden text).
2. Find the index entries and replace them with themselves colored as, say, plum, so your Find and Replace won't move across entry borders later:

Find What:

   (XE "*")

Replace With:

   \1 (formatted as plum)

Use Wildcards:

   Checked

3. Replace escaped colons and quotation marks with arbitrary symbols to be changed back later ("escaped" means they have a backslash in front of them, telling Word to treat them as characters, which is how you can use colons and quotation marks in your index entries!):

Find What:

   \:

Replace With:

   &&&

Use Wildcards:

   Unchecked

Find What:

\"

Replace With:

@@@

Use Wildcards:

Unchecked

4. Put a colon after main-only (but actually, after all) entries:

Find What:

(XE "*)(")

Replace With:

\1:\2

Use Wildcards:

Checked

5. Find plum-colored, multiple-word index entries and enter semicolon entries, going from three spaces to one space, which ought to be enough for anybody (and besides, Word can only handle up to five "Find What Expression" wildcards):

Find What:

(XE ")([! :]@) ([! :]@) ([! :]@) ([! :]@): (formatted as plum)

Replace With:

\1\2 \3 \4 \5;\2\3\4\5:

Use Wildcards:

Checked

Find What:

(XE ")([! :]@) ([! :]@) ([! :]@): (formatted as plum)

Replace With:

  \1\2 \3 \4;\2\3\4:

Use Wildcards:

  Checked

Find What:

  (XE ")([! :]@) ([! :]@): (formatted as plum)

Replace With:

  \1\2 \3;\2\3:

Use Wildcards:

  Checked

6. Clean up colons at ends of entries:

Find What:

  (XE "*):(") (formatted as plum)

Replace With:

  \1\2 (formatted as Automatic, which gets rid of all plum)

Use Wildcards:

  Checked

7. Restore escaped colons and quotation marks, if any:

Find What:

  &&&

Replace With:

  \:

Use Wildcards:

  Unchecked

Find What:

@@@

Replace With:

\"

Use Wildcards:

Unchecked

Now move to the bottom of your document and have Word generate your index (Insert > Index and Tables > Index). Well, look at that: The entries are sorted letter by letter. Neat!

If you want to work manually, you can insert a semicolon and alternate spelling after a main index entry to force Word to sort in any way you like. For example, let's say you've got some numbers in your index, ordered like this:

8123
835
86

Ordinarily, that's how they'd sort. But if you edit your index entries like this—

{XE "835;0835"}
{XE "86;0086"}
{XE "8123;8123"}

—you'll make them sort like this:

86
835
8123

If you really wanted to, you could even do something weird like this—

{XE "Zebra;1"}

—and force "Zebra" to the top of your index.

Pretty handy, no? At any rate, you now have an automated way to sort Word's index entries letter by letter. Enjoy!

Here's the prerecorded macro to make index entries sort letter by letter.

```
Sub IndexEntriesLetterByLetter()
' IndexEntriesLetterByLetter Macro
' Macro recorded 8/21/2002 by Jack M. Lyon
Selection.HomeKey Unit:=wdStory
```

```
Selection.Find.ClearFormatting
Selection.Find.Replacement.ClearFormatting
Selection.Find.Replacement.Font.Color = wdColorPlum
With Selection.Find
.Text = "(XE "")([! :]@) ([! :]@):"
.Replacement.Text = "\1\2 \3;\2\3:"
.Forward = True
.Wrap = wdFindContinue
.Format = True
.MatchCase = False
.MatchWholeWord = False
.MatchAllWordForms = False
.MatchSoundsLike = False
.MatchWildcards = True
End With
Selection.Find.ClearFormatting
Selection.Find.Replacement.ClearFormatting
Selection.Find.Replacement.Font.Color = wdColorPlum
With Selection.Find
.Text = "(XE ""*"")"
.Replacement.Text = "\1"
.Forward = True
.Wrap = wdFindContinue
.Format = True
.MatchCase = False
.MatchWholeWord = False
.MatchAllWordForms = False
.MatchSoundsLike = False
.MatchWildcards = True
End With
Selection.Find.Execute Replace:=wdReplaceAll
Selection.Find.ClearFormatting
Selection.Find.Replacement.ClearFormatting
With Selection.Find
.Text = "\:"
.Replacement.Text = "&&&"
.Forward = True
.Wrap = wdFindContinue
.Format = False
.MatchCase = False
.MatchWholeWord = False
.MatchWildcards = False
.MatchSoundsLike = False
.MatchAllWordForms = False
End With
Selection.Find.Execute Replace:=wdReplaceAll
With Selection.Find
.Text = "\"""
.Replacement.Text = "@@@"
.Forward = True
.Wrap = wdFindContinue
.Format = False
.MatchCase = False
```

```
.MatchWholeWord = False
.MatchWildcards = False
.MatchSoundsLike = False
.MatchAllWordForms = False
End With
Selection.Find.Execute Replace:=wdReplaceAll
Selection.Find.ClearFormatting
Selection.Find.Replacement.ClearFormatting
With Selection.Find
.Text = "(XE ""*)("")"
.Replacement.Text = "\1:\2"
.Forward = True
.Wrap = wdFindContinue
.Format = False
.MatchCase = False
.MatchWholeWord = False
.MatchAllWordForms = False
.MatchSoundsLike = False
.MatchWildcards = True
End With
Selection.Find.Execute Replace:=wdReplaceAll
Selection.Find.ClearFormatting
Selection.Find.Font.Color = wdColorPlum
Selection.Find.Replacement.ClearFormatting
With Selection.Find
.Text = "(XE "")([! :]@) ([! :]@) ([! :]@) ([! :]@):"
.Replacement.Text = "\1\2 \3 \4 \5;\2\3\4\5:"
.Forward = True
.Wrap = wdFindContinue
.Format = True
.MatchCase = False
.MatchWholeWord = False
.MatchAllWordForms = False
.MatchSoundsLike = False
.MatchWildcards = True
End With
Selection.Find.Execute Replace:=wdReplaceAll
Selection.Find.ClearFormatting
Selection.Find.Font.Color = wdColorPlum
Selection.Find.Replacement.ClearFormatting
With Selection.Find
.Text = "(XE "")([! :]@) ([! :]@) ([! :]@):"
.Replacement.Text = "\1\2 \3 \4;\2\3\4:"
.Forward = True
.Wrap = wdFindContinue
.Format = True
.MatchCase = False
.MatchWholeWord = False
.MatchAllWordForms = False
.MatchSoundsLike = False
.MatchWildcards = True
End With
Selection.Find.Execute Replace:=wdReplaceAll
```

```
Selection.Find.ClearFormatting
Selection.Find.Font.Color = wdColorPlum
Selection.Find.Replacement.ClearFormatting
With Selection.Find
.Text = "(XE "")([! :]@) ([! :]@):"
.Replacement.Text = "\1\2 \3;\2\3:"
.Forward = True
.Wrap = wdFindContinue
.Format = True
.MatchCase = False
.MatchWholeWord = False
.MatchAllWordForms = False
.MatchSoundsLike = False
.MatchWildcards = True
End With
Selection.Find.Execute Replace:=wdReplaceAll
Selection.Find.ClearFormatting
Selection.Find.Font.Color = wdColorPlum
Selection.Find.Replacement.ClearFormatting
Selection.Find.Replacement.Font.Color = wdColorAutomatic
With Selection.Find
.Text = "(XE ""*):("")"
.Replacement.Text = "\1\2"
.Forward = True
.Wrap = wdFindContinue
.Format = True
.MatchCase = False
.MatchWholeWord = False
.MatchAllWordForms = False
.MatchSoundsLike = False
.MatchWildcards = True
End With
Selection.Find.Execute Replace:=wdReplaceAll
Selection.Find.ClearFormatting
Selection.Find.Replacement.ClearFormatting
With Selection.Find
.Text = "(XE ""*):("")"
.Replacement.Text = "\1\2"
.Forward = True
.Wrap = wdFindContinue
.Format = False
.MatchCase = False
.MatchWholeWord = False
.MatchWildcards = False
.MatchSoundsLike = False
.MatchAllWordForms = False
End With
Selection.Find.ClearFormatting
Selection.Find.Replacement.ClearFormatting
With Selection.Find
.Text = "&&&"
.Replacement.Text = "\:"
.Forward = True
```

```
    .Wrap = wdFindContinue
    .Format = False
    .MatchCase = False
    .MatchWholeWord = False
    .MatchWildcards = False
    .MatchSoundsLike = False
    .MatchAllWordForms = False
  End With
  Selection.Find.Execute Replace:=wdReplaceAll
  With Selection.Find
    .Text = "@@@"
    .Replacement.Text = "\"""
    .Forward = True
    .Wrap = wdFindContinue
    .Format = False
    .MatchCase = False
    .MatchWholeWord = False
    .MatchWildcards = False
    .MatchSoundsLike = False
    .MatchAllWordForms = False
  End With
  Selection.Find.Execute Replace:=wdReplaceAll
End Sub
```

Find and Replace

Searching with Character Codes

In the article "Changing Note Number Format," I explained how to find Microsoft Word footnote numbers using the character code ^02. But there are other character codes you can use to find certain items:

- For a carriage return, you can use ^013.
- For a section break, you can use ^012.
- For a word space, you can use ^032.

Of course, you can also use Word's built-in codes, which you can insert into the Find dialog's "Find what" box by clicking the "Special" button:

- For a carriage return, you can use ^p.
- For a section break, you can use ^b.
- For a word space, you can use ^w for a word space (actually, any white space).

So why would you want to use the first codes? Because if you're searching with wildcards, the second ones won't work. For example, let's say that (for some reason) you're searching for "wh" followed by any other character (the wildcard for which is "?"), followed by a carriage return. In the Find dialog's "Find what" box, you enter this:

wh?^p

And to make Word search for the wildcard rather than an actual question mark, you put a check in the box labeled "Use wildcards."

Finally, you click the Find button. What happens? You get an error message: "^p is not a valid special character for the Find What box or is not supported when the 'Use wildcards' checkbox is selected."

"Well then, how," you politely ask your computer, "am I supposed to find what I'm looking for?"

As usual, it doesn't reply, but here's the answer anyway. In the "Find what" box, you enter this:

wh?^013

And that will do the job.

Ordinarily, you should probably use Word's built-in codes, such as ^p and ^b. But when those don't work, now you've got an alternative.

Searching with Microsoft Word's Built-in Codes

The previous article explained how to search for special characters (such as carriage returns and section breaks) using character codes. Why should you, as an editor, writer, or publisher, care about something as "technical" as searching with codes? Because they make it possible to find and replace things you ordinarily couldn't, such as paragraph breaks, dashes, and symbols. This can be a big help in cleaning up all kinds of editorial and typographical problems that you'd otherwise have to fix by hand.

After reading the previous article, Bruce White wrote: "Next obvious question: Where can we find a full list of codes?"

There are actually two different kinds of codes:

1. Microsoft Word's built-in codes (such as ^p for paragraph breaks and ^t for tabs).
2. ANSI character codes (such as ^013 for paragraph breaks and ^009 for tabs).

Both kinds of codes are useful, but the list of ANSI codes includes every character you can use in Microsoft Word. In the next article, I'll provide a list of these codes and explain how to use them.

Here, I'll give you a list of Word's built-in codes, which you can use in Microsoft Word's Find and Replace dialog (Edit/Replace). For example, if you wanted to find an em dash, you'd enter the following code in the "Find what" box:

^+

To replace it with an en dash, you'd enter this in the "Replace with" box:

^=

You can also insert Word's built-in codes by clicking the Special button in the Find and Replace dialog and then selecting the item you need. Please note that you can use some of the codes only in finding text, others only in replacing, and others in either one.

You can also use combinations of codes. For example, you could search for tabs followed by paragraph breaks (^t^p) and replace them with paragraph breaks alone (^p).

And now, here's the list. Enjoy!

Codes You Can Use in the "Find What" Box

Annotation mark ^a
Any character ^?
Any digit ^#

Any letter ^$
Caret character ^^
Column break ^n
Em dash ^+
En dash ^=
Endnote mark ^e
Field ^d
Footnote mark ^f
Graphic ^g
Line break ^l
Manual page break ^m
Nonbreaking hyphen ^~
Nonbreaking space ^s
Optional hyphen ^-
Paragraph mark ^p
Section break ^b
Tab character ^t
White space ^w

Codes You Can Use in the "Replace with" Box

Caret character ^^
Clipboard contents ^c
Column break ^n
Contents of the Find What box ^&
Em dash ^+
En dash ^=
Line break ^l
Manual page break ^m
Nonbreaking hyphen ^~
Nonbreaking space ^s
Optional hyphen ^-
Paragraph mark ^p
Tab character ^t

Readers Write

PHIL RABICHOW:

Here is a list of Find/Replace codes:

These you can use when you don't use wildcards:

^p Paragraph mark
^t Tab character
^a Annotation (comment) mark
^0nnn ANSI (4 digit) or ASCII (3 digit) characters, where nnn is the character code
^? Any character
^# Any digit
^$ Any letter
^^ Caret character
^c Clipboard contents
^& Contents of the Find What box
^e Endnote mark
^d Field
^f Footnote mark
^g Graphic

Breaks

^n Column break
^l Line break
^m Manual page break
^b Section break

Hyphens and Spaces

^+ Em dash
^= En dash
^s Nonbreaking space
^~ Nonbreaking hyphen
^- Optional hyphen
^w White space

These you can use when using wildcards:

^1 Picture (Except pictures with Float Over Text property, Word 98
Macintosh Edition)
^2 Auto-referenced footnotes
^5 Comment mark
^9 Tab
^11 New line
^12 Page OR section break
^13 Carriage return
^14 Column break
^19 Opening field brace (when the field braces are visible)
^21 Closing field brace (when the field braces are visible)
^? Any single character (not valid in the Replace

box)

^- Optional hyphen

^~ Non-breaking hyphen

^^ Caret character

^# Any digit

^$ Any letter

^& Contents of Find What box (Replace box only)

^+ Em Dash (not valid in the Replace box)

^= En Dash (not valid in the Replace box)

^u8195 Em Space Unicode character value search (not valid in the Replace box)

^u8194 En Space Unicode character value search (not valid in the Replace box)

^a Comment (not valid in the Replace box)

^b Section Break (not valid in the Replace box)

^c Replace with Clipboard contents (Replace box only)

^d Field

^e Endnote Mark (not valid in the Replace box)

^f Footnote Mark (not valid in the Replace box)

^g Graphic

^l New line

^m Manual Page Break

^n Column break

^t Tab

^p Paragraph mark

^s Non-breaking space

^w White space (space, non-breaking space, tab; not valid in the Replace box)

^nnn Where "n" is an ASCII character number

^0nnn Same as above, but uses ANSI characters (ALT+nnn PC only)

^unnnn Unicode character search where "n" is a decimal number corresponding to the Unicode character value.

Searching with Numeric Character Codes

The previous article explained how to search for special characters (such as carriage returns and section breaks) using Microsoft Word's built-in codes. But you can also search for special characters using numeric character codes (technically ANSI numbers). I'm including the list below, with codes for both PC and Macintosh, although I make no guarantees about how the characters themselves will show up in this email message.

Also, you'll notice that I haven't included the codes for such ordinary characters as letters of the alphabet, since you can search for these by using the characters themselves. No code is needed.

To use the codes for finding or replacing special characters, simply insert them, preceded by a carat and a zero, in the "Find what" or "Replace with" boxes in Microsoft Word's Find and Replace dialog box.

For example, if you wanted to find a u with an umlaut, you'd enter the following code in the "Find what" box on a PC:

^0252

On a Macintosh, you'd enter this:

^0159

You can also use the codes to insert many of the special characters into your documents. To do so:

1. Turn on Num Lock for the numeric keypad.
2. Hold down the ALT key.
3. On the numeric keypad, type a zero followed by the code.
4. Release the ALT key.

The character will be inserted into your document.

Warning: Use numeric codes to replace paragraph returns and section breaks only when absolutely necessary, because Word stores formatting information in these characters. Try to stick to Word's built-in codes when you can. Also, be aware that some fonts assign different characters to the numeric codes. The list below should be accurate for Times New Roman on a PC and Times on a Macintosh. But what if you're trying to find and replace some obscure character in an unusual font? In the next article, as the final installment about finding special characters, I'll give you a macro that will tell you the code for any character in your document, no matter what font is applied.

And now, here's the list:

CHARACTER NAME	MAC	PC
footnote reference	2	2
tab	9	9
line break	11	11
page/section break	12	12
paragraph break	13	13
column break	14	14
- nonbreaking hyphen	30	30
- optional hyphen	31	31
space	32	32
, comma	226	130
folio	196	131
„ double comma	227	132
... ellipses	201	133
† dagger	160	134
‡ double dagger	224	135
^ caret	246	136
‰ per thousand	228	137
Š cap S hacek	138	
‹ open angle bracket	220	139
Œ capital oe diphthong	206	140
' open single quote	212	145
' close single quote	213	146
" open double quote	210	147
" close double quote	211	148
• bullet	165	149
– en dash	208	150
— em dash	209	151
˜ tilde	247	152
™ trademark	170	153
š l/c s hacek	154	
› close angle bracket	221	155
œ l/c oe diphthong	207	156
Ÿ cap Y umlaut	217	159
nonbreaking space	160	160

¡ inverted exclamation	193	161
¢ cent	162	162
£ pound	163	163
¤ cell	219	164
¥ yen	180	165
¦ pipe	124	166
§ section	164	167
¨ umlaut	172	168
© copyright	169	169
ª ordinal, feminine	187	170
« left chevrons	199	171
not	194	172
- soft hyphen	248	173
® registered	168	174
¯ macron	248	175
° degree	161	176
± plus or minus	177	177
¹ superscript 1	49	185
² superscript 2	50	178
³ superscript 3	51	179
´ acute accent	171	180
µ micro	181	181
paragraph	166	182
· middle dot	225	183
¸ cedilla	252	184
º ordinal, masculine	188	186
» right chevrons	200	187
1/4 one-fourth	188	
1/2 one-half	189	
3/4 three-fourths	190	
¿ inverted question	192	191
À cap A, grave	203	192
Á cap A, acute	231	193
Â cap A, circumflex	229	194
Ã cap A, tilde	204	195

Ä cap A, umlaut	128	196
Å cap A, angstrom	129	197
Æ cap AE, diphthong	174	198
Ç cap C, cedilla	130	199
È cap E, grave	233	200
É cap E, acute	131	201
Ê cap E, circumflex	230	202
Ë cap E, umlaut	232	203
Ì cap I, grave	237	204
Í cap I, acute	234	205
Î cap I, circumflex	235	206
Ï cap I, umlaut	236	207
Đ cap eth	208	
Ñ cap N, tilde	132	209
Ò cap O, grave	241	210
Ó cap O, acute	238	211
Ô cap O, circumflex	239	212
Õ cap O, tilde	205	213
Ö cap O, umlaut	133	214
× multiply	120	215
Ø cap O, slash	175	216
Ù cap U, grave	244	217
Ú cap U, acute	242	218
Û cap U, circumflex	243	219
Ü cap U, umlaut	134	220
Ý cap Y, acute	89	221
Þ cap thorn	222	
ß sharp s	167	223
à l/c a, grave	136	224
á l/c a, acute	135	225
â l/c a, circumflex	137	226
ã l/c a, tilde	139	227
ä l/c a, umlaut	138	228
å l/c a, angstrom	140	229
æ l/c ae, diphthong	190	230

ç l/c c, cedilla	141	231
è l/c e, grave	143	232
é l/c e, acute	142	233
ê l/c e, circumflex	144	234
ë l/c e, umlaut	145	235
ì l/c i, grave	147	236
í l/c i, acute	146	237
î l/c i, circumflex	148	238
ï l/c i, umlaut	149	239
ð l/c eth	240	
ñ l/c n, tilde	150	241
ò l/c o, grave	152	242
ó l/c o, acute	151	243
ô l/c o, circumflex	153	244
õ l/c o, tilde	155	245
ö l/c o, umlaut	154	246
÷ divide	214	247
ø l/c o, slash	191	248
ù l/c u, grave	157	249
ú l/c u, acute	156	250
û l/c u, circumflex	158	251
ü l/c u, umlaut	159	252
ý l/c y, acute	121	253
þ l/c thorn	254	
ÿ l/c y, umlaut	216	255

Finding All Unicode Characters

Have you ever needed to know what Unicode characters are being used in a Word document? Maybe you need to tag them in some way. Maybe you need to replace them with other characters. Maybe you need to change their font. Whatever the reason, you can find them all with this procedure:

1. Click Edit > Find to display Word's Find dialog.
2. In the Find What box, enter the following string:

   [!^0001-^0255]

4. Click the More button if it's available.
5. Put a check in the "Use wildcards" checkbox.
6. Click the Find Next button.

Word will find the next Unicode character in your document.

What's going on here is that the Find string tells Word to find any character whose number is not (!) in the range of 0001 through 0255. By definition, that means any Unicode character, since characters within that range are ANSI characters. Note, however, that some characters may have a value in *both* ranges—em dashes and quotation marks, for example. Seems pretty weird, but perhaps some astute reader will explain this.

If you need to tag the Unicode characters in some way, you can use the basic procedure explained in "Find What Text."

If you want to learn more about Unicode characters, you'll find additional information in the chapter on "Special Characters."

Finding and Replacing Unicode Characters

I'm seeing more and more documents that use Unicode characters for all kinds of things—fractions, Greek, Hebrew—since these characters are so easy to use in Word 2000 and 2002. You can learn more about Unicode in the "Unicode" article.

Sometimes I need to find and replace these characters with something else. How to do so isn't readily apparent, but there are actually two different methods that will work.

Method 1: Unicode number

You're probably aware that you can find ASCII characters using numeric codes. For example, to find an e with an acute accent, you could do this:

1. Click the "Edit" menu.
2. Click "Find."
3. In the "Find What" box, enter ^0233 (on a PC) or ^0142 (on a Mac).
4. Click the "Find Next" button.

You can learn more about this in "Searching with Numeric Character Codes."

The procedure for finding Unicode characters is similar, but you'd use a "u" instead of a "0" in front of the number, and of course you'd need to know the Unicode decimal number for the character. You can look up Unicode numbers at Alan Wood's Unicode Resources site here:

http://www.alanwood.net/unicode/search.html

For example, to find a small Greek alpha in Microsoft Word, you'd search for ^u945.

Method 2: Copy and Paste

If you can see an example of the character in your document (or insert one), you can actually copy the character and then paste it into the "Find What" box. Then just search as usual.

Replacing Text with Unicode Characters

Replacing text with Unicode characters can be a little trickier than finding them, as Word won't let you use a numeric code (like ^u945) in the Replace dialog's "Replace With" box. I've usually had success, however, in pasting the character into the "Replace With" box. If you can't do that with a certain character, you may be able to follow this procedure instead:

1. Find an example of the character in your document (or insert one).
2. Copy the character.
3. Click the "Edit" menu.
4. Click "Replace."
5. In the "Find What" box, enter the text you want to find.
6. In the "Replace With" box, enter ^c to tell Word you want to replace with the contents of the Clipboard—in other words, with the Unicode character you copied.
7. Click the "Replace All" button.

Using Wildcards—the Basics

Allene Goforth wrote, "I use your 'Searching with Microsoft Word's Built-In Codes' list all the time, but Word's restrictions on what codes can be used in the 'Replace with' box are a pain. I'd love to see an article that deals with wildcard searching."

Thanks for the suggestion, Allene. Here goes:

When I was in the fifth grade in wintry Idaho, rather than venturing out into the cold, some fellow students and I often spent recess playing poker. (Did our teacher know about this? I can't remember.) Being *extremely* sophisticated players, we often designated jokers, deuces, *and* one-eyed jacks as wild cards—that is, they could represent any card in the deck. With the help of these wild cards, we had plenty of royal flushes, hands with five aces, and so on. Now that was poker!

Microsoft Word, too, has a bunch of "wild cards" (which Microsoft spells as one word) that you can use to find various combinations of characters in a document. Wildcards can get pretty complicated, but for now we'll cover just the basics.

The simplest wildcard is the question mark (?), which represents any single character. If you want to see how it works, try this:

1. Open a document with some text that you can play around with.
2. Click the "Edit" menu.
3. Click "Find."
4. In the "Find What" box, enter a question mark (?).
5. Put a check in the "Use wildcards" checkbox. (You may need to click the "More" button first.) Checking this box tells Microsoft Word that you're going to use a wildcard. If you didn't check the box, Microsoft Word would assume you were trying to find a question mark.
6. Click the "Find" button.

Microsoft Word will find the first character after your cursor position. Click the "Find" button again. Microsoft Word will find the next character. And so on.

That doesn't seem very useful, but let's suppose you're editing a document that was scanned from a magazine article and is riddled with typos. You notice that the word "but" shows up in various ways, including "bat" and "bet." Let's say that this is a technical article with no references to baseball, winged mammals, or games of chance, so you decide to use the ? wildcard to find "bat" and "bet" and replace them in a single pass. Here's the procedure:

1. Click the "Edit" menu.
2. Click "Replace."
3. Enter "b?t" in the "Find What" box.

4. Enter "but" in the "Replace With" box.
5. Put a check in the "Use wildcards" checkbox.
6. Click the "Replace All" button.

Both "bat" and "bet" will be replaced with "but." The problem is, so will "bit." And, unfortunately, since you can't specify "Find Whole Words Only" when the "Use wildcards" checkbox is checked, Microsoft Word will replace "better" with "butter," "combat" with "combut," and who knows what else. So, instead of clicking the "Replace All" button, you should click the "Replace" button for each individual item as needed.

Now you begin to see the power—and the danger—of using wildcards. Like cutthroat poker, they are not for the faint of heart. But if you know what you're doing, they can be very useful. Unfortunately, they won't help much in the "Replace With" box. In fact, you can't use them there at all. Why? Because Word has no way of knowing what you want them to represent.

Let's say you want to find "but" and replace it with either "bet" or "bat," so you put "b?t" in the "Replace With" box and click the "Replace All" button. Word doesn't know whether you want to replace "but" with "bet" or "bat," so it just replaces it with the actual text "b?t." So, basically, the only thing you can use in the "Replace With" box is actual text or certain built-in codes, mentioned earlier. You'll find the list of codes in the article "Searching with Microsoft Word's Built-in Codes."

In the next article, I'll explain wildcard searching in more depth. Until then, here's a list of wildcards for you to play with (on some junk text—don't use a real document):

? Finds any single character:
"c?t" finds "cat," "cut," and "cot."
* Finds any string of characters:
"b*d" finds "bad," "bread," and "bewildered."
[ ] Finds *one* of the specified characters:
"b[ai]t" finds "bat" and "bit" but not "bet."
[-] Finds any single character in the specified range (which must be in ascending order):
"[l-r]ight" finds "light," "might," "night," and "right" (and "oight," "pight," and "qight," if they exist).
[!] Finds any single character *except* those specified:
"m[!u]st" finds "mist" and "most" but not "must."
"t[!ou]ck" finds "tack" and "tick" but not "tock" or "tuck."
[!x-z] Finds any single character *except* those in the specified range:
"t[!a-m]ck" finds "tock" and "tuck" but not "tack" or "tick."
{n} Finds *exactly* n occurrences of the previous character or expression:
"re{2}d" finds "reed" but not "red."
{n,} Finds *at least* n occurrences of the previous character or expression:
"re{1,}d" finds "red" and "reed."
{n,m} Finds from n to m occurrences of the previous character or expression:
"10{1,3}" finds "10," "100," and "1000."
@ Finds one or more occurrences of the previous character or expression:

"me@t" finds "met" and "meet."
< Finds the beginning of a word:
"<inter" finds "interest" and "interrupt" but not "splinter."
> Finds the end of a word:
"in>" finds "in" and "main" but not "inspiring."

Readers Write

CALLIE JORDAN:

It's true that Word doesn't have "whole word" as an option, but if you include a space before and after the word(s) you're looking for, it won't find butter when you're looking for b?t—it also won't find "bat" [in quotation marks] though, because that word isn't followed by a space. So there's still a limit. But there aren't as many words in quotes as there are just plain whole words. . . . It also won't find words at the end of a sentence, or with any punctuation. You could just run the Find/Replace a second time and don't do a global replace, verifying each find. There wouldn't be as many words to check after most of them had been replaced.

Wildcard Combinations

The previous article discussed the basics of using wildcards to find text in a Microsoft Word document. Now let's talk about how to combine wildcards, which will let you get pretty fancy about the stuff you want to find. Basically, you just need to know that you *can* combine wildcards. Then you can get as crazy as you like.

In the previous article, we used the "?" wildcard to find every three-letter combination starting with b and ending with t—"bet," "but," "bit," "bat," and so on—by searching for "b?t" with "Use wildcards" turned on in the Find dialog box. Now let's say we wanted to find the same characters but add others as well. For example, we might want to find every three-letter combination starting with b and ending with d—"bed," "bud," "bid," "bad," and so on—in *addition* to the combinations ending in t. Can we really do that? Sure!

After bringing up the Find dialog (Edit > Find) and turning on "Use wildcards," we'll start by entering the letter b into the "Find What" box, telling Microsoft Word to find that letter.

Next, we'll enter the ? wildcard, which tells Microsoft Word to find any single character.

Finally, we'll enter a new wildcard: [td]. Microsoft Word will find any *one* of the characters specified in the brackets.

Altogether, the string of characters looks like this—

   b?[td]

—and there we are, doing wildcard combinations! This particular combination tells Word to find the letter b followed by any other single character followed by t or d.

How will something like this help you in editing? Suppose you're working on a manuscript in which the author has misspelled a name in nearly every way possible. You could comb through the manuscript over and over, hoping to catch all the variations. Or, you could be *sure* to catch them all by searching with wildcards. For example, let's say your manuscript is a book about India and the name in question is Gandhi. Your author has misspelled it as "Ghandi," "Gahndi," and "Ganhdi." (Not possible? Hah!) You can find every last one of them with the following string:

   G[andh][andh][andh][andh]i

Then, if you've put the correct spelling, "Gandhi," in the "Replace With" box, you can find and replace each wrong spelling with the right one in a single pass, which is much more efficient than finding and replacing each variation separately.

You may be wondering why you couldn't just use the * wildcard to represent the whole string of letters, like this:

   G*i

You could. But remember, the * wildcard represents *any* string of characters—including spaces. It's not limited to characters within a word (and neither are other wildcards). That means, in addition to finding the misspelled names, it will find the first 14 characters of the following phrase: "Go to the officer's hall." So be careful, especially if you're planning to use "Replace All" rather than finding and replacing one item at a time.

There is a way to simplify the wildcard combination, however. Consider this string:

G[andh]{3}i

It's functionally the same as G[andh][andh][andh][andh]i. The {3} tells Word to find exactly three more occurrences of the previous "expression," which is [andh].

But now a complication: Suppose that our slapdash author has also spelled Gandhi's name as "Gandi." Uh-oh. Our original string won't catch that, because this new misspelling is one character shorter than our string specifies. But consider this:

G[andh]{2,3}i

The {2,3} tells Word to find from 2 to 3 occurrences of the previous expression, so this string will catch all of our misspelled variations so far.

What if we want to allow for more or fewer characters, being particularly unsure of our author? We can use this string:

G[andh]@i

The @ wildcard tells Microsoft Word to find *one or more* occurrences of the previous expression. That ought to cover nearly anything our author throws at us. If we want to get a little more specific, we can use {2,}, which tells Word to look for *at least* two occurrences of the previous expression.

By this time you've probably noticed a pattern to these wildcards, but if not, I'll summarize:

A question mark ? finds any single character.
An asterisk * finds any string of characters.
Square brackets [] specify the characters to find.
Curly braces {} specify how many occurrences of the characters to find.
{n} finds an exact number (such as 2) of the preceding character or expression.
{n,} finds at least n occurrences (such as 3) of the preceding character or expression.
{n,n} finds from n to n occurrences (such as 3 to 5) of the preceding character or expression.
@ finds one or more occurrences of the preceding character or expression.

Here's a parting tip: What would happen if we put a lowercase rather than a capital G at the beginning of our string? Word wouldn't find the misspelled names. Why? Because with "Use wildcards" turned on, Word automatically matches case—a useful thing to know.

That brings us to the subject of finding a range of characters—something we'll talk about next.

Readers Write

GLADE LYON [MY DAD]:

It seems to me that your string should be G[andh][hand][ahnd][anhd]i.

I RESPONDED: I see what you're thinking—that each set of bracketed letters is an alternative spelling. No, *each set* of bracketed letters represents *one* letter in the word. [andh] will find either an "a," an "n," a "d," or an "h," whichever it comes to first. So, G[andh] will find:

Ga
Gn
Gd
or Gh

G[andh][andh] will find:

Gaa
Gan
Gad
Gah
Gna
Gnn
Gnd
Gnh
Gda
Gdn
Gdd
Gdh
Gha
Ghn
Ghd
Ghh

And so on. So the point of using G[andh][andh][andh][andh]i is to find every possible four-letter combination of a, n, d, and h. That way, no matter *how* many ways our author has misspelled "Gandhi," we'll catch them all.

In other words, the order of the characters inside the brackets doesn't matter. The strings you suggested—

[andh]
[hand]
[ahnd]
[anhd]

—are all functionally identical. Each one tells Word to find either an "a," an "n," a "d," or an "h."

MEG COX:

I just set up my first wildcard combination for a search and replace, and it works! I figured now was the time to take my walk on the wild side because I have a manuscript full of dates that are styled every which way. Now here's my question: I came up with the following to change various versions of month/day/year to day/month/year—but only for January.

Find what:

    (Ja[.a-z]@) ([0-9]{1,2}), ([0-9]{4})

Replace with:

    \2 January \3

I'd like to use this for all dates. I wonder if there's something like that [andh] combination that I can use to capture pairs of letters that begin months: Ja, Fe, Ma, Ap, and so on. But then again, maybe it won't work because I won't be able to specify the proper month in the "Replace with" box. This looks like the perfect opportunity to learn to do macros. Is a macro indeed the only one-click solution here?

I RESPONDED: You're right—there's no easy way to do this with one click. You might consider recording a macro to do all of the combinations. Once you have it recorded, you can use it whenever you need it:

1. Click the "Tools" menu.
2. Click "Macro."
3. Click "Record New Macro."
4. Type a name for your macro (something like "TransposeDates") in the "Macro name" box.
5. If you want, assign the macro to a toolbar or keyboard combination.
6. Click the "OK" button. (The macro recording toolbar will appear.)
7. Record the Replace routine for each month. In other words, run your Replace routine for January, then for February, and so on.
8. Click the "Stop" button (the button with the blue square) on the macro recording toolbar.

In other words:

1. Start recording your macro.
2. Do the search-and-replace for January.
3. Do the search-and-replace for February.
4. Do the search-and-replace for March.
5. And so on through December.
6. Stop recording your macro.

Now, if you assigned the macro to a toolbar or key combination, you can use the toolbar or key combination to run the macro in the future. Or, you can do this:

1. Click the "Tools" menu.
2. Click "Macro."
3. Click "Macros."
4. Click the name for your macro (say, "TransposeDates") in the list of macros so it's selected.
5. Click the "Run" button.

That should do the job.

At this point, you'll have transposed all of the dates in the current document. But you'll also have created a macro that you can run in one step on any document in the future—a very handy thing to have.

After responding to Meg, I realized that there is one possible way to do what she was asking—transpose all of the dates in one fell swoop—*if* all of the months have been spelled out. Consider this wildcard string:

([JFMASOND][a-z]@) ([0-9]{1,2}), ([0-9]{4})

[JFMASOND] represents the first letter of each month, with duplicate letters removed. [a-z]@ represents lowercase letters following the capital letter that starts the word. There's a space after the name of the month.
[0-9]{1,2} represents the day of the month, whether one or two digits.
There's a comma and a space after the day.
[0-9]{4} represents four consecutive digits—in other words, the year.
The parentheses group the items so you can transpose them using "Find What Expression" wildcards in the "Replace With" box (after turning on "Use wildcards," of course):

\2 \1 \3

If some of the months have been abbreviated (Jan., Feb., Mar., etc.), you could transpose them by finding this (notice the period following the @ sign)—

([JFMASOND][a-z]@.) ([0-9]{1,2}), ([0-9]{4})

—and replacing with this:

\2 \1 \3

If you've got a mix of abbreviated and unabbreviated dates, this string will find them all—

([JFMASOND][.a-z]@) ([0-9]{1,2}), ([0-9]{4})

—and you can transpose them with this replacement string:

    \2 \1 \3

But of course, that won't spell out the abbreviated months. To do that, you'd need to record a macro that finds and replaces each month.

If you're going to use any of these wildcard strings, be sure to run them on some test documents to make sure they do what you need—and *don't* do what you don't need.

Wildcard Ranges

The previous article discussed using wildcard combinations to find text in a Microsoft Word document. Now let's talk about wildcard ranges, which you'll probably use a lot.

Wildcard ranges are fairly simple. You just use the [-] wildcard to tell Microsoft Word what to find. Let's continue with our example from the previous article:

b?[td]

As you probably recall, this tells Word to find the letter b followed by any single character followed by either t or d. In other words, it will find "bet," "but," "bit," "bat," "bed," "bud," "bid," "bad," and so on.

But what if we wanted to find "bat," "bad," "bet," and "bed" but NOT "bit," "bid," "bud," and "but"? After bringing up the Find dialog (Edit > Find) and turning on "Use wildcards" (you may need to click the "More" button before this is available), we could use this wildcard combination in the "Find What" box:

b[a-e][td]

This tells Word to find the letter b followed by any letter from a to e (in other words, a, b, c, d, or e) followed by t or d. (The range *must* be in ascending order—in other words, from a "lower" letter [such as a] to a "higher" letter [such as z].)

Here's another way to approach this:

b[!f-z][td]

Notice the exclamation mark at the front of the "range" wildcard. The exclamation mark tells Word to find every character *except* those specified—in this case, the letters f through z. This wildcard combination, too, will find "bat," "bad," "bet," and "bed" but not "bit," "bid," "bud," and "but."

Here's a range that I use all the time:

[0-9]

This little beauty finds any occurrence of a digit. What's that good for? Let's say you're editing a document with lots of numbered lists, like this:

1. Lorem ipsum dolor sit amet.
2 Ut wisi enim ad minim veniam.
3. Duis autem vel eum iriure dolor.

Did you notice that the number 2 has no period? Good! You must have "the eye." But if you have several long lists, you might want to let Word find these problem numbers for you. To do so, try this wildcard string:

^013[0-9]@[!.]

Pretty cryptic. But you can probably figure this out:

^013 is the numeric code for a carriage return.
[0-9] represents any digit.
@ tells Word to find one or more occurrences of the previous expression (in this case, any digit). This is necessary in case you have lists with two-digit (or longer) numbers.
[!.] tells Word to find any character *except* a period.

Piece of cake.
Here are two other wildcard ranges you might find useful:

[a-z] represents any occurrence of a lowercase letter.
[A-Z] represents any occurrence of an uppercase letter.

Remember, too, that you can use the [] wildcard (without a hyphen) to specify a whole group of characters *without* using a range. For example, this wildcard will find various kinds of punctuation:

[.,;:\?\!]

You may be wondering about the backslash (\) in front of the question and exclamation marks. The backslash tells Word to treat the following character *as* a character and not as a wildcard. (Remember, ? is the wildcard for a single character, and ! is the wildcard for "except.")

Don't be afraid to try all of these wildcard combinations and ranges for yourself (on some junk text, of course). As you experiment, you'll better understand what works and what doesn't. Then, when the need to use wildcards arises (which it will), you'll be ready.

In the next article, we'll look at wildcard grouping and the little-known "Replace With" wildcard.

You can learn more about using numeric codes (such as that ^013 representing the carriage return) in "Searching with Numeric Character Codes."

And you can learn more about using junk text (such as "Lorem ipsum dolor sit amet") in "Sample Text."

Wildcard Grouping

Wildcard grouping is simply a way of telling Word that you want certain wildcards to be used together as a unit.

Continuing with our example from the previous article, let's say that you're editing a document with lots of numbered lists, like this:

1. Lorem ipsum dolor sit amet.
2. Ut wisi enim ad minim veniam.
3. Duis autem vel eum iriure dolor.

Now let's say that you want to replace the space after each number and period with a tab. After calling up the Replace dialog (Edit > Replace) and putting a check in the "Use wildcards" checkbox, you could enter the following string of characters into the "Find What" box:

^013[0-9]@.

(You can't see it, but there's a space on the end of that string, and it needs to be included.) As you probably recall, this tells Microsoft Word to do the following:

1. Find a paragraph mark (^013)
2. followed by a number ([0-9])
3. followed by one or more numbers (@)
4. followed by a period (.)
5. followed by a space ( ).

But that still won't let us replace that space with a tab. Why? Because there's no way to replace the space independently of the rest of the string—whatever the string finds *includes* the space.

So let's try this:

(^013[0-9]@.)( )

Notice that we've grouped the wildcards and other characters together with parentheses. (In case you can't tell, that's our uncooperative space between the last two parentheses.) Such groups, for reasons known only to the mathematically minded, are called "expressions," and in this case there are two of them:

(^013[0-9]@.)
( )

Grouping things together like this makes it possible to refer to each group independently in the "Replace With" box—a wonderful thing! So in the "Replace With" box, we'll enter this string:

    \1^t

That "\1" is an example of the little-known "Find What Expression" wildcard, which lives deep in the wilds of Redmond, Washington, and only comes out at night. It's a backslash followed by the number one, and it tells Word to replace whatever is found by the first expression—

    (^013[0-9]@.)

—with whatever the first expression finds. (Yes, you read that correctly.) In other words, Word replaces whatever the first expression finds with *itself.* That seems strange, but it means we can treat the second expression—

    ( )

—as an independent unit, which is exactly what we need to do. (By the way, "Find What Expression" wildcards are the only wildcards that can be used in the "Replace With" box. They are simply a backslash followed by a number.)

The ^t, of course, is the code for a tab, as explained in "Searching with Microsoft Word's Built-in Codes."

You'll notice that we haven't included a "\2" code, which would replace something with whatever is found by our *second* expression, the space in the parentheses. Since we haven't included that code, the space will be replaced by nothing—in other words, it will be *deleted* during the Find and Replace. So the relationship between the wildcards in the "Find What" string and the "Replace With" string is something like this:

    FIND WHAT: REPLACE WITH:
    (^013[0-9]@.) > \1 (followed by a tab: ^t)
    ( ) > [nothing]

Now let's try using them:

1. Start the Replace dialog (Edit > Replace).
2. Put a check in the "Use wildcards" checkbox (you may need to click the "More" button before this is available).
3. In the "Find What" box, enter this:

    (^013[0-9]@.)( )

4. In the "Replace With" box, enter this:

    \1^t

5. Click the "Replace All" button.

Presto! All of the spaces after your numbers will be replaced with tabs, and your list will now look like this:

1.\<tab\>Lorem ipsum dolor sit amet.
2.\<tab\>Ut wisi enim ad minim veniam.
3.\<tab\>Duis autem vel eum iriure dolor.

To me, this is like magic, and it comes in handy more often than you might think. I hope you'll find it useful! In the future, I'll try to provide other examples that you can apply in your day-to-day work. Next I'll show you how to use "Find What Expression" codes to move things around.

Using the "Find What Expression" Wildcard

In the previous article, I introduced the "Find What Expression" wildcard (\n) and promised to show you how to use it to move things around.

Let's say you've got a list of authors, like this:

Emily Dickinson
Ezra Pound
Willa Cather
Ernest Hemingway
and you need to put last names first, like this:
Dickinson, Emily
Pound, Ezra
Cather, Willa
Hemingway, Ernest

You can use the "Find What Expression" wildcard to do this in a snap.

Start the Replace dialog (Edit > Replace) and put a check in the "Use wildcards" checkbox (you may need to click the "More" button before this is available). Then, in the "Find What" box, enter this:

   ˆ013([A-z]@) ([A-z]@)ˆ013

If you've been reading the previous articles, you'll probably understand these codes and wildcards:

   ˆ013 represents a paragraph mark.
   [A-z] represents any single alphabetic character, from uppercase A to lowercase z.
   @ represents any additional occurrences of the previous character—in this case, any single alphabetic character, from uppercase A to lowercase z.
   () groups [A-z]@ together as an "expression" representing an author's first name. (This grouping is the key to using the "Find What Expression" wildcard in the "Replace With" box.)

The space after the first ([A-z]@) expression represents the space between first name and last name.

The next ([A-z]@) group represents the author's last name.

The final ˆ013 represents the paragraph mark after the name.

Now, in the "Replace With" box, enter this:

   ˆp\2, \1ˆp

The ^p codes represent paragraph marks. "Wait a minute," you say. "You just used ^013 for a paragraph mark. Why the change?"

Excellent question. The answer has two parts:

1. If we could use ^p in the "Find What" box, we would. But since Word won't let us do that when using wildcards (it displays an error message), we have to resort to the ANSI code, ^013, instead. You can learn more about this in "Searching with Character Codes."

2. If we use ^p in the "Replace With" box, Word retains the formatting stored in the paragraph mark (a good thing). If we use ^013, Word loses the formatting for the paragraph (a bad thing). In a list of author names, this probably doesn't matter, but you'll need to know this when finding and replacing with codes in more complicated settings.

Continuing with our example, ^p\2, \1^p:

\2 is the "Find What Expression" wildcard for our *second* expression (hence the 2) in the "Find What" box—in other words, it represents the last name of an author in our list.

The comma follows this wildcard because we want a comma to follow the author's last name.

A space follows the comma because we don't want the last and first names mashed together, like this: "Pound,Ezra."

\1 is the "Find What Expression" wildcard for our *first* expression (hence the 1) in the "Find What" box—in other words, it represents the first name of an author in our list.

Now click the "Replace All" button. The authors' names will be transposed:

Dickinson, Emily
Pound, Ezra
Cather, Willa
Hemingway, Ernest

You've always wondered how to do that, right? But now you're wondering about middle initials. And middle names. And Ph.D.s.

All of those make things more complicated. But here, in a nutshell, are the Find and Replace strings you'll need for some common name patterns (first last, first middle last, first initial last, and so on). First comes the name pattern, then the Find string, and finally the Replace string, like this:

NAME PATTERN
FIND WHAT
REPLACE WITH

William Shakespeare
^013([A-z]@) ([A-z]@)^013
^p\2, \1^p

Alfred North Whitehead
^013([A-z]@) ([A-z]@) ([A-z]@)^013
^p\3, \1 \2^p

Philip K. Dick
^013([A-z]@) ([A-Z].) ([A-z]@)^013
^p\3, \1 \2^p

L. Frank Baum
^013([A-Z].) ([A-z]@) ([A-z]@)^013
^p\3, \1 \2^p

G. B. Harrison, Ph.D.
^013([A-Z].) ([A-Z].) ([A-z]@,) (*)^013
^p\3 \1 \2, \4^p

J.R.R. Tolkien
^013([A-Z].)([A-Z].)([A-Z].) ([A-z]@)^013
^p\4, \1\2\3^p

That list doesn't show every pattern you'll encounter, but it should provide enough examples so you'll understand how to create new patterns on your own—which is the whole point of this article. Once you've created all of the patterns you need, you could record all of that finding and replacing in a single macro that you could run whenever you need to transpose names in a list.

Readers Write

Niquette Kelcher:

I have a wildcard question for you that I haven't been able to figure out. I'd like to supply the answer to my students, who have been trying to figure it out with me.

If I have a manuscript with "Titles in Quotations Like This", how do I italicize the title AND get rid of the quotation marks at the same time? My incorrect approach is as follows—it italicizes the text but doesn't get rid of the quotation marks. I feel I'm missing something obvious!

Find: "*" (use wildcards)

Replace: ^& (CTRL + I)

Your help would surely be appreciated!

I responded: You'll need to put the asterisk inside parentheses so it functions as a "group":

Find: "(*)" (use wildcards)

Then use the "Find What Expression" code as the replacement for the text found by the group:

Replace: \1 (CTRL + I)

MARY L. TOD:

Is it necessary to enclose the space in parentheses? Since it isn't being replaced by itself, can't the expression in the Find box be reduced to

(^013[0-9]@.)

(with just the space entered after the first expression)?

I REPLIED: You're absolutely right about this. I put the space in parentheses because I wanted to briefly introduce the idea that you could have more than one "Find What Expression" wildcard—in this case, \2. For that to work, the space has to be in parentheses so it's recognized as an expression. But I didn't actually *use* the \2 in the example, so a simple space would have worked just fine.

MARY CONTINUED: In a related question, does the @ symbol in the wildcard field also allow for no repeats of the previous character? Otherwise, it would start the list at 10, wouldn't it?

- followed by a number ([0-9])
- followed by one or more numbers (@)

I REPLIED: Again, this is right on the mark. The @ really means "followed by one or more numbers *if there are any.*" A more technical way to put it is "followed by *zero* or more numbers."

LEW GOLAN:

The ^& function in Word's find and replace is certainly useful—but is it possible to insert something *within* a string that was found?

The specific problem that brought this up: an author gave me a file containing the index for a book. Unfortunately, there was no comma between each entry and its page numbers. So, for example, I want to change

Jones, Jack 34, 56, 90
Smith, John 45, 56, 78

to

Jones, Jack, 34, 56, 90
Smith, John, 45, 56, 78

I tried putting ^$ ^# in the Find field—any letter, space, any digit. This found what I wanted—for example, "k 3" and "n 4".

But in the replace field, ^& invokes the entire found string, so I can insert a comma either before or after the string—but not within the string (to put a comma after the k and after the n).

Any thoughts?

I RESPONDED: You can easily do what you need with the Find What Expression wildcard. In the example you provided:

Jones, Jack 34, 56, 90
Smith, John 45, 56, 78

You can search for this—

([a-z]) ([0-9])

and replace with this—

\1, \2

with "Use wildcards" turned on.

Numbers by Chicago

I recently worked on a manuscript with lots of source citations, many of which had page numbers formatted like this:

122-123

I prefer the shorter style recommended in the Chicago Manual of Style (8.69):

122-23

And besides, the manuscript was inconsistent, sometimes using one style, sometimes the other. Not wanting to fix all of these by hand, I decided to put the old wildcard search to work. The first thing I needed to do was simplify things. Consider the style for even hundreds:

100-109
100-119
100-201

In all such cases, the numbers were already in the correct style, so I decided to just get them out of the way, like this:
Find What:

00-

Replace With:

~~-

(Those tildes are just arbitrary placeholders to be turned back to zeroes later.)
With that taken care of, I originally thought I could change all the other numbers like this:
Find What:

([0-9]{3}-)[0-9]([0-9]{2})

Replace With:

\1\2

That "Find What" string finds any set of three {3} numbers [0-9] followed by a hyphen, followed by a single number [0-9], followed by any set of two {2} numbers [0-9]. The items in parentheses are treated as as a group.

The "Replace With" string replaces the first \1 parenthetical group with itself and the second \2 parenthetical group with itself, leaving out any number [0-9] that was not grouped in parentheses.

That will definitely change 122-123 to 122-23, but it will also change 308-309 to 308-09, so we'll need to get a little fancier. How about this?

Find What:

([0-9]{3}-)[0-9]([1-9]{2})

Replace With:

\1\2

Notice that I've changed that last number range to [1-9] rather than [0-9]. That means numbers like 308-309 will not be found but numbers like 308-319 will. (Come to think of it, that single number in the middle could probably be [1-9] as well, since there shouldn't be any page numbers like 308-019. Of course, you never know.) Now, does that solve the problem?

Well, no. We still need to deal with numbers like this:

398-415

We certainly don't want that changing to 398-15. And what about this?

247-517

Unlikely, I'll admit, but still possible.

And that means we can't do our find and replace all in one shot. Instead, we'll have to do 18 specific searches:

(1[0-9]{2}-)1([1-9][0-9])
(2[0-9]{2}-)2([1-9][0-9])
(3[0-9]{2}-)3([1-9][0-9])
(4[0-9]{2}-)4([1-9][0-9])
(5[0-9]{2}-)5([1-9][0-9])
(6[0-9]{2}-)6([1-9][0-9])
(7[0-9]{2}-)7([1-9][0-9])
(8[0-9]{2}-)8([1-9][0-9])
(9[0-9]{2}-)9([1-9][0-9])
(10[1-9]-)10([1-9])
(20[1-9]-)20([1-9])
(30[1-9]-)30([1-9])
(40[1-9]-)40([1-9])
(50[1-9]-)50([1-9])

```
(60[1-9]-)60([1-9])
(70[1-9]-)70([1-9])
(80[1-9]-)80([1-9])
(90[1-9]-)90([1-9])
```

At least that's how it looks to me. You can do the searches by hand if you like. You've got 20 chapters, all in separate files? Let's see—20 x 18 = 360 separate searches. Ouch! Of course, you could use my MegaReplacer program to do them all at once, freeing up your time for something more interesting.

Don't forget, we still need to turn those tildes back into zeroes:

Find What:

~~

Replace With:

00

Now all of those page numbers should be in Chicago style. How beautiful!

"What about four-digit numbers?" you ask. I leave it as an exercise for you to work out.

If you'd like this whole thing ready to run in MegaReplacer, here it is:

```
00-|~~-
(1[0-9]{2}-)1([1-9][0-9])\1\2+m
(2[0-9]{2}-)2([1-9][0-9])|\1\2+m
(3[0-9]{2}-)3([1-9][0-9])|\1\2+m
(4[0-9]{2}-)4([1-9][0-9])|\1\2+m
(5[0-9]{2}-)5([1-9][0-9])|\1\2+m
(6[0-9]{2}-)6([1-9][0-9])|\1\2+m
(7[0-9]{2}-)7([1-9][0-9])|\1\2+m
(8[0-9]{2}-)8([1-9][0-9])|\1\2+m
(9[0-9]{2}-)9([1-9][0-9])|\1\2+m
(10[1-9]-)10([1-9])|\1\2+m
(20[1-9]-)20([1-9])|\1\2+m
(30[1-9]-)30([1-9])|\1\2+m
(40[1-9]-)40([1-9])|\1\2+m
(50[1-9]-)50([1-9])|\1\2+m
(60[1-9]-)60([1-9])|\1\2+m
(70[1-9]-)70([1-9])|\1\2+m
(80[1-9]-)80([1-9])|\1\2+m
(90[1-9]-)90([1-9])|\1\2+m
~~|00
```

Numbers by Chicago, Part 2

The previous article outlined a fairly lengthy Find and Replace routine to make sure inclusive (elided) numbers follow the style outlined in the Chicago Manual. Astute reader Andrew Lockton responded with a technique that is so important, it deserves a second article. Andrew suggested taking the "Find What Expression" wildcard, which takes the form \1, \2, and so on, and putting it not in the Replace With box, where it is ordinarily used, but in the *Find What* box—something I did not know was possible. Hats off to you, Andrew.

Andrew's discovery opens up all kinds of possibilities for various problems I've previously been unable to solve, but let's look specifically at getting numbers by Chicago. The previous method required 18 separate searches. Andrew's brilliant methodology requires only three. Here's the explanation:

1. Numbers that take the form 104-105 need to be converted to 104-5:

Find What:

([1-9])0([1-9])-\10([1-9])

Replace With:

\10\2-\3

What's going on there is that the first number grouping, ([1-9]), is being referred to by the \1 that follows the hyphen—in the Find What string. See it? Just before the 0 there? That tells Word to find (again) whatever was found by the first number grouping. For example, when the search hits something like "203-205," it says, "Hey, my first number group finds 2 [the first number in 203]. Let's see, is there also a 2 after the hyphen? Yes, there is!" Slicker than snake shoes, as expert word whacker Hilary Powers is fond of saying.

2. Numbers that take the form 104-110 need to be converted to 104-10:

Find What:

([1-9])0([1-9])-\1([1-9])([0-9])

Replace With:

\10\2-\3\4

3. Numbers that take the form 111-112 or 119-120 need to be converted to 111-12 or 119-20:

Find What:

([1-9])([1-9])([0-9])-\1([1-9])([0-9])

Replace With:

\1\2\3-\4\5

At first I thought it might be possible to combine 2 and 3:

([1-9])([0-9])([0-9])-\1([1-9])([0-9])

But that would also find even hundreds (100, 200), which need to be ignored (100-114 rather than 100-14).

Readers Write

JEANNE PINAULT:

What I do with elided numbers is just replace all the hyphens with en dashes and then fix whatever comes up wrong when I edit the notes. That's because every set of endnotes I see is wrong in a slightly different way from every other set of endnotes I ever saw, so I have to read every character anyway. I can see that your marvelous find and replace would be a godsend with consistently formatted and voluminous endnotes produced on a regular basis, though. Are en dashes in there someplace?

I RESPONDED: In the Find string, use ^150 (the en-dash code) instead of the hyphen.

MARGARET BERSON:

I just was looking at your sequential replacement operation for page numbers. Why would you not use a macro that would go through and use the string position functions to evaluate the first digit of the first page number against the first digit of the second page number, deleting the unneeded first digit of the second number if it's the same, and leaving it alone if it's higher?

STEVE HUDSON:

The following solution was designed to not just satisfy the English world with its 0-9 numerics. Use it to reduce hexadecimal addresses, Japanese, or anything. Even if the numbers aren't sequential, like hex, we just use ranges for the find such as "0-9A-F".

It is as simple as possible whilst being as generic as possible. Simpler solutions cannot work for non-English solutions as we cannot guarantee ASCII status. It is fully commented and written for clarity and education rather than speed. It will still run like greased lightning but . . . :-)

```
Public Sub NumberCruncher()
'Link this one to your toolbar
'Change any parms as needed from here
NumberCrunch ActiveDocument.Content
End Sub
Public Function NumberCrunch( _
Scope As Range, _
Optional NumberSeparator As String = "-", _
Optional Numbers As String = "0-9" _
) As String
'Another document solution from WordHeretic.com
'Produces short form number ranges anywhere in the provided
'document range. Eg 309-310 into 309-10 and 307-308 into 307-8
'You can use Unicode nnnn by using "^nnnn"
'NumberRange and architecture is for true I18N
'Known Issues: n-n will end up being n-. Eg 300-300 to 300-
'--------------------
'Declare
'--------------------
Const EndOfWord As String = ">"
Dim NumberRange As Range
Dim FirstNumber As Range
Dim SecondNumber As Range
Dim Separator As Range
Dim AnyNumber As String
Dim LenFirst As Long
Dim LenSecond As Long
'--------------------
'Initialise
'--------------------
Set NumberRange = Scope.Duplicate
Set FirstNumber = Scope.Duplicate
Set SecondNumber = Scope.Duplicate
'--------------------
'Clarity
'--------------------
AnyNumber = "[" & Numbers & "]@"
With NumberRange.Find
.Text = AnyNumber & NumberSeparator & AnyNumber & EndOfWord
.MatchWildcards = True
End With
'--------------------
'Main program loop
'--------------------
While NumberRange.Find.Execute(Replace:=wdReplaceNone)
Set Separator = NumberRange.Duplicate
With Separator.Find
.Text = NumberSeparator
```

```
      .Execute(Replace:=wdReplaceNone)
      End With
      'So now we have the entire number range AND
      'the separator range, we can calc the numbers
      FirstNumber.Start = NumberRange.Start
      FirstNumber.End = Separator.Start
      SecondNumber.Start = Separator.End
      SecondNumber.End = NumberRange.End
      'Counting chars is NOT the same as an offset
      LenFirst = FirstNumber.Characters.Count
      LenSecond = SecondNumber.Characters.Count
      'Now lets work out what's the same
      'First up, if the second number is shorter than
      'the first, it's already been done or is irrelevant.
      'Eg 200-7
      'If the second number is longer we cannot find common ground
      'Eg 97-101
      'Thus, we can ONLY operate on equal length numbers.
      'Then, test for the number being a dynamic field
      'as we can't really change those
      If LenFirst = LenSecond And NumberRange.Fields.Count = 0 Then
      'Now we need to match every character or finish
      'We will shrink our FirstNumber range as we go,
      'and delete the secondnumber range as we go
      'Char comparisons DO use unicode
      While FirstNumber.Characters(1) = SecondNumber.Characters(1)
      FirstNumber.MoveStart
      SecondNumber.Characters(1).Delete
      Wend
      End If
      Wend
      '--------------------
      'Destroy all objects
      '--------------------
      Set FirstNumber = Nothing
      Set SecondNumber = Nothing
      Set Separator = Nothing
      Set NumberRange = Nothing
      End Function
      Steve later added:
      We may also want to include something like this if the user
wants to run the macro on a range of text:
      Public Sub NumberCruncherSelection()
      NumberCrunch Selection.Range
      End Sub
```

PATRICK LaCOSSE:

In "Numbers by Chicago, Part 2" you provided a link to two scripts one might use to eliminate duplicates in a list. Although I'm not too familiar with WordBasic commands, I noticed that your examples were able to handle only duplicates that are adjacent to one another in the list. No problem if you've sorted the list, but what if sorting the list is not necessary or desirable? (There are times, for example, when preserving the order of occurrence is desirable.)

I thought I'd share a technique I've grown to prefer, which eliminates duplicates no matter where they are found in the list. It utilizes VB's dictionary object, and it is fast. I've run scripts similar to the one below on files that are 11 MB big, and the difference in speed as a result of using the dictionary object (as opposed to recursively iterating through each paragraph) is remarkable. The dictionary object's comparemode property provides a convenient way for the filtering to be case sensitive if need be. One can read more about the dictionary object's properties and methods in Word's VBA help file. I should mention that I've used the dictionary object only on Windows machines running Word 2000 and 2002. I don't know how available the dictionary object is for other platforms and versions, but those who have access to it will find it quite useful for a variety situations. I use it to create concordances, audit documents for special characters, etc., all the time.

Here is an example with comments. Normally I try to be much more modular in my programming. For example, I would usually put the core functionality here into a sub or function to which I could pass a range object (allowing me to pass it the range of an entire document or merely that of a selection within a document). And I'd make the comparemode an optional argument to pass. Because the purpose here is simply to show the dictionary object in action, I've adapted some code to be a situation-specific script, which allows it to be tested easily on a document. With that disclaimer, here it is:

```
Sub ListEliminateDuplicates()
'Pat LaCosse
'Adapted from my ConcordanceTools template
'and submitted to the Editorium newsletter
'on June 17, 2004.
Dim para As Paragraph
Dim dict
'Create an instance of the dictionary object
Set dict = CreateObject("Scripting.Dictionary")
'Set comparemode; use vbBinaryCompare
'for case-sensitive filtering
dict.comparemode = vbTextCompare
'Iterate through all the paragraphs in the doc.
For Each para In ActiveDocument.Paragraphs
'If we've already encountered this item,
'then delete the paragraph.
If dict.Exists(para.Range.Text) Then
para.Range.Delete
Else
'If we haven't already encountered this item,
'then add it to the dictionary's keys.
dict.Add para.Range.Text, ""
```

```
    End If
    Next para
    Set dict = Nothing
    MsgBox "Done!"
    End Sub
```

Wildcard Dictionary

If you've read the "Find and Replace" articles, you know about wildcard searches and some of the neat things you can do with them. Even though I use wildcard searches all the time, I don't do a very good job of saving my wildcard entries so I can use them again. But that's going to change when I make my wildcard dictionary. The dictionary will include entries in the following format:

- A description of what the Find and Replace wildcard strings do.
- The wildcard Find and Replace strings themselves.
- Some keywords I can search for if I'm looking for wildcard strings for a certain purpose.
- Before-and-after examples of what the wildcard strings do.
- Other comments.

Here's an example, with a wildcard string you may be able to use:

DESCRIPTION: Find parenthetical publishing information in source citations and replace it with nothing to help in changing citations to short form.

FIND WHAT: \([A-z ,.]@:[!)]@[0-9]{4}\)

RELACE WITH: [nothing]

KEY WORDS: publishing information, source, citation, footnotes, endnotes, books, parentheses, long, short, delete

BEFORE: Jack M. Lyon, *Total Word Domination* (Edina, Minn.: PocketPCPress, 2001), p. 237.

AFTER: Jack M. Lyon, *Total Word Domination,* p. 237.

COMMENTS: Won't find or delete other parenthetical text. *Note that the Find string includes a space in front of it, and that space is necessary.*

I'll save this kind of information for all of my wildcard strings henceforth and forever. Maybe you'd like to do something similar with yours.

Wildcard Dictionary Entries

In the previous article I suggested the need for a "wildcard dictionary." Rosalie Wells, Hilary Powers, Eric Fletcher, Allene Goforth, Michael Coleman, and Steve Hudson sent some great wildcard strings and commentary on their use. Many thanks to them, and, if I missed anyone, many apologies.

And now, the wildcard dictionary entries! (Before using any of these in the real world, be sure to try them on some test documents to make sure they will do what you need. You should do that with any wildcard string, of course.)

ROSALIE WELLS:

I use this one all the time in my translations into Spanish to change the decimal separator "period" to a "comma" separator as required for many Spanish-speaking countries:

Find what: ([0-9]).([0-9])
Replace with: \1,\2

HILARY POWERS:

I tend to design strings from scratch when needed, but here are a couple that I use often enough to more or less remember them:

.([A-Z]). \1

opens up initials on reference lists; requires fixing things like U.S. and N.Y. after.

([0-9]). |^t\1.^t

indents hand-typed list numbers.

[!.]^013

review one by one and add periods by hand where needed. There's a way of scanning for more end-sentence punctuation and doing the change automatically, but I'm usually too lazy to look it up and this is what I remember. A complete punctuation scan would be quite welcome. . . .

It'd be a good idea to emphasize that the Wildcard and Revision Tracking features do bad things to each other, at least in Word 97. Some simple replaces will work with tracking on, but it's hard to predict which ones are safe and which ones will scramble the new info. Before running any wildcard replace operation, it's best to save the file and then turn the tracking off. Run the replace, check to see if it worked, then *turn the tracking back on.*

Eric Fletcher:

I have my favourites in various Word files I seem to never get around to consolidating. But here are a few I found without having to look very hard:

DESCRIPTION: Finding a telephone number formatted as 123-4567.
FIND WHAT: ([0-9]{3})(-)([0-9]{4})
REPLACE WITH:
KEY WORDS: Telephone number
BEFORE:
AFTER:
COMMENTS: This is handy for doing a quick review of phone numbers. In Word 2002, you can choose to select all occurrences so you can see them easily in context.

DESCRIPTION: Changing telephone numbers formatted as (123) 456-7890 or (123)456-7890 to 123-456-7890.
FIND WHAT: ([(])([0-9]{3})([)])(*)([0-9]{3})(-)([0-9]{4})
REPLACE WITH: \2-\5\6\7
KEY WORDS: Telephone number
BEFORE: Telephone numbers formatted as (123) 456-7890 or (123)456-7890.
AFTER: Telephone numbers formatted as 123-456-7890 or 123-456-7890.
COMMENTS: Note that the (*) looks after catching situations where there may or may not be a space after the area code portion.

DESCRIPTION: Find formatted text and change it to use HTML codes.
FIND WHAT: Font=Italic
REPLACE WITH: <i>^&</i>
KEY WORDS: Italic, HTML, formatting
BEFORE: Change the italicized words to use HTML codes.
AFTER: Change the <i>italicized</i> words to use HTML codes.
COMMENTS: If you include Font=Not italic in the Replace with, the italics will be removed as well. Use variations of this for any formatting and other HTML codes.

DESCRIPTION: Find text coded with HTML and change it to Word formatting.
FIND WHAT: (\<i\>)(*)(\</i\>)
REPLACE WITH: \2 Font=Italic
KEY WORDS: HTML, italic, formatting
BEFORE: Change the <i>italicized</i> words to regular Word formatting.

AFTER: Change the italicized words to regular Word formatting.

COMMENTS: Use variations of this for any formatting and other HTML codes.

ALLENE GOFORTH:

Here are five of my wildcard routines. I use more than those, but some are specific to various publishers, and others are of the half-baked variety.

DESCRIPTION: In APA-style references lists, find volume numbers in roman and change them to italic. Retain the issue numbers in roman.

FIND WHAT: , [0-9]{1,}

REPLACE WITH: [nothing]; change font to italic

KEY WORDS: APA, references, volume numbers

BEFORE: Developmental Neurobiology, 13(2)

AFTER: Developmental Neurobiology, 13(2)

COMMENT: Find string includes a space between the first comma and the bracket.

DESCRIPTION: In APA-style references lists, find issue numbers in italics and change to roman.

FIND WHAT: \([0-9]@\)

REPLACE WITH: [nothing]; change format to roman

KEY WORDS: APA, references, issue numbers

BEFORE: Developmental Neurobiology, 13(2)

AFTER: Developmental Neurobiology, 13(2)

DESCRIPTION: In APA-style references lists, find initials in names that need a space inserted after the period.

FIND WHAT: ([A-Z].[!A-Z])

REPLACE WITH: \1

KEYWORDS: APA, references, initials

BEFORE: Brown, A.C.

AFTER: Brown, A. C.

COMMENTS: A space is needed at the beginning of the Replace string.

DESCRIPTION: In APA-style references lists, find name strings containing "&" that need commas inserted before the "&."

FIND WHAT: ([&])

REPLACE WITH: ,\1

KEY WORDS: APA, references, &, comma

BEFORE: Smith, A. B. & Gordon, D. J.

AFTER: Smith, A. B., & Gordon, D. J.

COMMENTS: In the Find string, there is a space between the opening parenthesis and the bracket.

DESCRIPTION: Find and close up space between journal volume number and issue number in APA-style references lists.
FIND WHAT: (\([0-9]@\))
REPLACE WITH: \1
KEY WORDS: APA, references, space, volume, issue
BEFORE: 45 (3)
AFTER: 45(3)
COMMENTS: In the Find string there should be a space before the opening parenthesis. There should not be a space before the first character in the Replace string.

MICHAEL COLEMAN:

Right now I'm working on an index. There's not a lot of work to be done, but it was exported from Quark to Word, so all the formatting was stripped. (If there's a way to avoid that, I'd love to learn about it.) So I set styles for the four levels. Simple enough. The only other trick is to get back all of the italics. There are a few titles that need to be italicized, and fortunately I know that they all have names with at least three words, so I searched for a string

[A-Z]([a-z]@) [A-Z]([a-z]@) [A-Z]

I didn't make any automatic changes because several titles fit the string but don't get italicized.

We used to have a lot of tables, figures, and exhibits in our books, but now they're all called figures. In the index, the appropriate first letter—t, f, or e—appeared in italics after the page number, such as 11-11e. (We use chapter-page pagination.) So I searched for

([0-9])[e,f,t]

I set the replace string to italic and replaced with

\1f

Then I searched for ([0-9]) formatted as italic and changed it back to roman using \1.

Our old style was to use en dashes to show a range of pages, but that was hard to read because of the hyphens in the chapter-page pagination format. So we changed it to "to." I therefore searched for

^=([0-9])

and replaced it with

to \1

STEVE HUDSON:

Remove Time stamping from most logs:

F: [[]*[]]
R: nothing

Kill excessive blank paras

F: ^p^p^p
R: ^p^p

Locate some passive voice instances

Find: be <*ed>

Convert a list of Firstname Lastname to Initial. Lastname

Find <(?)(*)> <(*)>
Replace \1. \3

Find manually formatted numbering (hand tweak)

F: [0-9]@.^t
R: Pass 1 List style, pass 2, nil.

Straight Quotes to Curly Quotes
To turn curlies to straight:

1. Turn off the Autocorrect
2. Go to your find and replace dialog and replace " with ".

SHARON KEY:

After selecting the option fo smart quotation marks, finding and replacing of quotation marks with themselves didn't work to trigger the replacement from straight to curly. Yes, your FnR (find and replace) is *not* triggering the smart quote function. To do that it needs something before or after the quote to help the smart quote system dope it out. It's actually triggered by an "end of word" condition. So to replace straight quotes with curly quotes, use these FnR's with Wildcards enabled (select More and then look at options near the lower left)

Find: "(<*>)

Replace: "\1

Find: ([!])"
Replace: \1"

Both formulae use the () to force capture of that segment to be referred to in the replace section as \1 (or whatever left -> right position it holds if there are multiple bracketed entries).

The first finds quotes followed by a word (a < is a start of a word, * is anything, a > is the end of a word), and replaces the quote with the word (now referred to as \1 from being bracketed) after it. You can't use that same trick for the second, as it selects the whole string of words afore it, and the smart quote feature is confused as the last typed character was in a range. So, we find any non blank character followed by a quote, and replace the single character and the quote. This will take care of most of your problems.

FnR CheatSheet
?= Any 1 character
*=Any string of characters
@ any number of repeats of the previous character
<=the beginning of a word
>=the end of a word
{n}=n repeats of the previous char
{n,}=at least n repeats
{n-m}= between n and m repeats
[ ] marks a set of characters. A - used inside this means an ascending range between the two hyphenated characters. A !, only valid at the set's start, means 'any character except'.

() groups the expressions and indicates the order of evaluation. It is used with the \n wildcard to rearrange expressions. The result of the 1st () pair is represented by \1, the next pair \2 and so on.

The easiest way is to use a special character as a literal, e.g. to find a bracket character, use ASCII code 40 instead. ASCII codes are specified in ANY sort of search with the caret ^.

\= ^92
(=^40
)=^41
?=^63
{=^123
}=^125
[=^91
]=^93
@=^64

```
<=^60
>=^62
*=^42
^=^94
```

To find some relevant information in Word's help file, Contents > Editing and Sorting text > Finding and Replacing Text. A few links later you can get some wildcard information.

10{1,3} finds "10", "100", and "1000".
[10]@ finds any binary number
<[a-zA-Z]{1,3}> finds words of three letters or less.
<[A-Z][a-z]@> finds any title-cased word.
<[0-9]@> finds any whole number, <[0-9]{1,3}> from 0-999

Find: <([0-9]@[/.-])([0-9]@[/.-])([0-9]@>)
Replace with: \2 \1 \3

Changes all numeric dates from DD/MM/YY(YY) to MM/DD/YY(YY) and back again.

Wildcard Searching with Tracked Changes

Have you ever put together a clever wildcard Find and Replace routine that you *know* should work, but when you run the routine, you end up with something unexpected? You do it all the time? So do I, but that's not quite what I meant. I'm thinking specifically about routines that use the Find What Text code or the Find What Expression code, which you can learn more about in the "Find and Replace" chapter.

Let's say you've got a document that has revision tracking turned on (Tools > Track Changes), and in that document is a numbered list, like this:

1. First
2. Second
3. Third

Let's also say you want to use a wildcard Find and Replace to change the list to this:

(1) First
(2) Second
(3) Third

You should be able to do it like this:

1. Click Edit > Replace to bring up Word's Replace dialog.
2. In the "Find What" box, enter this:

([0-9]@)(.)

3. In the "Replace With" box, enter this (with a space after it):

(\1)

4. Put a checkmark in the "Use wildcards" checkbox.
5. Click the button labeled "Replace All."

But it won't work. What you'll get is a list that looks like this:

1() First
2() Second

3() Third

How frustrating!

The problem is a bug in Word's wildcard Find and Replace engine. The easy way around the problem is to turn off revision tracking before doing the Find and Replace. So there you go!

If you *need* the changes to be tracked, however, you're in trouble. I know of one possible solution:

1. Keep a backup copy of your original document.
2. Do your Find and Replace with revision tracking turned off.
3. Use Tools > Track Changes > Compare Documents to mark the differences between the changed document and your backup copy.

If you're interested in trying this approach, you might want to know that Compare Documents has been much improved in Word 2002. For example, let's say Document 1 contains a bunch of parenthetical figure references, like this:

(Fig. 8)

Let's also say you want to use a wildcard Find and Replace to put bold tags around each one, like this:

<b>(Fig. 8)<b>

With revision tracking turned on, Word 2000 will give you the following, with the bold codes marked as additions and "(Fig. 8)" marked as a deletion (here represented by consecutive hyphens):

--------<b>(Fig. 8)<b>

Word 2002, however, will give you this, pure and simple, with the bold codes marked as additions and no unnecessary deletion:

<b>(Fig. 8)<b>

No matter what version of Word you're using, now maybe the next time you need to use revision tracking with wildcard searching, you can avoid some of the fuss.

Thanks to Karen L. Bojda and Allene M. Goforth for the examples and the idea for this article.

Replacing with "Find What Text"

If you're faced with a complex task using Microsoft Word's Find and Replace feature, the "Find What Text" replacement code may come in handy. For example, let's say you need to add the HTML italic tags <I> and </I> around anything formatted with italic. (If you don't understand HTML, don't worry. You'll soon see the point of this article.) You might think you'd need a macro to add the tags, but you don't. You can easily do it like this:

1. Open the document you want to tag.
2. Open the Find and Replace dialog (click on the Edit menu; then click "Replace").
3. With your cursor in the "Find What" box, turn on italic formatting (CTRL + I) so that the word "Italic" is displayed below the box. Make sure the box itself is empty.
4. In the "Replace With" box, enter "<I>^&</I>" (if you want, you can also set this box to "Not Italic" by pressing CTRL + I a couple of times).
5. Click the "Replace All" button.

Any italicized text will be surrounded by the HTML italic tags.

The ^& code in the "Replace With" box represents the text you specified in the "Find What" box. In this case, that's any text with italic formatting. What you're saying is, "Find any text in italic and replace it with *itself* surrounded by HTML italic codes."

As a specific example, let's take the following line, with "see" in italic formatting:

This is a test to *see* what will happen.

When you use the Find and Replace procedure above, you'll get the following result:

This is a test to <I>see</I> what will happen.

You can use the same principle to manipulate text in a variety of ways:

• Put quotation marks around the titles of magazine articles that an author has italicized.
• Insert a bullet in front of every paragraph formatted with Heading 3 style. (You knew you could find style formatting, right? In the Find or Replace dialog, click the "More" button [if available], then "Format," and then "Style.")
• Insert "Chapter" in front of every number formatted with Heading 1 style.

And so on. Any time you need to add something to unspecified text that's formatted in a specific way, try using "Find What Text."

Readers Write

SAGE ROUNTREE:

When we insert notes to compositor and authors in electronic manuscript files, we want those inserts to be bold and in either angle brackets (for coding and notes to compositor) or curly brackets (for queries to authors). Sometimes, our freelance copyeditors neglect to toggle on the bold for these queries, and we go through and manually convert them to boldface. (By manually, I mean we search for the opening bracket, highlight, and toggle—a big waste of time.)

I'm able to figure the search-and-replace for toggling short coding with fixed letters (<A>, <B>) to boldface, but how can I replace all text between the brackets < > and {} *with the brackets themselves* and the text they contain in bold? The substance of the note can sometimes be a few sentences long, and I don't know how to denote that with wildcards. It's like the opposite of the process you outlined in the article on replacing with "find what text."

This has been an interesting mental puzzle for me, but I'm ready to throw in the towel.

[Minutes later, before I could respond, Sage wrote again:]

Jack, I spoke too soon about throwing in the towel, and I added the backslash so Word would recognize the angle brackets as characters, not as the start and end of words. To that end, I wrote this macro:

```
Selection.HomeKey Unit:=wdStory
Selection.Find.ClearFormatting
Selection.Find.Replacement.ClearFormatting
Selection.Find.Replacement.Font.Bold = True
With Selection.Find
.Text = "\<*\>"
.Replacement.Text = "^&"
.Forward = True
.Wrap = wdFindContinue
.Format = True
.MatchCase = False
.MatchWholeWord = False
.MatchWildcards = True
.MatchSoundsLike = False
.MatchAllWordForms = False
End With
Selection.Find.Execute Replace:=wdReplaceAll
```

If your comments are between curly brackets, you could replace the sixth line with this:

```
.Text = "\{*\}"
```

Changing Note Number Format with "Find What Text"

In the article "Replacing with Find What Text," I explained how to use the "Find What Text" code to change formatted text in Microsoft Word. Now I'll show you how to use the "Find What Text" feature to change the format of note numbers. (I'm going to use footnotes as an example, but you can do the same thing with endnotes.)

When you create footnotes in Microsoft Word (Insert menu/Footnotes/Footnote), the footnote numbers are formatted in superscript, like this:

[1] This is the text of note 1.
[2] This is the text of note 2.

And so on. But sometimes you might want your footnote numbers to have regular formatting and be followed by a period, like this:

1. This is the text of note 1.
2. This is the text of note 2.

Microsoft Word has no numbering option that will do this. Nevertheless, there *is* a way to do it, using "Find What Text":

1. Open a document containing footnotes (be sure to keep a backup copy of the document, just in case).
2. Make sure you're viewing the document in Normal mode (View menu/Normal).
3. Open the footnote pane (View menu/Footnotes).
4. Make sure your cursor is at the top of the footnote pane.
5. Open the Find and Replace dialog (Edit menu/Replace).
6. In the "Find what" box, enter "^02" (don't include the quotation marks). ^02 is the code that represents a footnote number.
7. In the "Replace with" box, enter "^&." (don't include the quotation marks). Be sure to include the period after the ampersand. Also, in earlier versions of Word, you may need to follow the period with a space. The ^& code itself represents any text that was found, or in other words, the "Find What Text."
8. With your cursor in the "Replace with" box, click the "Format" button. (You may need to click the "More" button first.)
9. Click "Font."
10. In the Find Font dialog, clear the "Superscript" checkbox so that the replacement text won't be formatted in superscript.
11. Click the "OK" button to close the dialog.
12. In the Find and Replace dialog, click the "Replace All" button.

Your footnotes will now be formatted like this:

    1. This is the text of note 1.
    2. This is the text of note 2.

Pretty neat! Remember, however, that if you now add another footnote, its number will be formatted in the superscript default, and you'll have to fix it by hand. To do so:

    1. Select the number.
    2. Press CTRL + SPACE to remove the superscript format.
    3. Type a period after the number.

Warning: Be careful not to delete a note number or type a note number by hand. Microsoft Word uses a special code to represent a note number, and if you fool around with this code, you risk corrupting your file. You can, however, delete or move a note *reference* number that appears in the *body* of your document, like this,[3] and Microsoft Word will automatically renumber your notes, leaving their new formatting intact.

I ordinarily advise people not to mess around with automatic note numbers, because it's fairly easy to corrupt a document by doing so. If you know what you're doing, however, you can at least change the formatting of the note numbers if you really need to. Now you know how!

Finding "Whole Words Only" with Wildcards

If you often use wildcards with Microsoft Word's Find and Replace feature, you probably know that Word won't let you specify "Find whole words only" when the "Use wildcards" option is checked. This is more than an annoyance; sometimes you really *need* to be able to find whole words only while searching with wildcards.

One solution to the "Find whole words only" problem is to include a space before and after the words you're looking for. Of course, not every word begins or ends with a space. Words are often preceded or followed by quotation marks, dashes, and other characters, which would require multiple searching and replacing.

That suggests another solution: Use a wildcard "group" that includes every possible character that might precede or follow a word. For example, if we were searching for the word "bet," we could use a group like this before the word in the "Find What" box:

["-_\/]

That group (preceding "bet") would find the following text:
bet [preceded by a space]

    "bet
    -bet
    _bet
    /bet

We'd need a similar group after the word:

[.,;:\!"-_\/]

That group (following "bet") would find the following text:

    bet [followed by a space]
    bet.
    bet,
    bet;
    bet:
    bet!
    bet"
    bet-
    bet_
    bet/

So our entire "Find What" string would look something like this:

["-_\/]bet[.,;:\!"-_\/]

So far so good, but there ought to be an easier way. How about using a group to specify what *not* to find before and after the word we're looking for—like this:

[!A-z]bet[!A-z]

That string tells Word to find the word "bet" preceded and followed by any nonalphabetic character, which would certainly omit "bet" as part of another word. If we wanted to find "bet" both capped and lowercased, we could use this string:

[!A-z][b,B]et[!A-z]

These approaches are clever, and they will certainly work. In some situations, they (or variations of them) may be the best way to go, which is why I've included them here. However, we also need to remember that Microsoft Word includes a wildcard code for "beginning of word" (<) and "end of word (>)."

So, if we needed to find the whole word "bet" in a wildcard search, we could put this in the "Find What" box:

<bet>

That string would find "bet" but not "better" or "sorbet"—in other words, it would find "bet" as a whole word only!

Using < and > is probably the most elegant (and the easiest) way to find whole words only while searching with wildcards.

Thanks to Pamela Angulo and Michael C. Coleman for contributing to this article.

What's Your Handle?

When faced with a situation requiring a complex find and replace in Microsoft Word, many people have no idea even where to begin. If you're one of those people, here's the secret: Find the handle.

What do I mean by "handle"? Something your find and replace routine can grab onto to do what it needs to do. For example, a few years ago I was faced with a 500-page manuscript that had no style formatting for its different text levels—something I'm sure your authors would *never* give you.

Basically, the text looked like this (but there was a lot more of it, of course):

This Is a Heading
This is some text. And more text. And more. And really several paragraphs more.
JML
This Is a Heading
This is some text. And more text. And more. And really several paragraphs more.
ED
This Is a Heading
This is some text. And more text. And more. And really several paragraphs more.
CBD

So there I am, badly needing styles to be applied and yet not wanting to do it by hand. The first thing I looked for was a handle—some regularly occurring pattern that I could find and then replace with itself but now with a style applied. Since this author, like most authors, was utterly ignorant of the proper way to put line spacing in front of a heading (by modifying "space before" in the heading style), he'd inserted two extra carriage returns in front of every main heading—and nowhere else. There was my handle!

So, after calling up the Replace dialog (Edit > Replace), I typed this into the "Find What" box:

^13^13^13(*)^13

And I typed the Find What Expression code, surrounded by carriage returns, into the "Replace With" box:

^p\1^p

After typing in my find and replace strings, I clicked the More button to display the other Find and Replace options. I clicked the Format button, then "Styles," and then "Heading 1" so the replaced text would be formatted with that style. I put a check in the "Use Wildcards" checkbox. Then I clicked the "Replace All" button.

Ta-da! All of my main headings (and author attributions) were now formatted with the Heading 1 style.

So, how about those author attributions? There sure were a lot of them—each on its own line at the end of each short article. And each one was simply the author's initials—JML, ED, CBD, and the like. There was my handle—two or more capital letters preceded and followed by a carriage return.

In the "Find What" box I typed this:

```
^13([A-Z]{2,})^13
```

And in the "Replace With" box I typed this:

```
^p\1^p
```

Again, I clicked the Format button, then "Styles," and this time "Heading 2" so the replaced text would be formatted with that style. I made sure the check was still in the "Use Wildcards" checkbox. Then I clicked the "Replace All" button, which formatted all of those authors' initials with the Heading 2 style.

The final thing I needed to style was the paragraphs between each occurrence of Heading 1 text and Heading 2 text. There were no obvious handles associated with that text, but it did have those styled headings above and below it. Could I use those for my handles? Yes, but first I'd need to mark them with some arbitrary codes. Why? Because there's no way to find Heading 1 *and* some text *and* Heading 2, all in one pass. So here are the searches (this time with "Use wildcards" turned *off*) that I used to mark those headings:

Find What:

Heading 1 formatting

Replace With:

```
^&<H1>
```

Find What:

Heading 2 formatting

Replace With:

```
<H2>^&
```

That left me with an <H1> code at the end of each Heading 1 (really, at the beginning of the paragraph following it) and an <H2> code at the beginning of each Heading 2. Excellent handles indeed!

My final step was to search for those codes and the text between them, removing the codes and styling the text as Body Text. Piece of cake:

Find What (with "Use wildcards" turned on):

\<H1\>(*)\<H2\>

Replace With (formatted with the Body Text style):

\1

And that did the job. I still had some cleanup to do (like eliminating double carriage returns), but by looking for the handles in the text I was editing, I was able to style a 500-page document in less than five minutes.

The next time you're faced with a similar chore, don't just slog through the document doing everything by hand. Instead, see if there are some handles that will let you automate the whole process. You won't always find them, but you'll find them often enough to make the effort well worth your while. Please note that you should always back up your documents and run your find and replace routines on some test documents before proceeding with the real thing.

Readers Write

ANONYMOUS:

As a veteran of many find-and-replace operations, I enjoyed your article about "handles" and I thought that that's a very good way of explaining the concept. However, in this particular example, if I had been doing it, I would have first selected all the text in the document and made it all Body Text. In this way, I wouldn't have had to do your last step.

Wildcards in the Real World

After all of these articles on using wildcard find and replace, I thought you might be interested in seeing some of the wildcard combinations I've used recently in an actual editing project. Maybe you'll find them useful too.

Example 1

The manuscript I've been working on has lots of parenthetical references like this:

(Thoreau, *Walden,* p 10.)

You'll notice that there's no period after the p. To fix these references, I used the following string in Microsoft Word's "Find What" box in the Replace dialog (Edit > Replace), with "Use wildcards" turned on:

p ([0-9]@.\))

That's an odd-looking thing with its double parentheses, but its meaning becomes clear when you consider that the first closing parenthesis represents the closing parenthesis of the reference. The backslash in front of it tells Word to treat it as a character rather than the end of a group "expression." So the whole string says this:

1. Find a p followed by a space.
2. Find, as a group, one or more digits followed by a period followed by a closing parenthesis.

I put this in the "Replace With" box:

p. \1

And that string says this:

1. Replace the p followed by a space with p followed by a period and a space.
2. Replace the rest of the "Find What" string (the group in parentheses) with itself.

When I was finished finding and replacing, the references looked like this:

(Thoreau, *Walden,* p. 10.)

Example 2

Here's another example from the manuscript I've been working on:

(Genesis 8:26)

You'll notice that there's no period before the closing parenthesis. Wanting to fix these, I put this string in the "Find What" box:

([0-9]@:[0-9]@)\)

It says:

1. Find, as a group, any number of digits followed by a colon followed by any number of digits.
2. Find a closing parenthesis character.

I put this in the "Replace With" box:

\1.)

And that string says:

1. Replace the group with itself.
2. Replace the closing parenthesis with a period and a closing parenthesis.

When I was finished finding and replacing, the references looked like this:

(Genesis 8:26.)

"Why," you may be wondering, "did you have to use wildcards? Why didn't you just find a closing parenthesis and replace it with a closing parenthesis and a period, like this: Find What:

)

Replace With:

.)

I couldn't do that because the manuscript had other parenthetical items (like this one) that didn't need a period. Using wildcards makes it possible to find exactly the items you want and ignore those you don't.

Example 3

The manuscript had Bible references that looked like this:

II Corinthians

II John
II Kings

I wanted them to look like this:

2 Corinthians
2 John
2 Kings

I put this in the "Find What" box:

II ([A-Z])

The string says:

1. Find I followed by I followed by a space.
2. Find any capital letter.

And I put this in the "Replace With" box:

2 \1

That string says:

1. Replace the II with a 2.
2. Replace the capital letter with itself.

Worked like a charm.

"Why," you ask, "didn't you just replace II with 2 throughout the manuscript rather than use wildcards?" Well, I could have. But I was also thinking about other entries like these:

I Corinthians
I John
I Kings

Obviously, I couldn't just replace I with 1 throughout the manuscript, so I used this string in the "Find What" box:

I ([A-Z])

And I used this string in the "Replace With" box:

1 \1

And that took care of the problem.

I hope you're beginning to see how powerful wildcards can be and how much time they can save while you're editing a manuscript. Using wildcards, you can quickly fix repetitive problems that would take hours to correct by hand. I highly encourage you to try them, but I also urge you to back up your documents and experiment on some junk text before using wildcards in the "real world." Also, try finding and replacing items individually before replacing all of them globally. Then you'll know that the wildcards you're using actually do what you need to have done.

Readers Write

NANCY ADESS:

Why would there be periods at all at the end of references in parens in the text? Why not just (Thoreau, *Walden,* p. 10)?

I RESPONDED: I realize I'm at odds with the *Chicago Manual of Style* (10.77) on this, but I think Chicago is wrong. Chicago style is like this, with no period at the end of the quotation and a period after the source citation:

"The improvements of ages have had but little influence on the essential laws of man's existence" (Thoreau, *Walden* [New York: Time Reading Program, 1962], p. 10).

To me, the period is *part* of the quotation—but we've just put it after the citation. However, if the sentence ends with a question or exclamation mark, Chicago keeps it with the quotation where it belongs:

"What is the nature of the luxury which enervates and destroys nations?" (Thoreau, *Walden* [New York: Time Reading Program, 1962], p. 13).

The placement of the question mark reveals the faulty reasoning behind moving the period—we didn't move the question mark, right? Also, we now have another problem: Since we're not going to move the question mark, how do we punctuate our citation? Chicago does it by leaving that period there—but in this case the period was never part of the sentence to begin with. This makes no sense at all—and besides, the period looks stupid hanging out there by itself. I think the sentence and the citation should be punctuated independently, like this:

"The improvements of ages have had but little influence on the essential laws of man's existence." (Thoreau, *Walden* [New York: Time Reading Program, 1962], p. 10.)
"What is the nature of the luxury which enervates and destroys nations?" (Thoreau, *Walden* [New York: Time Reading Program, 1962], p. 13.)

Simple. Sensible. Neat. Consistent. And not ugly. (And besides, I was trained by a marvelous, independent-thinking editor, and that's the way she did it.)

In addition, using this style makes electronic manipulation simple because the sentence and the citation are both self-contained. For example, it's now an easy matter to write a macro that will turn parenthetical source citations into footnotes—or vice versa. If we take our first sentence, punctuated like this—

"The improvements of ages have had but little influence on the essential laws of man's existence." (Thoreau, *Walden* [New York: Time Reading Program, 1962], p. 10.)

—we can use a macro to:

1. Delete the space before the citation.
2. Delete the opening parenthesis.
3. Cut to the closing parenthesis.
4. Delete the closing parenthesis.
5. Create a footnote.
6. Paste the cut citation into the footnote.
7. Close the footnote.

That leaves our sentence looking like this:

"The improvements of ages have had but little influence on the essential laws of man's existence."[1]

And our note looking like this:

[1] Thoreau, *Walden* [New York: Time Reading Program, 1962], p. 10.

We could also use the macro successfully on our second sentence (the one with the question mark). But if we had followed Chicago style, we'd have to create separate macros for each kind of sentence and citation, and they'd be more complicated, too. (My NoteStripper program includes macros that do this kind of stuff.)

JEFFREY WHITE:

I am an attorney who writes appellate briefs. That often involves cutting and pasting from other sources. I need to make sure that case names appear in italic. For instance, General Motors Corp. v. Ford Motor Co., 123 F.2d 456 (1990).

It occurs to me that I could use search-replace. Using your discussion of wildcard searching, I have tried to construct a command that will find the most common pattern: One or more words beginning with an initial capital letter, followed by "v. ", followed by one or more capitalized words, ending with a comma.

I have been able get one capitalized word, followed by "v. " Is there any way to ask Word 2000 to find a string of one or more capitalized words?

I RESPONDED: The following string will find three capped words in a row (including any periods, commas, and spaces):

([A-Z][a-z.,]@ [A-Z][a-z.,]@ [A-Z][a-z.,]@)

However, when you put in the "v. " and then *repeat* the string, like this—

([A-Z][a-z.,]@ [A-Z][a-z.,]@ [A-Z][a-z.,]@)v. ([A-Z][a-z.,]@ [A-Z][a-z.,]@ [A-Z][a-z.,]@)

—Word will tell you that the string is "too complex." (Theoretically what you want to do should be possible, but in practice it's not. MS Word just ain't that smart, unfortunately.) I haven't been able to get variations to work either. For example, you'd think that you could use this string to find from 1 to 4 occurrences of a capped word followed by a space:

([A-Z][a-z]@){1,4}

But no—at least not in Word 2000. And this *should* work. The wildcard search and replace definitely has some minor bugs, especially with complex searches. I've also tried using the "start of word" and "end of word" wildcards (<, >) without success.

There is a workaround you may be able to use, however:

1. Identify all of the names used in the case names in your document (General Motors Corp., Ford Motor Co., etc.).
2. Find and Replace them with uppercase abbreviations (GMC, FMC, etc.).
3. Use a wildcard Find and Replace to italicize the abbreviations. To do so, put this (possibly with some tweaking to fit your situation) in the "Find What" box:

(<[A-Z]{2,}>) v. (<[A-Z]{2,}>)

Put this (possibly with some tweaking) in the "Replace With" box:

\1 v. \2

Format the "Replace With" box as italic (CTRL + I).

4. Click the "Replace All" button.
5. Find the abbreviations and Replace them with the actual names.

JEFFREY RESPONDED: Building on your suggestion, the following will select the one capitalized word preceding the v. , along with the rest of the case name.

[A-Z][a-z]@ v. [A-Z]*,

That probably does the job for 90% of my case names. If I replace one at a time, instead of Replace All, I can keep an eye out for preceding words that also need italics. That's still a time savings over a wholly manual edit. Or I can make a second pass, repeating the initial string to find case names beginning with 2 words:

[A-Z][a-z]@ [A-Z][a-z]@ v. [A-Z]*,

And then 3, and so on. It's hard to know when to stop, because some case names are quite lengthy.

MEG COX:

Newly committed to automating whatever I can, I tried to automate changing a word or phrase in quotes to italics and removing the quotes. But with wildcards turned on, Find wouldn't find quotation marks at all. Any idea of where I might be going wrong?

I RESPONDED: If your document has curly quotes, use ^0147 (for opening) and ^0148 (for closing). Those are the ANSI codes for curly quotation marks. If your document has straight quotes, use " in your find and replace.

As I tested this, I used this string in the Find What box:

"(*)"

And this string in the Replace With box (formatted as italic):

\1

Or, if you have curly quotes, you could find this:

^0147(*)^0148

And replace with the same thing (formatted as italic):

\1

This will cause you trouble if you have unmatched quotation marks. If that's the case, you might need to do something like this:

"([!"]@)"

Or this:

^0147([!^0147]@)^0148

Two-Step Searching

While editing in Microsoft Word, I often need to find something that's *partially* formatted and replace it with something else. For example, let's say a manuscript has a bunch of superscript note numbers preceded by a space that's *not* in superscript. Here's an example:

Lorem ipsum dolor sit amet. [1]

I'd like to have Word find all such spaces and replace them with nothing (in other words, delete them), but that doesn't seem possible. I can open Word's Replace dialog (Edit > Replace) and set the "Find What" box to superscript, but the space isn't superscript, and the manuscript has thousands of spaces that *don't* precede a superscript number. It also has numbers that aren't superscript (like 2001), so I can't just find spaces preceding numbers. What's an editor to do?

Find and replace the spaces in two steps rather than one:

1. Mark the superscript with codes.
2. Delete the spaces and codes.

Step 1

To mark the superscript with codes, do this:

1. Open Word's Replace dialog by clicking the "Edit" menu and then "Replace."
2. Put your cursor in the "Find What" box and make sure the box is empty.
3. Click the "Format" button. (You may need to click the "More" button first.)
4. Click "Font."
5. Put a checkmark in the "Superscript" box.
6. Click the "OK" button. The "Find What" box should now be set to superscript.
7. Put your cursor in the "Replace With" box.
8. Type the following string in the "Replace With" box:

   ^&

9. Click "Replace All."

All of your superscript numbers will be replaced with themselves, preceded by <S>, which is a code I just made up to indicate superscript. In other words, your sentences will now look like this:

Lorem ipsum dolor sit amet. [<S>1]

Feel free to make up your own codes for whatever you need (italic, bold, paragraph styles, and so on).

The other code in the "Replace With" box, ^&, is Microsoft Word's "Find What Text" code, which represents the text that was found (the superscript numbers). You can learn about it in "Replacing with Find What Text."

Step 2

To delete the spaces and codes, do this:

1. Open Word's Replace dialog by clicking the "Edit" menu and then "Replace."
2. Put your cursor in the "Find What" box by clicking it.
3. Type the following string in the "Find What" box:

    <S>

(You can't see it, but there's a space in front of that code, and it needs to be there.)

4. Click the "No Formatting" button so you're no longer finding superscript, which is now represented by the <S> code.
5. Put your cursor in the "Replace With" box and make sure the box is empty.
6. Click "Replace All."

All of the spaces in front of the codes (and thus in front of the superscript numbers) will be deleted, as will the codes themselves, leaving your sentences looking like this:

Lorem ipsum dolor sit amet.[1]

You can use this little two-step trick any time you need to find and replace partially formatted text. Now that you know how, that will probably be quite often.

PRU HARRISON:

I have a recurring problem with italicised commas. Unfortunately your FileCleaner fixes it the wrong way, as far as I'm concerned! The problem is this: many authors when wanting to put a book title into italics are careless with their highlighting and include a final comma (when present), which is *not* part of the title. It is extremely tedious looking out for this error (at least, as far as I'm concerned because I know very little about programming in Word). Can anybody come up with a program to fix this for me?"

I RESPONDED: It depends on which style you prefer. The old printer's rule is that punctuation follows the format of the text preceding it. The *Chicago Manual of Style* used to follow the rule, but the latest edition goes the other way. I'm planning on releasing a version of FileCleaner that gives you the option, along with many other new alternatives. For now, I'd recommend fixing the problem with a two-step Find and Replace:

1. Click Edit > Replace to bring up the Replace dialog.
2. Leave the Find What box empty but format it as Italic (CTRL + I).
3. In the Replace With box, put this:

   ^&~

4. Click the Replace All button.
5. In the Find What box, put this, with No Formatting (click the button labeled that):

   ~
  ,

6. In the Replace With box, put this, formatted as Not Italic (press CTRL + I twice):

  ,

7. Press the Replace All button.

That should do the trick.

JEANNE PINAULT:

Pru Harrison asked about how to make sure commas following italicized text are not themselves italicized. Replace [any letter] [comma] [italic] with [^&,] [not italic] and you get two not italic commas for every italic comma you started with. Then replace the double commas with single commas and run through and fix the relatively few that need to stay italic. I got a bunch of tildes when I tried it your way, but I have Windows XP, and it won't let FileCleaner replace hyphens in number ranges in live notes, where I need it most, either. (My cure for that is to replace all the hyphens with en dashes and go back and fix the few places that need hyphens.)

WALLACE SAGENDORPH:

In a long scientific paper an author writes "m3" when in fact "m^3" (where the 3 is in superscript) is intended. The editor says "OK, I will just find all instances of "m3" and replace them with "m^3". Not so fast! Using the font menu in "find and replace" and changing the "replace" 3 in "m3" to superscript, the result is ^{m3}—that is, the entire expression is superscripted. The editor can just enter 3 in "find" and a superscripted 3 in "replace," but that necessitates finding every 3 in what we said was a long document and replacing only those that are exponents of "m"—drudgery!

I'm sure there's a way to use "find and replace" to change m3 to m^3, but I'm not quite sure what it is. When you have a moment, I and perhaps others of your readers would appreciate learning the secret.

I RESPONDED: This requires what I call a two-step find and replace.

In your case, search for "m3" and change it to something like "m3~"

Then search for "3˜" and replace it with "3" formatted as superscript.

You can also do a wildcard search that will catch any such combinations:

Find What:

([a-z][0-9])

Replace With:

\1˜

Then:
Find What:

([0-9])˜

Replace With (formatted as superscript):

\1

ERIC FLETCHER:

I bet I won't be the only one to let you know about a much easier method to solve Wallace Sagendorph's superscript problem! [Editor's note: Several readers responded, including Mary Eberle, Eric Fletcher, Shirley S. Ricks, and Iwan Thomas.]

I would just change one instance manually, then select and copy it. Then, in the F&R dialog, put "m3" in the Find what and "˄c" in the Replace with. The caret c replaces each instance found with the content of the clipboard.

Of course, your two-step method works for the general case, but I'd be a little hesitant to use it unless I was pretty sure the manuscript didn't include other constructions that would get messed up. For example, $H2O$ would end up with a superscript 2 with your wildcard method. I once discovered (luckily just before press!) that the 2 in all instances of "V2 rocket" had inadvertently been changed to a superscript because of an earlier fix to km2.

I really like the "Highlight all items" feature of Word's Find dialog as a tool to easily check the total number of items about to be changed. If it looks a bit too high or I'm not sure, I tick it to cause all found items to be highlighted, drop out of the dialog, copy and then paste into a new Word document. This gives me a list of all found items that is easy to sort or review before committing to the replace. We've done several jobs where URLs and email addresses are sprinkled throughout the ms. I tag them with "URL text" character styles (displayed in purple during editing). Not only is it easier to see this way, but the "highlight all/copy/paste to new doc" procedure gives me a sortable list of all such items—always very handy for confirming currency of such items. I also use a similar method for pulling all citations for easier checking.

MELISSA L. BOGEN:

For one client, I have to insert coded text at the top of each file. I want to write a macro (or find some other fast way) to add this big chunk of text. Up until now I have been copying and pasting the chunk of text from an old manuscript and updating it for the ms being edited. I think automating this step will speed things up. I'd like to write a macro that will go to the top of a file and insert the copy. Then using your MultiMacro program, I can run that macro along with some other macros I've written.

I'm a tad rusty on recording macros. I tried to write a macro that searched for a character string (this client always inserts the same character string at the top of every file) and replaced it with the desired basic chunk of text. However, I crashed Word twice now. Maybe MS Word doesn't like that the "insert what" field in my search and replace that I tried to run while recording the macro had a lot of "^p" for hard returns. (The chunk of text includes about 8 lines of text.)

Can you point me to a place where I can find a solution to adding a chunk of text to the top of every file?

I RESPONDED: The number of times you use ^p shouldn't matter. The ^p code should work fine.

Are you really writing the macro, or just recording it? If you're just recording it, you should be able to:

1. Go to start of document (CTRL + HOME).
2. Replace [character string] with [your chunk of text] (CTRL + H).

And then run the macro.

But that reminds me: The longest chunk of text you can have in the Replace With box is 255 characters. So if your chunk of text is longer than that, that could be the problem. The sneaky way around this is to:

1. Select and copy the chunk of text to the Clipboard.
2. Find [character string].
3. Replace with ^c (which is the magic code for "whatever is on the Clipboard."

MELISSA REPLIED: Yup, the chunk of text is long. I tried your sneaky way around it (recorded that as a macro) and it worked great. So now I have a macro, but there needs to be something on the clipboard for it to work. Thus I also saved the chunk of text as AutoText, using Brad Hurley's instructions. Now I can insert the AutoText into one document, highlight the inserted boilerplate and hit CTRL + C to add the boilerplate to the clipboard, then run the macro with a bunch of others using your MultiMacro. All the files in a folder have the text inserted.

APRIL KARYS:

Our authors frequently write "the Java programing language," and just as frequently leave out the "the." I'm looking for a wildcard that will identify only the instances of this phrase that occur without the "the" and then insert it. That way I won't have to go through manually for this one correction item, but can include a wildcard with the macro that's cleaning everything *else* up. Whew. Anyway, is this possible to achieve with wildcards? Is nothing impossible to achieve with wildcards? (Will one of them make me dinner tonight?)

I RESPONDED: As far as I know, there's no elegant (wildcard) way to do what you're describing. You just have to grit your teeth and do a two-step find-and-replace. You *can* record it in a macro, however.

To achieve what you want:

Find: Java programming language
Replace with: the Java programming language.

And then:

Find: the the Java programming language
Replace with: the Java programming language

In other words, you'll be putting an extra "the" in front of some of your "Javas" but then removing them. That will leave *all* of the occurrences looking like this:

the Java programming language

That should do the job.
In the meantime, I'll be working on some wildcards that will make duck à l'orange.

HILARY POWERS:

Is there any chance of making MegaReplacer see Language settings? My latest oops is in U.K. English throughout, and it'd have been pleasant to use MegaReplacer to fix the files in one fell swoop. (It turns out that AutoCorrect, where a lot of my shortcuts lurk, is language specific, so I can't wait to find out—but it'd be a real enhancement.)

I REPLIED: How about using MultiMacro to do this? You could record a macro that:

1. Selects all.
2. Sets language.

Then have MultiMacro run the macro on your files.

HILARY RESPONDED: I recorded the guts of the macro you described, which turned out to be

```
Selection.WholeStory
Selection.LanguageID = wdEnglishUS
Application.CheckLanguage = True
```

and stuffed it into the macros I use (via MultiMacro, of course) to set the working template for each job at the beginning. Hey presto! No more need to think about language settings.

JOHN EAGLESON:

I'm trying to do something that is a kind of variation on MegaReplacer, but I haven't yet found a tool in your arsenal that does it.

A simple example:

I want to search for "January," and when I find it I want to be able to stop and edit the term. Depending on the context I may want to precede it with a nonbreaking space (20 January), follow it with a nonbreaking space (January 21), abbreviate it, or leave it as is.

When I'm finished I want to then hit ENTER or some other key and find the next instance of January.

When I'm finished January I want the macro to do the same with February, and so on.

Do you have a way to do that?

I REPLIED: My Go2Text macro will kind of do what you need. You can use it to find a word, such as "January," and all succeeding instances of "January," but once the word was found, you'd have to make the changes manually.

http://www.editorium.com/freebies.htm (scroll to the bottom of the page)

You wrote that the replacement would depend on the context, so one way to approach the problem is to figure out what the context is in each case. For example, one context would be "January" preceded by a space and one or more numbers. Another context would be "January" *followed* by a space and one or more numbers. In wildcard terms:

Find what:

([0-9]{1,2}) (January)

Replace with:

\1<nonbreaking space>\2

Find what:

(January) ([0-9]{1,2})

Replace with:

\1<nonbreaking space>\2

And so on.

Then, once you've identified the various contexts, it's a fairly simple matter to set up the wildcard Find and Replace strings (with February, March, etc.) to feed to MegaReplacer.

If you need more information on Find and Replace with wildcards, see the paper on advanced searching that came with MegaReplacer.

You might also be able to use some of the information in the article "What's Your Handle?"

JOHN RESPONDED: I think I found one way to do what I'm trying to do with MegaReplacer.

In my example of finding all the names of the months and pausing at each one to allow editing, I want to be able to do this without typing the names of the months each time. Solution:

1. Set up a file with the names of the months:

    January|
    February|
    etc.

(Only the pipe is needed here since I'm not going to be replacing anything yet.)
2. Run MegaReplacer with Mark Automatically checked. Now all the months are marked.
3. Search for the CheckMe character style. I use CTRL+PGDN to move from one month to the next (aka BrowseNext).

ERIC FLETCHER:

When I recently referred someone to your tips about using wildcards in Find and Replace, it reminded me that I had intended to send you some tips about techniques I use frequently.

MULTI-STEP F&R TO SET STYLES: I often need to rationalize formatting in jobs I do: setting styles, sometimes reducing the number of styles, frequently setting up styles for translation to html. I use the wildcard features to simplify the process but sometimes need to do it in several steps. One "routine" saved an enormous amount of work in removing the typed numbers in ordered lists and setting the style from Normal to List number.

1. The first F&R used "(^013[0-9]@.)( )" in Find; "\1þ" in Replace and used wildcards. The result is a unique code in each of the ordered list paragraphs. (The pattern was from one of your tips. I choose to use þ (ALT + 0254) as a unique character for later steps.)

2. The second F&R used "þ" in both Find and Replace without wildcards and had Style=List Number set in the Replace with. This caused the lines that had been flagged as starting with the number-period pattern to be set in the desired style.

3. The final F&R used "[0-9]@.þ" in the Find and nothing in the Replace with no styles but with wildcards. This caused the numbers and my unique flag to be stripped, leaving the paragraphs formatted with the List Number style as intended.

I use a similar technique for bullet lists. When the document is converted to html, having the appropriate styles set saves a huge amount of effort.

USE CHARACTER STYLES TO FLAG ITEMS: I find character styles very useful. When phrases or words need to be flagged for in-context review on-screen, I often use F&R to tag them with a special character style. Then, during review, I set the flag style definition to something that really stands out—a bold colour—so I can see it in a zoomed view of many pages at once. The items stand out and I can just click and scroll-zoom in to examine them. To finalize the document, I replace the style with the default character style to remove any remaining flagging. (The other advantage of this method is that I can find the flag style and rapidly skip from one to the next instance.)

HIGHLIGHT STYLES TEMPORARILY: When I have assembled a set of documents for conversion to html, I use F&R to set the styles (above) whenever possible. Then, to be able to see the potential problems, I redefine the style colours so I can see them in the zoomed-out view. For example, by setting the List Number style to green type, I can easily spot all instances of ordered lists—and elements like bullet paragraphs within an ordered list stand out clearly. I used to set resolved styles in hidden text to make the document shrink as I dealt with it but it introduces too many problems with tabular material. The nice thing about this technique is that the style changes can be temporary: just reset the template to update the styles to their normal definition.

Wildcard Carriage Returns

I've occasionally mentioned this in passing, but based on recent questions from readers, it seems worth making a fuss about: Yes, you *can* use a carriage return in a wildcard search.

People who use Microsoft Word often get stymied by this. They try doing a wildcard search with a string like this one:

^pSee(*)^p

What do they get? An error message: ""^p is not a valid special character for the Find What box or is not supported when the 'Use wildcards' checkbox is selected."

Then they give up: "Dang! Guess I can't look for carriage returns in a wildcard search." In the immortal words of Winston Churchill, "Never, never, never give up." There's almost always a solution if you'll just hang in there and look for it. In this case, the solution is to use the ASCII character code for a carriage return. That code is:

^013

So our theoretical wildcard search would look like this:

^013See(*)^013

And that will work—unless you're using a Macintosh. On a Mac, Word simply won't find anything or (as just happened to me when I was testing this) your computer will lock up. But, surprisingly, there is a solution, which took a considerable amount of messing around to figure out. Use the ^013 but "escape" it with a backslash and treat it as a range with square brackets. In other words, use this:

[\^013]

If you're a Mac user, you know what a breakthrough that is.

Finally, a caution: If you're *replacing* with carriage returns, don't use the ASCII code. Instead, use the good old paragraph code, ^p. Why? Because ^013 and ^p are *not* the same thing. ^p is a Word carriage return, and as such it holds formatting information that ^013 doesn't. If you replace with ^013, that formatting may be lost.

Readers Write

PHIL RABICHOW:

You mentioned that you can search for ^013 when you're looking for a paragraph mark. You can also use ^13 (just one keystroke less, I know).

LINDA DUGUAY:

I was recently faced with a request to create a macro to get rid of multiple blank lines in a document. This could happen when a document comes in as a text file or during a merge etc. I went to work on the problem using wildcards.

A caveat in this case: there were blank lines between paragraphs (it was a text file so no paragraph spacing) and we wanted to delete them (the first Find command). But we didn't want to delete the actual carriage return at the end of the paragraph, so we searched for two carriage returns and replaced them with one. With all of the double carriage returns out of the picture, we could now search for all occurrences of three or more carriage returns and delete those (the second Find command). It was very fast and did the job. We had over 1,000 pages reduced to 1 page in seconds.

In the case where you want two carriage returns to separate paragraphs, you can either not use the first Find routine or using a message box to ask if this is wanted.

Here is what I came up with:

```
Dim myRange As Range
ActiveDocument.Bookmarks.Add Name:="TempDBP", Range:=Selection.Range
Selection.Find.ClearFormatting
Selection.Find.Replacement.ClearFormatting
With Selection.Find
.Text = "^13{2}"
.Replacement.Text = "^13"
.Forward = True
.Wrap = wdFindContinue
.Format = False
.MatchCase = False
.MatchWholeWord = False
.MatchAllWordForms = False
.MatchSoundsLike = False
.MatchWildcards = True
End With
Selection.Find.Execute Replace:=wdReplaceAll
Selection.HomeKey Unit:=wdStory
With Selection.Find
.Text = "^13{2,}"
.Replacement.Text = ""
.Forward = True
End With
Selection.Find.Execute Replace:=wdReplaceAll
With ActiveDocument.Bookmarks("TempDBP")
.Select
.Delete
End With
```

Wildcard Searching and Multiple Paragraph Breaks

Steve Hudson

In trying to explain how Word's Find and Replace (FnR) wildcard mechanism works, I'll also present a practical solution to the multitude of problems encountered by the seemingly innocuous ^p^p to ^p, whose usual objective is to remove unnecessary blank lines. In doing so, we shall traverse the width of Word's pitfalls that never fail to trip up a traveller.

First up, the Word Help system has some excellent help on wildcards. It is a complete pain to access, but you can find something. In Word 2000: F1 - help > Answer Wizard Index > Search on: wildcard. The second topic down is the master list of all FnR stuff. Select it. Pick the Wildcard Characters topic down that list. Now select the *type a wildcard* hyperlink. Hooray! Print it out, fast, and use it as a guide from now on. You have just found the first excellent Quick Reference in the Help system.

The very last two paragraphs are the key to what I am attempting here.

To replace double paragraph breaks with a single one, we would think that finding ^p^p and replacing with ^p would do the job, right?

Well, not really. If you do it via VBA, you find yourself stalling forever if your document is terminated by a blank paragraph, as you have to perform it iteratively until you get a Not Found condition. Why does it fail to replace the last paragraph mark? Well, you *can't* delete the last paragraph mark—ever. When you a start a brand new virgin document and turn on View Formatting, that paragraph mark you see is the End Of Document paragraph mark. As the document does exist and thus has a finite end point, that magic pilcrow (backward P) has to appear. It is also the marker point in memory to place the nasty little objects we infest our nice clean ASCII text with: style definitions, table formatting, list templates, graphical objects, and the list goes on. See ALT + F11 > F2 > Enter for more information.

So, to get around the VBA problem, we simply pre-process the final paragraph. If it is blank (just a paragraph mark), then kill the second-to-last character—which must be the penultimate paragraph mark. Manually, press CTRL + END and use the backspace key as often as required.

The main problem with the simple FnR replace postulation is similar. If you just delete a paragraph mark, you lose the style for that paragraph. So, we can get around that by ensuring it is always the trailing paragraph that gets deleted. It won't do the final blank paragraph in a document, but that is solved above.

First, we need to understand how the brackets work, and the Help topic explains that nicely. So let us put the guide into good use. (^p)^p means that we have marked the first paragraph mark as our first "text chunk." If we use \1 in the replace string, it means to leave the first text chunk—the paragraph mark with the holy styling applied—in place. Unfortunately for us, we still haven't got there yet.

Why? We get an error: We can't use ^p if we are using wildcards. ($#%*! Microsoft.) So we have to use ^013 instead. Herein lies our next problem—paragraph marks that aren't! Oh, yes, kiddies, just because you see a pilcrow does not mean you are looking at a paragraph mark. Oh no. Not with Paste Special and even weirder applications handing in Clipboard data streams without thought. Word dutifully displays a pilcrow when it encounters an ASCII 013, but the background machinery may not have resolved into a paragraph object to be kept dynamically updated.

How do I know it is ASCII 013? Well, I cheat. I select the paragraph mark, or whatever character I need to know, and use VBA: ALT + F11 (VB Editor or the VBE), CTRL + G (Immediate Window), Enter: ? ASCW(Selection)

I use ASCW() rather than ASC() because I want the full Unicode value. For ASCII characters, the Unicode value is the same. Go ahead, work out the wildcards' ASCII numbers and write them on your guide.

So, if we are going to use replace (^013)^013 with ^013, we have to make sure every ASCII 13 is a bona fide paragraph mark. Without wildcards on, find ^013 and replace it with ^p. Honest paragraphs will see no change; fake paragraphs get converted to your will on the spot.

Now you can get serious and stick your wildcard search on. Replace (^013)^013 with \1 and we're in the clear. Done.

In a similar fashion, the much simpler exercise of replacing a colon that occurs after a ket—a ")" character—without destroying the ket itself, would be to use wildcards and replace (^041)^058 with \1.

However, if we were searching for a bra—a "(" character—we would run into another peculiar little Word problem with managing RTF strings. If you insert a symbol from the Wingdings range, or many other non-Unicode graphical fonts, Word actually stores a marker there instead, and then it stores the actual font character off beyond the end of the section mark. That marker is ASCII 40, our unfortunate bra. So an ^040^058 sequence could very well be *any* symbol followed by a colon.

If we were using two blank paragraphs before every heading and no space before to ensure that our new pages always start at the very top, no matter the method used to page break, and we wanted to get rid of scads of three or more blank paragraphs in excess of a single hit (are we listening, VBA people?), we could do something evil and wicked like this: find (^013{2,2})(^013)@ and replace it with \1. That leaves us with a maximum of two following blank paragraphs anywhere in the document, even at the end—in one single Find operation.

Interestingly enough, for those still able to follow, (^013{2,2})^013{1,} fails with an invalid pattern. I forced it with the brackets for the above solution.

That brings us to the final solution for editors and writers seeking to mass destroy all blank lines. It has taken a while, but boy haven't we learned a lot of useless stuff about Word on the way! Find (^013)(^013)@ and replace it with \1 to kill all blank paragraphs in a single pass, with the exception of the first paragraph (there is no start-of-document paragraph mark to give us a two-in-a-row target) and the last paragraph mark (which is excluded from the Find range).

Adding Periods to Lists

A book I recently edited had lots of lists—with no terminal punctuation. The lists looked something like this:

1. Text of the first item
2. Text of the second item
3. Text of the third item

As I worked, I found myself jumping to the end of each line and typing in a period, like this:

1. Text of the first item.
2. Text of the second item
3. Text of the third item

Then this:

1. Text of the first item.
2. Text of the second item.
3. Text of the third item

And finally this:

1. Text of the first item.
2. Text of the second item.
3. Text of the third item.

After two or three lists, I realized how silly this was. The solution is elementary, but I suspect that many readers haven't thought of it. Here it is:

1. Select all the items in your list, including the paragraph mark on the final item.
2. Click Edit > Replace.
3. In the Find What box, enter this (the code for a paragraph mark):

    ^p

4. In the Replace With box enter this (a period followed by the code for a paragraph mark):

    .^p

5. Click Replace All.

6. If Word asks if you want to search the rest of your document, click No; all you want to search is the list you selected.

That should do the trick.

And, of course, if you want to *remove* periods rather than add them, follow the same procedure but swap the contents of the Find What and Replace with boxes.

Macros

Microsoft Word's Secret Macros

Microsoft Word comes with a collection of secret macros. Well, okay, they're not really secret, but they're often overlooked. And they can be pretty useful if you know they exist and understand how to use them. Editors may be particularly interested in the following:

FindSymbol: A macro that allows you to find and replace symbols in your documents.

InsertFootnote: A wizard that helps you create footnotes in the MLA or Chicago Manual of Style format.

CopySpike: A macro that changes Word's spike functionality to copy to the spike rather than cut to the spike. (If you don't know what the spike is, please see your Word documentation. You'll find the feature very useful.)

The path and template names where you can find these macros are:

For Word 8 (97), C:\Program Files\Microsoft Office\Office\Macros\Macros8.dot

For Word 9 (2000), C:\Program Files\Microsoft Office\Office\Macros [or Samples]\Macros9.dot

If you don't find the template in the folder for your version of Word, you may need to install it from your Word installation disks. For Word 2000 or later, you may need to download it from the Microsoft Web site:

http://tinyurl.com/3kq8q

To use the macros, simply open the template into Microsoft Word. You'll see complete instructions in your Word window.

You'll find other useful macros at:

The Electric Editors: http://www.electriceditors.net/macros/index.php

The Microsoft Word MVP FAQ: http://word.mvps.org/faqs/MacrosVBA/index.htm

And, of course, the Editorium: http://www.editorium.com

Macro Recording: The Basics

Macros—the mysterium tremendum, the sanctum sanctorum of Microsoft Word. Or, hey, just a great way to automate those mind-numbing, finger-breaking tasks you've been doing manually for so long. Recording a macro is like recording a song from the radio, only you're recording keystrokes instead of music. Here's the basic procedure:

1. Start the macro recorder (just like starting your tape recorder).
2. Do the stuff you want to record (such as typing text and running Word features).
3. Stop the macro recorder (just like stopping your tape recorder).

Well, shoot, that's not so hard.

Now let's take a simple but real (and useful) example. As you edit, you probably transpose characters a lot—I know I do. But it takes several keystrokes to do it:

1. Select the character you want to move. (Hold down SHIFT and press the RIGHT ARROW key.)
2. Cut the character. (Hold down CTRL and press X.)
3. Move to the place you want to put the character. (Press the LEFT ARROW key.)
4. Paste the character. (Hold down CTRL and press V.)

That's seven keystrokes altogether—keystrokes you do over and over, all of the time. Let's make life easier by recording them in a macro:

1. Start the Macro Recorder

a. Click the "Tools" menu.

b. Click "Macro."

c. Click "Record New Macro" (in older versions of Word, click the "Record" button).

d. Type a name for your macro (something like "TransposeCharacters") in the "Macro name" box. (You can't use spaces in a macro name.) If you're using my Editor's ToolKit or Editor's ToolKit Plus program, don't call the macro "TransposeCharacters," as my programs already use that name.

e. Under "Assign macro to," click the "Keyboard" button.

f. With your cursor in the "Press new shortcut key" box, press the function key or key combination you want to use to run the macro. I like function key 12 (F12) for this macro, but you can use CTRL + T (for "Transpose") or something else. Word will show you if the key or key combination is already assigned. If it is, you can try a different one or overwrite the current assignment. It's up to you. You may want to avoid combinations using the ALT key, which works with various letters to activate menu items and dialog controls. You can, however, use ALT + CTRL, ALT + SHIFT, or SHIFT + CTRL as part of your combination.

g. Click the "Assign" button.

h. Click the "Close" button. The macro recording toolbar will appear with two buttons—the first to stop recording and the second to pause recording if you need to. That means the macro recorder is now recording what you do.

2. Do the Stuff You Want to Record

a. Select the character you want to move. (Hold down SHIFT and press the RIGHT ARROW key.)

b. Cut the character. (Hold down CTRL and press X.)

c. Move to the place you want to put the character. (Press the LEFT ARROW key.)

d. Paste the character. (Hold down CTRL and press V.)

Notice that this is the same procedure we used previously when we *weren't* recording a macro. In other words, we transposed the two characters just as we ordinarily would. Be careful not to use the cursor keys to move to a certain character before following this procedure. If you do, those keystrokes will become *part* of the procedure, and you'll end up recording all of those cursor movements. The idea is to record only the keystrokes you want the macro to do for you.

2. Stop the Macro Recorder

a. Click the "Stop" button (the button with the blue square) on the macro recording toolbar to stop recording.

That's it! You've recorded a macro. Now let's play it back:

1. Put your cursor between two characters you want to transpose.
2. Click the "Tools" menu.
3. Click "Macro."
4. Click "Macros."
5. Click the name of your macro to select it.
6. Click the "Run" button. (If you wanted to delete your macro, you could press the "Delete" button instead.)

That's one way to play back your macro. But since you assigned a key combination to the macro, it's a lot easier to do it like this:

1. Put your cursor between two characters you want to transpose.
2. Press the function key or key combination you've assigned to run the macro.

Presto! The two characters will be transposed.

In a way, what you've just done is create a feature (Transpose Characters) that Microsoft Word didn't have before. Are you beginning to see the possibilities?

Thanks to Meg Cox, Allene Goforth, and Dan A. Wilson for suggesting this topic.

Readers Write

DAVID M VARNER:

Not only can you choose to assign hot keys while you are creating a macro, but you can also create hot keys for existing macros. I discovered the latter a couple of years ago while trying to remember the hot keys I had assigned to a certain macro. To my dismay, the answer was not to be found in the Macros dialog box—a strange oversight.

This oversight was so strange, in fact, I was convinced that macro hot-key assignments still must exist somewhere. Well, they do, and their location was not obvious, but not too far away. In short, I found them in the "Customize" dialog box. So, to find the forgotten hot keys you assigned to a macro:

1. Click "Tools" on the menu, then select "Customize" to access the "Customize" dialog box.
2. Click the "Keyboard" button to access the "Customize Keyboard" dialog box.
3. In the "Categories" field, scroll down to and select "Macros."
4. In the "Macros" field, scroll, if necessary, down to the macro you want and select it. Your assigned hot keys now appear in the "Current keys" field.

You can probably now figure out how to assign (or modify) hot keys to existing macros using the "Customize Keyboard" dialog box: Using the "Press new shortcut key" field, select "CTRL," "ALT," and/or "SHIFT" keys in combination with other keyboard characters to make that hot-key assignment.

Recording a Find-and-Replace Macro

If you've been editing in Microsoft Word, you've probably come up with a list of items you find and replace on every manuscript. These might be picky little things like replacing multiple spaces with a single space, replacing underlining with italic, or replacing the word "catalogue" with "catalog" (or vice versa). If you're now doing such replacements manually, one after the other, you could record them all as a macro that you could run on any manuscript that needs it, saving yourself many hours over the course of a year. To do so, just follow the basic procedure outlined in the previous article:

1. Start Word's macro recorder.
2. Do the stuff you want to record—in this case, find and replace all of the items on your list.
3. Stop the macro recorder.

Got your list? Let's do it (on some junk files, of course):

1. Start the Macro Recorder

a. Click the "Tools" menu.
b. Click "Macro."
c. Click "Record New Macro" (in older versions of Word, click the "Record" button).
d. Type a name for your macro (something like "ReplaceMyStuff") in the "Macro name" box. (You can't use spaces in a macro name.)
e. Click the "OK" button. The macro recording toolbar will appear with two buttons—the first to stop recording and the second to pause recording if you need to. That means the macro recorder is now recording what you do.

2. Do the Stuff You Want to Record

Here's where you're going to find and replace all of those items on your list:
a. Go to the top of your document by pressing CTRL + HOME.
b. Click the "Edit" menu.
c. Click "Replace."
d. In the "Find What" box, type the string of characters or set the formatting you want to find. You can use wildcard strings if you like. For example, if you wanted to find multiple spaces (to be replaced by a single space), you could enter a space followed by {2,} (which means "at least two") and then put a checkmark in the "Use wildcards" checkbox (you might have to click the "More" button before the checkbox is visible).

c. In the "Replace With" box, type the string of characters or set the formatting you want to use to replace the contents of the "Find What" box. For example, if you wanted to replace multiple spaces with a single space, you'd enter a single space.

f. Click "Replace All."

Now repeat those steps for each item you want to find and replace, setting the options and checkboxes in the Replace dialog as needed. (For a wonderfully useful example of transposing dates in a find-and-replace macro, see today's Readers Write column following this article.)

As you replace your items, don't forget that you're recording what you do. It's easy to get sidetracked and start editing, which would create a very strange (and potentially dangerous!) macro indeed. Resist the temptation. Just mechanically find and replace your items, one at a time. Don't think about anything else. *Be* the computer.

If you do make a mistake, don't panic. Just press CTRL + Z to undo the last find-and-replace operation. Your macro will record that, too, so no damage will be done, although your macro will later take longer to run because it includes that unnecessary find-and-replace operation and its reversal. Of course, you can always start over again if you really need to.

2. Stop the Macro Recorder

Click the "Stop" button (the button with the blue square) on the macro recording toolbar to stop recording.

That's it! You've recorded a macro to find and replace all those items you've been cleaning up manually. To play it back:

1. Click the "Tools" menu.
2. Click "Macro."
3. Click "Macros."
4. Click the name of your macro to select it.
5. Click the "Run" button. (If you wanted to delete your macro, you could press the "Delete" button instead.)

All of the items you recorded will be fixed automatically.

If the items you want to find and replace are fairly complicated (using wildcards, for example), you should try each one by hand and make sure it's working correctly before recording your macro.

If you don't have a list of items you regularly need to clean up, you might consider making one. As you edit your next project, just make a note every time you come across something you need to change more than a couple of times. Then use your list to record a find-and-replace macro that will do the work for you from now on.

Got that macro running? Sit back and sip your diet soda. Life is sweet.

Recording a Complex Macro

Dan A. Wilson and Jack Lyon

The title "Recording a Complex Macro" looks intimidating, but actually *recording* a complex macro isn't really that hard. You just have to get firmly in mind what you want to do, step by step, and then do it. Even so, the example in this article is intentionally complex. It's a nightmare task of repetitive processes. And it's long. But it's designed to teach you some things about recording macros.

The Scenario

Suppose you have a Word document to edit—a 350-page dissertation with the title *Derived Humor: On the Roots of George Carlin's Comedy in the Works of Mark Twain.* The document has no block quotations, but it does have two hundred short Twain quotations and two hundred short Carlin quotations. The project editor wants you to make two lists of quotations so a couple of drudges can verify their accuracy. She wants the Twain quotations in one list and the Carlin quotations in another.

You'll have to create two new, blank documents. Save one with the name Twain and the other with the name Carlin. Twain will (eventually) contain all of the Twain quotations, and Carlin will (eventually) contain all of the Carlin quotations. After creating your new files, you'd have to do this (if you were doing the work by hand):

1. Scan through the dissertation file and find every Twain or Carlin quotation.
2. Select it (with its source citation).
3. Copy it to the clipboard.
4. Switch to Twain or Carlin, as appropriate.
5. Paste the quotation and source citation.
6. Hit ENTER to jump down a line so you're ready to paste the next quotation.
7. Switch back to the dissertation and hunt for the next quotation.

Whew! You'd have to select four hundred quotations, copy four hundred times, switch documents four hundred times, paste four hundred times, hit ENTER four hundred times, and switch back to your dissertation four hundred times. It would take you forever, and you'd have RSI pain before you were done. Well, suppose we reduce that list to two tasks:

1. Select four hundred quotations (still a lot of work, but bear with us).
2. Record two macros that will do everything else when we hit their keyboard shortcuts.

That should reduce the time required for the job by at least eighty percent—maybe ninety! Not bad for a few seconds of macro recording.

Since we're going to select the quotations by hand, items 3 through 7 in the list above will make up the steps of our Twain macro:

3. Copy the quotation and citation to the clipboard.
4. Switch to Twain.
5. Paste the quotation and source citation.
6. Hit ENTER to jump down a line so you're ready to paste the next quotation.
7. Switch back to the dissertation and hunt for the next quotation.

Recording the First Macro

You've got three documents open, right?

1. The dissertation itself. (We recommend that you actually create such a document to use while working through these instructions. It can include a bunch of junk text with the sample quotations from this article pasted here and there so you can actually see what happens when you record and use these macros.)
2. The empty Twain document.
3. The empty Carlin document.

You can check this by clicking the "Windows" menu on Word's menu bar, which should display a drop-down menu listing the three documents. You can switch to any of the documents by clicking its name on the menu. For now, switch to the dissertation, our starting place, and select the first Twain quotation:

"God, if you forgive my little jokes on thee, I'll forgive your great big joke on me" (ATS, p. 35).

With the quotation selected, let's record our first macro:

1. Click the "Tools" menu.
2. Click "Macro."
3. Click "Record New Macro."
4. Type a name for the macro ("Twain") in the "Macro name" box.
5. Under "Assign macro to," click the "Keyboard" button.
6. With your cursor in the "Press new shortcut key" box, press the function key or key combination you want to use to run the macro, such as CTRL + ALT + T (for Twain).
7. Click the "Assign" button.
8. Click the "Close" button. The macro recording toolbar will appear with two buttons—the first to stop recording and the second to pause recording if you need to. That means the macro recorder is now recording what you do.
9. Copy the quotation and citation to the Clipboard by pressing CTRL + C.
10. Switch to the Twain document by clicking the "Windows" menu and then clicking "Twain."
11. Paste the quotation and citation by pressing CTRL + v.

12. Hit ENTER to jump down a line so you're ready to paste the next quotation.
13. Switch back to the dissertation by clicking the "Windows" menu and then clicking "Dissertation."
14. Click the "Stop" button (the button with the blue square) on the macro recording toolbar to stop recording. If you can't find it (it is rather small), click "Tools > Macro > Stop Recording."

Recording the Second Macro

Now let's get ready to record our Carlin macro. In the dissertation, select the first Carlin quotation:

"One tequila, two tequila, three tequila, floor" (BFP, p. 29).

With the quotation selected, let's record our second macro:

1. Click the "Tools" menu.
2. Click "Macro."
3. Click "Record New Macro."
4. Type a name for the macro ("Carlin") in the "Macro name" box.
5. Under "Assign macro to," click the "Keyboard" button.
6. With your cursor in the "Press new shortcut key" box, press the function key or key combination you want to use to run the macro, such as CTRL + ALT + C (for Carlin).
7. Click the "Assign" button.
8. Click the "Close" button. The macro recording toolbar will appear with two buttons—the first to stop recording and the second to pause recording if you need to. That means the macro recorder is now recording what you do.
9. Copy the quotation and citation to the Clipboard by pressing CTRL + c.
10. Switch to the Carlin document by clicking the "Windows" menu and then clicking "Carlin."
11. Paste the quotation and citation by pressing CTRL + v.
12. Hit ENTER to jump down a line so you're ready to paste the next quotation.
13. Switch back to the dissertation by clicking the "Windows" menu and then clicking "Dissertation."
14. Click the "Stop" button (the button with the blue square) on the macro recording toolbar to stop recording.

Running the Macros

Now, with both macros recorded, we're ready to go to work. Here's the procedure:

1. In the dissertation document, select a quotation, either by Twain or by Carlin.

2. If the quotation is by Twain, press CTRL + ALT + T.

3. If the quotation is by Carlin, press CTRL + ALT + C.

4. Keep going until all of the quotations are done.

When you're finished, your Twain document will have all of the Twain quotations, and the Carlin document will have all of the Carlin quotations.

Automatically Selecting the Quotations

Still too much work? Let's see if we can get the macros to select the quotations automatically.

We'll start with the Twain quotations. What do they have in common? (See the article "What's Your Handle?") They're all in quotation marks, and they're all followed by an ATS source citation in parentheses. If you've read the wildcard articles, you know we could find (and thus automatically select) those quotations with this wildcard string:

"[!"]@" \(ATS*\).

What's that mean?

" is a quotation mark (which opens a quotation).

[!"]@ means "Find any additional characters except a quotation mark." (We need this to keep from including parts of other quotations.)

" is another quotation mark (which closes a quotation).

Then there's a space.

\(represents an opening parenthesis. (Remember, since a parenthesis is itself a wildcard, we have to use a backslash to tell Word to treat this one as a character.)

ATS is our Twain source.

* represents any other characters following the source.

\) represents a closing parenthesis.

Finally, there's a period.

Taken together, this string of characters will find our Twain quotation and others like it. And we can do the same thing with our Carlin quotations, using BFP rather than ATS in our wildcard string. So let's record our macros again, this time including this fancy way of finding and selecting them. Remember, you'll need to have three documents open:

1. The dissertation itself.

2. The empty Twain document.

3. The empty Carlin document.

Re-recording the First Macro

Then, with the dissertation as the active document, follow this procedure:

1. Click the "Tools" menu.

2. Click "Macro."
3. Click "Record New Macro" (in older versions of Word, click the "Record" button).
4. Type a name for the macro ("Twain") in the "Macro name" box. If Word asks if you want to replace the existing macro, click "Yes."
5. Under "Assign macro to," click the "Keyboard" button.
6. With your cursor in the "Press new shortcut key" box, press the function key or key combination you want to use to run the macro, such as CTRL + ALT + T (for Twain).
7. Click the "Assign" button.
8. Click the "Close" button. The macro recording toolbar will appear with two buttons—the first to stop recording and the second to pause recording if you need to. That means the macro recorder is now recording what you do.
9. Click the "Edit" menu.
10. Click the "Find" menu item.
11. In the Find dialog's "Find What" box, enter the string we discussed:

"[!"]@" \(ATS*\).

12. Put a checkmark in the "Use wildcards" checkbox. (You may need to click the "More" button before this is available.)
13. Click the "Find Next" button. Word will find and select the first Twain quotation and citation.
14. Click the "Cancel" button to close the Find dialog.
15. Copy the quotation and citation to the Clipboard by pressing CTRL + c.
16. Switch to the Twain document by clicking the "Windows" menu and then clicking "Twain."
17. Paste the quotation and citation by pressing CTRL + v.
18. Hit ENTER to jump down a line so you're ready to paste the next quotation.
19. Switch back to the dissertation by clicking the "Windows" menu and then clicking "Dissertation."
20. Click the "Stop" button (the button with the blue square) on the macro recording toolbar to stop recording.

Re-recording the Second Macro

Again, with the dissertation as the active document, follow this procedure:

1. Click the "Tools" menu.
2. Click "Macro."
3. Click "Record New Macro" (in older versions of Word, click the "Record" button).
4. Type a name for the macro ("Carlin") in the "Macro name" box. If Word asks if you want to replace the existing macro, click "Yes."

5. Under "Assign macro to," click the "Keyboard" button.

6. With your cursor in the "Press new shortcut key" box, press the function key or key combination you want to use to run the macro, such as CTRL + ALT + C (for Carlin).

7. Click the "Assign" button.

8. Click the "Close" button. The macro recording toolbar will appear with two buttons—the first to stop recording and the second to pause recording if you need to. That means the macro recorder is now recording what you do.

9. Click the "Edit" menu.

10. Click the "Find" menu item.

11. In the Find dialog's "Find What" box, enter this string:

    "[!"]@" \(BFP*\).

12. Put a checkmark in the "Use wildcards" checkbox. (You may need to click the "More" button before this is available.)

13. Click the "Find Next" button. Word will find and select the first Carlin quotation and citation.

14. Click the "Cancel" button to close the Find dialog.

15. Copy the quotation and citation to the Clipboard by pressing CTRL + c.

16. Switch to the Carlin document by clicking the "Windows" menu and then clicking "Carlin."

17. Paste the quotation and citation by pressing CTRL + v.

18. Hit ENTER to jump down a line so you're ready to paste the next quotation.

19. Switch back to the dissertation by clicking the "Windows" menu and then clicking "Dissertation."

20. Click the "Stop" button (the button with the blue square) on the macro recording toolbar to stop recording.

Finishing Up

Now you can go through the dissertation pressing CTRL + ALT + T to automatically select and copy the Twain quotations and then pressing CTRL + ALT + C to automatically select and copy the Carlin quotations. It will still take some time, but it will be *much* faster than doing all of the work by hand. Most important, by going through all of this, you've probably learned quite a bit about how to record macros and use them to simplify your work. And that's what we were *really* trying to accomplish.

Dan A. Wilson is the proprietor of The Editor's DeskTop:

http://www.editorsdesktop.com/

Repeating Macros

If you record macros to help automate your editing, you've probably bumped into a seemingly insurmountable problem: You can get a macro to find something, and then do something, but not more than once. For example, let's say you want a macro to do this:

1. Find text formatted with the Heading 1 paragraph style.
2. Move to the next paragraph.
3. Insert these characters: "Tip. "
4. Repeat steps 1 through 3 until there aren't any more Heading 1 paragraphs to find.

You can get a macro to do steps 1 through 3, just by recording those steps. But how do you get it to do step 4 (other than running the macro 587 times)?

Well, you can't just record that part. You have to go *into* the macro and insert the commands that will make it repeat. Here's how to proceed:

1. Record the steps you want your macro to take (find something, then do something).
2. After you've stopped the macro recorder, click "Tools > Macro > Macros."
3. Click the macro you just recorded (you may need to scroll down the list to find it).
4. Click "Edit." The macro editor will open on your screen, showing the commands you've recorded. For example, if you recorded steps 1 through 3, above (way above: "1. Find text formatted with the Heading 1 paragraph style," and so on), here are the commands you'd see:

```
Selection.Find.ClearFormatting
Selection.Find.Style = ActiveDocument.Styles("Heading 1")
With Selection.Find
.Text = ""
.Replacement.Text = ""
.Forward = True
.Wrap = wdFindContinue
.Format = True
.MatchCase = False
.MatchWholeWord = False
.MatchWildcards = False
.MatchSoundsLike = False
.MatchAllWordForms = False
End With
Selection.Find.Execute
Selection.MoveDown Unit:=wdParagraph, Count:=1
Selection.TypeText Text:="Tip. "
```

(Note: If your version of Microsoft Word inserts the following command as the third line in the macro—"Selection.Find.ParagraphFormat.Borders.Shadow = False"—take it out. As far as I can tell, this comes from a bug in Microsoft Word, and you don't want it in there.)

You can probably tell by reading these commands what they do. All but the last three set up the parameters for your search. The third command from the bottom executes the search. All of this constitutes the "find something" part of the macro.

The last two commands constitute the "do something" part. In this example, they move down one paragraph and type in the string of characters. Our challenge, of course, is to get these commands to repeat—and then get the Find command to repeat. And to keep repeating everything until there's nothing left to find.

So here's the secret: Just before the "do something" part of the macro, insert the following command:

```
Do While Selection.Find.Found
```

That tells Word to keep doing the "do something" part as long as ("While") Word finds the "find something" part.

Of course, you also want Word to keep doing the "find something" part, too. So, you have to include the following command at the end of the "do something" part:

```
Selection.Find.Execute
```

That tells Word to execute the Find command again—as long as something continues to be found.

Finally, to tell Word where to *stop* repeating, you have to insert this command:

```
Loop
```

When you're finished, the whole thing will look like this (except that I've added an X to show you each command we've added):

```
Selection.Find.ClearFormatting
Selection.Find.Style = ActiveDocument.Styles("Heading 1")
With Selection.Find
.Text = ""
.Replacement.Text = ""
.Forward = True
.Wrap = wdFindContinue
.Format = True
.MatchCase = False
.MatchWholeWord = False
.MatchWildcards = False
.MatchSoundsLike = False
.MatchAllWordForms = False
End With
Selection.Find.Execute
X Do While Selection.Find.Found
Selection.MoveDown Unit:=wdParagraph, Count:=1
```

```
Selection.TypeText Text:="Tip. "
X Selection.Find.Execute
X Loop
```

That's it. Click "File > Close and Return to Microsoft Word."

Now, when you run the macro, it will *keep* running until it's finished all of the paragraphs you specified.

Using "Found" Macros

The past few articles have talked about recording macros to automate repetitive tasks in Microsoft Word. What you may not know is that there are lots of "prerecorded" macros that will do all kinds of neat things. For example, subscribers to the Word-PC email list often post useful macros. You can learn more about the list (and search the list archives) here:

http://listserv.liv.ac.uk/archives/word-pc.html

You can also find macros on the Web by searching for the keywords "microsoft word macro" in your favorite search engine.

The macros you find will probably look something like this:

```
Sub CopyToSpike
If WordBasic.GetSelStartPos() <> _
WordBasic.GetSelEndPos() Then 'Text is selected
WordBasic.Spike 'Add entry to spike
WordBasic.EditUndo 'Undo the cut
Else
WordBasic.MsgBox "Please select text before running this
macro.", _
   "No Text Selected"
End If
End Sub
```

That particular macro copies text to the Spike. You can learn more about it in "Copying to the Spike."

However, you don't have to understand how the macro works in order to use it. Here's how to put it (or any other macro) into Microsoft Word so it will be available when you need it:

1. Copy the text of the macro, starting with the first "Sub" and ending with the last "Sub." If the macro doesn't have those "Sub" lines at the beginning and end, skip step 8 in these instructions.
2. Click the "Tools" menu at the top of your Microsoft Word window.
3. Click "Macro."
4. Click "Macros."
5. Make sure "Macros Available In" shows "Normal.dot."
6. Type a name for the macro in the "Macro Name" box—probably the name used after the first "Sub." For this macro, that's "CopyToSpike."
7. Click "Create."

8. Delete the "Sub [macro name]" and "End Sub" lines that Word created in the macro window. The macro window should now be completely empty.
9. Paste the macro text at the current insertion point.
10. Click "File," then "Close and Return to Microsoft Word."

The macro is now stored in your Normal template, ready for use.
To actually run the macro, do this:

1. Click the "Tools" menu.
2. Click "Macro."
3. Click "Macros."
4. Click the name of your macro to select it.
5. Click the "Run" button. (If you wanted to delete the macro, you could press the "Delete" button instead.)

And now, some cautions:

1. Make sure the macro was created for the version of Word you are using. Macros created for Word 97 and later versions will not run in earlier versions, and you can't just paste macros written for earlier versions into Word 97 and later. Also, later versions of Word have certain features that earlier versions don't, so a macro that uses features specific to Word 2000 won't run in Word 97.
2. Try to make sure the macro comes from a reasonably reliable source.
3. Before using a macro on a real document, test it on a backup copy of the document to *make sure* it does what you need it to do.

Readers Write

JEFF ROSS:

Here's a macro to clean up text copied into Word from an email message:

```
Sub CleanMyMessage()
'Macro recorded 3/11/02 by Jeff Ross
'Remove angle brackets with spaces
With Selection.Find
.Text = "> "
.Replacement.Text = ""
.Forward = True
.Wrap = wdFindContinue
.Format = False
.MatchCase = False
.MatchWholeWord = False
.MatchWildcards = False
.MatchSoundsLike = False
.MatchAllWordForms = False
End With
```

```
Selection.Find.Execute Replace:=wdReplaceAll
'Remove other angle brackets
With Selection.Find
.Text = ">"
.Replacement.Text = ""
.Forward = True
.Wrap = wdFindContinue
.Format = False
.MatchCase = False
.MatchWholeWord = False
.MatchWildcards = False
.MatchSoundsLike = False
.MatchAllWordForms = False
End With
Selection.Find.Execute Replace:=wdReplaceAll
'Remove spaces before paragraph breaks
With Selection.Find
.Text = " ^p"
.Replacement.Text = "^p"
.Forward = True
.Wrap = wdFindContinue
.Format = False
.MatchCase = False
.MatchWholeWord = False
.MatchWildcards = False
.MatchSoundsLike = False
.MatchAllWordForms = False
End With
Selection.Find.Execute Replace:=wdReplaceAll
'Mark true paragraph breaks with unique character
Selection.Find.ClearFormatting
Selection.Find.Replacement.ClearFormatting
With Selection.Find
.Text = "^p^p"
.Replacement.Text = "§"
.Forward = True
.Wrap = wdFindContinue
.Format = False
.MatchCase = False
.MatchWholeWord = False
.MatchWildcards = False
.MatchSoundsLike = False
.MatchAllWordForms = False
End With
Selection.Find.Execute Replace:=wdReplaceAll
'Replace other (false) paragraph breaks with spaces
With Selection.Find
.Text = "^p"
.Replacement.Text = " "
.Forward = True
.Wrap = wdFindContinue
.Format = False
.MatchCase = False
```

```
      .MatchWholeWord = False
      .MatchWildcards = False
      .MatchSoundsLike = False
      .MatchAllWordForms = False
    End With
    Selection.Find.Execute Replace:=wdReplaceAll
    'Replace unique character with paragraph break
    With Selection.Find
      .Text = "§"
      .Replacement.Text = "^p"
      .Forward = True
      .Wrap = wdFindContinue
      .Format = False
      .MatchCase = False
      .MatchWholeWord = False
      .MatchWildcards = False
      .MatchSoundsLike = False
      .MatchAllWordForms = False
    End With
    Selection.Find.Execute Replace:=wdReplaceAll
    'Turn double hyphens to em dashes
    With Selection.Find
      .Text = "--"
      .Replacement.Text = "^+"
      .Forward = True
      .Wrap = wdFindContinue
      .Format = False
      .MatchCase = False
      .MatchWholeWord = False
      .MatchWildcards = False
      .MatchSoundsLike = False
      .MatchAllWordForms = False
    End With
    Selection.Find.Execute Replace:=wdReplaceAll
    'Turn straight single quotation marks into curly ones
    'Note: For this to work, the AutoFormat option
    'to replace straight quotes with curly quotes must be on
    '(Click Tools > AutoCorrect > AutoFormat As You Type >
    'Replace as you type > straight quotes with smart quotes)
    Selection.Find.Execute Replace:=wdReplaceAll
    With Selection.Find
      .Text = "'"
      .Replacement.Text = "'"
      .Forward = True
      .Wrap = wdFindContinue
      .Format = False
      .MatchCase = False
      .MatchWholeWord = False
      .MatchWildcards = False
      .MatchSoundsLike = False
      .MatchAllWordForms = False
    End With
    Selection.Find.Execute Replace:=wdReplaceAll
```

```
'Turn straight double quotation marks into curly ones
'Note: For this to work, the AutoFormat option
'to replace straight quotes with curly quotes must be on
'(Click Tools > AutoCorrect > AutoFormat As You Type >
'Replace as you type > straight quotes with smart quotes)
Selection.Find.Execute Replace:=wdReplaceAll
With Selection.Find
.Text = """"
.Replacement.Text = """"
.Forward = True
.Wrap = wdFindContinue
.Format = False
.MatchCase = False
.MatchWholeWord = False
.MatchWildcards = False
.MatchSoundsLike = False
.MatchAllWordForms = False
End With
Selection.Find.Execute Replace:=wdReplaceAll
End Sub
```

Macros in Add-in Templates

The previous article explained how to put the text of a "found macro" into Microsoft Word on your computer. Often, however, when you find a macro on the Internet, it won't be lines of text. Instead, the macro will be stored in a Word template (usually along with other macros) that you can "add" to Word. You'll find some useful examples at the Electric Editors Web site, here:

http://www.electriceditors.net/macros/index.htm

And at Microsoft:

http://office.microsoft.com/downloads/2000/supmacros.aspx

And, of course, at the Editorium:

http://www.editorium.com

Microsoft calls such templates "global templates and add-ins" or "add-in templates." They work kind of like an electric screwdriver, which comes with all kinds of little tools that make it do different things. For example, you can insert a screwdriver blade if you want to turn a screw. You can insert a drill bit if you want to drill a hole. Or you can insert a sausage grinder if you want to make sausage (just kidding).

Think of Microsoft Word as the electric screwdriver. And think of add-in templates (with their macros) as the tools that fit into the screwdriver to make it do different things. (Thanks to Hilary Powers for this analogy.) If you've used QuarkXPress, you're familiar with XTensions. If you've used PageMaker, you've seen Plug-ins. Global templates and add-ins are the same kind of thing.

Once you've found an add-in template (and its macros) that you want to use, here's how to add it to your system:

1. Put the template into Word's Templates folder. (If you don't know where that is, you can find out by clicking the "Tools" menu, then "Options," and then "File Locations." You'll find the location of the folder on the line labeled "User templates." If you can't see the full path to the folder, click the "Modify" button.)
2. Click the "Tools" menu (the "File" menu in earlier versions of Word).
3. Click "Templates and Add-ins" ("Templates" in earlier versions of Word).
4. Click the "Add" button.
5. Click the template you want to add.
6. Click the "OK" button.
7. Click the next "OK" button to finish up.

(Note: If your macro security level is set to high, you may need to change it to medium or low before you can use the template and its macros. You can do this by clicking "Tools," then "Macro," and then "Security." You may want to read more about this in Word's Help file or check with your system administrator before proceeding.)

Once you've added the template, you may see new menu items or toolbars on your Word screen that run the macros included with the template (be sure to read any accompanying documentation). Or, you may need to run the macros like this:

1. Click the "Tools" menu.
2. Click "Macro."
3. Click "Macros."
4. Click the name of your macro to select it.
5. Click the "Run" button.

Before using any add-in template and its macros, please heed these cautions:

• Make sure the template comes from a reliable source.
• Make sure the macros you want to use were created for the version of Word you are using. Macros created for Word 97 and later versions will not run in earlier versions, and macros created for earlier versions may not work in later versions. Also, later versions of Word have certain features that earlier versions don't, so a macro that uses features specific to Word 2000 won't run in Word 97.
• Before using a macro on a real document, test it on a backup copy of the document to *make sure* it does what you need it to do.

Creating Add-in Templates

If you've been recording your own macros, you've probably been saving them in your Normal template, where they'll be available to use with any document. The Normal template may not be the best place to save them, however. Since it's used a lot, it can become corrupt. (You should back up your Normal template frequently.) Also, saving macros in your Normal template makes it hard to keep them organized.

What's the alternative? Create your own add-in templates as a place to keep your macros. Doing so has several advantages:

1. It makes organizing your macros easy. You can keep all the macros for a particular project or task in a single add-in template.
2. It makes backing up your macros easy. Just keep copies of your templates in several locations.
3. It makes sharing your macros easy. Just give a copy of a template to a colleague or friend.

So how do you create an add-in template? Here's the way I like to do it:

1. Create a new document in Microsoft Word.
2. Save the document as a Microsoft Word template, which has a ".dot" extension. Be sure to give it a name that describes the purpose of the macros you're going to store in the template (for example, Cleanup.dot or MyProject.dot).
3. Click the "Tools" menu.
4. Click "Macro."
5. Click "Macros."
6. Click the "Organizer" button.

On the "Macro Project Items" tab, you'll see two windows. The name of the template you just created should be displayed above the left window, which should be empty since the template doesn't contain any macros yet. If the name of your template isn't displayed, click the drop-down list under the window and select it.

The window on the right should show the macros available in Normal.dot (as indicated above the window). If the window isn't displaying Normal.dot, click the drop-down list under the window and select it. Then, do this:

1. Select the macros in Normal.dot that you want to copy to your new template. (To select several at once, hold down the CTRL key while clicking the macro names.)
2. Click the "Copy" button. The macros should now be displayed in the left window as being in your new template. (You can also delete or rename macros if you like.)

3. Click the "Close" button.

4. Save your new template, which now contains the macros you copied to it.

You've just created your own add-in template containing your own macros.

Adding a Template Automatically

The previous article explained how to add macros to Microsoft Word in a "global template" or "add-in." The problem is, every time you start Word, you'll have to reactivate the global template before you can use its macros. Here's the procedure:

1. Click the "Tools" menu (the "File" menu in earlier versions of Word).
2. Click "Templates and Add-ins" ("Templates" in earlier versions of Word).
3. In the list of global templates and add-ins, put a checkmark in the checkbox for the template you want to use.
4. Click the "OK" button.

Wouldn't it be nice, though, if you could have Word add the template automatically? You can. Just follow this procedure:

1. Close Microsoft Word.
2. Copy the template you want to add automatically.
3. Navigate to Word's Startup folder.
4. Paste the template into the Startup folder.
5. Restart Microsoft Word.

The macros in the template should now be available for you to use, and they'll be available automatically every time you start Word.

If you don't know where the Startup folder is, here's how to find out:

1. Click the "Tools" menu (in any version of Word).
2. Click the "Options" menu item.
3. Click the "File Locations" tab.

You'll see the location of the Startup folder on the line labeled "Startup." (If you can't see the full path to the folder, click the "Modify" button.)

Readers Write

BRIAN VICARY

As part of our business I visit our clients' sites to install software and to perform updates when necessary. We supply a Word template with predefined macros to make the use of our software easier. On networks we prefer our template to be shared so that we only have one location to update. While this can be accomplished by pointing the Word Startup path to this shared location, it is often not possible if the users already have templates in their Startup folder. Often users already have slightly different Startup templates for their own use or do not need access to a particular template.

You can add templates using the Tools, Templates and Add-Ins option, but you have to manually activate them each time you run Word.

To get round this problem this is what I do:

1. Open Word and then close the blank document that is open.
2. Go to the Tools menu and select the Macro option; from there select the Record New Macro.... option.
3. Give the macro a name appropriate to the macro—for example, AddMyMacro.
4. Click OK to begin recording the macro.
5. Click the Tools menu and select the Templates and Add-Ins option.
6. Click the Add button.
7. Navigate to where the Template document is stored on the network and select it. It should appear in the Add-ins list with a tick.
8. Click the OK button.
9. Stop recording the macro.
10. Go to the Tools menu and select the Macro option; from there select the Macros.... option.
11. Enter the name AutoExec in the Macro Name box and click the Create button. This will open the Visual Basic Editor with the new macro AutoExec.
12. In the sub for AutoExec, enter the name of the new macro you recorded above—for example, AddMyMacro.
13. Close the Visual Basic Editor.
14. Close and restart Word.

Now when Word starts, it automatically runs the macro AutoExec. This in turn runs the macro name you entered, AddMyMacro, which loads and activates the required template.

If you already have an AutoExec macro, just add a new line to it with the name of your macro. Any number of macros can be added this way, and you also have control over who loads what macros, as well as allowing them to maintain a personal Startup path.

You can also add the template in the usual manner without recording a macro, then record a macro of your activating it. The process is exactly the same, and the result is also exactly the same.

The only drawback can be the speed of the network if your macros are complex, but in practice I have not found this to be a major problem. Also, you have to get everyone to close their Word if you need to update any of the Add-on templates. However, this is true whatever method you use for sharing templates.

Miscellaneous Stuff

Where to Get Help

If you need help with Word, there are actually lots of places to go. Some of the best include:

Allen Wyatt's WordTips:

http://WordTips.VitalNews.com

The Word-PC List:

http://listserv.liv.ac.uk/archives/word-pc.html

The McEdit list:

http://groups.yahoo.com/group/McEdit/

Microsoft's Word discussion groups:

http://www.microsoft.com/office/community/en-us/FlyoutOverview.mspx\#13 (Look in the lower right of the page.)

The Word MVP site:

http://word.mvps.org/

Woody's Lounge:

http://www.wopr.com/cgi-bin/w3t/postlist.pl?Cat=\&Board=wrd

The Electric Editors

http://www.electriceditors.net/

Copyediting-L

http://www.copyediting-l.info/

Index